# British queer history

MANCHESTER
1824

Manchester University Press

# British queer history

## New approaches and perspectives

Edited by Brian Lewis

Manchester University Press

Manchester and New York

*distributed in the United States exclusively by Palgrave Macmillan*

Published by Manchester University Press
Oxford Road, Manchester M13 9NR, UK
and Room 400, 175 Fifth Avenue, New York, NY 10010, USA
www.manchesteruniversitypress.co.uk

Distributed in the United States exclusively by
Palgrave Macmillan, 175 Fifth Avenue, New York,
NY 10010, USA

Distributed in Canada exclusively by
UBC Press, University of British Columbia, 2029 West Mall,
Vancouver, BC, Canada V6T 1Z2

British Library Cataloguing-in-Publication Data
A catalogue record for this book is available from the British Library

Library of Congress Cataloging-in-Publication Data applied for

ISBN 978 07190 8894 0 hardback

ISBN 978 07190 8895 7 paperback

First published 2013

Typeset in 10/12 Scala by
Servis Filmsetting Ltd, Stockport, Cheshire
Printed in Great Britain by
Bell & Bain Ltd, Glasgow

# Contents

# List of figures

# List of contributors

**Justin Bengry** is a Social Sciences and Humanities Research Council of Canada Postdoctoral Fellow in History at McGill University, Montreal. His research on the relationship between homosexuality and consumer capitalism in twentieth-century Britain has appeared in *History Workshop Journal* and *Socialist History*. His book project, based on his U. C. Santa Barbara PhD thesis, is entitled *The Pink Pound: Queer Profits in Twentieth-Century Britain*.

**Paul R. Deslandes** is Associate Professor of History at the University of Vermont. He is the author of *Oxbridge Men: British Masculinity and the Undergraduate Experience, 1850–1920* (2005) and a number of articles and essays on the history of British education, masculinity and male sexuality. He is currently writing a book on the cultural history of male beauty in Britain from the 1840s to the present.

**Laura Doan** is Professor of Cultural History and Sexuality Studies at the University of Manchester. She is the author of *Fashioning Sapphism: The Origins of a Modern English Lesbian Culture* (2001) and *Disturbing Practices: History, Sexuality, and Women's Experience of Modern War* (2013) and co-editor of several essay collections, including *Sexology in Culture* (1998) and *Sapphic Modernities* (2006). Her new work in the historiography of sexuality addresses the epistemological challenges in attempts to historicise heterosexuality and heteronormativity.

**Matt Houlbrook** is Senior Lecturer in Modern British History at the University of Birmingham. He is the author of *Queer London: Perils and Pleasures in the Sexual Metropolis, 1918–57* (2005) and (with Harry Cocks) editor of *Palgrave Advances in the Modern History of Sexuality*

(2005). His more recent research explores the relationship between subjectivity and culture after the Great War and he is currently completing a monograph entitled *The Prince of Tricksters: Cultures of Confidence in Interwar Britain.*

**Jongwoo Jeremy Kim** is Associate Professor of Modern Art at the University of Louisville, Kentucky. He is the author of *Painted Men in Britain, 1868–1918: Royal Academicians and Masculinities* (2012). His current work focuses on representations of male friendship in the works by Walter Sickert, Edgar Degas and James McNeill Whistler.

**Brian Lewis** is Professor of History at McGill University, Montreal. He is the author of *The Middlemost and the Milltowns: Bourgeois Culture and Politics in Early Industrial England* (2001) and *'So Clean': Lord Leverhulme, Soap and Civilization* (2008), guest editor of a special edition of the *Journal of British Studies* on queer history (July 2012) and editor of *Wolfenden's Witnesses: Homosexuality in Postwar Britain* (forthcoming). He is currently working on a book entitled *The First Queer Revolution: George Ives and Homosexuality in Britain from Wilde to Wolfenden.*

**Ryan Linkof** is Ralph M. Parsons Curatorial Fellow in the Photography Department at the Los Angeles County Museum of Art. He received his PhD in 2011 from the University of Southern California. His dissertation is a study of the origins of photojournalism in the British tabloids in the first half of the twentieth century. His published work has appeared in *Photography and Culture, Études photographiques* and the *New York Times.*

**David Minto** is a PhD candidate in History at Yale University. His thesis is provisionally entitled *Special Relationships: Transnational Homophile Activism and Anglo-American Sexual Politics, 1948–73.*

**Mo Moulton** is Associate Director of Studies in History and Literature at Harvard University. Her PhD thesis (Brown University, 2010) is entitled *Private Irelands: The Legacies of the Anglo-Irish War in Interwar England,* and she is currently revising that work for publication.

**Amy Tooth Murphy** completed her PhD, *Reading the Lives Between the Lines: Lesbian Oral History and Lesbian Literature in Post-War Britain,* at the University of Glasgow in 2012. She is currently based at the University of East London where she is coordinating an oral history and public engagement project on the Bethnal Green Tube disaster and the Home Front in East London during the Second World War.

**Charles Upchurch** is Associate Professor of British History at Florida State University. He is the author of *Before Wilde: Sex between Men in Britain's Age of Reform* (2009), 'Forgetting the unthinkable: Cross-dressers and British society in the case of the Queen vs. Boulton and others' (in *Gender and History*) and other scholarly articles. His current work continues to explore the multiple ways in which accusations of sex between men factored into mainstream politics in 1820s Britain.

**Chris Waters** is Hans W. Gatzke '38 Professor of Modern European History at Williams College, Massachusetts. He is the author of *British Socialists and the Politics of Popular Culture, 1884–1914* (1990), co-editor of *Moments of Modernity: Reconstructing Britain 1945–1964* (1998) and author of some thirty articles on various aspects of modern British cultural and social history. He has published several articles on homosexuality in Britain and is currently at work on a book tentatively entitled *Queer Treatments: Homosexual Selfhood and the Therapeutic Ideal in Britain, 1890–1980*.

# Acknowledgements

Many of the essays in this collection are extended versions of papers presented at a conference on 'British Queer History' hosted by myself at McGill University in October 2010. The conference was made possible by generous support from the Maxwell Cummings Distinguished Lectureship fund, the Dean of Arts, the Department of History and the Institute for Gender, Sexuality and Feminist Studies. I would like to thank all those involved in ensuring the smooth running and the success of the conference. I am very grateful to the participants, to those who have worked up their papers into chapters in such a punctual fashion and to those who subsequently accepted invitations to contribute to the collection. I thank also the anonymous reviewers for their perceptive and very helpful comments and the staff of Manchester University Press for their patience and efficiency at every step of the way.

Brian Lewis
Montreal

# Introduction: British queer history

*Brian Lewis*

In a 2002 article in the *Independent*, the author and columnist Philip Hensher latched on to a recent government decision about how to refer to gay people in legislation. 'Homosexuality' was to be replaced with 'orientation towards people of the same sex'. Otpotss? 'I suppose it could catch on, given time.' But if not that, then what? What do we call ourselves? Homosexual? Too medical, 'and no one wants to go round with a diagnosis round his neck'. Gay? 'One puts up with it ... dopey as it is, so long as it stays an adjective.' Queer? The brave attempt to reclaim it, and turn it into a political rallying cry, was rather dated; moreover, 'it is one of those words, like "poof", that we cheerfully use to each other, but that we would certainly not want anyone else to use.' Part of the problem, he thought, was that the language of 'orientation' and labels of stable identity had become increasingly problematic, failing to encompass everyone all of the time. In stating his preference for a word with historical resonance, that described what people do rather than claiming to know what they are, Hensher suggested, tongue firmly in cheek: 'sodomite'.[1]

Well, sodomite has no more chance of resurrection than otpotss of adoption. But, as Hensher rightly indicates, there has been no shortage of terms nor dearth of controversy surrounding the delicate question of nomenclature – an arresting development for acts or identities that once struggled (at least in official discourse and polite circles) to be named at all: for 'the love that dare not speak its name', for '*peccatum illud horribile, inter christianos non nominandum*', for the 'nameless offence' committed by 'unspeakables of the Oscar Wilde sort'.[2] A recent thesaurus gaily mixes together desires, deeds and descriptors in coming up with more than eight hundred synonyms for gay male (from 'A-gay' to 'zebrajox') and 230 for lesbian (from 'Amazon' to 'zamie girl').[3] The 'Juliet question' – 'What's in a name?' – is just as pertinent and unresolved a decade after Hensher wrote; but he exaggerated the demise of 'queer', at least in the academy and upon university campuses, where it remains in robust health.

Of all the possible terms, queer is perhaps the most contentious. Before the rise of gay liberation, queer – as in odd, bent or peculiar – served a dual function as a mode of self-address by same-sex-desiring males and as an expression of hostility and contempt by ill-disposed others. But, for post-Stonewall sexual minorities, queer was the language of oppression and of internalised self-loathing; they abandoned it without regret in favour of gay. Only in the late 1980s did it start to make a comeback. Radical grassroots activists in organisations like Queer Nation and ACT UP (in the US) and Outrage! (in Britain) began to deploy it as a calculated and edgy act of reclamation. It represented a defiant two-fingered gesture to reactionary and stigmatising governments, slow to respond to the AIDS crisis, and to the bile spewed out by many moral and religious commentators in a largely unsympathetic media.[4] It also reflected a deep sense of alienation from and a challenge to the assimilationist tendencies of the mainstream gay movement. In this it shared some affinities with the work of a new generation of scholars elaborating a queer theoretical perspective from circa 1990 who similarly staked out their opposition to the 'normal'. Historians influenced by queer theory not only dismissed any notion of an unchanging and recognisable homosexual personhood across history (already demolished by a generation of social constructionists) but also stressed the fictitious nature of hetero- and homosexual binaries and identities, arguing for their historical specificity and the fluidity of sexual desire and expression.[5]

Much of this was (and is) controversial. Some older gay rights militants were offended by the rehabilitation of a despised term from an unlamented past. Some feminists saw queer as effacing and demoting the position of lesbians. Some pragmatists wondered how the civil rights of sexual minorities could be defended and forwarded if the categories of gay and lesbian are exploded as unreal 'fictions'. Some progressive community-builders noted that, even if queer had stormed the academy, it had little traction outside, suggesting a huge and problematic disconnect between public and ivory tower.[6] Still, not only in scholarly discourse but also among student organisations, queer became well entrenched. As the number of subdivisions within the ranks of sexual and gender nonconformists proliferated, and as the LGBT alphabet-soup categories became ever more refined and ever more complex (yet always falling short of the much-desired inclusivity), queer was co-opted as an all-encompassing umbrella expression. 'Queer McGill' (née 'Gay McGill' in 1972) at my own university, for example, strikes a familiar universalising, politically sensitive note in its mission statement:

> Queer McGill is a university-wide support service for queer students and their allies. Queer is a broad term which includes anyone who chooses to identify with it. This includes those who identify simply as queer, and includes – but is by no means limited to – those who identify as queer and/or any combination of agender, ally, ambigender ... [and then all the way through no fewer than forty-nine different permutations to] transgender, trigender, and Two-Spirit. In addition, Queer McGill welcomes any students whose identities do not fit into the Western heternormative gender binary, whether or not they identify as queer. We operate our services from an anti-racist, anti-classist, anti-ageist, anti-ablist, anti-sizeist, pro-feminist and sex-positive orientation.[7]

This collection of essays starts from the premise that, in spite of its problems and limitations, queer is indeed a useful category of analysis for students of modern British history and sexuality, both as a big-tent term and because it builds on a body of recent scholarship that differs in significant ways from the pioneering gay and lesbian history of the 1970s. But, like the 2010 conference on 'British Queer History' at McGill University from which it arises, it avoids prescription, imposes no party line and encourages a thousand flowers to bloom. The conference stemmed from a conviction that historians of sexual diversity in Britain had, since the 1970s, established a distinctive and innovative field of investigation and that it was time to take stock. Anything broadly 'British', 'queer' (however one chose to define it) and 'history' was fair game. The quality and diversity of the papers were impressive, and a selection of them – supplemented by an additional call for papers and individual invitations – now forms the core of two companion collections: the current volume (with its more focused timeframe) and a special queer edition of the *Journal of British Studies* (which stretches back to the early seventeenth century).[8] As the first collections specifically to focus on British queer history over an extended period, and showcasing challenging think-pieces from leading luminaries in the field alongside some of the most original and exciting research being undertaken by emerging young scholars, together they demonstrate the richness and promise of current British queer historical scholarship.[9]

Each of these authors owes a substantial debt to the seminal work of the sociologists and historians of the 1970s.[10] As historians began to take the 'sexual turn', expanding the remit of social history by examining and integrating neglected groups and topics, the first wave of gay and lesbian scholars attempted to recover a usable past in the service of gay liberation, making use of the critical insight of the social constructionist perspective: that same-sex activities can be understood only in a historical and cultural context. Still, during the 1980s and 1990s, modern British historians tended to cede the territory to literary historians and theorists or to popular and polemical history.[11] At the turn of the millennium, a gathering of modern (nineteenth- and twentieth-century) British gay and lesbian or queer historians would barely have filled a taxi and collections such as this would not have been possible. But, since then, there has been a remarkable efflorescence of important, archivally based, theoretically savvy studies. Joseph Bristow has dubbed this the 'new British gay history', Chris Waters (rather more felicitously), the 'new British queer history'.[12]

As Jeffrey Weeks points out, the epistemological rupture between the first and second waves should not be exaggerated nor nuance sacrificed to the thrill of bayoneting straw men.[13] Nevertheless, the new generation was researching and writing with the queer theoretical notions of the 1990s to heart and after social history's failure of nerve in the face of the culturalist onslaught of the 1980s.[14] Influenced perhaps above all by Eve Kosofsky Sedgwick, these scholars especially took aim at the key sociological and Foucauldian arguments that modern homosexual and heterosexual categories were 'made' in the late nineteenth century (or, following Randolph Trumbach, in the early eighteenth century), that acts gave way to identities.[15] The trend was away from grand narratives, great explanatory schema and satisfying teleologies towards an emphasis on fragmented experiences, self-understandings, desires and behaviours. Deep burrowing in archives and a theoretical mindset conducive to a bonfire of taxonomies have vastly expanded our localised knowledge of the multiplicity of sexual practices and beliefs but rendered 'our queer ancestors' less knowable. Recent attempts by Rebecca Jennings and Matt Cook to map out *A Lesbian History of Britain* and *A Gay History of Britain* respectively have produced excellent syntheses but – as the authors readily acknowledge – they constantly encounter the conundrum of what 'lesbian' and 'gay' actually mean in the centuries before their current usage, and raise the question of whether such histories are possible at all.[16] The desire of publishers, the reading public, undergraduates and harried lecturers for a straightforward story and the big picture sits uneasily beside the scholarly urge to complicate, to twist the kaleidoscope.

What, then, does this collection bring to the table? In siding with the kaleidoscope twisters, it aims for complexity (but also accessibility), to give a clear sense of the state of play and to offer pointers and suggestions for the next generation of research. It highlights a considerable diversity of thematic, methodological and theoretical approaches while retaining a strong geographical and chronological focus. It does not claim to be all-inclusive: the intersection of sexuality and gender with race and ethnicity, for example, is barely represented, analysed or even problematised here, reflecting how little work has been done and needs to be done in this area in the British context.[17] And, although all of the authors are comfortable working under a 'British Queer History' rubric, the chapters reflect a real tension between those scholars seeking and finding flashes of recognition and identifiable queer forebears (however hedged around with caveats) and those insisting on the irreducible alterity and foreignness of the past, between those who want to cling to and those who want to disrupt bounded queer subjectivities, between those who register few qualms about and those eager to deconstruct the hetero/homo binary, between the direct heirs of first-wave gay history (for whom 'queer', 'gay' and 'homosexual' are little more than interchangeable synonyms) and those who have put the most distance between themselves and these genealogical roots. This is merely to indicate that there is plenty of scope for continuing debate and expansion of research topics into the foreseeable future in this, one of the richest seams of recent modern British historiography.

Charles Upchurch begins the collection with a topic of concern to all the authors: the effective interrogation of archival sources in pursuit of British queer history. In previous studies of the nature and frequency of the discussion of sex between men in leading London newspapers between 1820 and 1870, Upchurch highlighted the pros and cons of full-text electronic searches of books, periodicals and government documents.[18] Although such searches allowed historians to expand dramatically the hunt for references to same-sex activity, in often unlikely or unpromising places, Upchurch noted that they were far from infallible and warned against overconfidence in the power of full-text searching. In this chapter, he again notes that the digitisation of newspaper archives enables researchers to map the multiple and often oblique ways that sex between men was publicly discussed during the eighteenth and nineteenth centuries. But full-text searching often overlooks allusion and innuendo. Detailed archival research and knowledge of the period are thus required in addition, greatly expanding the observable instances of such cases. Using his combined strategies, Upchurch locates the 1820s as the critical decade in which the tropes of eighteenth-century reporting of same-sex cases gave way to new conventions of policing and reporting – to innovative practices and procedures in the prosecution of sex that would dominate the next half century. He focuses on incidents involving a number of socially prominent individuals – including the notorious Bishop of Clogher affair in 1822 – to make his case.

Jongwoo Jeremy Kim's chapter demonstrates a fruitful cross-fertilisation of ideas between queer history and art history. His subject is Henry Scott Tuke's naturalist paintings of working-class Cornish life, in particular *All Hands to the Pumps!* (1889), *The Message* (1890) and *The Run Home* (1902). His contention is that these paintings of ordinary people performing everyday tasks on land or on sea, or heroically battling storms, which are often considered separately from Tuke's depictions of nude youths, should instead be viewed as a whole – as a consistent pursuit of Uranian ideals through the pictorial examination of the male body. The homoeroticism of this naturalism, Kim argues, was all part of Tuke's attempt to recapture for late Victorian England the Greek idyll of manly love for beautiful youths. The paintings, carefully decoded and backed by the documentary evidence of diaries and interviews, become replete with same-sex desire. And in his analysis of another painting, *A Woodland Bather* (1893), Kim borrows Walter Pater's idea of diaphanous, 'sexless beauty' to link the eponymous nude young man with the telegraph boy in *The Message*, tying the Uranian admiration for the seductive power of sexual indeterminacy to the sexual transgression of the Post Office messenger (in the wake of the Cleveland Street Scandal of 1889), an invitation to escape from the conventional boundaries and disciplines of heteronormativity.

If Chapter 1 draws principally on digitised newspapers and Chapter 2 on visual representations, the third chapter continues the exploration of different types of sources by focusing on autobiography.

Mo Moulton's study undertakes a meticulous reading of Katherine Everett's life-story, *Bricks and Flowers*. It is a prime example of the new queer history in its differentiation from gay and lesbian history: that is, it does not assume that an individual's sexuality in the past is knowable, it lays stress on alternative expressions of difference and it demonstrates the queer potential of de-normalising identity terms such as lesbian, gay and homosexual. Everett, a scion of the Anglo-Irish upper classes who later made a public, professional career as a successful building contractor, married briefly and had two sons; but she apparently never entertained other suitors after her husband left her at the beginning of the First World War. She lived for a time with her 'dear friend', Ina Jephson, and in 1949 dedicated her memoirs to her. Moulton recognises clearly enough that modern readers, attuned to the possibilities of same-sex relationships and habituated to the practice of recovering lost lesbians written out of the past, would be quite happy to draw conclusions; but she resists the temptation. While reading between the lines of Everett's memoir for whatever hints and whispers it might impart, and amassing the available evidence for any notion of her subject's sexual orientation, Moulton takes us no further than the surviving evidence will allow. Instead, she underlines the need to attend to what Everett herself broadcast at high volume: the richness of an unconventional, 'eccentric' life that relied on the support of misfit women and breached conventions of gender. This was a queer life, Moulton argues, whether or not Everett transgressed normative sexual behaviour, whether or not her personal life and sexual identity are legible to a modern readership.

Laura Doan's recent work has drawn a critical distinction between 'queerness as being' and 'queerness as method'. Queer scholarship over the last quarter of a century has effectively disrupted the stability of queer categories and targeted and dissected the hetero/homo binary, but it has tended to measure a queer fluidity against a fixed, unchanging heterosexuality. Her 'queerness as method' seeks to interrogate the production of heteronormativity and to disturb its universal, transhistorical status; she makes a powerful case for the queering of heterosexuality just as much as for homosexuality.[19] In this chapter her starting point is how, with the late nineteenth- and early twentieth-century medicalisation of sexuality, sexologists needed a 'normal' against which to measure deviance, but that this normal was an absent presence: heterosexuality was defined by what it was not. She zeroes in on a crucial moment, in 1918, when the binary began to

emerge in a form that has persisted ever since. In comparing and contrasting two texts by British feminist writers – Marie Stopes's *Married
Love* and a paper by Stella Browne on the 'problem of feminine inversion' – Doan demonstrates how the hetero and homo parts of the
binary have separate histories that evolved erratically and unevenly.
Browne used the sexologists' case study method to validate her theory
of female congenital inversion, to produce a knowable sexual subject
in contrast to its 'normal' opposite. But Stopes, in her hugely popular
marital advice tracts, was not interested in making the heterosexual
a case and remained sceptical of a scientific discourse that privileged anomaly and aberration. Her aim was to describe what married
couples *do* – and how they could and should do it more effectively
– rather than to define what they *become* as a result of their acts,
desires and bodily differences. These acts and desires of the normal
resided outside the classificatory system; to borrow from Foucault,
her analysis rested more on '*ars erotica*' than on '*scientia sexualis*' for
the production of sexual truth. This left the married lover as natural
and normal, defined by the act of coitus, rather than a category of
identity, a species, a knowable sexual subject. Doan concludes that
sexological knowledge alone does not account for the hetero/homo
distinction, complicating the task of explaining how and when the
normal began to exert its power in the social regulation of sexuality.

In Chapter 5, Ryan Linkof takes us into the camp, dandyish world
of the gossip columnist in British national newspapers and magazines between 1910 and the Second World War. Starting with 'Mr
Gossip' in the *Daily Sketch*, gossip writers established a reputation
for themselves in the late Edwardian era as cultivated, witty, urbane
decadents existing in a symbiotic relationship with London Society
hostesses who were eager to see their social gatherings recapitulated
in the press. As the genre developed and blossomed it attracted a
disproportionately large number of men with avowed same-sex identities or who indulged in same-sex acts. Linkof argues that gossip
columnists, to perform their jobs well, needed to operate on the
margins: sufficiently inside High Society so as to be welcomed at its
social events and rites of passage but, simultaneously, sufficiently
outside so as to speak with objective authority. As popular demand
for revelations about the private lives of celebrities accelerated in the
interwar period, queer men were particularly adept at discerning and
revealing hidden secrets and truths behind public façades. Since they
themselves performed a false identity for public approval on a daily

basis – in a hostile world where queer sex was illegal and homosexual expression frequently vilified – they were well attuned to the social masks and hypocrisies necessitated by custom and protocol. At the same time, as many of the writers were from privileged backgrounds, often Oxbridge graduates and protected by wealth and acclaim, many of them were able to deploy the advantages of class and connection to carve out a relatively protected space for themselves – so long as they kept their guards up and behaved with all due decorum.

In *Queer London*, Matt Houlbrook provided one of the most significant examples of the 'altericist reaction' fomented by the new British queer history. He sought to defamiliarise the past, to disrupt continuities, to problematise categories of identity and to dissect the 'modern homosexual' in order to reveal the contrasting sexual practices and subjectivities in the different social layers of post-1918 London. Yet, as he puts it in his chapter in this collection, his work remained wedded to binary understandings of difference. He and other practitioners of the new queer historiography had explored shifting formations of 'homosexuality', had complicated and nuanced the picture, but they had scarcely moved beyond an identitarian framework or troubled the homo/hetero binary. Now he wants to trouble it and trouble us. Drawing on Laura Doan's notion of 'queerness as method', he challenges us to 'think queer' in our practice as historians – to abandon the chimerical quest for a bounded queer (or straight) subject that only serves to reiterate inappropriate, restrictive binaries. Like Doan and Moulton he resorts to case studies, highlighting once again queer history's increasing preoccupation with the particular and the peculiar, implying that anything more representative is illusory. He focuses on two particular life-histories – Sydney Fox, a confidence trickster who was executed in 1930 for murdering his mother, and Josephine O'Dare, a Society beauty and 'sexualised vamp' who was gaoled for fraud in 1927 – to explore what happens when we think queer about subjects that cannot be subsumed into LGBT identity categories. He insists on the importance of a queer historical practice in elucidating social, cultural and political formations that engage with issues of sexuality only occasionally, tangentially or sometimes not at all. Thinking queer, he argues, is much too useful to be confined to the study of the queer.

This theoretical and analytical approach perhaps lends itself best to the interwar period and becomes more complicated in recent decades by the greater readiness of historical subjects to claim and cling to sexual identities as such categories gained greater cultural credence. Bringing us into the postwar world, Amy Tooth Murphy's chapter engages with self-identified lesbians and with another highly important source for queer history: oral history. In a series of interviews with women born before 1955, Murphy takes us beyond the social and political worlds of 'out and about' lesbians into the lesbian experience of domesticity. Scholars have largely neglected the home and the domestic side of queer lives, partly because of the paucity of testimonies, partly because of a privileging of the public over the private in narratives documenting an increasing lesbian and gay visibility. This, Murphy argues, downplays the significance of the sites where people lived most of their lives, obscures those women who were not (until later at least) visible or 'out' lesbians and perpetuates the notion that, in the wake of the Second World War, the domestic sphere could be equated simply and unproblematically with the reinforcement of heteronormative and gender-specific roles. In drawing a distinction between 'hetero-domesticity' and 'homo-domesticity' – between those women who were previously married to men and those who only had same-sex relationships – Murphy compares and contrasts the ways in which the women in her sample brought narrative composure to their life-stories. Those who had avoided hetero-domesticity tended to project a more coherent sense of self, a more stable identity as lesbian women; those who had to work around such a central life-phase and cultural trope as marriage by and large had a less composed, more fractured sense of their sexual selves. With such insights, Murphy sheds light on the ways in which her narrators envisioned and created domestic spaces, providing a more complete and complex picture of lesbian lives in postwar Britain.

Chris Waters's chapter approaches historical recuperation from another angle – not the recuperation of the lives and experiences of gays and lesbians but of those forms of knowledge that rendered their lives intelligible in particular ways. His concern is with how and why 'experts' reconceptualised the male homosexual in the two decades after 1945, transforming him from a biological, psychosexual and often pathological problem into a social being. In meticulous detail, Waters traces how the homosexual became seen as part of a minority pursuing a particular way of life – as a social problem amenable to social solutions and forms of management. He argues that this process of uncovering, dissecting and mapping the homosexual's social relations took place relatively late in Britain, with tentative prewar beginnings only producing significant studies in the 1950s and 1960s. All this was in the context of a dramatic expansion of the human sciences during and after the war and the perceived need to address a range of social problems – a declining birth-rate, divorce, juvenile delinquency, race relations and homosexuality among them – that appeared to threaten the rational, ordered landscape of postwar Britain. But, Waters contends, much of this new approach to and understanding of homosexuality (initially as a problem, increasingly couched in more positive terms of tolerance, acceptance and advocacy) has been obscured. Scholars of queer history have paid so much attention to the radical gay-liberationist paradigm shift of the late 1960s, and its denigration of most of what went before, that they have overlooked the pivotal work of those earlier postwar writers who carved out a space for the study of homosexuality as a social phenomenon.

Waters gestures towards international comparisons in speaking of the 'relatively late' advent of the homosexual as a social being in Britain, and all the authors in this collection draw extensively on a scholarly literature that freely trespasses over national borders. Yet none of them would dissent from the proposition that the nation state is crucially important in framing the discourse, practices and experiences of queer history – not even David Minto, who comes closest to troubling the boundaries of 'British' queer history. His chapter is built around the papers of Antony Grey, secretary of the Homosexual Law Reform Society, and in particular Grey's correspondence with homophile organisations in continental Europe and the United States in the 1960s. Minto reminds us that in the pre-Stonewall decade, before gay liberation caught fire and spread, these organisations – and in particular the Anglo-American network – shared magazines, letters, people and strategies in a mutual search for inspiration, support and legitimacy. In the wake of the 1967 Sexual Offences Act, which partially decriminalised gay sex in Britain, Grey set off on a speaker's tour of the US at the invitation of American activists committed to law reform. He was broadly welcomed, but his tour brought out not only the infighting between competing US homophile factions but also the differences in tactics on both sides of the Atlantic – between Grey's politics of respectability, for example, and the Washington activist Frank Kameny's more militant, in-your-face approach. Minto's chapter highlights the international dimension of what to date has been told as a classic British tale of homosexual law reform – but also illuminates the choices made and constraints imposed at the national level.

Sticking with pre-decriminalisation Britain, in the penultimate chapter Justin Bengry focuses on the 'pink pound' – the queer marketplace – in the 1950s and 1960s. In exploring the print culture of magazines, yet another critical source for queer history, Bengry zeroes in on *Films and Filming*, in its heyday an internationally respected and successful film journal. *Films and Filming* could be, and was, read on two different levels by two different audiences: as a mainstream publication devoted to the promotion and review of films; and as a magazine catering for a queer clientele, with all kinds of barely encoded information easily legible to those who were looking or who were in the know. Interviews with editors and contributors and reminiscences from readers leave no doubt that the magazine's producers knew what they were about, that they were deliberately targeting a potential market while flying under the radar of censors. Thus *Films and Filming* at various times included photo spreads featuring generous proportions of male flesh, articles on the censorship of queer themes in film and theatre, advertisements for queer-friendly businesses and discreet bachelor ads from men seeking men. But closeted gay men, purporting to have a fascination with film, could have it delivered or purchase it in newsagents and read it openly on the Underground, in a bus or in the office, without raising suspicion. Bengry argues that *Films and Filming* was the longest-running pre-decriminalisation magazine to be successful and respected in the mainstream while courting a queer market segment. It is an important example of one of the many ways in which queer-identifying men could find information and could connect, even in an age of repression.

In the final chapter, Paul Deslandes continues the investigation of magazines and queer market niches, but this time in the post-decriminalisation, post-Stonewall era of the 1970s. There was nothing coy, ambiguous or coded about the gay pornography on open display in *Him Exclusive, Him International* and *Him Monthly*. Produced by gays for gays, these magazines promoted what they saw as a politically progressive, sex-positive gay identity through a celebration of erotic pleasure, hyper-masculine bodies and frank sexual education. Many self-identifying gay men, in letters to the editor and in submissions to the Williams Committee on Obscenity and Film Censorship, set up in 1977, praised the virtues of such publications for depicting an alternative reality enabling gay men a momentary escape from the negativity of a largely hostile society. But some gay socialists and feminists were among those who expressed qualms about the exploitative and body-worshipping implications of this new explicitness. More significantly, the magazines also ran afoul of morality crusaders and anti-obscenity legislation; they were subject to periodic closures, arrests, seizures and fines as agents of the state sought not only to police the boundaries of propriety but also to regulate queer political expression. In response, the magazines positioned themselves as unlikely defenders of multiple freedoms against oppression. Deslandes concludes that, in the new-found assertiveness of homosexuals and in the struggle to expand a public, gay culture after 1967, questions of aesthetics, censorship and the politics of liberation formed a potent mix – and gay pornography was central to these debates.

The gay porn of the 1970s is a fitting way to round off this introduction, since it is indicative of the range of sources at play in this volume and the distance travelled from the cagily phrased accounts in the public prints of the 1820s. Collectively, these essays provide a variety of fresh perspectives and a wealth of new information, suggest enticing avenues for research and challenge us to rethink the parameters of the field. As British queer history grows from adolescence into maturity, encompassing more and more practitioners, moving beyond the identitarian comfort zone and making bigger and bigger claims, today is a good time to be a queer historian.[20]

## Notes

1 *Independent* (3 December 2002).
2 'The love ...' is a line from Lord Alfred Douglas's poem 'Two Loves' (1894); the 'horrible sin not to be spoken of among Christians' most famously appears in William Blackstone, *Commentaries on the Laws of England*, vol. IV (1769), p. 215; and the 'unspeakable' is Maurice Hall's self-description in E. M. Forster, *Maurice* (begun 1913, published 1971).
3 A. D. Peterkin, *Outbursts! A Queer Erotic Thesaurus* (Vancouver: Arsenal Pulp Press, 2003), pp. 54–64, 77–81. An 'A-gay' is an A-list gay man who has money, looks and power; a 'zebrajox' is a black male who likes white males, or vice versa; a 'zamie girl' is a West Indian term for a lesbian.
4 See Simon Watney, *Policing Desire: Pornography, AIDS, and the Media* (Minneapolis: University of Minnesota Press, 1987); Richard Davenport-Hines, *Sex, Death and Punishment: Attitudes to Sex and Sexuality in Britain since the Renaissance* (London: Collins, 1990), chapter 9.

5   See Jeffrey Weeks, *The Languages of Sexuality* (London: Routledge, 2011), pp. 144–6.

6   See, for example, Sally R. Munt, 'Introduction', in Andy Medhurst and Sally R. Munt (eds), *Lesbian and Gay Studies: A Critical Introduction* (London: Cassell, 1997), pp. xi–xvii; Terry Castle, *The Apparitional Lesbian: Female Homosexuality and Modern Culture* (New York: Columbia University Press, 1993), pp. 12–13; Sheila Jeffreys, 'The queer disappearance of lesbians: Sexuality in the academy', *Women's Studies International Forum*, 17:5 (1994), 459–72; Joshua Gamson, 'Must identity movements self-destruct? A queer dilemma', *Social Problems*, 42:3 (August 1995), 390–407; Steven Epstein, 'A queer encounter: Sociology and the study of sexuality', *Sociological Theory*, 12:2 (July 1994), 188–202; Adam Isaiah Green, 'Gay but not queer: Toward a post-queer study of sexuality', *Theory and Society*, 31 (2002), 521–45.

7   http://queermcgill.ca/about/faq/, accessed 28 June 2012.

8   *Journal of British Studies*, 51:3 (July 2012).

9   Though there have, of course, been landmark collections or readers on gay history more broadly, such as Martin Bauml Duberman et al. (eds), *Hidden from History: Reclaiming the Gay and Lesbian Past* (New York: NAL Books, 1989) and on the history of sexuality more generally, such as Kim M. Phillips and Barry Reay (eds), *Sexualities in History: A Reader* (London: Routledge, 2002).

10  Especially Jeffrey Weeks, *Coming Out: Homosexual Politics in Britain, from the Nineteenth Century to the Present* (London: Quartet Books, 1977); Kenneth Plummer (ed.), *The Making of the Modern Homosexual* (Totowa, NJ: Barnes and Noble Books, 1981).

11  Chris Waters, 'Distance and desire in the new British queer history', *GLQ*, 14:1 (2007), 140–1. Prominent examples of the former include Joseph Bristow, *Effeminate England: Homoerotic Writing after 1885* (New York: Columbia University Press, 1995); Richard Dellamora, *Masculine Desire: The Sexual Politics of Victorian Aestheticism* (Chapel Hill: University of North Carolina Press, 1990); Linda Dowling, *Hellenism and Homosexuality in Victorian Oxford* (Ithaca: Cornell University Press, 1994); Alan Sinfield, *The Wilde Century: Effeminacy, Oscar Wilde and the Queer Moment* (London: Cassell, 1994) and of the latter include Hugh David, *On Queer Street: A Social History of British Homosexuality, 1895–1995* (London: HarperCollins, 1997); Emily Hamer, *Britannia's Glory: A History of Twentieth-Century Lesbians* (London: Cassell, 1996); Patrick Higgins, *Heterosexual Dictatorship: Male Homosexuality in Postwar Britain* (London: Fourth Estate, 1996); Stephen Jeffery-Poulter, *Peers, Queers and Commons: The Struggle for Gay Law Reform from 1950 to the Present* (London: Routledge, 1991); Alkarim Jivani, *It's Not Unusual: A History of Lesbian and Gay Britain in the Twentieth Century*

(Bloomington: Indiana University Press, 1997); Lisa Power, *No Bath But Plenty of Bubbles: An Oral History of the Gay Liberation Front 1970–73* (London: Cassell, 1995).

12  The evolution of the field is traced by Joseph Bristow, 'Remapping the sites of modern gay history: Legal reform, medico-legal thought, homosexual scandal, erotic geography', *Journal of British Studies*, 46:1 (January 2007), 116–42; H. G. Cocks, 'Homosexuality between men in Britain since the eighteenth century', *History Compass*, 5:3 (2007), 865–89; Barry Reay, 'Writing the modern histories of homosexual England', *Historical Journal*, 52:1 (2009), 213–33; Waters, 'Distance and desire', 139–55; Jeffrey Weeks, 'Queer(y)ing the "modern homosexual"', *Journal of British Studies*, 51:3 (July 2012), 523–39. Leading works in the field since 2000 include Chiara Beccalossi, *Female Sexual Inversion: Same-Sex Desires in Italian and British Sexology, c. 1870–1920* (Houndmills, Basingstoke: Palgrave Macmillan, 2011); Sean Brady, *Masculinity and Male Homosexuality in Britain, 1861–1913* (Houndmills, Basingstoke: Palgrave Macmillan, 2005); H. G. Cocks, *Nameless Offences: Homosexual Desire in the Nineteenth Century* (London: I. B. Tauris, 2003); Deborah Cohler, *Citizen, Invert, Queer: Lesbianism and War in Early Twentieth-Century Britain* (Minneapolis: University of Minnesota Press, 2010); Matt Cook, *London and the Culture of Homosexuality, 1885–1914* (Cambridge: Cambridge University Press, 2003); Laura Doan, *Fashioning Sapphism: The Origins of a Modern English Lesbian Culture* (New York: Columbia University Press, 2001) and *Disturbing Practices: History, Sexuality, and Women's Experience of Modern War* (Chicago: University of Chicago Press, 2013); Matt Houlbrook, *Queer London: Perils and Pleasures in the Sexual Metropolis, 1918–57* (Chicago: University of Chicago Press, 2005); Rebecca Jennings, *Tomboys and Bachelor Girls: A Lesbian History of Post-War Britain, 1945–71* (Manchester: Manchester University Press, 2008); Morris Kaplan, *Sodom on the Thames: Sex, Love and Scandal in Wilde Times* (Ithaca: Cornell University Press, 2005); Sharon Marcus, *Between Women: Friendship, Desire, and Marriage in Victorian England* (Princeton: Princeton University Press, 2007); Frank Mort, *Capital Affairs: London and the Making of the Permissive Society* (New Haven: Yale University Press, 2010); Alison Oram, *Her Husband Was a Woman! Women's Gender-Crossing in Modern British Popular Culture* (London: Routledge, 2008); Lucy Robinson, *Gay Men and the Left in Post-War Britain* (Manchester: Manchester University Press, 2007); Charles Upchurch, *Before Wilde: Sex between Men in Britain's Age of Reform* (Berkeley: University of California Press, 2009); Martha Vicinus, *Intimate Friends: Women Who Loved Women, 1778–1928* (University of Chicago Press, 2004); Jeffrey Weeks, *The World We Have Won* (Abingdon: Routledge, 2007).

13  Weeks, 'Queer(y)ing the "modern homosexual"', 538.

14  See Annamarie Jagose, *Queer Theory: An Introduction* (New York: New York University Press, 2006); Geoff Eley, *A Crooked Line: From Cultural History to the History of Society* (Ann Arbor: University of Michigan Press, 2005); Brian Lewis, 'The new social history: A new *kind* of history' and 'The newest social history: Crisis and renewal', chapters 6 and 14 of Sarah Foot and Nancy Partner (eds), *Sage Handbook of Historical Theory* (London: Sage, 2013).

15  Eve Kosofsky Sedgwick, *Between Men: English Literature and Male Homosocial Desire* (New York: Columbia University Press, 1985) and *Epistemology of the Closet* (Berkeley: University of California Press, 1990); Michel Foucault, *The History of Sexuality*, vol. 1: *An Introduction*, trans. Robert Hurley (New York: Penguin, 1980); David M. Halperin, *How to Do the History of Homosexuality* (Chicago: University of Chicago Press, 2002); Randolph Trumbach, *Sex and the Gender Revolution*, vol. 1: *Heterosexuality and the Third Gender in Enlightenment London* (Chicago: Chicago University Press, 1998).

16  Rebecca Jennings, *A Lesbian History of Britain: Love and Sex between Women since 1500* (Oxford: Greenwood, 2007); Matt Cook (ed.), *A Gay History of Britain: Love and Sex between Men since the Middle Ages* (Oxford: Greenwood, 2007); Reay, 'Writing the modern histories of homosexual England', 214–15.

17  In contrast to the work done in the US. See, for example, E. Patrick Johnson and Mae G. Henderson (eds), *Black Queer Studies: A Critical Anthology* (Durham, NC: Duke University Press, 2005); George Chauncey, *Gay New York: Gender, Urban Culture, and the Making of the Gay Male World, 1890–1940* (New York: Basic Books, 1994); John Howard, *Men Like That: Southern Queer History* (Chicago: University of Chicago Press, 1999); Marc Stein, *City of Sisterly and Brotherly Loves: Lesbian and Gay Philadelphia, 1945–1972* (Chicago: University of Chicago Press, 2000).

18  See Charles Upchurch, 'Full-text databases and historical research: Cautionary results from a ten-year study', *Journal of Social History*, 45 (2012), 1–17.

19  See Laura Doan, 'Sex education and the Great War soldier: A queer analysis of the practice of "hetero" sex', *Journal of British Studies*, 51:3 (July 2012), 641–63.

20  Eric Hobsbawm, 'From social history to the history of society', *Daedalus*, 100 (1971), 43, famously made the same claim about social history. Equally famously, the gods soon punished such hubris and social history came under prolonged assault. At the risk of giving a hostage to fortune, I remain more sanguine about the future of British queer history.

**1**

# Politics and the reporting of sex between men in the 1820s

*Charles Upchurch*

There is something of a paradox in the discussion of sex between men in Britain in the nineteenth century. For generations it was thought to have been unspeakable and unspoken-about in this period, and the discussion of it is almost entirely absent from nineteenth-century diaries, novels, parliamentary papers and other sources. Yet for most of the nineteenth century, sex between men was regularly discussed in the mainstream newspapers, primarily through articles about court cases ranging in length from one paragraph to multiple columns of text. These stories were carried in newspapers directed at the upper, middle and working classes, although the amount of detail and the frequency of coverage varied from paper to paper. Over six hundred substantial reports relating to sex between men were printed in *The Times* between 1822 and 1871 alone, with some years seeing as few as three or four reports and others having as many as thirty-seven or thirty-eight.[1] The *Weekly Dispatch* had about two-thirds as many as *The Times*, while the *Morning Post* had just under half as many. There was some coverage of court cases related to sex between men before 1822 and after 1871, but in those periods the number of reports dropped substantially, and the amount of detail in most reports was often only skeletal.

The volume of the discussion that occurred between 1822 and 1871 was largely forgotten by later generations of historians, but the events that led to it were not. The regular publication of the details of trials related to sex between men in London ended because of the 1870–71 Boulton and Park prosecution, which inadvertently revealed the way that large numbers of middle-class male cross-dressers and their admirers made use of the pubic and private spaces of the West End.[2] Fifty years earlier, it was the arrest and the failed prosecution of the Bishop of Clogher in 1822 that was the catalyst for the regular publication of such detailed coverage in the liberal daily newspapers.

The identification of these two well-known cases as transition points in the public discussion of sex between men has been made possible using full-text searching for dozens of newspapers, although accurate results for this type of analysis take time to establish. *The Times* is a unique resource for mapping the accuracy of full-text searching, since in addition to being full-text searchable within the *Times Digital Archive*, there also exists an index to *The Times* that was created over a forty-year period in the late nineteenth and early twentieth centuries. During the creation of the *Palmer's Index to the Times*, individuals read every story, and categorised them under terms devised by an understanding of the meaning of the sentences and paragraphs. By contrast, full-text databases should be understood as possibly imperfect catalogues of the words appearing in the newspaper, which is not the same information, especially if journalists have used vague terms to discuss uncomfortable topics.[3] Given these differences, it has taken years to piece together what seems like a reliably accurate understanding of how sex between men was reported for all of the decades of the nineteenth century, and only with such a picture do the Boulton and Park case of 1870–71 and the Bishop of Clogher prosecution of 1822 become distinct as transitional moments.

Also apparent from this more detailed understanding of what actually appeared in the newspapers is the political origins of this type of reporting. It was not just the hypocrisy of a bishop of the Church of Ireland being caught having sex with a soldier that made his case such a sensation in 1822, although that is the primary way it has been discussed in more recent scholarship. It was rather that when the events of 1822 were linked in the public sphere with an earlier trial that occurred in Ireland in 1811, as they were after just a few days in the major London newspapers, they showed in a shockingly graphic way the injustice perpetrated by the judicial system as it then operated in this area of the law. It was an injustice so galling, and so perfectly illustrative of the abuses of aristocratic government, that radical publications like *Cobbett's Political Register*, Richard Carlile's *Republican* and Thomas Wooler's *Black Dwarf* seized on the issue and found ways to keep it before the public for months. Even more dangerous for the government than the anger of the radicals, however, was that the liberal middle-class newspapers, heretofore extremely circumspect in their reporting of trials related to sex between men, matched and then exceeded the radical press in the attention given to these events. Just as the murderous excesses of Peterloo in 1819 were

the catalyst for *The Times* to move more forcefully towards supporting
a liberal reform agenda, so too should the increased coverage of sex
between men in *The Times* and other liberal newspapers be seen as
a critique of the system of unnatural assault prosecutions as it had
existed up to 1822, and an attempt to end the secrecy that created the
potential for abuses of power.[4]

The evidence for this exists not only in the sustained level of
increased reporting from that point forward, but also in the content
of those reports in the months and years immediately after 1822. A
greater willingness on the part of individuals to bring these cases
seems evident in the volatile situation of 1822 and 1823, leading to
an alteration of the law, in 1823 and again in early 1825, designed to
strengthen the position of propertied men when accused of sexual
advances by their social inferiors. This was followed by what seems
like an aggressive reassertion of state authority in this area in 1825,
when reported cases of sex between men and related extortion accusations reached a one-year peak not exceeded until the 1840s. Caught
in this wave of new prosecutions were John Grossett Muirhead, Esq.,
and Lieutenant-Colonel Richard Archdall, both from aristocratic families, and both prosecuted for making sexual advances on working-
class young men. The Muirhead and Archdall prosecutions are the
two most prominent trials related to sex between men in the 1820s
not yet discussed in any detail in the scholarly literature, and, as analysed in the final pages of this chapter, their divergent fates illustrate
some of the effects of the greater newspaper attention to these cases.
By the end of the 1820s the advantages of the wealthy in these cases
were largely restored, but the abuses that could stem from those
advantages were tempered by sustained and dispassionate publicity,
spearheaded by a liberal press reluctant to publicise these events, yet
obligated to bring the check of public opinion into even this area of
the exercise of state power.[5]

To argue that 1822 represented a break requires first establishing
what the earlier pattern had been. State statistics for prosecutions
of sodomy and attempted sodomy became consistent only in 1810,
putting the total number of cases before the criminal courts at around
forty per year for England and Wales, with on average fifteen of those
occurring in London and Middlesex. The number of cases increased
steadily if erratically over the 1820s, so that by 1830 just over eighty
cases were recorded per year for the criminal courts of England

and Wales, with just over forty of those occurring in London and
Middlesex.[6]

Given time and patience, the newspaper record can be reconstructed
for a significantly longer period of time. Randolph Trumbach's extensive search of the eighteenth century using full-text searching within
the newspapers of the *Burney Collection* generally aligns in its findings with my own work with the *Times Digital Archive*, *Palmer's Index
to the Times*, *British Newspapers, 1800–1900* and the names of the men
gleaned from the HO 26 series of government documents housed in
the National Archives.[7] Incidents involving sodomy and attempted
sodomy were recorded in eighteenth-century newspapers, but most
often with only a line or two noting the occurrence, or the verdict if a
trial was held. Before 1822 there was on average only one story with
any amount of detail related to sex between men in *The Times* in any
given year, with those stories most often involving libel or extortion
charges. Radical or Ultra-Tory newspapers might publish rumour
or innuendo pertaining to same-sex desire, as the *New Times* did
regarding a political ally of Major John Cartwright, the *True Briton*
did regarding the bibliophile and MP Richard Heber, and the *Weekly
Dispatch* did regarding the Rev. John Church, but such references
were most often fleeting, and were also primarily about critiquing
the behaviour of individuals rather than recounting the actions of the
state.[8]

There was one major exception to this pattern of minimal trial
coverage before 1822, but more than anything it seems to show that
sensationalism alone was not enough to change the approach of the
liberal press to the reporting of these cases. On 8 July 1810 twenty-
seven men were arrested at the White Swan, a London molly house
located on Vere Street. Most of the victims of the police raid were
released or otherwise acquitted, but six of these men were sentenced
to stand in the pillory for an hour, in addition to serving prison sentences of two to three years. The description of the violent anger and
insults hurled at them both before and especially during their time in
the pillory has become one of the most indelible images shaping our
understanding of sex between men in the early nineteenth century.[9]

There were at least some significant parallels in the coverage of
Vere Street in *The Times* and the patterns associated with the 1822
Bishop of Clogher coverage. Both led to a spike in coverage of other
cases related to sex between men in the following months. Of the
fourteen substantial reports related to sex between men present in

*The Times* that year, ten related to individuals not connected to Vere Street, making 1810 the year with the largest number of these smaller stories, by far, between 1800 and 1822. Also as in 1822, the spate of short articles began only after the major event. Yet if the Vere Street incident initially led to *The Times* paying increased attention to a wide range of prosecutions involving sex between men, the former pattern of minimal coverage was re-established within a few months. Only two reports related to sex between men were detected in the following year, only one per year in 1815, 1817 and 1818, and none in 1812, 1813, 1814, 1816 or 1821.[10]

The reason Vere Street did not create a lasting change in the reporting of the law in this area was because the prosecutions and punishments showed the law operating in a way consistent with its own rules, and in alignment with public and popular opinion. In a time of war, economic hardship and government repression, the spectacle of the Vere Street prosecutions united the government and a large segment of the London population in a vengeful humiliation of these men. The reports that it took over two hundred constables to keep the crowd at bay, that the crowds packed the streets for the entire route to the pillory to taunt the convicted men and that the men became bloodied and nearly indistinguishable as human forms from the amount of mud, vegetables, animal parts and other objects hurled at them as they stood defenceless, all displayed a disturbing consensus on the issue of punishment of men thought to be sodomites.[11] Because of this it was a political asset for the government rather than a political threat.

The 1822 arrest of the Bishop of Clogher and related revelations concerning James Byrne had entirely the opposite effect. On the night of 19 July 1822 Percy Jocelyn, the Bishop of Clogher, was caught in the White Lion public house in London having sex with John Moverley, a twenty-two-year-old Grenadier Guard. The two had planned to meet there at nine o'clock that evening, each going separately to a back parlour. Moverley was in his military uniform, while Jocelyn, who had spent the day in the House of Lords, was wearing clothes that gave him 'the appearance of a gentleman'.[12] It was the son-in-law of the landlord who first suspected the men, and saw them in the act through a window in the back yard of the public house. The landlord, a watchman and several other regular patrons of the public house all watched Jocelyn and the soldier through the window for some time before finally breaking in and making the arrest. A mob had formed around Jocelyn and the soldier on their way to the St James's watch house, and, despite Jocelyn's efforts to keep his identity secret, a letter in his possession soon revealed his identity.

News that a bishop had been arrested with a common soldier spread throughout the capital, fanned primarily by word of mouth and the radical press in the first days. Outrage over Jocelyn's actions was augmented on the following day with the reports that he was allowed bail of only £1,000, an amount so low for a man of his fortune that it all but assured he would flee the country, as he almost immediately did. In the following days clergymen found themselves taunted in the streets of London, with the private secretary to the Home Secretary remarking that no event in the last one hundred years was potentially more damaging to the system of deference binding the lower and higher social orders.[13] Yet despite this firestorm and the attention that the radical press and word of mouth was bringing to these events, the daily newspapers remained almost entirely silent in the first week.

By mapping the timing and the amount of press coverage stemming from Percy Jocelyn's arrest, it becomes apparent that the revelations concerning James Byrne were what brought the liberal press to cover the bishop's story.[14] Within a few days the newspapers were reporting that in 1811 James Byrne had been prosecuted for accusing Jocelyn, then the Bishop of Ferns and Leighlin, of attempting to commit an 'unnatural act'. Byrne had worked as a coachman for Jocelyn's brother, and the circumstances by which Jocelyn was able to get Byrne alone and make his sexual advance were not that different from those in hundreds of reports that would be published in the London newspapers from 1822 forward. Byrne did not attempt to make an accusation with only his word against the bishop's, but two letters that he had as additional evidence of Jocelyn's advances 'were taken from him by a stratagem, and he, being thus deprived of the only documents by which he could support his charge against the Bishop, was brought to trial for defamation and found guilty'.[15] Byrne was sentenced to two years' imprisonment and two or three floggings. It was reported that after the first flogging, where 'he was bled and tortured until the last spark of life and feeling had nearly become extinct', he was persuaded to recant his accusation on the promise that the other floggings would not follow. Even then 'he did not yield until after repeated menaces of utter destruction, and until his wife and four children were brought to his dungeon, and had

thrown themselves on their knees, and actually *wept him* into acqui-
escence'. On signing the confession, it was reported that Byrne told
the Sherriff 'but mind, *I am about to put my name to a falsehood!!!*'[16]

These were the details that constituted the first substantial reports
in *The Times* on the Bishop of Clogher incident, with the liberal and
the radical press now almost equal in their expressions of outrage.
The readers of the liberal and the radical press were shown in detail
how the character of Byrne was denigrated in 1811, while the personal morality and noble heritage of Jocelyn were repeatedly praised.
In some 1822 reports up to one-third of the total text was taken
up with reprinted statements from the 1811 trial documents where
'the attention of the jury [was called] to every act of [Percy Jocelyn's]
life, and they would find them marked by the display of *virtue, piety,
and benevolence*'. Jocelyn himself was praised, as were his family,
'the other noble branches of this stock' and 'the unusual purity of
their sires', and all this was used as 'the most undeniable evidence
to prove, that every tittle which this most atrocious wretch [Byrne]
has alleged is utterly false'.[17] And yet exactly the opposite was true.
Someone of the highest birth, with one of the highest positions in
the state church, was shown in paragraph after paragraph to be lying
remorselessly, sending an innocent man to be flogged to a point near
death, all to protect himself and hide his lustful advances. Not only
did all this happen, but the legal procedures that ratified it were still
very much in place in 1822, and potentially continuing to facilitate
similar injustices.

Radical politicians not only seized on Byrne's story, but when it
was discovered that he was still alive in Ireland he was brought to
London and given a hero's welcome. William Cobbett presided over
a London banquet given in Byrne's honour, attended by over two
hundred individuals. A public subscription was also set up for Byrne,
raising over £300 to compensate him. Advertisements for the ban-
quets and subscription kept Byrne's name and his story before the
public, as did more substantial publications like William Benbow's
1822 *Crimes of the Clergy*, or the retelling of Byrne's story in a pamphlet with commentary written by William Cobbett.[18] Even *The Times*
argued that part of the property of Jocelyn should be seized and given
in compensation to Byrne, while the more radical *Bell's Life in London*
argued that the case 'cannot but be viewed as a most important lesson
to judges, magistrates, and counsellors'.[19]

It is within this charged atmosphere that we need to consider the suicide of Robert Stewart, Viscount Castlereagh, Foreign Secretary from 1812 to 1822. On 12 August 1822, just over a week after the publication of the revelations about James Byrne in the radical and liberal newspapers, Castlereagh cut his own throat at his country retreat in Kent. Some have argued that the suicide was sparked from exhaustion caused by his parliamentary responsibilities, but it seems likely that Matthew Parris and Nick Angel, John Derry and H. Montgomery Hyde are correct in arguing that the suicide was also due to Castlereagh being blackmailed over the accusation that he had approached another man for sex.[20] Among the most compelling evidence for this is in the diary of Harriet Arbuthnot, prominent Tory hostess and close friend to Castlereagh, who recorded his confession to her that he was guilty of the same crime as Jocelyn, that everyone knew it and that he expected to have a warrant issued for his arrest in the near future.[21] The denial of homosexual blackmail as the reason for Castlereagh's suicide has most often been coupled with a dismissal of the idea that Castlereagh had homosexual desires, but the issue of Castlereagh's personal sexual preferences is in large part immaterial to the political significance of the event and what it tells us of the political climate of 1822 and the years immediately following.

For radicals, Castlereagh was one of the most hated political figures of the day owing to his longstanding opposition to parliamentary reform, his support for foreign autocratic regimes at the expense of liberal movements, his role supporting George IV in the Queen Caroline Affair and, most recently, for his introduction into Parliament of some of the most repressive legislation following the 1819 Peterloo Massacre. As the Mary Anne Clark Affair and the Queen Caroline Affair had recently demonstrated, accusations of sexual misconduct could be far more effective as a weapon for criticising high political officials than attacks on their policies or competence.[22] Any defence Castlereagh would have mounted against a charge of having solicited sex from another man would have been one man's word against another's, and would have involved witnesses speaking to the good character of Castlereagh and against that of his accuser. Given the then-current uproar over just such a defence that had proved to be a fabrication, Castlereagh may have wondered if such an argument would have been possible at that moment, and what the political consequences would be for mounting it. Castlereagh's suicide possibly prevented such an explosive situation from following directly on the heels of the Bishop of Clogher revelations, and the idea that the suicide was linked to accusations of sex between men was not reported in the press.

But a great deal else was. Just a few weeks later liberal and radical newspapers reported that the Duke of Newcastle had personally taken action against his valet and other men accused of having sex with one another. Newcastle had come in to the possession of a letter from Henry Hackett, a nineteen-year-old apprentice to a local draper, which addressed Newcastle's valet as 'my beloved Benjamin'. It was ultimately determined that the men were 'part of a gang; and that the number of individuals already implicated in the affair amounted to thirty-six'.[23] The final months of 1822 also saw newspaper reports on cases that included accusations of sodomy in a long-running debt dispute, reports of unnatural assaults in a house where men newly arrived in London from the country were invited to sleep, several more cases involving soldiers and sailors, several more involving clergymen and extortion cases related to charges of sex between men.[24]

The number of extensively reported cases remained elevated throughout 1823 and 1824, even as the law was being altered in this area to try and address the increased threat to propertied men that this represented. In 1823 the eighteenth-century law governing attempts to rob by use of threats was modified, making it more applicable to cases of threatening to accuse another man of an infamous crime. An 1824 court case, however, determined that the wording of the new law made it applicable only if the threat involved an accusation of sodomy, the felony related to sex between men, but not attempted sodomy, the misdemeanour, making it inapplicable in the majority of cases.[25] New legislation was passed correcting this problem in early 1825, coinciding with the dramatic increase in the reporting of unnatural assault cases and related extortion accusations in that year.

Individuals at the time noticed this increased coverage. In August 1825 it was reported in *The Times* that 'scarcely a week passes but the magistrates of this office have individuals brought before them, (and those of most respectable connexions in society), charged with indecent assaults on the sentries in the park'. Less than two weeks later, a report from a different police court noted that 'the disgusting propensity to practices at which human nature revolts, and which were formerly seldom or ever heard of among Englishmen, is again evidently upon the increase in the metropolis'. The report went on to say that 'in addition to the instances that have recently transpired at Bow-street and other public offices, two charges for offences of similar descriptions have occurred at this Justice-room within the course of the present week'. One week later at another police court 'the Magistrate was occupied for a considerable time in the investigation of one of those revolting and unnatural cases, so many of which have recently been heard at the different police offices in town'.[26] Three weeks later, a man was acquitted on a charge related to 'this horrible and increasing crime' while yet another court a few weeks later also dealt with 'disgusting charges of human depravity, which has unhappily, in so many recent instances, engaged the attention of police magistrates'. Finally, in one of the many threatening-to-accuse cases that occurred in 1825, 'the Judge, in summing up, remarked upon the increase of crimes of this nature since the passing of the act of the 4$^{TH}$ Geo. IV'.[27] Finding even one such statement that these cases were on the increase in any given year between 1800 and 1870 is extremely rare, and the repetition in 1825 indicates that such comments were not simply rhetoric but reflected actual change.

No fewer than thirty-four separate reports related to sex between men appeared in *The Times* in 1825, and no fewer than twenty-four in the *Weekly Dispatch*. The largest single category of reported cases in this year was those involving extortion with threats to accuse of an infamous crime. One of the earliest in that year was described 'as deserving the particular attention of the jury, from its being the first instance of a prosecution under the late statute (4 George IV)'.[28] In this case Frederick Denman and Joseph Mould were put on trial for threatening to accuse Thomas Cozens of an infamous crime; in another trial of that same year Charles Houlder and David Gardener were indicted on 4 Geo. IV for feloniously sending a letter to the Rev. Edmund Cartwright; in another James Dovey and Roger Adams were put to death after having been found guilty of threatening to accuse another man of an infamous crime; in another case Thomas Dunkley, a journeyman baker, and Samuel Bird, a butcher, were indicted for extorting John Axx; and in still another case George Kelly, a carpenter, was accused of extorting money from Edward Turner. These and other cases involving extortions related to unnatural assault were extensively reported in 1825. Sexual assaults in front of picture-shop windows, cases involving soldiers and sailors and one molly house raid were also reported in that year.[29]

The raid on the Barley Mow was the most publicised attack on a molly house since the 1810 Vere Street arrests, and yet surprisingly it was not the most shocking incident related to sex between men that appeared in the papers on 23 August 1825. Judging by the public reaction, that distinction belonged instead to the story of John Grossett Muirhead, Esq., a member of the Society for the Suppression of Vice, Vice President of the Auxiliary Bible Society and brother-in-law of the Duke of Atholl. In August 1825, newspaper readers learned of the techniques he had been using to pick up young men for the better part of two decades. His encounters with several of them were described in detail, including his three meetings with Charles Lane, sixteen years of age, who was first approached by Muirhead as he stood in front of a picture-shop window. After striking up a conversation about some of the more 'sporting' prints in the window, the two went on several subsequent occasions to the second floor of a nearby oyster shop where they settled down in a more private room, 'looked at prints of the most indecent and shocking nature' and did things that could not be described in the newspapers. Similarly, Thomas Hodson was a sixteen-year-old apprentice to a surgeon and apothecary whom Muirhead had spoken to for several months in his master's shop before asking if he ever had a day off from work. Muirhead took Hodson to the same oyster shop in Leicester Square at least three times, showing him indecent prints, buying him food and drink, giving him money and carrying out acts too 'shocking to mention any particulars of'.[30]

Muirhead's pursuit of young men had not gone unnoticed, and he was well known to many in the neighbourhood, including the owner of a local picture shop, located on the corner of Sackville Street in Piccadilly. On one occasion the picture-shop owner attempted 'to shame him away from the place, by holding up to his face a print of the Bishop of Clogher; but instead of going away in consequence, he stood and looked at it with the utmost unconcern'. The shop owner yelled at Muirhead 'I know you well, and have seen your practices at my window, with boys, often; and you know that as long as 16 years ago – you were the talk of the town.' The shop owner had previously approached magistrates about having Muirhead arrested, but was informed by them that his evidence alone was not enough. When the law finally did catch up with Muirhead, he not only had on him indecent prints but 'in his pockets were several letters, which, from their contents, evidently came from other youths who had meetings' with him.[31] Multiple other witnesses provided similar stories of Muirhead's advances going back twenty years, while one elderly gentleman, Muirhead's former steward, said that he had left Muirhead's service decades before after witnessing similar practices.

The details of another trial, published in the same month, about advances made in front of a different picture-shop window, reveal some of the assumptions individuals made in such situations. This shop, by the Broadway, Blackfriars, was described as having 'for a longtime been the nightly resort of wretches of this description' and one man was identified 'as one of those constantly infesting the house'.[32] 'Several persons had been similarly assaulted, but fearful of having their names connected in any manner with such disgusting transactions, had declined taking any notice publicly.' The same story included an account of the arresting constable who had been sexually assaulted in the same location by a 'country gentleman', but declined to prosecute after he pleaded to be let go. The story of another man was recounted, who 'knocked [a similar] fellow down, and contenting himself with that summary punishment, suffered him to make his escape'.[33]

The fact that Muirhead's case was carried out under greater scrutiny by the press and the public seems to have made unavailable some of the usual means by which men of his station avoided prosecution. The magistrate at the Marlborough Street police court set the bail excessively high at £4,000, to ensure that his great fortune would not allow him to escape from trial without difficulty. The request to have the hearing held as a private examination, which might have helped in recruiting prominent individuals to speak favourably on his character, was also refused owing to the great public interest that was already building.[34] Because Muirhead had explicit prints in his possession when he was arrested, and because so many witnesses, including respectable property owners, came forward to speak against him after learning of his arrest, he could not easily claim that one or two lower-class men had fabricated a charge to extort money from him. At one of the police court hearings Muirhead did claim to be the victim of a conspiracy and he said prominent individuals would be willing to speak for his character, but at the later trial he did not make a counter-charge of extortion. Also important was that Muirhead was not able to get the case moved to the Court of King's Bench. An attempt to do this was made at the trial itself, by questioning the technical features of the indictment, but the objection was dismissed and the case went ahead at the Westminster Sessions. This meant that, instead of having the case decided by a special jury comprised of men of his own class, the jury that heard the case was much closer in economic and social circumstances and outlook to Muirhead's accusers.

Arguably no other man between 1822 and 1870 of Muirhead's rank and fortune was so thoroughly vilified and punished (serving a sentence of fifteen months' imprisonment). Many presumably guilty men instead fled and forfeited their bail; many unjustly yet successfully destroyed the character of their accusers; and some of those actually convicted in a criminal court, like the magistrate John Richmond Seymour, Esq., were able to reopen their case and prevail at subsequent proceedings.[35] Wealthy men were regularly disgraced by their association with these cases, and some were forced to disappear or were ostracised from former associations, but in only a very few cases were they actually made to serve the type of sentences regularly handed down to men of lesser wealth or social status. Muirhead's fate seems further evidence of the exceptional nature of the prosecutions of 1825.

Lieutenant-Colonel Richard Archdall's experiences were more typical. Archdall's actions first came to public attention ten months after Muirhead's conviction, when two brothers, Frederick and Samuel Withers, one fifteen and the other a year older, went to the Marlborough Street police court late in the afternoon to apply for a warrant against a 'gentleman of rank and fortune' for an 'assault of an indecent nature' on Frederick. They said that the warrant had to be given then, as the man was about to leave town, and might escape prosecution altogether.[36] Finding merit in their story, the magistrate dispatched two police officers to a Mayfair address, and there found the Lieutenant-Colonel packing for a trip. Because of his rank and since no felony was charged, they allowed him to stay the night in his own house, under their watch, until going before the Marlborough Street magistrate the next morning.

The association between Frederick Withers and Archdall had begun in July of that year when Archdall 'had requested a servant fitting Withers's description' from the National Guardian Institution. A few weeks into his service Archdall told Withers to accompany him to the baths in Harley Street, and had baths drawn for them both in the same room. The attendant had raised a question over this, and Withers said that he 'resisted the propositions made to him' by Archdall once the two men were naked and alone. Later that evening, Archdall called Withers into his parlour, as he did every day, and brought up the earlier 'adventure' they had had at the baths. Archdall stated that he had only done what he had as a test of Withers, and he was 'highly pleased' with how Withers had conducted himself. Because of his 'virtuous conduct' Archdall said he wished to give Withers a gift of a new pair of jockey boots, and he said 'he would never attempt any thing of the sort again'. But just a few nights later Archdall returned home drunk at about eleven o'clock in the evening and made a similar sexual advance on Withers. Frederick told his brother about this the next day, and together they went to the magistrate.

The Marlborough Street magistrate they spoke to, Henry Moreton Dyer, was the same man who had set Muirhead's bail excessively high, and he did the same for Archdall's, since the 'case appeared to be one of the greatest enormity [and so] many cases of this nature have of late occurred, when the guilty have eluded punishment by a forfeiture of their bail, that the Magistrates were determined in future that the ends of justice should not be defeated except at the more considerable expense than usual to the parties'.[37] Archdall was required to produce £1,000 himself, and an additional £1,000 to be provided by two or four sureties, whose names were required to be published. Archdall's solicitor petitioned repeatedly to have the bail reduced, but Dyer was unmoved by multiple arguments.[38] The father of Frederick came to the court to argue against the release of Archdall on bail, but his efforts were unnecessary given Dyer's stance.

Some of the pressures that poorer men were subject to when prosecuting wealthier individuals became apparent in the plea that the father of Frederick Withers made to the Marlborough Street magistrate. While Archdall was still incarcerated, unable to make bail, his coachman, another man and two other women were 'eternally on the watch' for Frederick, harassing him at the National Guardian Institution, where he was returning daily in an effort to find new employment. They also followed him elsewhere in an effort to find something that could discredit him and his story. Frederick's father expressed 'fear that some personal injury may befall him' and wished to keep his son in the house and away from such harassment, but did not have the financial resources to keep him idle.[39]

Despite the desire of the magistrates of the Marlborough Street police court to hold Archdall to ensure his trial, in the end the decision was taken out of their hands. Almost a month after Archdall had been committed to prison, Dyer was informed by the Lord Chief Justice that the trial of Archdall would be held before the Court of

King's Bench, and that in the meantime Archdall was to be released on £500 bail, without the need of additional sureties.[40] This could be done because the Court of King's Bench had the power to issue a writ of certiorari on behalf of a defendant who made the compelling case that an impartial trial was not possible in the lower court. Unlike the method by which Muirhead attempted to get his case moved to the Court of King's Bench, so long as a defendant followed the correct procedures when filing the petition, judges had limited discretion over whether or not to accept it. Archdall's solicitor filed for such a writ, and from this point on, up to and including the 1870–71 Boulton and Park trial, the writ of certiorari would become a regular feature of these prosecutions when they involved men of rank and fortune.[41]

The next day saw the appearance of Frederick Withers and his father at the police court, dumbfounded at the release of Archdall and shocked that they had learned of this only through the newspapers. Withers pleaded that his case was now seriously compromised, and that people would think that he and his son were taking money from Archdall to allow the prosecution to be undone. Withers said that already the governors of the National Guardian Institution had expressed their displeasure, and 'they suspected that he or his father had been induced to consent' to Archdall's release. Withers pleaded that 'my character and that of my son are at stake ... all my son has to depend on through life is his character'.[42] Dyer assured Withers that they were still convinced of the merits of the charges against Archdall, but there was no choice but to comply with any order issued from the Court of King's Bench.

The Lord Chief Justice allowed bail for Archdall in part because of the counter-charges Archdall now made against Withers, including allegations of an anonymous note left for Archdall requesting money to drop the case. The fact that Archdall was 'by birth, education, and rank in life, a gentleman, and one whose moral and general character has hitherto been unspotted' was alluded to, as were the prominent family connections of Archdall and his father, which included the Marquis of Hastings. It was also claimed that a trial at the Westminster Sessions would be biased against Archdall, as the hearings before the Marlborough Street magistrates were extensively reported in the newspapers, and that 'hand-bills' with excerpts of the newspaper reports were printed up and posted around the neighbourhood of Westminster. The previous newspaper reporting, it was argued, would prejudice the minds of potential jurymen of the

Westminster Sessions, who were anyway 'taken from a class in society much more nearly connected with that of the prosecutor and his friends'. Archdall requested a jury of *his* peers, which a special jury before the Court of King's Bench could provide.[43]

There was an effort made by the Marlborough Street magistrates not to lose control over the case entirely. After Archdall had his trial successfully moved to the Court of King's Bench, a second indictment was proffered against him by the Marlborough Street office for the incident that had happened in Archdall's lodging several days after the visit to the baths, again making him subject to trial at the Westminster Sessions. This second case too, though, was moved to the Court of King's Bench, on the same argument that the newspapers and handbills that had circulated were 'calculated to excite a prejudice in that class of society likely to act as petty jurors' at the Westminster Sessions.[44]

The subsequent trial before the Court of King's Bench took the whole day and was widely reported, yet by that point the pieces were already in place to allow for a decision in favour of Archdall. To discredit Frederick, the prosecution argued that the whole Withers family exhibited a pattern of criminal behaviour, and it was also argued that Frederick might have had prior sexual experience with another man. The defence also played on the common background between Archdall and the jury, claiming that there were many villains in the metropolis fabricating charges such as Archdall faced, so that 'when a man of fortune, rank, and distinguished honour, came forward publicly to brave a charge like the present, it furnished a strong presumption of his innocence'. The defence did agree that Archdall had placed himself in a compromising position with Frederick, but attributed this to his Irish upbringing and years of foreign travel in the military. It was said that 'Colonel Archdall, it was clear, was unacquainted with London Life ... or else he would never have taken the boy into the bathing room with him'. The Duke of Wellington himself appeared at the trial, and related that he had a highly favourable opinion of Archdall, and multiple other character witnesses also came forward and related similar stories. The jury took only a few minutes to find Archdall not guilty.[45]

The vilification of the Withers family and the celebration of the character of Archdall looked a great deal like a restoration of the patterns from the unjust 1811 contest between the Bishop of Clogher and James Byrne, and in some ways they were, but there were also important differences. The tone of *The Times* reporting shifted to favouring Archdall just before the trial at the Court of King's Bench, but that coverage remained extensive and both sides of the case were presented. The radical press did not champion the cause of the Withers family as martyrs, but neither were they persecuted and made an example of as Byrne had been. The acquittal of Archdall left them open to prosecution for making a false charge, but no further prosecutions resulted. Too many of the details damaging to Archdall were too well known for him to seek retribution against the Withers family. In this way, public opinion was not sufficient to prevent the reassertion of class privilege in this area of the law, but the new regular reporting could and did act as a check on the worst abuses of that privilege.

This use of the press to check state power should be seen as the lasting legacy of the Bishop of Clogher incident. For the next five decades the liberal press set a dispassionate and detailed tone for the mainstream discussion of sex between men in Britain. It was not that this new attention from the liberal press ended other forms of reporting on this behaviour, but rather it eclipsed those other forms with its volume, frequency and prominence. H. G. Cocks has previously identified the tension in the nineteenth century over the desire of the liberal press to bring greater transparency to the workings of government and the deep misgivings of those who controlled the liberal newspapers over spreading knowledge of sex between men.[46] Through this more detailed understanding of the Bishop of Clogher incident and its aftermath, we can better understand why publicity ultimately won out over silence.

Five decades after they were established, the political rationales for this detailed reporting were swept away by the 1870–71 Boulton and Park prosecution. The reporting ended in part because the radical critique of state corruption was no longer so potent a force in politics, but the change was primarily due to the unprecedented nature of the information revealed at Boulton and Park's 1870 police court hearing. That weeks-long proceeding attracted many witnesses who had first heard of it through the newspapers, and whose testimony described significant numbers of effeminate middle- and upper-class men pursuing other men for sex with relative impunity in London's West End.[47] Nothing so damaging to middle- and upper-class men's self-perceptions had been published in the previous fifty years, and it led to a one-year spike in the reporting of sex between men rivalled only by the increases in the years 1822, 1825, 1842–43 and 1895. After the 1871 Boulton and Park trial, which tried to contain the damage by omitting previous witnesses who had spoken of the larger gatherings of cross-dressed men, the reporting of sex between men in the liberal press was greatly diminished, and those reports that were published had nothing like the previous level of detail. In at least this respect the Victorian silence over sex between men that was broken by the 1895 Oscar Wilde trials was only established after 1871. Knowing this kind of overall context and establishing the chronological relationship between the hundreds of big and small cases makes it increasingly possible to use this material not simply to document the scandal of an event like the 1822 Bishop of Clogher incident but also to understand how it and events like it factored into the broader political struggles of the period.

## Notes

1  Charles Upchurch, *Before Wilde: Sex between Men in Britain's Age of Reform* (Berkeley: University of California Press, 2009), pp. 129–56.
2  Dozens of authors have written on the prosecution of Ernest Boulton and Frederick Park, although for an account that stresses the accidental process by which the police court hearing got out of the control of state authorities, see Charles Upchurch, 'Forgetting the unthinkable: Cross-dressers and British society in the case of the Queen vs. Boulton and others', *Gender and History*, 12:1 (April 2000), 127–57.
3  Charles Upchurch, 'Full-text databases and historical research: Cautionary results from a ten-year study', *Journal of Social History*, 45 (2012), 1–17.
4  Oliver Woods and James Bishop, *The Story of The Times: Bicentenary Edition: 1785–1985* (London: Michael Joseph, 1985), p. 47.
5  In attempting to analyse these cases of sex between men in a way that ties them more directly to the political tensions of the time, this chapter builds on the analysis and methodology of Dror Wahrman and Anna Clark. See Dror Wahrman, 'Public opinion, violence and the limits of constitutional politics', in James Vernon (ed.), *Re-Reading the Constitution: New Narratives in the Political History of England's Long Nineteenth Century* (New York: Cambridge University Press, 1996), pp. 83–122; and Anna Clark, *Scandal: The Sexual Politics of the British Constitution* (Princeton: Princeton University Press, 2004).
6  Parliamentary Papers: Command Papers, Criminal Offender and Judicial Statistics, Annual Returns, 1805 to 1880.
7  Special thanks to Randolph Trumbach for sharing his unpublished

research on eighteenth-century newspaper reporting, and to Andrew
McCarthy for assistance in collecting the nineteenth-century material.

8  *The Times* (15 April 1820), p. 3; Arnold Hunt, 'A study in bibliomania:
   Charles Henry Hartshorne and Richard Heber', *Book Collector*, 42
   (1993), 25–43, 185–212; Matthew Parris and Nick Angel, *The Great
   Unfrocked: Two Thousand Years of Church Scandal* (London: Robson
   Books, 1998), pp. 168–9.

9  Rictor Norton, *Mother Clap's Molly House: The Gay Subculture in England,
   1700–1830* (London: GMP, 1992), pp. 187–98.

10 The year 1819 saw twenty-eight prosecutions in London and Middlesex,
   more than double as many as in the two years before or the two years
   after, but sixteen of these prosecutions stemmed from a single raid on
   a house in Marylebone. Despite the scale of this raid, comparable to
   the Vere Street raid of 1810, 1819 and 1820 saw only small increases in
   newspaper coverage of trials related to sex between men.

11 Robert Holloway, *The Phoenix of Sodom, or the Vere Street Coterie*
   (London, 1813); *The Times* (6 July 1815), p. 2.

12 Parris and Angel, *The Great Unfrocked*, pp. 146–8.

13 *Ibid.*, p. 144. See also Brian Lacey, *Terrible Queer Creatures: Homosexuality
   in Irish History* (Leopardstown, Dublin: Wordwell, 2008).

14 For just some of the stories appearing in only two newspapers for the
   remainder of 1822 related to the Bishop of Clogher incident, see *The
   Times* (26 July 1822), p. 3; *The Times* (30 July 1822), p. 3; *The Times* (31
   July 1822), p. 3; *The Times* (3 August 1822), p. 3; *Bell's Life in London and
   Sporting Chronicle* (4 August 1822); *The Times* (8 August 1822), p. 3; *Bell's
   Life in London* (11 August 1822); *The Times* (27 August 1822), p. 3; *The
   Times* (31 August 1822), p. 3; *Bell's Life in London* (1 September 1822);
   *The Times* (6 September 1822), p. 3; *The Times* (10 September 1822), p. 3;
   *The Times* (20 September 1822), p. 3; *Bell's Life in London* (29 September
   1822); *The Times* (2 October 1822), p. 2; *The Times* (8 October 1822),
   p. 3; *The Times* (11 October 1822), p. 3; *Bell's Life in London* (13 October
   1822); *The Times* (14 October 1822), p. 3; *The Times* (24 October 1822),
   p. 2; *The Times* (29 October 1822), p. 2; *The Times* (30 October 1822),
   p. 2; *The Times* (2 November 1822), p. 1; *Bell's Life in London* (3 November
   1822); *The Times* (5 November 1822), p. 2; *The Times* (8 November 1822),
   p. 3; *Bell's Life in London* (10 November 1822); *The Times* (12 November
   1822), p. 3; *The Times* (13 November 1822), p. 3; *Bell's Life in London* (17
   November 1822).

15 *Bell's Life in London* (4 August 1822), p. 191; *The Times* (3 August 1822),
   p. 3.

16 *Bell's Life in London* (11 August 1822), p. 191.

17 *Bell's Life in London* (4 August 1822).

18 William Benbow, *The Crimes of the Clergy; or, the Pillars of the Priest-Craft*

*Shaken* (London: Benbow, 1823); James Byrne, Percy Jocelyn and William Cobbett, *The Trial of Unfortunate Byrne, (Late Coachman to the Hon. John Jocelyn,)... Which Is Annexed the Opinion of That Great Political Writer Mr. Cobbett on the Late Abominable and Disgusting Transaction* (Dublin, 1811).

19 *Bell's Life in London* (4 August 1822); *The Times* (26 July 1822), p. 3.
20 John Bew, *Castlereagh: Enlightenment, War, and Tyranny* (London: Quercus, 2011), pp. 552–6; Parris and Angel, *The Great Unfrocked*, pp. 151–2; John W. Derry, *Castlereagh* (New York: St Martin's Press, 1976); H. Montgomery Hyde, *The Strange Death of Lord Castlereagh* (London: Heinemann, 1959).
21 Parris and Angel, *The Great Unfrocked*, p. 152; Bew, *Castlereagh*, p. 553.
22 Clark, *Scandal*, pp. 148–76.
23 *The Times* (14 September 1822), p. 2; *Weekly Dispatch* (15 September 1822), p. 292; *Bell's Life in London* (22 September 1822), p. 237; *Weekly Dispatch* (16 March 1823), p. 85; *The Times* (17 March 1823), p. 3; *Annual Register* (1823), p. 30; *Ipswich Journal* (22 March 1823).
24 *The Times* (16 August 1822), p. 3; *The Times* (23 September 1822), p. 3; *The Times* (25 September 1822), p. 3; *The Times* (16 October 1822), p. 3; *The Times* (3 December 1822), p. 3.
25 In that case, one man threatened to reveal that another had 'made overtures' to him to commit sodomy. Such overtures constituted the misdemeanour of attempted sodomy, but not the felony of sodomy. A felony charge of sodomy required the act to take place, while an attempted sodomy charge could stem from a broad range of physical or spoken acts. See Upchurch, *Before Wilde*, pp. 95–100.
26 *The Times* (16 August 1825), p. 3; *The Times* (26 August 1825), p. 3; *The Times* (2 September 1825), p. 3.
27 *The Times* (21 September 1825), p. 3; *The Times* (18 October 1825), p. 3; *The Times* (4 August 1825), p. 3.
28 *The Times* (11 April 1825), p. 3.
29 *The Times* (9 November 1825), p. 3; *The Times* (16 November 1825), p. 3; PCOM, New Court, 18 February 1825, Middlesex Cases, 417; *The Times* (16 April 1825); *The Times* (18 April 1825); *The Times* (27 March 1825); *The Times* (4 August 1825), pp. 2–3. For the Barley Mow Public House raid see *The Times* (23 August 1825), p. 3; *The Times* (25 August 1825); *The Times* (2 September 1825); *The Times* (22 September 1825), p. 3.
30 *The Times* (23 August 1825), p. 3. For other newspaper stories discussing the Muirhead case, see *Morning Chronicle* (23 August 1825); *The Times* (25 August 1825), p. 3; *Morning Chronicle* (25 August 1825); *The Age* (28 August 1825), p. 126; *Weekly Dispatch* (28 August 1825), pp. 274–5; *Bell's Weekly Messenger* (28 August 1825), p. 278; *Examiner* (28 August 1825); *Bristol Mercury* (29 August 1825); *Weekly Dispatch* (4 September 1825),

p. 283; *The Times* (6 September 1825), p. 3; *The Times* (7 September 1825); *The Times* (24 September 1825), p. 3; *Examiner* (25 September 1825); *The Times* (26 September 1825), p. 3; *Morning Chronicle* (22 October 1825); *The Times* (22 October 1825), p. 3; *The Age* (23 October 1825), p. 189; *Bell's Weekly Messenger* (23 October 1825), p. 338; *The Age* (6 November 1825), p. 208; *The Times* (17 November 1825), p. 3; *Morning Chronicle* (21 October 1826); *The Age* (22 October 1826), p. 606; *Morning Chronicle* (26 April 1827); *Examiner* (29 April 1827); *The Times* (17 May 1827), p. 6; *Sun* (April 29 1830).

31  *The Times* (23 August 1825), p. 3.

32  *The Times* (26 August 1825), p. 3.

33  *The Times* (26 August 1825), p. 3.

34  *The Times* (23 August 1825), p. 3.

35  *The Times* (9 March 1831), p. 4; Upchurch, *Before Wilde*, pp. 29–33.

36  For coverage of the Archdall case, see *The Times* (4 September 1826), p. 3; *Morning Chronicle* (5 September 1826); *The Times* (14 September 1826), p. 3; *Weekly Dispatch* (17 September 1826), p. 299; *The Times* (18 September 1826), p. 3; *The Times* (19 September 1826), p. 3; *Morning Chronicle* (29 September 1826); *The Times* (29 September 1826), p. 3; *The Times* (30 September 1826), p. 3; *Weekly Dispatch* (1 October 1826), p. 316; *Morning Chronicle* (1 October 1826); *The Times* (2 October 1826), p. 3; *The Age* (8 October 1826), p. 589; *The Times* (9 October 1826), p. 3; *The Times* (20 October 1826), p. 3; *The Times* (10 November 1826), p. 3; *Weekly Dispatch* (12 November 1826), p. 362; *The Age* (12 November 1826), p. 626; *Morning Chronicle* (23 February 1827), p. 626; *The Times* (24 February 1827), p. 3; and *Weekly Dispatch* (25 February 1827), p. 59.

37  *The Times* (4 September 1826), p. 3.

38  *The Times* (14 September 1826), p. 3; *The Times* (18 September 1826), p. 3.

39  *The Times* (19 September 1826), p. 3.

40  *The Times* (29 September 1826), p. 3.

41  Other trials where upper-class men moved their cases to the Court of King's (or Queen's) Bench include the final trial of John Richmond Seymour, Esq., in 1831; the 1833 trial of Charles Barring Wall, MP; the 1841 Lowndes trail; the 1852 contest between Jackson and Surlari; the 1863 Whitehurst trial; and the 1871 Boulton and Park prosecution. The writ of certiorari had been used previously in less publicised cases involving sex between men and it is unclear why Muirhead's defence did not petition for it, although the aggravated nature of the evidence against him may have influenced the decision.

42  *The Times* (29 September 1826), p. 3; *The Times* (30 September 1826), p. 3.

43  *The Times* (2 October 1826), p. 3.

44  *The Times* (10 November 1826), p. 3.
45  *The Times* (24 February 1828), p. 3.
46  H. G. Cocks, *Nameless Offences: Speaking of Male Homosexual Desire in Nineteenth-Century England* (London: I. B. Tauris, 2003), pp. 79–88.
47  Upchurch, 'Forgetting the unthinkable', 137–40.

## 2

# Naturalism, labour and homoerotic desire: Henry Scott Tuke

*Jongwoo Jeremy Kim*

Henry Scott Tuke's career as an artist was deeply committed to the visual proliferation of youths – clad or unclad. 'You came to Falmouth to paint the sea, I suppose?' asked an interviewer from *The Studio* in 1895. Tuke replied, 'The sea is certainly the keynote of my pictures, but my object in living here is not to be a marine painter – I do not reckon myself one – but primarily to paint the nude in the open air; here there are quiet beaches, some of them hardly accessible except by boat, where one may paint from the life model undisturbed.'[1] This statement provides a strong impetus to re-examine Tuke's oeuvre, including those Newlyn School[2] paintings of working-class life in Cornwall which are often considered separately from his male nudes. If a pictorial examination of the male body was Tuke's ultimate goal, the inclusion of youths in 'marine paintings' of fishing, rigging and battling sea storms could have been also dictated by his interest in their physique. After all, he did not see himself as a marine painter like Stanhope Forbes or Charles Napier Hemy. Tuke's primary interest was not in visualising a narrative situation that revealed maritime workers' hard but respectable lives at a particular point in the class structure. Rather, his chief interest lay in the erotic valence of the working-class model, whether posing nude or acting out the role of a specific form of labour. Tuke sought Uranian male ideals in all his depictions of youths.[3]

The homoeroticism of Tuke's naturalism can be understood as part of his effort to contemporise what was considered to be a lost Hellenic tradition of 'man-manly love'. As John Addington Symonds celebrated male bathers in modern 'water-meadows' and the cadets of nineteenth-century military schools,[4] Tuke sought to revitalise Greek ideals by recapturing the beauty of Greek youths in the images of young men from his own time. In a poem attributed to Tuke, he confesses yearnings for the erotic freedom of Greece:

> Youth, beautiful and daring, and divine,
>   Loved of the Gods, when yet the happy earth
>   Was joyful in its morning and new birth;
> When yet the very odours of the brine
> Love's cradle, filled with sweetness all the shrine
>   Of Venus, ere these starveling times of dearth,
>   Of priest-praised abstinence made void of mirth,
> Had given us water where we asked for wine.[5]

The poet expresses his nostalgia for a time he has never experienced. In the imaginary ancient Greece, even the gods of Olympus adored young men. When the world was free of the Christian Church, there was no shame in the pursuit of 'beautiful' youths, and the 'divine' law sanctioned their 'daring' romance with men. In that idyllic past, the ocean was 'love's cradle', and bathers like Tuke's own celebrated the joy of Venus's 'brine' shrine. But, in the poet's present – these 'starveling times of dearth' – the 'wine' of natural (pre-Christian) desire is banned. Overcoming the sexual poverty of his time, however, the poet seeks to modernise the homoerotic beauty and freedom of the mythological past. He exclaims, 'Youth, make one conquest more; and take again / Thy rightful crown, in lovers' hearts to reign!'

Paintings of fishermen and other workers were central to Tuke's efforts to bring Greek homoeroticism to his modern time. By identifying his nude heroes – the life models of his endless bathers – as young fishermen, postal workers and hands on the deck in the contemporary scenes of Falmouth, Tuke was able to reintroduce the lost tradition of the homoerotic adoration of youths into the fabric of working-class reality. Even in what appears to be the Newlyn School's standard depictions of fishermen's daily life, Tuke seldom fails to embed a handsome young sailor. In *A Sailor's Yarn*, 1887,[6] Jack Rowling commands the foreground with his shining beauty of pubescence. In *The Midday Rest*, 1905,[7] a sailor sleeps languidly in the foreground, rendering himself vulnerable to any desiring eye.[8] Recent scholars have diminished this aspect of Tuke's art[9]; devaluing his eroticism, Marcia Pointon, for instance, emphasises the painter's class-consciousness and social commentary instead:

> We think of Tuke as the painter of bathing boys, which, indeed, he was. Yet his repertoire ... is a great deal wider than this reputation would

imply. A close look at, say, *All Hands to the Pumps!* rapidly dispels any
lingering disposition to regard Tuke as exclusively devoted to the *plein-air* male adolescent nude. This is a work of bold composition, a view of
labour, vigorously painted as a drama of daily life, albeit marine daily
life.[10]

*All Hands to the Pumps!* (see Figure 1), however, is not far removed
from Tuke's '*plein-air* male adolescent nude': a homoerotic romance
continues despite its 'view of labour'. In fact, it is more accurate
to say that such a romance is the cause of Tuke's 'bold' and 'vigorously painted' naturalism that treats working-class men and youths.
Analysing the 'romance mode' (an erotic structure that 'simultaneously quests for and postpones a particular end, objective, or
object')[11] in Tuke's paintings, Julia Saville examines *August Blue*,
1893, and *Ruby, Gold and Malachite*, 1902,[12] to argue that, 'While the
narrative paintings dwelt on manly activity – exemplified for instance
in *All Hands to the Pumps!* of 1889 and *The Run Home* of 1902 [see
Figure 2] – the colour compositions suggested the contemplative
suspension of activity in a moment of romance deferral'.[13] Saville is
mistaken, however. *All Hands to the Pumps!* and *The Run Home* are
not only colour compositions themselves – blue in the former and
beige in the latter – but also their 'manly activity' of labour and hard
life enables a distinctly homoerotic 'romance deferral'.

Tuke's romantic fantasy in what look like common naturalist scenes
of labour involves even his own image, intensifying the emotional
urgency as well as physical immediacy. Among the figures in *All
Hands to the Pumps!*, a fisherman holding the pump lever on the left –
his white shirt under a drab waistcoat is soaked in cold water – shows
Tuke's facial features, including the moustache and his signature
cap. If this fisherman is Tuke, the unusual tattoos on his forearms –
unusual, even ironic for a gentleman to sport tattoos when no 'real'
seamen in the painting do – suggest a fusion of embodiment and
representation. Tuke's self-portrait inserted in *All Hands to the Pumps!*
articulates the painter's longing – hidden but undeletable just like the
tattoos on Tuke's forearms – to be with Jack Rowling. Tuke's yearning
injects a subtle form of homoerotic fantasy into what is apparently a
dramatic narrative of working-class men in a storm. The vessel leaks.
To remove the water, sailors pump together up and down despite violent waves and the murderous wind. As the ship might capsize at any
moment and sink to the depths of the sea, bringing all men to their
death, Tuke in the picture takes perhaps the last look at Rowling, who

**1** Henry Scott Tuke, *All Hands to the Pumps!*, 1888–9. Oil on canvas,
1854 × 1397 cm, Tate Gallery, London.

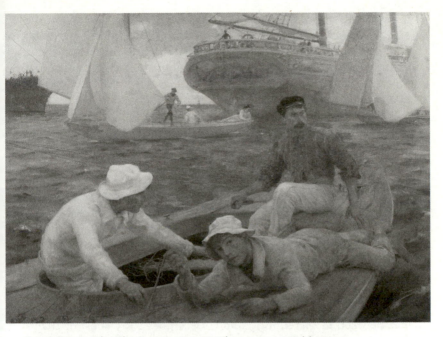

**2** Henry Scott Tuke, *The Run Home*, 1904. Oil on canvas, 117 × 160 cm.
The Royal Cornwall Museum, Truro.

seems oblivious of his intense attention. Rowling – one of his favour-
ite models – is cast in this scene as an unremarkable chap pushed to
the pictorial edge on the right. His red wind-blown hat emulates a
Phrygian cap, which he is shown to wear in his photographs and in
*Jack in the Rigging* (*Going Aloft*), 1888.[14] Rowling gravely observes the
mercilessly torn sail fluttering in the gale. The sail formally echoes
the tattered Union Jack equally struggling against the storm on the
upper left. Such symbolism raises the composition to a depiction
of heroism that rivals history painting. Determination and defiance
in the face of an unjust and unmatchable power recall images like
Eugène Delacroix's 1830 *Liberty Leading the People*[15] – a Phrygian cap
and a national flag are found in both paintings. In Tuke's *All Hands to
the Pumps!*, the long lever of the pump creates a bridge between Tuke
and Rowling – a link that paradoxically connects as well as separat-
ing them. This separated union or united separation of the painter
and the model – an example of 'romance deferral' – is witnessed,
even joined, by the brotherhood of seamen (the sensuality suggested

in the action of pumping as well as the water gushing out from the pipes must not be overlooked here). Perhaps the sea storm is a metaphor pictorialising an internal and external struggle Tuke experienced fighting his impossible longing for Rowling. Yet, frozen in pictorial time, the painter's romance is, in Saville's term, for ever incomplete, never coming to fruition, and thus that much more poignant.

Saville's categorisation of *The Run Home* (see Figure 2) as a painting of 'manly' labour devoid of desire is equally problematic. Like *All Hands to the Pumps!*, *The Run Home* contains what must be recognised as another self-portrait of Tuke, indicated by the figure's cap and sharp eyes, the shape of the head, his moustache and the clothes. *The Run Home* reflects the relationship between Tuke and his model John (also called Johnny) Jackett. *The Run Home* is Tuke's call to Jackett, who was with the Cape Mounted Rifles during the Second Boer War.[16] Jackett's military service in South Africa was deeply significant to the artist. Before Jackett's departure, Tuke took him and his friends out to spend a night in London. In his diary of 9 April 1901, Tuke described his farewell.[17] The entry may appear to be a straightforward jotting-down of a day's event, but, considering that, between 12 March 1899 and 31 December 1905, most of Tuke's diary entries hardly ever exceed two or three lines – many of them simply comprising a few words – the length and details given for the event of 9 April 1901 speak to the import of the night in London Tuke spent with Jackett, Christophus, Toy and Coleman. It was the artist's sincere sending-off. Tuke treated the working-class lads to dinner at Gatti's, a restaurant he frequently visited with his more gentlemanly friends such as Charles Kains-Jackson. Tuke also dazzled his young friends with a circus show at the Hippodrome, a newly opened fashionable theatre, and put them up at the Norfolk Square Hotel. Soon after their departure, according to Jackett's wife, Sallie, Tuke began to experience recurring dreams about John without understanding why. Sallie recollected that Tuke made sketches from the strong images reappearing in his nightly dreams. The painting *The Run Home*, Sallie said, was based on those sketches. Sallie believed that Tuke's uncanny dreams began when John was injured and hospitalised in South Africa.[18]

Taking these circumstances of absence and longing into account, *The Run Home* transcends the limits of the Newlyn School's naturalism. Tuke transcribed a young man, his model Jackett, from his dreams, overcoming the divide between illusion and reality and between pictorial reality and its physical counterpart. In the same painting, Tuke also inscribed another man in his own image, delivering Jackett safely home away from the harms of the battlefield. His composition helps magically realise Jackett's return. *The Run Home* is dramatically cropped at bottom, creating an ambiguous space.[19] Violating the picture plane, Tuke challenges the boundary of the pictorial illusion separated from the viewer's reality. By abruptly discontinuing the foreground, Tuke disables a conventional entrance into a pictorial space. Consequently, the viewer's spatial relation to the painting is severely disoriented, confusing the real space with its illusory counterpart. When the boundary blurs, dreams may come true.

Jackett in white stares daringly out at the viewer. His gaze is intense and direct. Many compositional axes converge on his face, which is positioned in the bottom centre of the painting (simply drawing lines from the two upper corners of the canvas to his face helps visualise many axes forming multiple upside-down triangles). Like so many ropes stretching in the picture, these hidden compositional diagonal lines radiate from Jackett's face, pulling the entire canvas forward. He becomes a bowsprit idol heading a ship. His intense stare asserts itself. The sail of this boat has already exceeded the limit of the pictorial space: it is outside the frame, and thus in the viewer's space. The rope Jackett holds in his right hand in Tuke's dreams pulls the vessel closer to the real space.

Jackett's body is recumbent on the side of the boat. He is neither quite in the vessel nor completely overboard. His legs are strikingly foreshortened; in fact the contraction seems exaggerated. His position is marginal and ambiguous as though he is floating. In this light the youth is literally a figure in transit. He is between the water and the vessel, between the pictorial space and the viewer's space, and between Tuke's dream and Tuke's reality. He is on the threshold. Indeed, the whole picture is about interstices created by the comings and goings of various vessels. This painting is at once Tuke's replication of and a remedy for his incessant dreams. Although Tuke in the picture looks away to compose a respectable uninterested gravity and to cloak the emotional urgency, it is Tuke who holds the rudder and who directs this action of the 'run home'. The return of Jackett is what Tuke desired desperately: it is what his inexplicable dreams revealed to him as his most urgent need. *The Run Home* is painted as though Jackett would be spilled into the real space as long as Tuke paints him pressed hard enough against the picture plane. Jackett is painted to look up and see the real Tuke. He must come back to Tuke.

In its expressions of longing and ciphers of absence, Tuke's Boer War picture *The Run Home* may be compared to John Byam Liston Shaw's *Boer War 1900*, 1901.[20] The lady of Byam Shaw's *Boer War 1900* is a passive observer of the calamity – what Tim Barringer calls 'the crisis of imperial masculinity'.[21] She stands still with an anguished and anxious countenance at Dorchester on the Thames; her longing and the purple yarn in her left hand approximate her to Penelope who awaited Odysseus while weaving and un-weaving a shroud. Shaw's painting represents the frustration that the nation felt during this time of war and the beginning of the grand disillusionment and decline of Britain's colonial power. In contrast, Tuke takes the matter into his own hands: he launches a rescue mission in his painting. He recovers Jackett and brings him home to Falmouth. Tuke did not see the point of losing in South Africa another man, a beautiful inspiration for his art and desire.[22]

The details of this episode also reveal the limitations on Tuke's realisation of his ideals of bonds between men, however. Despite the pictorial evidence of *The Run Home*, in Sallie's recollection, Tuke insisted he could not understand his dreams about Jackett. Tuke was ready to admit that he dreamed about his model, and the realism and the repetition of the nocturnal imaginings were no matters for him to hide, but, as to the cause of the dreams, Tuke sounds wilfully reticent. It is as though the dreams were not themselves inexplicable but any verbal explanation would inevitably lead to questions about why it was Tuke, not Sallie, who had them. Tuke's continuing dreams of John visualised an incessant but unacceptable longing, which must remain unacknowledged and unuttered because it is for another man. Imagery, in this case, offered a way to express what could not be expressed in words. In *All Hands to the Pumps!* and *The Run Home*, the conventions of Newlyn School naturalism offered a way to visualise homoeroticism in modern time. Relying on the imagery of fishing-village life, Tuke re-establishes in the present the forgotten and punished tradition of male beauty. The Cornish fisherlads are celebrated as heroes who restore the beauty of the male sex, and a homoerotic gaze is encouraged as an aesthetic virtue. Tuke's naturalism capturing 'views of labour' must be understood in this context of love between men.

**3** Henry Scott Tuke, *The Message*, 1890. Oil on canvas, 100 × 89.5 cm. Falmouth Art Gallery Collection.

The complex infusion of illicit desire in the depictions of the rural poor can be found even in Tuke's 1890 genre painting, *The Message* (see Figure 3), which is usually taken as exemplifying the Newlyn School. Indeed, Victorian critics saw Newlyn School naturalism as the salient aspect of Tuke's *The Message*. A *Pall Mall Gazette* review

noted, '[I]f the Newlyn School stands for anything it stands for literalness of treatment; of grace it attempts little, but of hard facts it gives
much'.[23] The evening newspaper's critic explained his approval of
Tuke:

> [I]n the hands of a really talented painter like Mr. H. S. Tuke, the anecdo-
> tal element, though always present, is attenuated to the smallest propor-
> tions. In his picture, for instance 'The Message', it is not at all suggested
> what the nature of the message is. The children look surprised and the
> telegraph boy leans against the wall with a nonchalance which are char-
> acteristic. The woman reads the telegram, but its nature and its effect
> upon her Mr. Tuke does not attempt to pourtray [sic].[24]

The critic is right in that the typical Victorian narratives driven by
'anecdotal elements' are weak in Tuke's *The Message*. The artist's
interest in the telegram or the woman's response to it appears mark-
edly inactive.

Comparisons to Victorian 'letter pictures' underscore this point.[25]
In Rebecca Solomon's *The Love Letter*, 1861 (see Figure 4), the letter
a young woman holds in her hands explains the desire and surprise
evident on her face, and identifies a suitor in the reflection of the
young man entering the room. The letters cascading down the wall
in a holder on the left and the small note tucked into the frame of
the mirror further suggest that the courtship has been carried on for
a while.[26] As articulate objects, these letters anchor the meaning of
Solomon's painting as a narrative of love. In John Everett Millais's
*Trust Me*, 1862 (see Figure 5), a letter creates a confrontational divide
between father and daughter, as visualised by the vertical golden line
thinly blazing between the two door panels in the back: the elderly
gentleman does not approve of the nature of the letter his daughter
safeguards from him. In his red hunting jacket with a symbol of
authority under his arm (a riding crop with the whip tightly coiling
around), the father tells his daughter, 'Trust me'. Or, perhaps, the
young woman defies her father with those two words, 'trust me',
as the crocuses on the table blossom to indicate the spring of love.
In contrast to these Victorian 'letter pictures' with popular narrative structures, Tuke's 'telegram picture' does not portray any legible
action or the feeling of the woman who has just received a message,
denying the viewer an explicit story, leaving the painting empty, 'lit-
eral', and 'hard'.

In the January issue of *The Artist*, another critic examined
Tuke's *The Message*: 'It is a thoroughly natural representation of

**4** Rebecca Solomon, *The Love Letter*, 1861. Oil on canvas, 54 × 41.9 cm. Private collection.

**5** John Everett Millais, *Trust Me*, 1862. Oil on canvas, 111.2 × 77.5 cm. Private collection.

an ordinary incident – a cottager's wife has received a telegram, the boy messenger in uniform waits at the door for any reply message, and the woman's juvenile son looks up from the breakfast table with curiosity. Mr. Tuke has not attempted to dramatise his subject, but has painted it as truthful as possible and as pictorially.'[27] Tuke's lack of dramatisation was well received, and his 'truthful' description of the humble cottage household and his documentary observation of the daily life of the poor were deemed appropriate.

Contrasting these responses from critics who welcomed Tuke's naturalism, a poem also appearing in *The Artist* addresses 'beauty' in *The Message* despite its pictorial 'literalness' and 'hard facts'. Entitled, 'The Message (Suggested by a picture in the Cornish Show at 160, New Bond Street)', this poem, in its first nine lines, alludes to the 'miracle' of 'the subtle fire', 'a tide electric', and 'flashing knowledge through a thousand wires' that quickly turns into 'a thing un-noticed' in the fast-paced modern life, even in 'a place remote' like Newlyn. But, in the fifteenth line of the poem, the 'painter' is singled out to be different: although he does not 'pause to wonder' at the 'strange new thing, a telegram', the 'painter' can see the power of 'older things' such as 'breath and being and beauty' in the cottage interior. The poem continues:

> Only the artist, in the wrinkled face
> Of toil sees beauty, in the curious child
> Still beauty, and sees beauty in the boy.
> ...
> Thus the true artist and true naturalist
> Sets nature down on canvas truthfully;
> Teaching no lesson, only saying 'see',
> And leaving hearts to profit as they will.[28]

The 'beauty' the poet perceives in Tuke's painting is problematic given that aesthetic concerns were considered incongruous with the kind of naturalism critics championed as the chief strength of the Newlyn School. Moreover, the beauty Tuke is said to recognise in the 'wrinkled face of toil' does not have the same kind of romantic narrative power found in the beauty of women in the Victorian genre paintings centring on letters. As such, this beauty Tuke visualises in the Cornish housewife is dissociated from desire. What about the beauty of her curious 'juvenile son', sitting at the breakfast table,

'looking up'? Is his beauty like his mother's? How about 'the telegraph boy' who 'leans against the wall with a nonchalance' while
boldly staring back at the painter and the viewer? Is his beauty
dissociated from desire? Is his 'nonchalance' natural or learned? To
the left of the telegraph boy stands the youngest child in the painting, gawking at the uniformed stranger. How truly naturalist is the
painter in his depiction of the three representative stages of a boy's
growth towards adulthood, and what is the nature of this boyish
beauty?

The two-tiered spatial structure of the painting helps separate the
ravaged 'beauty' of the woman from that of boyhood in three stages.
The kitchen in the foreground is the space of a family, occupied by
the mother and one of her two sons. In the centre of the painting
is a doorway to another room, which seems to lead to the main
entrance of this cottage. This back room with an entryway functions
as a threshold to what the telegraph boy promises outside the family.
In both Victorian 'letter pictures' by Solomon and Millais, doors are
used symbolically: Solomon's door signals the beginning of a new
chapter in life as a suitor enters the young lady's room after a sustained epistolary courtship, and Millais's white double door reveals,
through the thin gap between its panels, a golden light blazing in
the next room, implying the potential of the heroine's determination
for a new romance. What about Tuke's door in *The Message*? The
telegram may have been delivered to the working-class mother, but
the painting's symbolic 'letter' seems meant for the painter and the
viewer; the message of this unseen letter is the door – a passage to
different forms of beauty and pleasure that the uniformed youth with
a provocative stare represents. The right hand of the telegraph boy
lingers on the door as if he wants to see whether the painter or the
viewer will leave the space of the family and walk out of the cottage
with him. That the cottage interior is modelled after Tuke's own[29]
and that he and his Uranian viewer inevitably assume the patriarchal
role when looking at this scene of a fatherless home make the telegraph boy's subversive invitation that much more real, urgent and
irresistible.

The telegraph boy stands in the doorway, but he also embodies
boyhood itself as a threshold – a threshold of adulthood, masculinity and sexual desire. In the way Tuke pictorialises them, they are
outside heteronormativity. Tuke's 'beauty' in his cycle of boyhood culminating with the telegraph boy is thus contextualised in the politics

of illicit desire, which Charles Kains-Jackson effectively illustrated in his writing. In sympathy with many poets he published, Kains-Jackson, the editor of *The Artist*, published his own manifesto for a new model of masculinity, titled 'The New Chivalry', in his magazine on 2 April 1894.[30] The subversive nature of this essay was at least in part responsible for him losing his post as editor.[31] He argued that procreation – the goal of the 'old chivalry' – was no longer obligatory, and, therefore, that the masculine ideal must be redefined:

> The New Chivalry then is also the new necessity. Happily it is already with us. The advanced – the more spiritual types of English manhood already look to beauty first. In the past the beauty has been conditioned and confined to such beauty as could be found in some fair being *capable of increasing the population*. The condition italicized is now for the intelligent, removed. The New Chivalry therefore will not ask that very plain question of the Marriage Service. 'Will it lead to the procreation of children?' It will rest content with beauty – God's outward clue to the inward Paradise. No animal consideration of mere sex will be allowed to intrude on the higher fact. A beautiful girl will be desired before a plain lad, but a plain girl will not be considered in the presence of a handsome boy. Where boy and girl are of equal outward grace the spiritual ideal will prevail over the animal and the desire of influencing the higher mind, the boy's, will prevail over the old desire to add to the population. The higher form of influence will be chosen.[32]

The telegraph messenger is Kains-Jackson's 'handsome boy', a 'beauty – God's outward clue to the inward Paradise', rejecting the ideology of reproduction and family values.

Between the summer of 1889 and the spring of 1890, a sex scandal featuring policemen, aristocrats, prostitutes, court cross-examinations and high-profile cover-ups took place in London, commonly known as the Cleveland Street Affair or the West End Scandals.[33] At the centre of the scandal were telegraph boys. Between 1888 and 1889, on behalf of Charles Hammond, a telegraph boy named Harry Newlove recruited a group of young fellow postal messengers with last names such as Wright and Thickbroom for a homosexual brothel in London. The investigation began when a fifteen-year-old telegraph boy, Charles Swinscow, was caught on 4 July 1889, suspected of theft after being seen carrying eighteen shillings on his person, more cash than an ordinary postal worker could manage at the time. Swinscow told a Post Office constable that he 'got the money from Mr Hammond', who lived 'at nineteen Cleveland Street', 'for going to bed with gentleman at his house'.[34] The *Illustrated Police News* of 25 January 1890 shows three telegraph boys from the General Post Office headquarters. The caption reads, 'THE BOYS GIVING INFORMATION, SCOTLAND YARD'. In the centre of this illustration is a circle depicting a police raid at 'THE HOUSE OF CLEVELAND ST, A DEN OF INFAMY'.

Considering the press coverage of the Cleveland Street Affair and its impact on English minds, when Tuke painted a telegraph boy in 1890, it was not an innocent subject matter.[35] It would have been particularly hard for the typical readers and contributors of *The Artist*, including Uranian poets and writers, to look at Tuke's Cornish genre painting without thinking about the scandal involving Newlove, Thickbroom and their fellow postal workers. According to Timothy d'Arch Smith, among Uranian poets, writers and artists, telegraph boys indisputably symbolised and unfailingly encouraged homoerotic desire.[36] He lists a number of Victorian men who found that the young postal workers powerfully embodied their longing and forbidden pleasure. Alfred Douglas and Frederick Rolfe make his list of postal love, and so does Tuke because of his painting *The Message*. Smith identifies Tuke's model in the painting as William James Martin, an actual telegraph boy employed by a local Post Office in Falmouth, Cornwall.[37] Whether or not his employment status at the time can be verified, Martin has been also identified as the model for Tuke's *Woodland Bather* of 1893 (see Figure 6).

Martin, having modelled for *The Message* two years before, posed nude for Tuke's *A Woodland Bather*.[38] What is the implication of Martin posing as a uniformed, working-class youth and later as a nymph-like creature of woods and water? The answer to this question can be found in Tuke's treatment of the bather's skin, revealing the connections between labour, naturalism and homoerotic desire. Martin's body is marked by the chromatic anomalies in his otherwise ideally white and delicate complexion. The green tint found in his left arm, abdomen and right leg is particularly unnatural. Even considering Tuke's sympathy with French 'Salon Impressionists', the use of green for Martin's skin unbalances the whole colour composition. The vegetation, for instance, rendered in brushstrokes characteristic of Jules Bastien-Lepage, a painter Tuke knew and admired,[39] does not show similar distorting plays of the light or the mind on its hue, relying on the academically correct local colours despite their brightness. The dark brown used to describe the bather's right thigh and lower buttock is equally out of place, unless he is assumed to have slid on

**6** Henry Scott Tuke, *A Woodland Bather*, 1893. Oil on canvas, 152 × 84 cm. Private collection.

the mud and the wet earth has dried on his skin. Finally, the purple tone running down the entire length of the bather's left leg not only deviates in itself from conventions but also produces unrealistic tension against the green on the other leg, rendering his body chromatically incoherent.

Walter Pater's concept of 'diaphaneitè' helps explain Tuke's factually erroneous use of green, brown and purple, complicating claims for the painter's 'Impressionistic' naturalism. The Greek origin of the adjective 'diaphanous' incorporates *diaphanēs, dia* meaning 'through' and *phainein* 'to show'. Pater celebrated diaphanous man as an ideal of beauty. Tuke's unnatural colours marring the bather's body can be thus understood through Pater's idea as not inherent in his skin but lent from his surroundings. Every brushstroke bearing green renders the bather's skin diaphanous, like clear glass, through which the colour of foliage penetrates and on the surface of which other verdant shades reflect. Likewise, each brushstroke laying down brown on the bather's right buttock and thigh creates more transparent flesh, through which rich wet earth peeks. In the purple of the young man's left leg, even the surrounding shadow is captured. These are Pater's 'evanescent shades', for which the 'world has no sense fine enough', and they 'fill up the blanks between contrasted types of character'.[40]

'Diaphaneitè' is directly associated with Pater's idea of 'sexless beauty':[41] Pater cited as a 'diaphanous' type Praxitelean sculptures of male nudes from the fourth century BCE, which combined, according to Johann Johannes Winckelmann, 'the forms of prolonged youth in the female sex with the masculine forms of a beautiful young man'.[42] Pater argued that these marmoreal forms commanded 'sexless beauty', by which he meant not without a sex but of both sexes and thus beyond the binary sexual division. The 'diaphanous' body cannot be sexed because it possesses the powers of all sexes.[43] In this somatic ambiguity, sex disappears. By the same logic, a 'diaphanous' man becomes invisible because he transcends the specificity of the male – or female – sex. He is indescribable in the normative patriarchal mind because he cannot be pinned down to be like this man or like that woman. In other words, Pater's hero transcends all sexual bounds. In *A Woodland Bather*, Tuke constructed a visual equivalent of a speech act that makes this Aesthetic idea of the 'diaphanous' man pictorially urgent. It consists of a body of water pooled against the dark earth reflecting the bather's left foot. As the reflection of his body illustrates, validates and thus actualises the process of diaphanisation on the surface of the water, the bather's flesh becomes Pater's 'sexless beauty'.

The context of Pater's diaphanous beauty links Martin the tele-graph boy and Martin the bather. Historical specificities tie sexual transgression that young male workers at the Post Office represented with the fracturing of dichotomised desire in Tuke's male nude. In *The Message* as well as *A Woodland Bather*, Tuke consistently paints a male body that resists heteronormativity, materialising desire beyond conventional boundaries. Boyhood for Tuke and his admirers in the Uranian circle signifies the sexuality and seduction of indeterminacy. It is a bodily state in constant change manifesting characteristics of a child, 'sexless' in the Paterian sense, as well as a man. Set against the regulations of the normative gender and sexuality, the irresolu-tion of boyhood was potently alluring. The kind of boyhood Tuke represented was thus a threshold of subversion, a possible departure from patriarchy. The message in Tuke's painting *The Message* is then an invitation to fantasy, a mind-picture of escape from disciplines of heteronormativity.

In the 1895 interview quoted in the beginning of this chapter, the journalist from *The Studio* also asked Tuke, 'You set most store by your nude, I believe?' Tuke replied,

> Yes, at the time I first took up the subject ... it seemed to open up fresh vistas, and certainly gave new interest to the study of the undraped figure, to depict it with the pure daylight upon it, instead of the artificial lighting of the studio. Besides, as a matter of personal taste, I much prefer working in the open to the close air of a room, especially at the temperature which is necessary to maintain when you are working from the life. Sometimes one is tempted to inquire if the result com-pensates for the extra labour involved, and the disappointments and inconveniences of the changeable English climate. But I always return to my first opinion, that the truth and beauty of flesh in sun light by the sea, is offered to you in a way impossible to secure in pictures built up from hasty sketches, at leisure, in one's studio. Because, however much you may work indoors afterwards, whatever you add is with the outdoor impression strong upon you.[44]

This response from Tuke, establishing him as a serious painter of the nude, indicates a commitment to *plein-air* practice and manly 'labour' against the harshness of nature. But even this quotation rewards closer reading in the context of the rest of the article and the journal in which it appeared. The malleability of contemporary forms

of masculinity is evident in the way the article, for instance, characterises Tuke's 'Pink Cottage', 'with its blaze of flowers, carnations and
gladioli especially', as 'far more like the house of a coastguard than the
abode of an artist of note'. *The Studio* in its first few issues reflected
an Aesthetic ideology all but openly intrigued by eroticism between
men.[45] Invocations of such Aesthetic homoeroticism run through the
interview, part of which was purposely conducted at the site where *A
Woodland Bather* was painted. One such key phrase is Tuke's allusion
to 'the truth and beauty of flesh in sun light by the sea'. The 'truth and
beauty of flesh' reside in the 'diaphanous' body. This 'useless' (repro-
ductively inactive) and 'un-ideal' (sexually indefinable) body that is
'cruel-lovely, with half-angelic, half-dæmonic splendour' or the power
of its 'clear crystal nature', as Pater explained, 'is felt like a sweet
aroma in early manhood'.[46] A transgressive desire inspired by this
type of body is the engine of Tuke's creativity, whether or not such a
desire was ever physically fulfilled or for ever held back at the 'burning point'.[47] Tuke's naturalistic portrayal of Cornish working-class
lads and their lives, with its 'sexless' 'view of labour', is animated by
this complex homoerotic desire.

## Notes

An earlier version of this chapter was published as part of my book
*Painted Men in Britain, 1868–1918: Royal Academicians and Masculinities*
(Farnham: Ashgate, 2012).

1   *The Studio*, 5 (1895), 93.
2   Stanhope Forbes, Elizabeth Forbes, Frank Bramley, Thomas Cooper
    Gotch, Walter Langley and Tuke were some of the prominent artists
    who were associated with an artists' colony that was active in Newlyn, a
    Cornish coastal town, in the 1880s and 1890s. Forming what is known
    as the Newlyn School, these artists were committed to painting outdoors
    under natural light and capturing everyday events of ordinary people.
    See Betsy Cogger Rezelman, *The Newlyn Artists and Their Place in Late-
    Victorian Art* (PhD dissertation, University of Indiana, 1984); Caroline
    Fox, *Stanhope Forbes and the Newlyn School* (Newton Abbot: David and
    Charles, 1993).
3   For Uranians, see Karl Heinrich Ulrichs, *The Riddle of 'Man-Manly' Love*,
    2 vols, trans. Michael A. Lombardi-Nash (New York: Prometheus Books,
    1994). The German sexologist and activist Ulrichs argued that 'Uranian'
    men's attraction to their own sex was 'congenital'. In collaboration
    with Havelock Ellis, John Addington Symonds played a major role in

introducing Ulrichs's ideas to English readers. See Symonds, *A Problem of Modern Ethics* (London: privately printed, 1891).

4  See Peter J. Holliday, 'Symonds and the model of Ancient Greece', in John Pemble (ed.), *John Addington Symonds: Culture and the Demon Desire* (New York: St Martin's Press, 2000), p. 89.

5  Emmanuel Cooper, *The Life and Works of Henry Scott Tuke* (Swaffham: Editions Aubrey Walter, 1988), p. 26.

6  Tuke, *A Sailor's Yarn*, 1887. Oil on canvas, 87.6 × 63.5 cm. Art Gallery of New South Wales.

7  Tuke, *The Midday Rest*, 1905. Oil on canvas, 103 × 134 cm. Collection of Sir Elton John.

8  In the centre of this painting, a blond man in a red shirt smokes a pipe. Considering the facial features, this may well be Tuke's self-portrait despite the wrong hair colour.

9  For example, Catherine Dinn, David Wainwright and Catherine Wallace overlook or obfuscate Tuke's homoeroticism. See Dinn and Wainwright, *Henry Scott Tuke 1858–1929: Under Canvas* (Carshalton: Sarema Press, 1989); Wallace, *Catching the Light: The Art and Life of Henry Scott Tuke* (Edinburgh: Atelier Books, 2008); and Wallace, *Henry Scott Tuke: Paintings from Cornwall* (Wellington: Halsgrove, 2008). Against these scholars, Michael Hatt offers a critical alternative as he directly engages with Tuke's sexuality and art. See Hatt, '"A Great Sight": Henry Scott Tuke and his models', in Jane Desmarais, Martin Postle and William Vaughan (eds), *Model and Supermodel: The Artist's Model in British Art and Culture* (Manchester: Manchester University Press, 2006), pp. 89–104; Hatt, 'Uranian imperialism: Boys and empire in Edwardian England', in Tim Barringer, Geoff Quilley and Douglas Fordham (eds), *Art and the British Empire* (Manchester: Manchester University Press, 2007), pp. 153–68.

10  Marcia Pointon, foreword to Dinn and Wainwright, *Henry Scott Tuke 1858–1929*.

11  See Julia F. Saville's discussion of 'romance deferral' in 'The romance of boys bathing: Poetic precedents and respondents to the painting of Henry Scott Tuke', in Richard Dellamora (ed.), *Victorian Sexual Dissidence* (Chicago: University of Chicago Press, 1999), p. 254.

12  Henry Scott Tuke, *August Blue*, 1893. Oil on canvas, 122 × 183 cm. Tate Gallery, London; Henry Scott Tuke, *Ruby, Gold and Malachite*, 1902. Oil on canvas, 117 × 159 cm. Guildhall Art Gallery, City of London.

13  Saville, 'The romance of boys bathing', p. 257.

14  Henry Scott Tuke, *Jack in the Rigging (Going Aloft)*, 1888. Oil on panel, 23 × 13 cm. Trehayes Collection, Cornwall. For a photograph of Rowling wearing the hat in question, see Dinn and Wainwright, *Henry Scott Tuke, 1858–1929*, p. 45.

15  Eugène Delacroix, *Liberty Leading the People: 28 July 1830*, 1830. Oil on canvas, 260 × 325 cm. Musée du Louvre, Paris.

16  Brian D. Price (ed.), 'Tuke Reminiscences' (unpublished manuscript), Hyman Kreitman Research Centre for Tate Library and Archive, London, p. 27.

17  'Diary of Henry Scott Tuke, 12 March 1899–31 December 1905' (unpublished manuscript), Hyman Kreitman Research Centre for Tate Library and Archive, London.

18  Price, 'Tuke Reminiscences', p. 19.

19  In *Henry Scott Tuke*, p. 84, Dinn and Wainwright mistakenly attribute this daring composition to Charles Napier Hemy. But a survey of Hemy's oeuvre will immediately reveal that Tuke's 'fellow marine painter' never violates the picture plane as Tuke does in *The Run Home*. Hemy indeed relies on the 'device of showing a vessel at an acute angle and masking off the top portion of the mast to convey the sense of rapid motion', but he never transgresses the discrete boundary, the frame, of a picture, which segregates the viewers' space from the pictorial space.

20  John Byam Liston Shaw, *Boer War 1900*, 1901. Oil on canvas, 1002 × 737 cm. Birmingham Museum of Art Gallery.

21  Tim Barringer, *Reading the Pre-Raphaelites* (New Haven: Yale University Press, 1998), p. 169.

22  For Tuke and the Boer War, see Maria Tuke Sainsbury, *Henry Scott Tuke, R.A., R.W.S.: A Memoir* (London: Martin Secker, 1933), p. 126: 'The Boer War was of course very trying to the faithful Liberal and he [Tuke] writes, after meeting Horatio Brown, "I am glad to find he agrees with me in thinking this war was unnecessary[.]" ... The war was hateful to him, but he could respect and admire soldiers and at the end of it he let his model go with other Falmouth youths to join the South African Mounted Police.'

23  'Dowdeswell's', *The Artist*, 12:134 (1 January 1891), 12–13.

24  *Ibid.*, 12–13.

25  See Susan P. Casteras, *The Defining Moment: Victorian Narrative Paintings from the Forbes Collection* (Charlotte, NC: Mint Museum of Art, 1999), pp. 104–6, 124–6.

26  *Ibid.*, p. 124.

27  'Dowdeswell's', 12–13

28  *Ibid.*, 21.

29  Wallace, *Catching the Light*, p. 57.

30  See Richard Dellamora, *Masculine Desire: The Sexual Politics of Victorian Aestheticism* (Chapel Hill: The University of North Carolina Press, 1990), pp. 157–8.

31  See Laurel Brake, '"Gay discourse" and *The Artist and Journal of Home*

*Culture'*, in Brake, Bill Bell and David Finkelstein (eds), *Nineteenth-Century Media and the Construction of Identities* (New York: Palgrave, 2000), pp. 286–7.

32 *The Artist*, 15:173 (2 April 1894).

33 See Colin Simpson, Lewis Chester and David Leitch, *The Cleveland Street Affair* (Boston: Little, Brown and Company, 1976); Matt Cook, *London and the Culture of Homosexuality, 1885–1914* (Cambridge: Cambridge University Press, 2003), pp. 42–72; Morris B. Kaplan, *Sodom on the Thames: Sex, Love, and Scandal in Wilde Times* (New York: Cornell University Press, 2005), pp. 167–223.

34 Simpson, Chester and Leitch, *The Cleveland Street Affair*, p. 16.

35 On 5 July 1890, the *Scots Observer* stated that *The Picture of Dorian Gray* was 'false art' and Oscar Wilde could 'write for none but outlawed noblemen and perverted telegraph boys', demonstrating the extent to which the Cleveland Street Affair entered the cultural lexicon at the time.

36 Timothy d'Arch Smith, *Love in Earnest: Some Notes on the Lives and Writings of English 'Uranian' Poets from 1889 to 1930* (London: Routledge & Kegan Paul, 1970), p. 29.

37 *Ibid.*, p. 29. See also Dinn and Wainwright, *Henry Scott Tuke*, p. 47, and Wallace, *Catching the Light*, p. 59. For Tuke's portrait and oil sketches of Martin in uniform in the Royal Cornwall Polytechnic Society, Falmouth, see Wallace, *Henry Scott Tuke*, pp. 38–9.

38 For *A Woodland Bather* and its Classical and Biblical references in the context of British Aestheticism, see the introduction of my book *Painted Men in Britain, 1868–1918: Royal Academicians and Masculinities* (Farnham, UK: Ashgate, 2012).

39 See Dinn and Wainwright, *Henry Scott Tuke, 1858–1929*, pp. 24, 45, and Wallace, *Catching the Light*, p. 65.

40 Walter Pater, *The Renaissance: Studies in Art and Poetry*, ed. Adam Philips (Oxford: Oxford University Press, 1986), p. 154.

41 Pater, *The Renaissance*, pp. 154, 257; for a discussion of 'sexless beauty', hermaphroditism and androgyny, see J. B. Bullen, *The Pre-Raphaelite Body: Fear and Desire in Painting, Poetry, and Criticism* (Oxford: Clarendon Press, 1988), pp. 154, 187, 189–94.

42 Johann Joachim Winkelmann, *History of Ancient Art*, trans. G. Henry Lodge, vol. I (New York: Ungar, 1968), p. 208, quoted in Dellamora, *Masculine Desire*, p. 64.

43 See Herbert Sussman, *Victorian Masculinities: Manhood and Masculine Poetics in Early Victorian Literature and Art* (Cambridge: Cambridge University Press, 1995), pp. 190–2; for the connection between the hermaphrodite and the diaphanous type, see Dellamora, *Masculine Desire*, p. 67.

44  E. B[onney] S[teyne], 'Afternoon in studios: Henry Scott Tuke at
    Falmouth', *The Studio*, 5 (1895), 94.
45  See Christopher Reed, *Art and Homosexuality: A History of Ideas* (New
    York: Oxford University Press, 2011), chapter 3.
46  Pater, *The Renaissance*, p. 158.
47  For a discussion of Pater's concept of the 'burning point', a 'hard gem-
    like flame' and masculinity, see Dellamora, *Masculine Desire*, p. 68, and
    Sussman, *Victorian Masculinities*, pp. 193–202.

# 3

## *Bricks and Flowers*: unconventionality and queerness in Katherine Everett's life writing

*Mo Moulton*

Katherine Everett's 1949 memoir, *Bricks and Flowers*, narrates a remarkable life. Born into the Anglo-Irish gentry in the 1870s, Everett (1872–1953) escaped an abusive mother by moving to Britain as a teenager. Her memoir describes an art-school education, life as a single mother and a career as a building contractor, to name only a few of the highlights. The question of Everett's sexuality is never directly addressed, though for the modern reader it hovers in the background. Separated from her husband in 1914, Everett dedicated her memoirs to her 'dear friend Ina Jephson', with whom she lived for a time. A single woman, a dear friend, a tender dedication: perhaps inevitably, the question of whether Everett was involved in a lesbian relationship with Jephson emerges. Yet it was not only in her intimate relationships that Everett seemed a little different. By her own self-representation, she was utterly unafraid. In one striking passage, she travelled across civil-war-torn Ireland, actually bicycling the last sixty miles to Limerick, in order to confirm that her relative's castle at Macroom had been burned by the anti-Free State forces.[1] In conjunction with the rest of the memoir, Everett's epic bicycle trip signals that she was an individual defined, however understatedly, by unconventionality.

That unconventionality, I argue, provides a key to understanding a life like Everett's, which seems simultaneously to invite and to resist a queer reading. By listening carefully to what Everett has to say about her own life, as well as by trying to read between the lines, I argue that it is possible to arrive at a richer understanding of life outside the conventions of heteronormativity and, perhaps, of homonormativity as well. Everett was neither a typical upper-middle-class straight wife and mother, nor an entirely recognisable member of the emerging Sapphic subcultures of twentieth-century Britain. Instead, she was a daughter, wife, mother and companion; a builder, artist and writer; possibly lesbian, arguably gender-non-conforming in certain respects; and, ultimately, a valuable source of insight into the possibilities of queer life, broadly defined, in twentieth-century Britain. Laura Doan warns against 'attaching our own labels to past sexual lives' and so shaping those lives 'to look like our own'.[2] Noting the geneaological preoccupations (whether in the ancestral or Foucauldian sense) of much queer historiography, Doan calls for the practice of a queer critical history that could 'explain aspects of the sexual past that resist explanation in the context of identity history.'[3] After a brief biographical sketch, this chapter attempts an ancestral genealogy, amassing the available evidence for Everett's sexual orientation and reading between the lines to discern what her memoir and other writings might be whispering to us about homosexuality. The second part of the chapter, by contrast, embarks on a queer critical history, arguing for the centrality, in Everett's life-writing, of the strange-to-us category of unconventionality. While Everett is quiet on the subject of sexuality, she is clear about the importance of being unconventional, especially for women. Misfit women, Everett explains, saved her life, and rejecting conventions of gender, especially in regard to work, made her life rich and fulfilling. Ina Jephson is the female mystery at the heart of Everett's obscured personal life, but that mystery should not distract from the many women who provided Everett the wherewithal to pursue her eccentric and very public professional life. Ultimately, it matters whether Everett was a lesbian, and whether she wrote her memoir in a coded fashion to reflect a closeted relationship. In the practice of a genuinely queer history, however, it matters even more that we are able to understand Everett's own queerness on her own terms and to map out how her unconventionality made her life possible.

Everett was born at her family's home in Killarney in the early 1870s, and many of her short stories reflect her upbringing amidst the declining world of the Protestant Ascendancy. Educated largely at home, at the age of nineteen she fled to England, where she lived with her mother's relatives and began studying art formally. She married her cousin and fellow art-student Herbert Everett; the couple had two sons but the marriage was unhappy and fell apart at the outbreak of the First World War. In the meantime Everett had embarked upon a career as a building contractor, building and restoring houses in southern England, which she would pursue in various guises throughout her long life. In order to support herself and her two sons, however, Everett also took on other employment, including working as a nurse and serving as a companion to a wealthy relative, Lady Olive Ardilaun, in Ireland. Working as a lady's companion also brought her to Italy, where she stayed on to renovate a very old villa before returning to the Sussex countryside. Her memoir, *Bricks and Flowers*, ends at the Second World War, with Everett's two sons settled into careers and Everett retired in a country home she built for herself. *Bricks and Flowers* was published in London in 1949 and subsequently reprinted, and a book of short stories, *Walk With Me*, covering related material came out two years later.

## Looking for lesbians: homosexuality in Everett's writings

Homosexuality, or the possibility of it, appears only in muted and intermittent ways in *Bricks and Flowers*. Historians of sexuality in Britain frequently invoke two trials, that of Oscar Wilde in 1895 and of Radclyffe Hall's novel *The Well of Loneliness* in 1928, as milestones that mark the transition to a modern sensibility about sexual orientation, informed by medical and sexological discourses.[4] Indeed, Doan has argued that the 1928 obscenity trial profoundly changed the cultural landscape for women who lived with other women and for women who embraced aspects of masculinity, as 'the possibility of denial – so convenient for those who knew but preferred not to – began to slip away'.[5]

Yet although Everett wrote her memoir eleven years after the publication of *The Well*, neither Hall nor any other publicly recognised lesbian or female gender invert appears in the book. Poignantly, Wilde does make a cameo appearance, by way of Ireland. Lady Ardilaun had known Wilde through Anglo-Irish society, and late in the book Everett recalls asking her about her impressions of him. She describes Wilde's parents as 'strange people' who were 'not fit to bring up boys'.[6] After telling several anecdotes, Lady Ardilaun exclaimed, 'I had no suspicions about his character. It was so tragic. His trial was a great shock, and I couldn't bear to read about it. Poor, poor Oscar!' She confessed her lasting guilt and regret for refusing to answer a letter Wilde sent from France shortly before his death, asking for comfort and a little money.[7] In a book that generally eschews name-dropping, the passage on Wilde stands out, particularly for its emotional intensity. Many years after his death, Wilde's offence was still, to Everett, something that dared not speak its name. His fate was presented as an unequivocal tragedy, but also a tragedy that existed within the realm of family ties rather than the public world of authorship, celebrity and the debate over homosexuality.

Female homosexuality appears even more tangentially and uncertainly in Everett's writing. Her beloved aunt Louise Berens, with whom she travelled to Canada as a young woman, provided the occasion for one possible reference to same-sex love or at least exceptional companionship. Everett refers, in the memoir, to a friendly visit from 'the maid who subsequently became the lifelong friend and companion to Mrs Berens', adding that Mrs Berens referred to her as 'My blessed Virgin Mary'.[8] Such a sentence begs to be parsed: what would occasion the promotion from maid to permanent companion? Is it reasonable to read 'lifelong friend' as code for the kind of respectable romantic friendship described by Martha Vicinus?[9] And what are we to make of the nickname, 'my blessed Virgin Mary', with its connotations of religion, possessiveness and sexuality both deferred and made explicit? Everett's network of female relatives was tightly knit, and Mary had been transferred, by the time of the visit, to the management of another elderly aunt's affairs, raising the alternative scenario that Mary has been incorporated into the family along sisterly rather than marital lines. Indeed, characteristically, the rest of the passage is focused on the antics of the elderly Aurelia, reported by Mary in 'her slow, gentle way of speaking'.[10]

References to Wilde and a possible romantic friendship take on potential significance mainly in light of the same-sex mystery at the heart of the book: Everett's relationship with Jephson, the 'dear friend' to whom Everett dedicated *Bricks and Flowers*. She returned to the formulation later in the one episode featuring Jephson, describing her as 'a dear friend to whom I and my boys were devoted'. Jephson had moved from England to Ireland to live with Everett, who lived on Lady Ardilaun's estate in a smaller house named Sibyl Hall. Evidently this was a fairly serious undertaking, since Jephson brought her furniture over with her. Jephson joined Everett at a difficult juncture in Irish history. The Anglo-Irish War of 1919–21 had ended with a treaty that created the Irish Free State from the southern twenty-six counties of the island, but a bloody civil war between supporters and opponents of the treaty within Ireland raged through 1923. One feature of this conflict was the burning and raiding of homes belonging to loyalists, particularly to members of the Anglo-Irish Ascendancy. The point of this brief passage on Jephson, then, was ultimately more to explain why Jephson left Ireland, rather than to explain why she came in the first place or to describe her stay.

The chapter opens with a discussion of Everett's willingness to take risks on her cousin's behalf during this difficult time. She then turns to Jephson: 'At this time Ina Jephson, a dear friend to whom I and my boys were devoted, had brought her furniture over and was sharing Sibyl Hall with us.'[11] Interestingly, this section is one of the very few that was substantially rewritten in the 1950 edition. In the first edition, Everett explains, 'She was not strong and, unlike us, her nerves were unable to stand the strain of living through civil war.'[12] Such a statement allies Everett with her sons in a possibly gendered differentiation between the strong, masculine members of the household and the frailer Jephson. In the reprinting, however, Everett unifies the experience of the household: 'we were all of us labouring under the strain of living through a period of civil war, and houses were constantly being raided'. She also suggests instead that the cold, draughty house was challenging for Jephson's health. In both editions, she goes on to describe her sons' demonstration that the house was easily broken into, a humorous episode that served to explain why the situation was unsuitable for Jephson in the long run. Everett notes, however, that 'Ina's decision was taken reluctantly and only, I think because she knew it would relieve my mind'.[13]

Who was Jephson? Trained, like Everett, as an artist, Jephson became an expert in child guidance and a member of the council of the Society for Psychical Research (SPR).[14] As a researcher, she was particularly interested in clairvoyance. In a series of three articles published in the *Proceedings of the Society for Psychical Research*, Jephson used card-guessing as a method for demonstrating and describing the nature of clairvoyance. Although the experiments ultimately failed to prove the existence of clairvoyant card-guessing, a result in keeping with the SPR's tradition of restraint and scepticism, Jephson nonetheless argued that they pointed towards future research questions related to the conditions under which clairvoyance might be successfully observed.[15] She was almost certainly aware of Radclyffe Hall and her partner Una Troubridge and had probably encountered them. Hall's interest in psychical research was sparked by the sessions she and Troubridge held with a medium in order to communicate with Hall's deceased lover Mabel Batten.[16] In 1920, Hall sued the SPR member St George Lane Fox-Pitt for making slanderous allegations

against her, based on reports of the psychic communications with
Batten, in order to block her election to the SPR.[17]

Given this background, Jephson is certainly the character featured
in Everett's 1951 short story, 'Phantasmagoria', which opens with the
lines: 'My friend Margaret was staying with me in my Georgian house
in Ireland. She had studied psychology and was a sceptical member
of a group investigating spiritualism.'[18] At the narrator's instigation,
Margaret agrees to overcome her scepticism and participate in an
impromptu experiment with automatic writing, the popular spiritual-
ist practice of channelling dead spirits through apparently spontane-
ous handwriting.[19] At first, nothing happens, but when the narrator
puts her hand over Margaret's, the pencil instantly begins to move in
a moment charged with tension: '"Don't take your hand away," she
whispered.'[20] The results claimed to be from Jeremiah Doyle, who
loved a serving-maid in Sibyl Hall (the real-life name of the house
where Everett and Jephson briefly lived together in Ireland). Doyle
refers to money hidden in the roof of the house, but the narrator fails
to find anything; still, her belief is reinforced by the ornate quality of
the script. Margaret dismisses this: 'The subconscious can make us
do things beyond our normal capacity, and we have no doubt looked
at old deeds and observed the writing at some time.'[21] Still, Margaret
agrees to take part in one more writing effort before the narrator
must go on a journey to the west of Ireland to help an old lady. Their
touching hands again produce a message, this one warning against
taking a journey. Margaret insists that this, too, is a subconscious
message: 'I don't want you to go haring across Ireland; you do far too
much as it is.'[22] The narrator does fall seriously ill with influenza on
her journey, and receives dubious care from her hostess who prefers
not to call a doctor, 'a Ca-a-tholic and a Sinn Feiner', until, halluci-
nating, she nearly dies from fever.[23] On her return home, she and
Margaret are unable to repeat the automatic writing, and Margaret,
who argues that Doyle, too, was a hallucination, gets the last word: 'In
fact the whole business was just bunkum.'[24]

Tying all this evidence together with a lavender ribbon, it is easy to
imagine that Jephson and Everett, both unattached to men, were in
fact lovers moving through a social context in which such things were
not, and did not have to be, discussed openly. The 'automatic writing'
can be read as a touching metaphor for the suppressed, displaced, but
ultimately intimately personal expressions of desire and connection
between the two lovers. In her study of Hall's efforts to communicate

with the dead Batten, Jodie Medd uses the language of spiritualism to turn such metaphors into a source of empowerment: 'Rather than thinking of lesbian "ghosting" as the effacing or "murdering" of lesbian authenticity, I'd propose that it is the very discursive *conjuring* up of lesbianism as a ghostly possibility – incoherent, undefinable, diffuse, mobile, evasive, shaped by its invisibility – that performatively begins to *bring lesbianism into being,* historically as a cultural category of identity.'[25] And yet, appealing as such a conclusion is, without further evidence it must remain provisional at best. Like Margaret, the reader should be suspicious of his or her own subconscious hopes: is it Everett's truth, or ours, that threatens to emerge from the pattern of evidence?

The interwar years were a time of considerable cultural visibility for female homosexuality. Out of the two categories of 'romantic friendship and Sapphic sexuality', Vicinus has argued, women were able to fashion 'a personal identity based upon a sexualized, or at least recognizably eroticized, relationship with another woman', an identity that she suggests had come into existence by 1928.[26] Certainly such an identity was not rigid, even by the notoriously fraught standards of identity categories: in their volume on 'sapphic modernities', for example, Doan and Jane Garrity use the term sapphism 'to signal the discursive fluidity of female same-sex desire as an emergent cultural category' in these decades.[27] Doan warns that no category can be expected to reach everyone, and indeed the idea of even having a sexual identity might have been foreign to many people still in the 1920s and 1930s.[28] Yet Everett was precisely the sort of highly educated, privileged woman whom we would expect to have been aware of elite discourses on sex and gender and to have had the capacity for reflection and expression on those matters as they related to her own self-conception. Her approach to Jephson and to homosexuality in general might be coy or careful, but it is surely not clueless.

## A lineage of misfits

Fortunately, Everett's own words lead us out of this speculative territory and into the essence of her own ideas about what was important in her life. Her surfeit of information on her own unconventionality puts the queerness of her life in all senses of the word at centre stage. Queer is a rich and heavily laden term.[29] Unconventional is a more restrained and polite word, but its relationship to queer is undeniable.

Judith Halberstam, for example, has glossed the queer way of life as a series of 'willfully eccentric modes of being', a phrase that captures much of the appeal of Everett's memoir.[30] Lettice Fowler, writing in *The Spectator*, referred to the book's 'glorious touch of lunacy' and recommended it to '[c]onnoisseurs of the wilder bizarreries of family life'.[31] More seriously, *Bricks and Flowers* is a fable about overcoming adversity by learning at the feet of a sisterhood of strong female misfits and ultimately triumphing where they failed by utterly disregarding the limitations of gender. Importantly, Everett's own triumph is narrated, not in the realm of the personal, sexual or romantic, but rather firmly in the realm of professional life.[32]

The villain of Everett's young life was an abusive mother, driven to the edge by her isolation in Ireland and her high-strung temperament. Everett writes, 'As a child I was vaguely conscious of a sadness in our surroundings, but the earliest emotion that I can remember was fear, and that fear was focused on my mother.'[33] Years later an aunt explained why she and her sisters had never come to Ireland to aid their nieces: 'We were so thankful, my dear, to get rid of your mother ... that we all decided to have nothing to do with her or her vipers.'[34] Crucially, however, it was through the agency of women that Everett escaped her mother's grasp. By expanding the frame of reference out from Everett's possible romantic relationships with women to encompass all of her same-sex relationships, especially those with maternal or mentor-like dimensions, the centrality of women to her life becomes obvious.[35] In this, she certainly fits the category of 'lesbian-like' as defined by Judith Bennett: 'women whose lives might have particularly offered opportunities for same-sex love; women who resisted norms of feminine behavior based on heterosexual marriage; women who lived in circumstances that allowed them to nurture and support other women'.[36] Such a definition, however, raises once again the problem that Everett, living in the first half of the twentieth century, had a narrower definition of lesbianism available to her and chose not, in her writings, to make use of it. Moreover, it threatens to obscure what was, for her, the central point: the fact that she was mentored and raised up by a series of women, some of them related to her by blood and others by friendship, who fostered the value of unconventionality in their various ways. Although Everett herself and many of the women from whom she drew inspiration and guidance were certainly independent, in the ordinary sense, they do not fit Vicinus's category of 'independent women', middle-class women pursuing unmarried, independent lives outside the context of the family.[37] Everett was briefly married, and her connections and obligations to her two children form a major strand of motivation throughout her memoir. In this she is like the women who guided her, pursuing unconventional lives while still enmeshed in a dense context of family relationships.

A neighbour, Lady Kenmare, offered Everett a way out of her unhappy childhood home, inviting her to stay with her in order to help with a craft school for the children of the town. There, Everett received artistic encouragement for the first time.[38] In a significant exchange, Lady Kenmare linked, for Everett, the idea of earning money through work with the possibilities of personal and artistic fulfilment:

> Then she would add, 'You must study art, as you are so interested in it', and as I could not explain how hopeless the idea was with my home background, I only said, 'I haven't any money.'
>  'Well, you must earn some', she said, and secured me an order to copy miniatures, from which more orders followed.[39]

Building on the confidence thus engendered, Everett arranged to go to Leicestershire for an extended visit to Ina Ferrers, her mother's first cousin. Married to the wealthy Lord Ferrers, Lady Ferrers impressed Everett both with her kindness and with her unhappiness. Lady Ferrers had grown up in Bantry, on the west coast of Ireland, but ended up in a mismatched marriage to a possessive, highly formal Englishman. In a rare moment, she admitted to being 'a complete misfit' in her husband's world, 'caged' by climate, ill health and her husband's control.[40] Lady Ferrers thus became one example of an unhappy fate for a misfit, one trapped by a poorly chosen mate and the expectations of wealth and social class. Her visit, however, provided Everett with further skills. She records technical conversations with the gardener and the estate's agent, which foreshadow her future work in building and gardening. The sight of the 'lavish' stables sparked early ideas about housing: 'I thought how much better their buildings were than the cabins people lived in at home.'[41] Lady Ferrers also encouraged Everett's artistic talent, but Lord Ferrers became angry when she copied a painting out of his collection, sparking a domestic quarrel that forced her to leave.[42]

She travelled south to live with her next role model, her Aunt Aurelia, whose marriage to a rector only barely reined in her enormous eccentricity. Everett describes her first impression of Aurelia: 'She was about forty, very fat, though all her movements were vigorous; her cheeks were bright pink and her eyes very blue, and she was untidily dressed and wore men's boots.'[43] Aurelia's larger-than-life personality and multiple escapades form the comic highlight of the memoir, but, in the logic of Everett's own life-story, she was both a promise and a warning. Unlike Lady Ferrers, she was able to live her life to the full, exulting in her difference rather than watching it get strangled in an unsuitable marriage. Yet she was constantly a headache for others and occasionally got into potentially serious legal trouble, relying always on her charm and ingenuity and never on hard work or diligence. Her brief career at the Slade Art School, where she encouraged both Everett and her own son to enrol as well, was a humorous but also depressing disaster of high jinks and terrible art: Professor Henry Tonks described her as 'the only completely primitive adult he had ever known'.[44] Taking the freedom to wear men's boots is a wonderful thing, her example seems to say, but the crucial part is what you do next.

Seeking a different path, Everett took time off from her own much more serious art studies to travel across Canada with her other aunt, the highly respectable Louise Berens. There, the possibility of professional success and financial independence appeared before Everett for the first time. She had befriended the head of the Canadian Cable Company in Montreal and corresponded with him on her journey across Canada, asking technical engineering questions about a dam and passing along information about gold mines. On the strength of this, he offered her the position of personal agent, and Everett was attracted by the idea of finally being financially secure. Mrs Berens, however, invoked respectability and blocked that route, asking Everett, 'Don't you see that it is all very well for you to run about with a lot of young men and gain their confidence, with my eye always upon you, but it would be quite another thing to do this as a commercial business once you were alone?'[45] Everett's evident talent for succeeding in a professional and male-dominated world was thus temporarily deflected, inducing her to make a brief attempt at a conventional life-trajectory.

Returning to England, she married her cousin, Aurelia's son Herbert. Everett describes the self-effacement of the decision, which represented her attempt to become a traditional wife. Herbert, she explains, 'was thought to be one of the most promising students at the Slade', and so 'I transferred to Herbert my personal ambition regarding work, and never doubted his having a great future. That hope was not fulfilled.'[46] In fact, Everett struggles to make Herbert a compelling character in her life-story: Aurelia overshadowed even the wedding ceremony with her flamboyant clothing and behaviour and was mistaken for the bride by a heckling onlooker.[47] Female relationships remained central, in other words, even during a scene recounting the ritual triumph of heterosexuality. Settled with Herbert in the English countryside, Everett seemed at first on track to follow in Aurelia's footsteps, becoming a zany housewife with a distant husband. Her firstborn son failed to thrive and, in her zeal to save him, Everett finally hit upon fresh donkey's milk as the cure, but not before she ended up with a French wet nurse and two donkeys (one recalcitrant and one compliant) living with her in a state of chaos. When she saw her household as a 'lunatic's home' through the eyes of some visitors, though, she was shocked into action and quickly restored order. 'Well, it had all got to stop; the French woman … must be put on a train and made to go; the brown donkey and foal should be sold, and the grey treasure confined in a nearby paddock. I, too, must return to ordinary life and cease to focus solely on saving my baby.'[48]

## Bricks, flowers and the building of an unconventional life

Everett was not destined, however, for ordinary life as an upper-middle-class housewife. Even as a very young person she had said that 'I wanted to have a career and be independent', and her wish turned out to be a prediction.[49] Although she and Herbert had a second son together and remained in contact with their old colleagues from the Slade School, the marriage was not a success, and it ended when the First World War broke out. Everett explains the matter tersely: '[A]t the start of the war my marriage foundered. In the past if things had been uncomfortable, as for instance directly after my babies were born, Herbert went away, perhaps to Paris or to Cornwall, or I might not know where he was. This time he informed me that his disappearance was to be final.'[50]

The passage is suggestive in several ways. For one thing, the phrase 'my babies' unambiguously asserts Everett's sense of ownership and the lack of relevance of Herbert's role as father in the family structure. The description of their marriage also highlights the ways in which Everett functioned as a single mother and independent woman from the earliest days of the relationship. Finally, Everett leaves unanswered the question of what Herbert was doing in Paris, Cornwall, or wherever he went, raising the possibility that he might have been pursuing extra-marital relationships, whether with men or women. Everett felt 'very unhappy and distraught with anxiety' at this development, but characteristically, she dwells very briefly on feelings of failure and turns instead to discussing how she dealt with her financial position.[51]

While still married, Everett had embarked on a career as a builder. Dissatisfied with the builder she and Herbert had hired to build their home, she learned the business herself.[52] Her pursuit of this career was interrupted, most dramatically by the First World War and the end of her marriage. The war greatly expanded the opportunities for women working outside of the home.[53] For Everett, however, the war put a temporary break in her unconventional career as a builder and pushed her towards more typical means of earning a living for a woman: nursing and working as a personal companion.[54] Her choices were guided by her need to be available to her sons, a need that is sometimes voiced as a fear of Herbert's potential ability to take them from her and sometimes more sentimentally, as in anecdotes that convey how much they missed her when separated by employment.[55] Yet even in those moments she found ways to return to her central interest: when in Ireland with Lady Ardilaun, for instance, she renovated Sibyl Hall, at first over her cousin's misgivings.[56] In the eight years she spent there, Everett 'was quite content acting as lady-in-waiting to my cousin, both for her social and charitable efforts, and, in addition, doing a good deal of building work for her and for other people'.[57] Lady Ardilaun died suddenly in 1926, leaving Everett £5,000 and some furniture.[58] Everett travelled next to Italy as a companion to Nelly Baring, and decided to stay on, purchasing and renovating a very old villa.[59] Thus building and renovation formed a through-line of Everett's adult life, linking her first independent acts during her marriage to her ultimate renovation of a Sussex home and the building of a retirement cottage called Roughfield for herself on its grounds.

Work often absorbs more attention and time in daily life than personal relationships, but historians of gender and sexuality tend to privilege the latter as sites of identity formation. Although this is understandable, it risks overlooking important arenas of personal development. Georgine Clarsen finds that the female-staffed Alice

Anderson Motor Service of interwar Melbourne, Australia, was a place where 'a highly public exploration of youthful female masculinity ... was celebrated as stylish and enviable'.[60] Clarsen argues, ultimately, that it was in 'the garage that a new kind of lesbian subjectivity began to coalesce – not within the cramped spaces of the medical, moral, or criminal discourses' that have dominated scholarly work.[61] For Everett, too, work as a builder became the medium through which she explored issues of gender, politics and aesthetics.

Builders undertook the building of houses, with the aid either of an architect or of widely available designs.[62] Building contractors built to order, often with an architect, while speculative builders built to meet projected demand, increasingly to prospective owner-occupiers rather than landlords.[63] Speculative building and the rapidity with which small contracting firms were made and dissolved helped to tarnish the profession in the public view, though the industry remained a cornerstone of the British economy.[64] Between the wars, four million new homes were built in England and Wales, part of a massive expansion centred on the suburb, especially in southern areas that avoided the worst of the economic depression.[65] According to Christopher Powell, the interwar building industry enjoyed 'prosperity and independence', and it 'exerted an important stabilizing influence in troubled times'.[66] Mocked as 'bungaloid growth' and 'ribbon rash', these suburbs nonetheless have been seen as essential manifestations of some of the central concerns of interwar Britain. Todd Kuchta, for example, links fears about suburbia to 'the decline in imperial confidence during the 1920s and 1930s', as suburban homes seemed to colonise Britain from within.[67] Yet where Kuchta sees degeneration, Alison Light finds the essence of a new version of Englishness 'at once less imperial and more inward-looking, more domestic and more private – and, in terms of pre-war standards, more "feminine",' embodied by, among other figures, 'the suburban husband pottering away in his herbaceous borders'.[68]

While the ideal of the suburb might reflect a more feminine vision of Englishness, the business of building was resolutely male. Patrick Geddes, one of the leaders of British town planning, envisioned the modern suburb as a space defined by gender difference and separate spheres, a vision supported by the segregation of the workforce.[69] The British building industry employed some 1,219,000 people in 1901, of whom only 3,000, or 0.25 per cent, were women.[70] Women gained formal access to some professions related to building during the interwar decades. The 1919 Sex Disqualification (Removal) Act allowed women to train as chartered surveyors, while by the early 1930s the professional society of architects, RIBA, established a Women's Committee to deal with the slowly increasing number of female architects.[71] However, Elizabeth Darling has emphasised the importance of the voluntary sector in providing women with the opportunity to gain experience and expertise. Working in fields such as interior decoration and social work, women 'made a considerable impact on much of England's social and built landscape'.[72] Of the four women in her study, only one had formal design training, and Darling argues that the professionalisation and bureaucratisation of the building industry that occurred after the Second World War actually served to limit the growth of women's influence in this field.[73]

Everett's situation would not have been unfamiliar to her female contemporaries in the art and design world, many of whom pursued artistic careers while leaving issues of sexuality suppressed. Indeed, many leading interwar interior decorators 'were women who pursued same-sex relationships'.[74] In her study of four such women, one of whom also attended the Slade School, Bridget Elliott argues that their reticence can be attributed to possible fears of negative stereotypes, but also to the possibility that 'they were more absorbed in the practice of art than in sexual politics'.[75] Everett, too, was more absorbed in the practice of building than she was in just about anything else, and yet it was through that practice that many of her ideas on gender and politics ultimately emerged. Espousing a blend of paternalist socialism and Arts-and-Crafts-style artisanal work ethics, embracing her status as an exceptional woman, she nevertheless stopped short of consigning all other women permanently to the home. Unconventional to the end, she complicated ideas of conservative modernity in the interwar decades.

Everett entered the field of building through her commitment to 'the William Morris tradition, that as much as possible should be done by handcraft'.[76] Frustrated by her builder's lack of a similar commitment, she instead oversaw the construction herself, turning her training in the unconventional to a constructive end: 'Many small houses and villas are unattractive through having been built by men who have seen little better work and are obsessed by meaningless conventions'.[77] After a visitor offered a good price for the finished house, Everett's carpenter convinced her to start again and 'be your own builder'.[78] Her experience substantiates Darling's point that informality and lack of professionalisation provided opportunities for women: although Everett 'felt a complete fraud in calling myself a builder', she 'saw at once how essential it was, as it entitled me to a large commission on all I bought'.[79] Her work on this house led to commissions from others in the neighbourhood, and her career was launched.

Everett was interested in the question of economy, challenging herself to build homes more cheaply than the local authority and discussing her cost-saving measures with her employees, who suggested that her good management as well as her lack of overhead and need to support a family fully accounted for her success.[80] From there, she developed principles of management and ideas about housing policy that combined an interest in socialism inflected with a tone of paternalism. She argued that 'good relations with one's men is of vital importance, and apart from its being right, and making for happiness all round, costs are reduced'.[81] Just before the outbreak of the First World War, she began a project whereby she and her employees could buy and build houses for their own use under a co-partnership scheme: 'It would have been a scheme in keeping with William Morris' idea of how a socialist country would function', but it was dashed by the outbreak of war.[82]

Writing about her return to the building industry in the south of England in the 1930s, Everett admitted that she had 'sometimes been asked whether I have had trouble in controlling a gang of men. I never have.' She allowed only that her sex might have facilitated her theory of workers' investment: 'being employed by a woman they have found a sense of co-partnership, possibly more than they would have under a man', as well as enjoying the 'unusual circumstances' of working under the only female architect and builder they had ever encountered. Characteristically, she turned the whole thing into a congenial in-joke: 'Once a local contractor had said he was sure that the lady would make a muddle of the houses she was building, and the phrase became a catchword; when a job went particularly well the men would refer to it as "a nice piece of muddle".'[83]

Everett described her interactions with female clients as rather more troublesome. One woman demanded 'little extra fancies' and forced Everett to be 'firm and stern with her',[84] while another widow was frankly relieved when Everett took on the mantle of her dead husband and told her that her plans were impossible: 'Yes, I am quite, quite sure that you cannot do it, and that your husband would agree if he were here.'[85] Here Everett shows no awareness that she was overriding the wishes of her female clients much as her first builder ignored her desire for a handcraft approach. She writes approvingly, by contrast, of a friend who had saved up for a cottage and requested only that it be 'warm and easy to look after', leaving the rest in Everett's hands.[86] Everett was not passing as male in her profession, though, like the famous cross-dresser Colonel Barker, she relied implicitly on the eminently understandable need to provide for her children as one explanation for her gender-non-conforming professional efforts.[87] Yet she was, by her own account, essentially functioning as a man in a social sense: leading and bonding with her workmen and guiding the flighty women who sought her aid. The link between female masculinity and lesbianism is historically specific, and Doan argues that it really crystallised only after the *Well of Loneliness* obscenity trial, which linked images of Hall's masculine image with the book's lesbian content.[88] If Everett did have lesbian relationships, with Jephson or anyone else, this might explain her reticence to emphasise either those relationships or her own masculine professional role in her writing. At the same time, Everett retained her respect for unconventional women of all sorts. Travelling through France after she had sold the renovated Italian villa, she struck up an acquaintance with a woman out sun-tanning who turned out to be a sort of modern courtesan, having long-term, financially provident affairs with a series of married men. Another woman at the hotel was shocked and asked if Everett knew 'how the person she was walking with occupies herself?' In keeping with her own ancestral debts to women who flouted convention, Everett coolly replied, 'That is not my affair; I found her so well-mannered and so good-looking.'[89]

## Queer conservative modernity?

Yet Everett was no radical and in certain respects was deeply rooted in ideas about social hierarchy, even to the point of opposing democracy. Her account of the Ireland of her childhood reflects the typical politics of her class, longing for an imagined golden age when Paddy and his Anglo-Irish overlords lived in humorous tranquillity. Everett excused the violence of the Black and Tans, citing the IRA's provocation, and she regarded the treaty and subsequent civil war as senseless.[90] Horrified in general by the destruction in the civil war – when the Customs House was burned, she reflected that it 'was utterly horrible that these savages should enjoy such vandalism'[91] – she was particularly eloquent on the feelings of her distraught cousin when her family home, Macroom Castle, was destroyed. 'When people have been born and have grown up in a house on their own land, where their forebears have lived and died for generations, they may feel not only love for it, but a bond which ties them to every stone and tree and sod of the place.'[92]

More surprising, perhaps, is the fact that Everett opposed women's suffrage. In a striking indication of her connections with the feminist world, Everett was called upon at one point to provide shelter for Emmeline Pankhurst, who was then in hiding from arrest. When Everett told Pankhurst that she was not in favour of women voting, Pankhurst exclaimed, 'What can you mean? ... You, who are doing a man's work.'[93] But Everett rejected Pankhurst's argument that 'women would raise the whole tone of the electorate', replying, 'I should think that as a whole women are more ignorant than men, and they are unlikely to vote with any solidarity as women'. Everett was far from alone in being a woman who opposed suffrage: indeed, as Julia Bush argues, the claim that most British women did not want the vote 'has considerable plausibility'.[94] Like the anti-suffragists studied by Bush, Everett was anti-democratic, as evidenced by her suspicion of allowing the ignorant to vote, though her interest in co-operative, socialist housing schemes suggests that she did not share the anti-suffragists' 'deep hostility to the labour movement and to socialism'.[95] In her willingness to accept the privileges of her class, privileges that allowed her the status of 'exceptional woman' in a masculine working world, Everett was like her sapphic contemporaries Hall and Vita Sackville-West. Yet she was different both from the anti-suffragists in general and Hall and Sackville-West in particular in her impatience with gender essentialism. Hall and Sackville-West both espoused conservative ideas about the rightful domestic place of most women while themselves enjoying extraordinary careers.[96] Anti-suffragists, meanwhile, were concerned about women's 'naturally beneficial social function' and their inherent differences from men.[97] Everett, by contrast, mocks the notion that women would vote as a single block and opposes democracy on more general grounds: 'I think too many ill-informed people have the vote now,' meaning that voters were 'susceptible to propaganda and ready to accept bribes'.[98]

In her tone and approach, Everett fits comfortably into what Light has termed 'a conservative modernism'.[99] This brand of conservatism gave to middle-class femininity some 'distinctly masculine qualities: in particular the ethics of a code of self-control and a language of reticence', and Light argues

> that something generic and historic rather than simply individual might be read into the outright denials of autobiography, the silences, under-statements, and the 'refusal of interiority' which make up the place of femininity in the work of so many women of the day. Ironic dismissal, worldly wisdom, brisk competence and heroic disavowal could all be part of that reaction to the legacy of representations which had seen ladies as the softer and the frailer sex, the medium of the emotions and of 'higher things'.[100]

Upon her return to England, Everett bought and renovated a Sussex country house called Mumpumps. Listed with a guide price of £895,000 to £925,000, the house was described on a recent property-sale website as having been 'bought by an Irish lady who carried out extensive renovation work to the property'.[101] Her culminating satis-faction came, however, from the building of her 'permanent home', Roughfield, in 1934–35. The description of that process of building encapsulates Everett's aesthetic, historic and social ideals as well as her professional ethic:

> Every day I arrived early at the site, and stayed till the men had gone, and after I had finished going round each department, noting what materials were wanted, and seeing to the work at hand, I could rest under an oak-tree and feel an inner peace, as intimacy with the beauty of the distance grew upon me. All that summer the weather was perfect, the men were good-tempered and worked willingly, taking a pride in what they were doing.... Is it fanciful to believe that some special grace is given to a structure when such good feeling has gone to the making of it?[102]

She ends her book with a reflection on the present political situ-ation, arguing that England should reduce its population through colonial emigration in order to raise the standard of living and put people back in touch with nature: a William Morris utopian visionary to the end, she concluded that 'the promise of State insurance from cradle to grave will not foster self-reliance, which, together with good craftsmanship, are the native characteristics of the Englishman'.[103]

It is fair to say that Everett found them to be her own native char-acteristics as well. Having learned self-reliance from her unconventional female mentors, she forged a life and a building career founded on good craftsmanship. Everett titled her memoir *Bricks and Flowers*, explaining that the name referenced 'the building of houses and the making of gardens' as well as 'the lights and shadows of my long life'.[104] Yet the title also evokes masculinity and femininity, and accurately reflects Everett's insistence on her right to access both modes throughout her life. It is reasonable to conclude that her relationship with Jephson was something more than a platonic friendship. Yet it is not, in the end, necessary to resort to guessing games and semantics to read Everett's life as queer. Rooting herself in a lineage of nonconformist women, Everett built on their examples and converted their eccentricities into a solid professional career that crossed gender lines with studied casualness. The memoir reminds us of the importance of work and professional life to identity: the title *Bricks and Flowers*, again, redirects our attention to Everett's work, rather than her intimate relationships. Yet whether in the public or the private realm, she is an eminently worthy object of study for queer history in whatever register we might choose to pursue it.

## Notes

1   Katherine Everett, *Bricks and Flowers* (London: Constable, 1950), pp. 155–7. The memoir was first published in 1949 and was reprinted in 1950 with a few small changes. All references are to the 1950 edition unless otherwise noted. For readings of Everett's memoir that place her in a predominantly Anglo-Irish context, see Elizabeth Grubgeld, *Anglo-Irish Autobiography: Class, Gender, and the Forms of Narrative* (Syracuse: Syracuse University Press, 2004); Johannes Wally, *Selected Twentieth Century Anglo-Irish Autobiographies: Theory and Patterns of Self-Representation* (Frankfurt am Main: Peter Lang, 2004).

2   Laura Doan, 'Topsy-turvydom: gender inversion, sapphism, and the Great War', *GLQ: A Journal of Lesbian and Gay Studies*, 12:4 (2006), 525.

3   Laura Doan, *Disturbing Practices: History, Sexuality, and Women's Experience of Modern War* (Chicago: University of Chicago Press, 2013), p. 61.

4   See Deborah Cohler, *Citizen, Invert, Queer: Lesbianism and War in Early Twentieth-Century Britain* (Minneapolis: University of Minnesota Press, 2010), pp. xvi–xvii.

5   Laura Doan, *Fashioning Sapphism: The Origins of a Modern English*

*Lesbian Culture* (New York: Columbia University Press, 2001), p. 193.

6    Everett, *Bricks and Flowers*, pp. 228–9.

7    *Ibid.*, p. 230.

8    *Ibid.*, p. 223.

9    Martha Vicinus, *Intimate Friends: Women Who Loved Women, 1778–1928* (Chicago: University of Chicago Press, 2004), pp. 5–30.

10   Everett, *Bricks and Flowers*, p. 223.

11   *Ibid.*, p. 161.

12   *Ibid.*, p. 161 (1949 edition).

13   *Ibid.*, p. 162.

14   Leslie Shepard (ed.), *Encyclopedia of Occultism & Parapsychology: A Compendium of Information on the Occult Sciences, Magic, Demonology, Superstitions, Spiritism, Mysticism, Metaphysics, Psychical Science, and Parapsychology, with Biographical and Bibliographical Notes and Comprehensive Indexes* (Detroit: Gale, 1978), p. 482.

15   I. Jephson, 'Evidence for clairvoyance in card-guessing: a report on some recent experiments', *Proceedings of the Society for Psychical Research*, 38 (1928), 223–71; I. Jephson, S. G. Soal and T. Besterman, 'Report of a series of experiments in clairvoyance conducted at a distance under approximately fraud-proof conditions', *Proceedings of the Society for Psychical Research*, 39 (1931), 375–411; I. Jephson, 'A behaviourist experiment in clairvoyance', *Proceedings of the Society for Psychical Research*, 41 (1933), 99–114. On the SPR's tradition of scepticism see Shepard (ed.), *Encyclopedia of Occultism & Parapsychology*, p. 848.

16   Jodie Medd, 'Séances and slander: Radclyffe Hall in 1920', in Laura Doan and Jane Garrity (eds), *Sapphic Modernities: Sexuality, Women and National Culture* (New York: Palgrave Macmillan, 2006); Doan, *Fashioning Sapphism*, pp. 31–2, 201.

17   Medd, 'Séances and slander', 206.

18   Katherine Everett, *Walk With Me* (London: Constable, 1951), p. 47.

19   See Alex Owen, *The Darkened Room: Women, Power and Spiritualism in Late Victorian England* (Philadelphia: University of Pennsylvania Press, 1990), especially pp. 79–83; Shepard (ed.), *Encyclopedia of Occultism & Parapsychology*, p. 78.

20   Everett, *Walk With Me*, p. 47.

21   *Ibid.*, p. 48.

22   *Ibid.*, p. 49.

23   *Ibid.*, p. 52.

24   *Ibid.*, p. 54.

25   Medd, 'Séances and slander', 213 (italics original). But see Rebecca Jennings, *A Lesbian History of Britain: Love and Sex Between Women since 1500* (Westport, CT: Greenwood World Publishing, 2007), p. xi.

26 Vicinus, *Intimate Friends*, pp. xviii–xix.

27 Doan and Garrity, 'Introduction,' in Doan and Garrity (eds), *Sapphic Modernities*, p. 4.

28 Doan, 'Topsy-turvydom', 536.

29 For a summary of recent debates over the use of the term queer in the context of British history, see Barry Reay, 'Writing the modern histories of homosexual England', *Historical Journal*, 52:1 (2009), 215–17. See also Jennings, *A Lesbian History of Britain*, p. xvi. Historians such as Matt Houlbrook have embraced the idea of queerness as a way to avoid the anachronistic use of words of 'gay' or 'homosexual'. Houlbrook, *Queer London: Perils and Pleasures in the Sexual Metropolis, 1918–1957* (Chicago: University of Chicago Press, 2005), p. 7.

30 Judith Halberstam, *In a Queer Time & Place: Transgender Bodies, Subcultural Lives* (New York: New York University Press, 2005), p. 1.

31 Quoted in the advertising material at the back of Everett, *Walk With Me*.

32 Wally also highlights independent women and building as key themes of Everett's text. For him, they are crucial to the construction of a specifically female identity. Wally also focuses on the role of Everett's art professor, Henry Tonks, casting him as the source of her ideology and genre conventions. Wally, *Selected Twentieth Century Anglo-Irish Autobiographies*, pp. 156–8.

33 Everett, *Bricks and Flowers*, p. 5. On reasons for her mother's behaviour, pp. 12–13. See also Wally, *Selected Twentieth Century Anglo-Irish Autobiographies*, pp. 87–92; Grubgeld, *Anglo-Irish Autobiography*, pp. 51–3, 77–8, 83–4.

34 Everett, *Bricks and Flowers*, p. 7.

35 See Sharon Marcus, *Between Women: Friendship, Desire, and Marriage in Victorian England* (Princeton: Princeton University Press, 2007).

36 Judith M. Bennett, '"Lesbian-like" and the social history of lesbianisms', *Journal of the History of Sexuality*, 9:1/2 (2000), 9–10.

37 Martha Vicinus, *Independent Women: Work and Community for Single Women, 1850–1920* (Chicago: University of Chicago Press, 1985).

38 Everett, *Bricks and Flowers*, pp. 24–5.

39 *Ibid.*, p. 25.

40 *Ibid.*, p. 33.

41 *Ibid.*, p. 34.

42 *Ibid.*, pp. 38–9.

43 *Ibid.*, p. 43.

44 *Ibid.*, p. 62.

45 *Ibid.*, p. 70.

46 *Ibid.*, pp. 75 (first quote), 76 (second quote).

47 *Ibid.*, p. 77.

48   *Ibid.*, p. 102.
49   *Ibid.*, p. 228.
50   *Ibid.*, p. 121.
51   *Ibid.*, p. 121.
52   *Ibid.*, p. 114.
53   Doan, 'Topsy-turvydom', 517.
54   See Vicinus, *Independent Women*, p. 292.
55   Everett, *Bricks and Flowers*, pp. 121, 133. But see Grubgeld, *Anglo-Irish Autobiography*, pp. 68, 95. Grubgeld locates Everett in a tradition of Anglo-Irish women who avoid writing about their experiences of motherhood.
56   Everett, *Bricks and Flowers*, pp. 136–9.
57   *Ibid.*, p. 139.
58   'Wills and bequests. Lady Ardilaun and the "Black and Tans"', *The Times* (15 March 1926), p. 16e.
59   Everett, *Bricks and Flowers*, pp. 170–8.
60   Georgine Clarsen, '"The woman who does": a Melbourne motor garage proprietor', in Doan and Garrity (eds), *Sapphic Modernities*, pp. 55 (first quote) and 56 (second quote).
61   *Ibid.*, p. 56.
62   Richard Russell Lawrence, *The Book of the Edwardian and Interwar House* (London: Aurum, 2009), p. 12; Christopher Powell, *The British Building Industry Since 1800: An Economic History* (London: E. & F. N. Spon, 2nd edn, 1996), pp. 120–1.
63   Lawrence, *Edwardian and Interwar House*, pp. 11, 15, 69; Powell, *The British Building Industry*, p. 85. See J. W. R. Whitehand and C. M. H. Carr, 'The creators of England's inter-war suburbs', *Urban History*, 28:2 (2001), 218–34.
64   Powell, *The British Building Industry*, pp. 125–6.
65   Todd Kuchta, *Semi-Detached Empire: Suburbia and the Colonization of Britain, 1880 to the Present* (Charlottesville: University of Virginia Press, 2010), p. 150; Powell, *The British Building Industry*, p. 99. See also generally F. M. L. Thompson (ed.), *The Rise of Suburbia* (Leicester: Leicester University Press, 1982).
66   Powell, *The British Building Industry*, p. 119.
67   Kuchta, *Semi-Detached Empire*, p. 150; see also p. 15.
68   Alison Light, *Forever England: Femininity, Literature and Conservatism between the Wars* (London: Routledge, 1991), p. 8. See also Peter Mandler, *The English National Character: The History of an Idea from Edmund Burke to Tony Blair* (New Haven: Yale University Press, 2006), p. 143.
69   Helen Meller, 'Gender, citizenship and the making of the modern environment', in Elizabeth Darling and Lesley Whitworth (eds),

Women and the Making of Built Space in England, 1870–1950, (Aldershot: Ashgate, 2007), p. 13.

70 Powell, *The British Building Industry*, p. 74.

71 Elizabeth Darling, '"The house that is a woman's book come true": The All-Europe House and four women's spatial practices in inter-war England', in Darling and Whitworth (eds), *Women and the Making of Built Space*, p. 133. See Jill Seddon, '"Part-time practice as before": the career of Sadie Speight, architect', in Darling and Whitworth (eds), *Women and the Making of Built Space*.

72 Darling, '"The house that is a woman's book come true"', p. 127.

73 *Ibid.*, p. 133.

74 Bridget Elliott, 'Art Deco hybridity, interior design, and sexuality between the wars: two double acts: Phyllis Baron and Dorothy Larcher / Eyre de Lanux and Evelyn Wyld', in Doan and Garrity (eds), *Sapphic Modernities*, p. 109.

75 Elliott, 'Art Deco hybridity, interior design, and sexuality', p. 111.

76 Everett, *Bricks and Flowers*, p. 114.

77 *Ibid.*, p. 114.

78 *Ibid.*, p. 115.

79 *Ibid.*, p. 116.

80 *Ibid.*, p. 117.

81 *Ibid.*, p. 118.

82 *Ibid.*, p. 120.

83 *Ibid.*, p. 206.

84 *Ibid.*, p. 207.

85 *Ibid.*, p. 211.

86 *Ibid.*, p. 211.

87 On Colonel Barker, see James Vernon, '"For some queer reason": the trials and tribulations of Colonel Barker's masquerade in interwar Britain', *Signs*, 26:1 (2000), 37–62; Doan, *Fashioning Sapphism*, pp. 88–96.

88 Doan, *Fashioning Sapphism*, pp. 95–125. See also Jennings, *A Lesbian History of Britain*, pp. 78, 107; 'Topsy-turvydom', 518, 520–1; Judith Halberstam, *Female Masculinity* (Durham, NC: Duke University Press, 1998), p. 42; Alison Oram, *Her Husband Was a Woman! Women's Gender-Crossing in Modern British Popular Culture* (London: Routledge, 2007), pp. 154–7.

89 Everett, *Bricks and Flowers*, p. 197.

90 *Ibid.*, pp. 148–52. See Wally, *Selected Twentieth Century Anglo-Irish Autobiographies*, pp. 123–6.

91 Everett, *Bricks and Flowers*, p. 152.

92 *Ibid.*, pp. 152–3.

93 *Ibid.*, p. 237.

94   Julia Bush, *Women Against the Vote: Female Anti-Suffragism in Britain*
     (Oxford: Oxford University Press, 2007), p. 3.
95   *Ibid.*, p. 15.
96   Laura Doan, '"Woman's place *is* the home": conservative Sapphic
     modernity', in Doan and Garrity (eds), *Sapphic Modernities*, p. 100.
97   Bush, *Women Against the Vote*, pp. 15 (quote) and 13–14.
98   Everett, *Bricks and Flowers*, p. 237.
99   Light, *Forever England*, p. 11.
100  *Ibid.*, p. 210.
101  Property Search, Independent, at http://property.independent.co.uk/
     sales/2115829, accessed 22 December 2011.
102  Everett, *Bricks and Flowers*, p. 222.
103  *Ibid.*, p. 251.
104  *Ibid.*, dedication.

**4**

# 'A peculiarly obscure subject': the missing 'case' of the heterosexual

*Laura Doan*

The normal proves nothing, the exception proves everything.

Carl Schmitt (1922)

Nature has so created us.

Marie Stopes (1918)[1]

In 1990 the theorist Eve Kosofsky Sedgwick declared that any serious study of sexuality in the modern West was 'not merely incomplete, but damaged in its central substance' if it did 'not incorporate a critical analysis of the modern homo/heterosexual definition' – and for a quarter of a century this imperative has been duly observed.[2] For LGBT and queer scholars the homo/hetero binary has been a 'key problematic and political target' – their very effort to bring it 'to the point of collapse' sustaining rather than diminishing its centrality and power.[3] Elsewhere in the academy there has been resistance to privileging the homo/hetero distinction above other relationalities. Some historians, for example, express scepticism that queer studies, in their view, raises the binary to the 'status' of 'a quasi-anthropological principle of human culture'.[4] My recent work on British sexual cultures during the First World War and into the 1920s confirms that sexual practices were subject not to one but several regulatory regimes.[5] Nevertheless, if we are to understand fully the social regulation of sexuality across multiple domains – law, religion, medicine, morality, family and so on – we cannot overlook how the homo/hetero divide is itself historically contingent. Queer literary and cultural critics have been highly effective in theorising how heterosexuality secures its power through a perverse symmetry with its lexical counterpart but I see two shortcomings in this otherwise provocative critique. First, as I explain elsewhere, queer findings and assertions are often overdetermined by an epistemological system that organises sexuality as classifiable and identifiable.[6]

Second, detailed historical understanding of how the hetero evolves and establishes its dominance over the homo is sketchy. These intertwined problems are too complex and wide-ranging to be fully resolved here. More feasibly, I propose to split this familiar binary arrangement apart and inspect its workings by focusing on one crucial moment in 1918 in which the homo and hetero begin to emerge and converge in an oppositional logic that persists to this day.

With the medicalisation of sexuality in the late nineteenth and early twentieth centuries sexologists required an ideal social norm – called the 'normal' – against which perversion, anomaly or deviance might be measured. Conjured into existence through the taxonomical elaboration of the perversions, the normal would become a paradox – hegemonic as an absent presence, lurking obliquely in early twentieth-century references to 'regular sexuality'.[7] A product of negative identification, the category of the heterosexual would come to be perceived not for what it *is* but for what it is *not*. As historian Jonathan Ned Katz explains:

> Before the invention of 'heterosexuality,' the term 'contrary sexual feeling' presupposed the existence of a non-contrary 'sexual feeling,' the term 'sexual inversion' presupposed a noninverted sexual desire. From the start of this medicalising, 'contrary' and 'inverted' sexuality were problematised, 'sexual feeling' was taken for granted. This inaugurated a hundred-year tradition in which the abnormal and homosexual were posed as riddle, the normal and heterosexual were assumed.[8]

Assumed, yes – but identifiable, apparently no. Hugely important as a heuristic device, the heterosexual, queer scholars argue, is not an '*object* of knowledge' in its own right.[9] The heterosexual in sexology and queer studies achieves cultural visibility and legibility through strategic oppositionality only as a 'back formation' of the homosexual.[10] Hence, tellingly, the entries in the *Oxford English Dictionary* for the word heterosexual reference homosexual but not vice versa – the person attracted to the *opposite* sex is knowable because there exists 'a person who has a sexual propensity for his or her own sex'.[11] The history of the homo/hetero binary then speaks to the peculiar conditions of sexual knowing and unknowing from the vantage point of a knowledge apparatus that primarily values the heterosexual for its otherness, its ability to act as a blank canvas on which anything (or nothing) might be projected – and therefore, a category beyond and outside history.

In *The Invention of Heterosexuality* Katz implicates Foucault in this failure to give the heterosexual a history: *'how could he ... have said so little?* What specific arrangements of power stopped Foucault from explicitly problematising heterosexuality?'[12] Katz's frustration is palpable, but Foucault's purpose is not to account for the myriad discursive formations that made sexuality modern – he is most interested in elucidating the power inherent in the distinctive binary logic of sexology (even though early sexology was less invested in the binary than we might think[13]). In a well-known passage from the first volume of *The History of Sexuality*, Foucault distinguishes between 'two great procedures' in the production of sexual truth: *'ars erotica'* and *'scientia sexualis'*.[14] This analytic distinction enables Foucault to demonstrate how sexuality – as a system of knowledge – evolves in the West as opposed to, say, 'China, Japan, India, Rome, the Arabo-Moslem societies', utopic spaces he envisages as outside social regulation.[15] *Ars erotica* represents a tradition in which 'truth is drawn from pleasure itself' and passed from master to pupil, while *scientia sexualis* tells the 'truth of sex' as 'a form of knowledge-power', its procedures originating in the ritual practices of the confession.[16] By the late nineteenth century

> it is no longer a question simply of saying what was done – the sexual act – and how it was done; but of reconstructing, in and around the act, the thoughts that recapitulated it, the obsessions that accompanied it, the images, desires, modulations, and quality of the pleasure that animated it. For the first time no doubt, a society has taken upon itself to solicit and hear the imparting of individual pleasures.[17]

The (dubious) achievement of modern sexual science is its transformation of a sexual subject hitherto defined by acts (the sodomite, for instance) into 'a personage, a past, a case history, and a childhood, in addition to being a type of life, a life form, and a morphology' and, in this way, the 'homosexual' becomes 'a species'.[18] *Ars erotica* is not subject to the 'law of the permitted and the forbidden' and neither does it reference 'utility', but beyond this we learn little about how the master derives the truth of the pleasures that emanate from the human body.[19] What distinguishes sexology from *ars erotica* is its investment in establishing the 'norms of scientific regularity' to codify and classify the individual's sexual pleasures and desires 'under the rule of the normal and the pathological', deploying 'the listening technique, the postulate of causality, the principle of latency, the rule of interpretation, [and] the imperative of medicalisation' to disclose its truths about sex.[20]

Like a magic trick, Foucault draws the reader's attention to one tradition at the expense of a critical engagement with the other. Of paramount interest is *scientia sexualis* which, it turns out, is 'an extraordinarily subtle form of *ars erotica*' – meanwhile, the peculiarities of the latter tradition slip away unnoticed, with significant consequences to the history of heterosexuality.[21] In a rare comment on different-sex relations, Foucault recognises that the homosexual – as a 'case history' – relegates 'heterosexual monogamy' to the shadows.[22] Leaving aside the fact that heterosexual monogamy emerges several decades after the invention of the homosexual (conceptualised in the early twentieth century as marital monogamy), the neglect of *ars erotica* as a competing discursive practice greatly inhibits our ability to assess *its* distinctive features and impact on sexual knowledge in the context of modern Britain.[23] Heterosexuality is not a product of sexology alone, but evolves in other discursive domains. In this chapter I want to complicate the genealogy of the heterosexual in relation to its counterpart by looking closely at two distinctive but interconnected systems: sexology and marital advice literature. As a great classificatory project, sexology turns an undifferentiated sexual nature into multiple essences we now term sexual identities.[24] This is often achieved through 'caseness' – or, as Foucault puts it, 'lived experience as evidence' – which establishes a binary relationship between the exceptional and the normal, and confirms the knowability of the former while leaving the latter without anything to say for itself.[25] Marital advice literature, on the other hand, largely eschews caseness and, though there are fleeting glimpses of abnormality, hetero-relations gain substance as a force, the normal an index of what is 'natural, pure, and unproblematic'.[26] Neither discourse, of course, tells a truth about human sexuality – each constructs the various cultural meanings of sex – but their juxtaposition highlights more vividly the difference methodology makes, particularly the case study method.

In March 1918 two British feminist writers made different though equally significant contributions to the modern understanding of sex and sexuality: Marie Stopes (1880–1958) published *Married Love: A New Contribution to the Solution of Sex Difficulties* and F. W. Stella Browne (1880–1955) presented a paper on the 'problem of feminine inversion'.[27] In a book famously described by its author as having

'crashed English society like a bombshell', Stopes called for an end
to sex-ignorance to achieve women's sexual satisfaction.[28] Her marital advice manual discussed at length the mechanics of the normal
sexual act as a natural phenomenon in which the male and female
bodies are perfectly matched for the purpose of reproduction. In
the same month that the first print run of *Married Love* was flying off
the shelves, Browne, while critical of Stopes's exclusive interest in 'the
educated, prosperous, and privileged classes', addressed some thirty
members of the British Society for the Study of Sex Psychology on
the subject of gender variance and same-sex desire.[29] Later, in 1923,
she virtually buried her findings in a little-known American publication with a small circulation, the *Journal of Sexology and Psychanalysis*
[*sic*].[30] In building a picture of the invert based on five case studies,
Browne's method could not have been more different from Stopes's,
whose 'lyrical outpouring' of the natural order of 'bodies and life
processes' marks another pathway towards a common scientific
project.[31] Foucault characterises these discursive divergences as a
'strangely muddled zone' whereby the 'will to knowledge', in accounting for the 'biology of reproduction', collides with the 'stubborn will to
nonknowledge' in the 'medicine of sex'.[32] A trained botanist, Stopes
enters the arena of human sexuality through a different door from
Browne – well versed in 'animal and plant reproduction', Stopes
attempts to break away from a medical discourse she admonishes
for its obsession with pathology and, in so doing, attempts to forge a
new knowledge practice to account for what we perceive now as the
ontological antithesis of the exception, the heterosexual.[33]

Reading Stopes and Browne clarifies how LGBT and queer historiographies of sexuality effectively reverse the influence these writers
enjoyed in their lifetime. With the ascendance of sexology, an elite
and esoteric knowledge would gradually obscure the epistemological
paradigm showcased in the more popular form of interwar marital
advice. In shifting marital advice from the margins to the centre of
queer historical inquiry we can see more clearly how the binary distinction actually conflates separate histories that evolve erratically and
unevenly at different moments in the twentieth century. The homosexual develops circuitously as an object of history but so too does the
heterosexual, except the latter faces formidable obstacles in gaining
legibility. The history of straightness is not straightforward because
heterosexuality begins life as a social norm (later described by queer
scholars as heteronormativity) and achieves identity belatedly. In

sexology as well as marital advice, hetero-relations are all the more powerful in moving quietly 'behind the scenes', as a 'mystified, infrequently named, hidden persuader'.[34] The research methods of early theorists of inversion, whose system of knowledge more closely correlates to our own, easily achieve what is only a theoretical possibility in *Married Love*; however pervasive the sex lives of 'healthy, mating creatures', it takes an invert to carve out a conceptual space for the normal person (ML 11).[35] Today heterosexuality 'depends on homosexuality to lend it substance ... as a *lack of difference* or an *absence of abnormality*', but we should not underestimate the achievement of Stopes who elucidates what the married couple *do* together rather than defining who or what each *becomes* as a result of their acts, desires, bodily differences or imagined pleasures.[36] *Married Love* sets in motion a pioneering attempt to rethink the making of sexual knowledge outside the epistemological framework that organises sexuality as categorisable. Scrutiny of the pivotal role of the case study method and, conversely, the epistemological repercussions of its absence in marital advice, provides analytical purchase on the unruly historical processes at work in the making of homo *and* hetero identities.

## Sexology's case

In 'Studies in Feminine Inversion' Stella Browne uses the case study method to illustrate the validity of her theory of congenital inversion in women. Along with other early sex researchers, Browne sought to classify persons into 'diverse types', ever subdividing the 'immense complexity' of sexual expression into discrete categories and imposing order and coherence on to an array of 'temperamental and emotional shades and grades and blends'.[37] Practising the scientific method of 'close and careful observation', Browne believes her cases 'are absolutely distinguishable from affectionate friendship' and 'episodical homosexuality' (SFI 51; 56). Noting 'the pitch of the voice and outline of the body', her cases range from the 'entirely feminine' to the 'childish' or boyish – none exhibits mannishness or expresses a desire to be a man (SFI 52; 51; 53). Following Havelock Ellis, sexuality and gender are intermeshed – the latter category associated with the somatic rather than 'mental or emotional qualities': 'I use the adjectives masculine and feminine, only as referring to the pitch of the voice and outline of the body as modified by greater or less development of the secondary sexual characteristics'(SFI 52). The face too is important, as seen in references to Case B's 'beautiful eyes and classical features', Case D's 'big magnetic eyes' or Case E's 'chubby, fresh-coloured face' (SFI 53; 55). Cases A and B stand out from the rest 'to a very marked degree' in the intensity of their 'maternal instinct' (SFI 56). This quality further refines taxonomic distinctions within inversion but also reveals Browne's empathy for her subjects who, she speculates, will someday fulfil their maternal needs through 'artificial fertilisation': 'and I now see in reading Dr. Marie Stopes's interesting Essay "Married Love," that she makes a similar suggestion, though not with reference to inversion' (SFI 57).

Browne does not disclose why she chose these cases over others (other than to say she excluded cases told to her 'in confidence') and, more worryingly, unlike Ellis's participant-informants, the women seem to have been scrutinised as specimens without their consent or knowledge (SFI 51). Aware that the 'fragmentary' nature of her 'data' endangers its 'validity', Browne conjectures that her results would have been more 'illuminating' had the research been conducted by someone 'entirely or predominantly homosexual' – an admission that seems to undermine the value of impartiality (SFI 51). Despite her modest sample, she concludes that inversion is 'deeply rooted' and the 'homosexual impulse' is 'innate' rather than acquired or the result of opportunity, a position similar to Stopes, who regarded the normal as natural or instinctive (SFI 51; 57). Discreetly avoiding 'the physical side of sex', Browne nevertheless asserts that, unlike the 'heterosexual' whose 'normal erotic impulse' registers most saliently in cases of sexual frustration, the inverted body – not sexual activity – provides the researcher with clues to the psychosexual disposition (SFI 53; 57; 58). Never pathologised, the invert is envied for her greater opportunities for 'satisfaction' (SFI 57). Arguing that there is a deep human need for 'vital contact, mental and bodily', Browne pleads with her listeners to 'recognise this force, as frankly as we recognise and reverence the love between men and women' (SFI 58). Throughout 'Studies in Feminine Inversion', as well as in a paper presented three years earlier ('The Sexual Variety and Variability among Women and their Bearing upon Social Reconstruction'), the 'average' or normal woman gains legibility in comparison with her opposite: 'I repudiate all wish to slight or depreciate the love-life of the real homosexual; but it cannot be advisable to force the growth of that habit in heterosexual people.'[38] The desire at the core of the 'real homosexual' transmutes to an act or habit in the heterosexual, which is also how the normal is understood by Stopes.

For both writers, woman's sexual nature is variable and diffuse, psychological and physiological. Scientific research is an effective means to realise their aims and objectives – above all, to attain individual happiness through sexual fulfilment. Physical love produces 'perfect happiness' in the 'unity composed of a myriad essences' – essential for 'vigour, sanity, and serenity of body and mind, for efficiency, for happiness, for the mastery of life, and the understanding of one's fellow-creatures' (ML 24; SFI 57). Browne recognises this need for the normal *and* abnormal type, whereas Stopes, notably, does not. Browne goes so far as to suggest that the conditions of modern society – with its strict segregation of the sexes – '*artificially stimulate inversion*' among 'some women who *are not innately or predominantly homosexual*', because the desire for physical connection leads them to 'form more or less explicitly erotic relations with other women' (SFI 58). However, the sex act does not the invert make – in some of her cases, 'there has been ... no definite and conscious physical expression' (SFI 51). In other words, these case studies prove the invert possesses a nature or essence whether or not there is any physical contact 'beyond the kissing and embracing which is normal, and even, in some cases conventional, between women' (SFI 55).[39] The invert need not act on her desires to inhabit the category; in the sexological knowledge system, inversion is the 'self-confirming inner truth' of one's nature, whether or not physical contact occurs.[40]

Stopes, on the other hand, argues that physical expression is vital for normal types not simply because it produces happiness – the 'supreme purpose of nature' is to procreate, and the supreme purpose of procreation is to sanctify marriage (ML 78). This is why she is so concerned with what she identifies as 'contrariness', a disposition that Browne, grounded in sexual science, brands as a category, the frigid (ML 27). It is no coincidence that frigidity surfaces in writings on sexual inversion as well as marital advice, since female sexual pleasure was a major concern for feminists and sexual progressives at this time. Browne advocated sexual happiness for the normal and abnormal, but expressed concern that 'for at least a generation, the circumstances of women's lives and work will tend ... to favour the frigid, and next to the frigid, the inverted types', a comment that exhibits the usefulness of case study knowledge as well as its constraints in narrowing the complexity of the sexual subject to a label

(SFI 57). Critical of sexology's privileging of 'human variations and abnormalities', Stopes refuses to reduce the greater complexity of sexual aspirations, needs or desires to a generic category (ML 10). Instead, she constantly reiterates that she is concerned only with the normal and deliberately ignores *"femmes incomprises"* and all the innumerable neurotic, super-sensitive, and slightly abnormal people' (ML 23).[41] Consequently, references to specific cases in *Married Love* are rare and concern incidences of sexual dysfunction or frustration within a regime of normality or abnormality.[42] When the 'average man' notices his wife suddenly 'cold and incomprehensible' – and the average woman experiences emotions 'she cannot explain' – the cause is a lack of understanding of the woman's 'rhythms', a condition identified as a feeling rather than a type (ML 27; 31). Stopes turns to the case of Mrs G. to explain the conundrums of *'contrary'* behaviour to show that contrariness is an exception to natural law, while insisting, paradoxically, that the case is 'not exceptional' (ML 27; 32). Her normal does not map evenly on to Browne's because, in marital advice, the normal does not *possess* a nature but is a creature *of* nature by virtue of the act. The desires and acts of the normal, for Stopes, reside outside the classificatory system, and therefore the normal is not a thing.

## The missing case of X

In a chapter on 'Marriage Manuals and the Eroticisation of Marriage', the historian Angus McLaren calls Marie Stopes 'one of the main architects and defenders of modern heterosexuality' – a judgement at odds with the queer depiction of heterosexuality as only ever 'dimly perceived'.[43] In what sense does her detailing of the anatomical differences between the sexes, as well as the mechanics of the physical act of sex between a man and a woman, contribute to the making of modern heterosexuality? Stopes is undoubtedly a significant figure in the history of heterosexuality, and her book *Married Love* sold two thousand copies within a fortnight and went into six further editions before the year was out.[44] By 1928, with 406,000 copies in print, Stopes required a small staff to assist her in responding to 'nearly a thousand letters' per week, her public profile enhanced still further by a well-publicised libel action against a conservative Catholic physician who had attacked the tactics deployed at her Birth Control Clinic.[45] Between 1918 and 1928 Stopes produced no fewer than four best-selling books on marriage, family, motherhood and birth control.[46] She was named in 2010 by the *Independent on Sunday* as one of the top one hundred British women who 'have done most to shape the world we live in today', and *Married Love* still appears in bookshops as one of the Oxford University Press 'World's Classics'.[47]

Outing herself (probably disingenuously) as a woman who once suffered terribly owing to 'sex-ignorance', Stopes depicts her work as the culmination of 'long and complex investigations', relying on 'individual records' and the 'notes' of her informants (ML 11; 9; 42; 39).[48] Basing her conclusions on 'a large number of first-hand observations' of 'men and women of all classes and types', Stopes differentiates between the 'confidences' shared by her informants and the minority experiences that typify the case study (ML 9). A qualified researcher and scholar, Stopes credits her methodological rigour and 'wide reading' of the literature on physiology and medicine in allowing her to collect 'facts ... sufficient to overturn many ready-made theories about women', shrewdly appropriating the prestige of science (ML 9; 37). Further evidence that she observes scientific protocol is her breakdown of her informants' demographics in terms of gender and region (mostly women from 'our northern climate' who are 'less persistently stirred than southerners') as well as age, class and professional circumstance: around 'thirty years', drawn 'primarily' from the 'educated class', and often 'separated from their husbands for some months through professional or business duties' (ML 38; 9; 22; 39).

For all her emphasis on scientific methods and professional expertise, there is a persistent tug in Stopes's analysis toward *ars erotica*, as seen in her evaluation of 'pleasure' according to 'its intensity, its specific quality, its duration, its reverberations in the body and the soul'.[49] Seducing her readers with sensuous poetic flourishes, Stopes speaks of 'billowing curves' and 'regular ripples' in reference to the female sex drive, thereby enlivening a potentially arid subject – human biology and reproduction – with the passion and reverie of an Edwardian middlebrow novel (ML 38; 39). Dedicated to the 'ordinary untrained reader' (rather than medical or legal professionals, or colleagues in the sex reform movement), and written in a highly accessible and lyrical style, *Married Love* exhorts the 'married' and those 'about to be married' to master the art of lovemaking to achieve 'irradiating joy' in coital union (ML 10; 82). *Married Love* is 'less a record of research' than 'a reverent study of the Art of Love', even as it is presented 'in a clean scientific way' (ML 9; 26; 49). As a teacher and modern sex-guru Stopes guides her readers on the right path toward a profound understanding of the 'strange' and 'mystical interrelations between our bodies, our minds, and our souls' (ML 25). In this sense she closely approximates Foucault's 'master' whose possession of 'secrets is of paramount importance' and whose purpose is to 'transmit this art' of the erotic by guiding 'the disciple's progress' toward 'singular bliss' and 'obliviousness to time and limits'.[50] To achieve ecstasy, *Married Love* advises, lovers should avoid 'excessive speed': 'So deep-seated, so profound, are woman's complex sex-instincts as well as her organs, that in rousing them the man is rousing her whole body and soul. And this takes time' (ML 57). Stopes instructs couples with a clinical description of the sex act but also falls back on less scientific language ('slow and profound mutual rousing of passion' and 'perpetually recurring entrancement'), intermingling the traditions of *ars erotica* and *scientia sexualis* (ML 26). Moving seamlessly from the realm of science to the practicalities of lovemaking, Stopes explains that 'recent discoveries of physiology' provide a 'key' to 'unlock a chamber of the mystery and admit us to one of the halls of the palace of truth' (ML 103).

Expounding on the 'joys of marriage' and encouraging an appreciation of the beauty of the marital act, *Married Love* issues constant reassurance to middle-class readers, women especially, that social respectability is not compromised by gaining expertise in the 'supreme human art, the art of love' (ML 9; 11). According to Stopes, the physicality of 'perfect union' – the cornerstone of normal sexuality – is nature's perfect way: 'nature has so created us that we are incomplete in ourselves; neither *man nor woman* singly can know the joy of the performance of all the human functions; neither *man nor woman* singly can create another human being' (ML 103; 17, emphasis mine). However, modern lovers need instruction in the facts of life (information hitherto 'almost unobtainable') because civilised society has corrupted 'instinctive knowledge' (ML 9; 105). The origins of the 'normal way' have been lost in 'mists and shadowy darkness'; and, therefore, the rhythms of physical union are frequently mismatched (ML 81; 23). Discovering 'rottenness and danger at the foundations of the State', Stopes blames sex-ignorance for marital unhappiness – a point she hammers home relentlessly in the final chapter: young people must be given 'the necessary tool – knowledge'; the 'racial ideal' must be met 'with a store of knowledge';

'anguish' is preventable with 'knowledge' and 'wisdom'; civilisation robs the younger generation of 'instinctive knowledge'; ordinary people need 'access to the knowledge' on 'the first day of marriage'; and 'knowledge and love' go hand in hand (ML 9; 104; 105; 106). Because modernity effaces the 'primitive' instincts necessary for the survival of the race, for most people (though not all) the 'laws' of their 'physical being' remain 'completely hidden' (ML 94; 20).

Tutelage and mastery in the art of lovemaking are now required because 'an impersonal and scientific knowledge of the structure' of the body is insufficient (ML 54). Marital advice provides true knowledge of the 'strange and powerful' laws of nature and works like a tonic to revivify what has been pushed to 'the back of the mind' of 'lovers' as a result of the unnatural strains of modern life (ML 17; 54). Recognising that the needs of the individual for personal happiness are as important as the state's need to reverse the declining birthrate, Stopes introduces her 'Law of the Periodicity of Recurrence of desire in women' (which she touts as original) – this configuration of bodily rhythms as a Law produces a knowledge that Stopes believes will kick-start the 'primitive sex-tides' and rectify the difficulties in different-sex sexual relations (ML 39). In calling on readers to assist in the Law's verification, Stopes fosters a sense of belonging among a community of lovers whose shared impulses, yearnings and desires to generate 'new bodily life' define what is natural, normal, regular or ordinary (ML 21). And it is this impulse to shape and redefine the natural *as* normal that places Stopes squarely among the Moderns, who, according to the theorist Bruno Latour, 'mobilise Nature at the heart of social relationships, even as they leave Nature infinitely remote from human beings'.[51] For Stopes, Nature creates man and woman in a union that is 'incomprehensible' because the 'eternal' is always 'already-present' (ML 28).[52] The 'wisdom of the race' is known and unknown, describable and indescribable: the 'immemorial laws of our physical being' – 'fundamental' and 'ancient' – are subject to 'the exclusive transcendence of a Nature that is not our doing' (ML 104; 20; 32).[53] This doublethink frees the Moderns 'to make and unmake their society, even as they render its laws ineluctable, necessary, and absolute'.[54] Casting her decrees in a vague and spiritual language ('the innermost spirit of one and all so yearns as for a sense of union with another soul'), Stopes locates the truth of nature beyond human reason and, in so doing, posits an alternative knowledge system both congruent *and* incongruent with sexological thought (ML 95). The key to happiness for 'married lovers' is to accept unquestionably the sexual as part of the natural order (ML 17).

For a writer often described as a populariser of sexology, Stopes is remarkably ambivalent and contradictory: while accepting its structuring of the sexual as normal or abnormal, she also rejects what she perceives as its overinvestment in the abnormal. In an astonishing opening gambit, Stopes signals her move away from sexology's interests: 'I do not now touch upon the many human variations and abnormalities which bulk so largely in most books on sex, nor do I deal with the many problems raised by incurably unhappy marriages' (ML 10). Yet her use of sexology is highly strategic and she quickly realises that its logic is something she cannot do without. In arguing that married love is universal and transhistorical she requires an exception, and so she no sooner boldly proclaims that *Married Love* is for the 'great majority' than she immediately qualifies and narrows the boundaries to 'all young people, *unless* they have inherited depraved or diseased faculties' (ML 18; 17, emphasis mine). Although the reproductive function of differently sexed bodies is 'profound' and 'fundamental', Stopes cannot evade a different fact of nature: some individuals – inexplicably – possess instincts resistant to natural law (ML 20). Claims for the universal ('every heart' or 'one and all') are simultaneously advanced and undone (ML 18). Those who wilfully resist completeness are swiftly dismissed: the single person, the celibate, 'saints and sages, reformers and dogmatists' and 'the innumerable neurotic, super-sensitive, and slightly abnormal people' and 'many middle-aged unmarried women' – none of whom represent the 'standard of the *race*' (ML 20; 23; 63). Some in this motley group believe they strive for a 'higher ideal' in rejecting the 'love of home and children'; they are, however, unnatural since their bodies 'flower, but never fruit in a bodily form' (ML 19; 20). Also excluded are those who suffer 'sex anaesthesia', since their maladies represent an obvious violation of the 'profound physical laws' of complementarity (ML 19; 20). Stopes initially attempts to explain away these anomalies within the framework of the normal by arguing that such differences are the result of the 'immense' degree of variation 'in the sex-needs and the sex-ideas of different healthy people' (ML 54). Unable to tease apart the 'normal' and 'healthy' from those whose 'departure from the ordinary ranks of mankind is … more fundamental', Stopes must concede the presence of caseness in an otherwise 'widely various humanity' (ML 105; 19). To grasp how 'all have some measure' of desire for 'bodily union' demands the imagining of a minority who feel differently – the yearnings of most people become intelligible by recognising nature's quirks, among those who depart from 'the ordinary course of life' (ML 18; 17). Inevitably, 'the normal proves nothing' and 'the exception proves everything', and so the rule cannot establish its own identity and must turn to the exception.[55] In the end, the exceptional (its perversity privileged in knowledge production) is identifiable through an ontology denied to the 'majority of our citizens' who cannot know their own nature – and, thus, the universal is affirmed and problematised (ML 18). The normal maintains its power by defining an 'other' rather than defining itself – and this, in turn, empowers the normal to define as unnatural acts, feelings or desires that do not fulfil its purposes.

Stopes's disavowal of an epistemological framework enthralled by aberration and binary logic is innovative and conceptually bold but, ultimately, a failed venture if success is measured by the production of a knowable sexual subject. Never a category of identity, the married lover is natural and normal, qualities as inexplicable and opaque as sexology's normal individual. Despite its frequent appearance in *Married Love*, 'normal' works as an adjective to describe the 'sex relation' or 'sex-life', but the 'human sex union' is an action between differently sexed bodies and does not generate a personal or collective identity based on sexual object choice (ML 63; 62).[56] The purpose of marital advice literature is to show how bodily acts belong to the natural order, which means this genre – 'resolutely heterosexual' – proceeds differently from the taxonomising procedures enacted by the sexological case study.[57] There are no tell-tale signs, no distinctive psychosexual or somatic traits, to aid in the identification of a human who engages in such practices because commonality is unmarked. The 'average' and 'healthy' become knowable by anatomising the pleasures, passions, frustrations and difficulties of coitus, but an act cannot produce 'an idea of a person, a kind of person, a norm of personhood' (ML 11).[58] The author of *Married Love* may have been 'one of the first of the modern marriage counsellors who made it obligatory for the twentieth-century husband and wife to "adore" each other', but normal feelings, erotic desires or acts are not constitutive of a type of sexual subject, let alone a type who would recognise common bonds with others to form a collective identification.[59] Stopes unveils the secrets to perfecting what female and male bodies do together but the actors do not self-identify and are resistant to identification by others. Sexual relations between male and female bodies do not produce subjectivity outside ontology or represent 'a case of $x$'.[60] In later decades the normal would be seen as a recognisable type but its origins as a norm suggests its status as simultaneously like and unlike other categories, as the baseline by which the exception is known. What Stopes's marriage manual does demonstrate is that the love and physical union of the average requires a different knowledge system because – as with the term queer – sexology's heterosexual is 'an empty placeholder for an identity that is still in progress and has as yet to be fully realised'.[61]

## Peculiarly obscure subjects

Historicising the homo/hetero binary suggests a curious lop-sidedness since one half of the binary possesses a historical presence the other lacks. In this sense, the invention of the homosexual might be seen as a discursive success story against Stopes's failed effort to name the heterosexual. In the closing months of the First World War, sex reformers and sex educators actively developed and disseminated a scientific knowledge of sex by drawing on the work of Ellis and others, but Browne's interest in female sexual inversion appears to give her the conceptual edge. Using the sexological framework to impose order and substance on the messiness of human sexuality, Browne uses the case study method to produce a knowable sexual subject against its nameable (though 'peculiarly obscure') opposite. Stopes too endeavours to impose order and substance on the messi-ness of married love but her rejection of the case study method marks the normal in terms that are equally oblique in that she does not pro-duce a knowable subject – and, without a subject, no species of the normal can emerge. Hamstrung by her repudiation of the logic of a normalising discourse that produces the identifying and identifiable subject, Stopes finds herself 'entangled in a maze of abnormalities' and so cannot bestow personhood on the normal (ML 105). What can be established then is that, around 1918 and into the early 1920s, sexuality was understood (at least) in two ways: first, by the structur-ing habits and logic of an epistemology that positioned the sexual subject within a regime of normal and abnormal and, second, in a hugely popular form that organised sexuality in ways we do not recognise as modern. It is tempting to assess this latter discourse as something of an epistemological dud, an example of an interesting if flawed trajectory in the history of modern sexuality; even so, Stopes's articulations of different-sex desire and love seem the more successful in fleshing out the empty space of a merely oppositional normal.

Particularly striking about Browne's use of the case study method is its demonstration of the ways it was possible to speak – and not speak – about the sexual before normality's power was yet secure, its workings largely baffling and indecipherable. To understand the epistemology of sexuality in the early twentieth century we need to situate it both within the sexological framework as well as without. In the late nineteenth and early twentieth centuries, sexual science produced a startling array of categories – the fetishist, masturbator and transvestite, for instance – all measured against an unnamed practice or thing. Ordinary Britons at this time navigated sexual knowledge outside the structure produced by the sexological case study, which assigned labels to sexual tastes, feelings, preferences, inclinations, erotic fantasies, acts and so on. This is why Stopes positions her own project as a long overdue corrective to the early sexologists and her distaste of sexual variation was visceral. Famously, in her 1939 obituary of Ellis, she declared that reading his work on the abnormal felt 'like breathing a bag of soot: it made me feel choked and dirty for three months'.[62] Marital advice literature represents an attempt for heterosexuality to speak on its own behalf – a way of knowing that is absent in a homo/hetero binary that requires heterosexuality to know its place rather than to know itself. Our attentiveness to Stopes's project rectifies an imbalance in historical explanation and complicates our task of discerning how and when the normal begins to exert its considerable power as one regime of several in the multivalent, overlapping and contradictory layers of the social regulation of sexuality.

Whether we damn the homo/hetero binary for its purported pathologising effects *or* acknowledge its power to create subversive counter discourses to nurture collectivised political identities, neither of its component parts can remain 'peculiarly obscure' (SFI 51). Teasing out its fleeting appearances across diverse discursive realms poses an immense challenge for queer critics and historians whose practices are already shaped by the structure of modern sexuality. Browne's radical views on inversion in the context of sexual freedom for all women were controversial even among progressive thinkers, but her adumbration of the hetero is as stubbornly elusive as that of Stopes, whose discussion of conjugal love creates the conditions of hetero knowability rather than a heterosexual subject. Browne does not make the case for the heterosexual and Stopes is uninterested in making the heterosexual a case. This means that we cannot rely on sexological knowledge alone in accounting for the power of the homo/hetero distinction. More than this, we need to cultivate Stopes's scepticism of a scientific discourse that privileges anomaly and aberration. Browne's and Stopes's discussions of female friendship, courtship, marriage, chastity and perversion point to the sexual as a multifaceted landscape infused by scientific discourse as well as another discourse 'spoken of less and less'.[63] To recuperate the strangeness of the modern sexual past, we cannot forget that in Britain straightness – like queerness – did not always exist 'as an identity'; more 'a state of becoming rather than as the referent for an actually existing form of life'.[64] At present, queer interest in the homo/hetero binary shows little sign of abating – an apt reminder to historians of the risks in assigning homosexuality and heterosexuality to separate chapters in the history of sexuality.

## Notes

1   Carl Schmitt, *Politische Theologie: Vier Kapitel zur Lehre von der Souveränität* (Berlin: Duncker and Humblot, 1996), trans. and cited by Kirk Wetters, 'The rule of the norm and the political theology of "real life" in Carl Schmitt and Giorgio Agamben', *diacritics*, 33:1 (2006), 42; Marie Stopes, *Married Love* (Oxford: Oxford University Press, 2004), p. 17 (hereafter page numbers will be parenthetical, distinguished by ML).

2   Eve Kosofsky Sedgwick, *Epistemology of the Closet* (Berkeley: University of California Press, 1990), p. 1. According to the *Handbook of Lesbian and Gay Studies*, 'by the start of the twentieth century there was in widespread circulation a proliferation of medical, legal, literary, and psychological discourses for which the homo/hetero binary was axiomatic'; see Sasha Roseneil, 'The heterosexual/homosexual binary: Past, present, and future', *Handbook of Lesbian and Gay Studies* (2002), www.omnilogos.com/2011/06/15/the-heterosexual-homosexual-binary-past-present-and-future/, accessed 27 February 2012. Jeffrey Weeks, *Sexuality* (London: Routledge, 2003), pp. 28–9, writes, 'Northern European and American societies ... have since the nineteenth century at least been obsessively concerned whether a person is normal or abnormal, defined in terms of whether we are heterosexual or homosexual'. The queer scholar Annette Schlichter, 'Queer at last? Straight intellectuals and the desire for transgression', *GLQ: A Journal of Lesbian and Gay Studies*,

10:4 (2004), 544, similarly notes, 'A variety of scholars have convincingly argued that the dominant system of institutionalised heterosexuality operates through the hetero/homo divide.' Most recently, the historian Gert Hekma, 'Introduction', in Gert Hekma (ed.), *A Cultural History of Sexuality in the Modern Age* (Oxford: Berg, 2011), p. 1, characterises seismic shifts in sexual knowledge as a binary relation: 'During the twentieth century, the Western world saw some major changes in sexual practices and ideologies. The first and foremost was a heterosexualisation of society – the monogamous heterosexual became the social standard.'

3 Roseneil, 'The heterosexual/homosexual binary'; Diana Fuss, 'Inside/out', in Diana Fuss (ed.), *Inside/Out: Lesbian Theories, Gay Theories* (New York: Routledge, 1991), p. 1.

4 Lucy Bland and Frank Mort, 'Thinking sex historically', in Lynne Segal (ed.), *New Sexual Agendas* (Houndmills, Basingstoke: Macmillan, 1997), p. 23. For an important reassessment of the role of sexological writing in binary thinking see Chris Brickell, 'Sexology, the homo/hetero binary, and the complexities of male sexual history', *Sexualities*, 9:4 (2006), 423–47.

5 For a fuller discussion of this point see my book *Disturbing Practices: History, Sexuality, and Women's Experience of Modern War* (Chicago: University of Chicago Press, 2013).

6 As I discuss in *Disturbing Practices*, queer historical work on modern sexuality generally treats queerness as ontological rather than as methodological. Queer historiography has shown identity as unstable, but struggles to conceptualise modern sexuality outside the identity framework.

7 Michel Foucault, *The History of Sexuality*, vol. 1: *An Introduction*, trans. Robert Hurley (New York: Penguin, 1980), p. 38.

8 Jonathan Ned Katz, *The Invention of Heterosexuality* (New York: Plume, 1996), p. 55.

9 David M. Halperin, *Saint Foucault: Towards a Gay Hagiography* (New York: Oxford University Press, 1995), p. 47.

10 Annamarie Jagose, *Queer Theory: An Introduction* (New York: New York University Press, 1996), p. 16, emphasis mine.

11 *Oxford English Dictionary Online*, accessed 5 March 2012. Emphasis mine.

12 Katz, *The Invention of Heterosexuality*, p. 177.

13 Brickell, 'Sexology, the homo/hetero binary', is particularly good on this point.

14 Foucault, *The History of Sexuality*, pp. 57, 58.

15 *Ibid.*, p. 57.

16 *Ibid.*, pp. 57, 58.

17  *Ibid.*, p. 63.

18  *Ibid.*, p. 43.

19  *Ibid.*, p. 57.

20  *Ibid.*, pp. 65, 67, 68.

21  *Ibid.*, p. 71.

22  *Ibid.*, pp. 43, 38.

23  As Hekma, 'Introduction', p. 1, observes, 'The older patriarchal model of marriage and family was replaced by a new version of male and female lover'.

24  For a wonderfully concise and informative overview of sexology, see Chris Waters, 'Sexology', in H. G. Cocks and Matt Houlbrook (eds), *Palgrave Advances in the Modern History of Sexuality* (Houndmills, Basingstoke: Palgrave Macmillan, 2006), pp. 41–63.

25  Lauren Berlant, 'Introduction: What does it matter who one is?', *Critical Inquiry*, 34:1 (2007), 2; Foucault, *The History of Sexuality*, p. 64.

26  Jagose, *Queer Theory*, p. 16. Jagose continues, 'there is a sense in which heterosexuality is assumed to be a natural or unmarked form of sexuality *per se*'.

27  F. W. Stella Browne, 'Studies in feminine inversion', *Journal of Sexology and Psychanalysis [sic]*, 1 (1925), 57 (hereafter page numbers will be parenthetical, distinguished by SFI). 'Studies in feminine inversion' appeared in the first issue of this journal.

28  Marie Stopes, *Marriage in My Time* (London: Rich and Cowan, 1935), p. 44.

29  This phrase appears in Browne's largely favourable review of *Married Love*; see *International Journal of Ethics*, 29:1 (1918), 113. For an account of the event see Lesley A. Hall, *The Life and Times of Stella Browne: Feminist and Free Spirit* (London: I. B. Tauris, 2011), p. 75. This authoritative biography also includes an up-to-date and thorough review of the secondary literature on Browne. Also see Lesley A. Hall, '"Disinterested enthusiasm for sexual misconduct": The British Society for the Study of Sex Psychology, 1913–47', *Journal of Contemporary History*, 30:4 (1995), 665–86. An early discussion of Browne can be found in Sheila Rowbotham, *A New World for Women: Stella Browne, Socialist Feminist* (London: Pluto Press, 1977). Browne's lecture was a deliberately low-key affair owing to her insistence on the exclusion of non-members, an attempt perhaps to safeguard the anonymity of her five case studies drawn from personal acquaintance, though, as Hall conjectures, *The Life and Times of Stella Browne*, p. 73, Browne may have sought to distance her serious scientific project from the 'hot gossip and titillating speculation' arising from accusations of perversity in the sensational 'Cult of the Clitoris' case. In February 1918 an article in the *Vigilante*, a 'patriotic scandal-sheet' owned by the radical right-wing Member of Parliament

Noel Pemberton Billing, accused the Canadian dancer Maud Allan of
sexual perversity. For a concise account of the case, see Lucy Bland,
'"Trial by sexology?" Maud Allan, *Salome*, and the "Cult of the Clitoris"',
in Lucy Bland and Laura Doan (eds), *Sexology in Culture: Labelling Bodies
and Desires* (Chicago: University of Chicago Press, 1998), pp. 183–98.

30 I am grateful to Lesley Hall for this information. Personal correspondence, August 2011.

31 Foucault, *The History of Sexuality*, p. 64.

32 *Ibid.*, p. 55.

33 *Ibid.* For biographical details on Stopes's educational training and background, see Ross McKibbin, 'Introduction', in *Married Love* (Oxford:
Oxford University Press, 2004), pp. ix–xi.

34 Katz, *The Invention of Heterosexuality*, p. 176.

35 See, for instance, formulations by other sexologists in Lucy Bland and
Laura Doan (eds), *Sexology Uncensored: The Documents of Sexual Science*
(Chicago: University of Chicago Press, 1998), especially pp. 41–72.

36 Halperin, *Saint Foucault*, p. 44.

37 These phrases appear in F. W. Stella Browne's review of Havelock
Ellis's *Studies in the Psychology of Sex*, vol. II: *Sexual Inversion*, in the
*International Journal of Ethics*, 27:1 (1916), 114.

38 F. W. Stella Browne, 'The sexual variety and variability among women
and their bearing upon social reconstruction', reprinted in Rowbotham,
*A New World for Women*, pp. 99, 103.

39 For an intriguing look at the permissible boundaries in the late nineteenth century for the physical expression of affection between women
see Sharon Marcus, *Between Women: Friendship, Desire, and Marriage in
Victorian England* (Princeton: Princeton University Press, 2007).

40 David M. Halperin, *One Hundred Years of Homosexuality and Other
Essays on Greek Love* (New York: Routledge, 1990), p. 53.

41 McKibbin translates *'femmes incomprises'* as 'literally "misunderstood or
unappreciated women," that is, women who attribute their sexual and
marital failures to the refusal of others to understand their real qualities'; see his explanatory n. 23 in *Married Love*, p. 112.

42 Other cases Stopes cites include: Mrs A who is 'typical of a large class of
wives'; Mr C, who 'did not give his wife any orgasm'; and Mr and Mrs
D, a couple 'prevented ... from having any intercourse' (ML 62; 81; 82).

43 Angus McLaren, *Twentieth-Century Sexuality* (Oxford: Blackwell, 1999),
p. 52; Lauren Berlant and Michael Warner, 'Sex in public', *Critical
Inquiry*, 24:2 (1998), 552. The extensive bibliography on Stopes cannot
be adequately summarised here but a sampling of important work
includes Lucy Burke, 'In pursuit of an erogamic life: Marie Stopes and
the culture of *Married Love*', in Ann L. Ardis and Leslie W. Lewis (eds),
*Women's Experience of Modernity, 1875–1945* (Baltimore: Johns Hopkins

Press, 2003), pp. 254–69; Lesley A. Hall, 'Uniting science and sensibility: Marie Stopes and the narratives of marriage in the 1920s', in Angela Ingram and Daphne Patai (eds), *Rediscovering Forgotten Radicals: British Women Writers, 1889–1939* (Chapel Hill: University of North Carolina Press, 1993), pp. 118–36; Ellen M. Holtzman, 'The pursuit of *Married Love*: Women's attitudes toward sexuality and marriage in Great Britain, 1918–1939', *Journal of Social History*, 16:2 (1982), 39–51.

44 Publication details appear in McKibbin, 'Introduction', p. xxxvi. See also Alexander C. T. Geppert, 'Divine sex, happy marriage, regenerated nation: Marie Stopes's marital manual *Married Love* and the making of a best-seller, 1918–1955', *Journal of the History of Sexuality*, 8:3 (1998), 389–433.

45 This information appears in Ruth Hall's introduction to an edited collection of letters to Marie Stopes; see Ruth Hall (ed.), *Dear Dr Stopes: Sex in the 1920s* (London: André Deutsch, 1978), p. 9.

46 In addition to *Married Love* Stopes published *Wise Parenthood* (London: A. C. Fifield, 1918), *Radiant Motherhood* (New York: G. P. Putnam and Sons, 1920) and *Enduring Passion* (London: Putnam, 1928).

47 *Independent on Sunday* (7 March 2010), www.independent.co.uk/news/ people/news/a-century-of-distinction-100-women-who-changed-the-world-1917427.html, accessed 15 March 2012. The author Melvyn Bragg named *Married Love* on par with Charles Darwin's *Origin of Species*; see *12 Books That Changed the World* (London: Hodder and Stoughton, 2006).

48 McKibbin, 'Introduction', p. xii, notes, 'It is very unlikely that a scientist, much of whose work was on the reproduction of plants, would be quite so ignorant of human sexuality.'

49 Foucault, *The History of Sexuality*, p. 57.

50 *Ibid.*, pp. 57, 58.

51 Bruno Latour, *We Have Never Been Modern*, trans. Catherine Porter (Cambridge, MA: Harvard University Press, 1993), p. 37.

52 *Ibid.*, p. 81.

53 *Ibid.*, pp. 36–7.

54 *Ibid.*, p. 37.

55 Schmitt, *Politische Theologie*, p. 42.

56 In an early essay David M. Halperin observes, 'sexuality generates sexual identity: it endows each of us with an individual sexual nature, with a personal essence defined (at least in part) in specifically sexual terms; it implies that human beings are individuated at the level of their sexuality, that they differ from one another in their sexuality and, indeed, belong to different types or kinds of being by virtue of their sexuality'; see 'Is there a history of sexuality?', *History and Theory*, 28:3 (1989), 259.

57  McLaren, *Twentieth-Century Sexuality*, p. 55.

58  Berlant, 'Introduction: What does it matter who one is?', 2.

59  McLaren, *Twentieth-Century Sexuality*, p. 52. For an insightful discussion of 'sexological types', see Joseph Bristow, *Sexuality* (London: Routledge, 1997), especially pp. 12–61.

60  Berlant, 'Introduction: What does it matter who one is?', 1.

61  Halperin, *Saint Foucault*, pp. 112–13.

62  Marie Stopes, obituary of Havelock Ellis, *Literary Guide* (September 1939).

63  Foucault, *The History of Sexuality*, p. 38.

64  Halperin, *Saint Foucault*, p. 113.

# 5

# 'These young men who come down from Oxford and write gossip': Society gossip, homosexuality and the logic of revelation in the interwar popular press

*Ryan Linkof*

This chapter has a rather gossipy agenda. Its aim is to expose the queer implications of celebrity gossip writing. It might seem unnecessary and maybe even a bit offensive to assert that homosexual men make good gossips. In many ways, the 'gay gossip' is a common enough construct that it has fallen into the realm of cliché, used as a way of denigrating homosexual men as prone to engage in feminised, malicious behaviour that is, at its worst, seen to be corrosive to the social order. This stereotype has even been carried to the level of self-parody, seen most saliently in the celebrity gossip writing of the flamboyant blogger Perez Hilton. To offer historical and analytical 'proof' of the link between homosexual men and gossip would seem only to reify a cultural construct as somehow ontologically sound. Clearly, I have no intention of doing that, but I do want to start from the premise that homosexual men do, in fact, sit at the crux of a system of social meaning and communication circulated through gossip.

In this, of course, I am not alone. David Harris in his epic tome *The Rise and Fall of Gay Culture* has analysed gossip as a mode of attack and self-defence uniquely suited to the gay male sensibility, suggesting pithily that 'straight men punch, gay men quip'.[1] The historical encoding of gossip as a form of *female* power-knowledge, as Patricia Meyer-Spacks has shown, suggests that gossiping involves at least the partial surrendering of one's masculine identity.[2] The sociologist Jorg Bergmann writes, 'Men, it seems, do not gossip; they chat, discuss, have a talk, but they do not gossip – and if one should indulge in gossip he would make himself appear ridiculous ... because he then would be assuming a typically female mode of behavior.'[3] Taken to its logical conclusion, it might even be suggested that there is something profoundly queer at the core of gossip as a social mechanism. Eve Sedgwick has traced the links between homosexuality and gossip by suggesting that the logic of the 'closet' requires the recognition of a system of binaries defined by what is said and what is not said.[4] Gossip is an operation of knowingness that sits at the centre of the hidden/exposed dichotomy at the core of gay identity. Gossip attempts to define 'good' and 'bad' behaviour, those who are 'in' and those who are 'out'. It is a form of titillating revelation requiring a clear knowledge of both the socially accepted and the socially verboten.

Utilising such conceptual insights, this chapter offers a historical analysis of the link between homosexual men and gossip by examining the origins of the gossip column in the British tabloid press in the three decades after 1910. The so-called 'social' gossip column was a mode of class voyeurism, a whispery series of paragraphs all reporting on the latest High Society events, with commentary on clothes, behaviour and the social customs of the very rich.[5] Society gossip had particular purchase in Britain, as many commentators suggested at the time, because of the deeply entrenched popular fascination with the lives of the aristocratic and royal elite.[6] Celebrity and social class were much more intricately intertwined in Britain than elsewhere, and much of the desire to learn about the activities of celebrities was rooted in a preoccupation with the intimate details of upper-class social life. In order to transact this exchange of information, the gossip writer needed to be welcome in the world of High Society, yet not so much a part of that world that he or she could not speak about it with authoritative objectivity. As scholars such as Jack Levin and Arnold Arluke have suggested, celebrity gossip writers acted as anthropologists of sorts – 'going native' by immersing themselves in the culture that they were studying, becoming, in effect, what anthropologists refer to as 'marginal natives'.[7] To be simultaneously inside and outside – privy to the private conversations of those at the social centre, but not entirely *of* that world – was the essential position of the social gossip writer.

In the process of researching the interwar gossip column in Britain I was struck, as I read through the memoirs, archives, diaries, letters and biographies of early twentieth-century gossip writers, by how many of these figures were homosexual, or at least inclined to engage in the occasional homosexual act.[8] A remarkably disproportionate number of Fleet Street's gossip writers before the Second World War were queer[9] men: Beverley Nichols, Patrick Balfour, Tom Driberg, Brian Howard, Brodrick Haldane, Godfrey Winn. The list could easily go on. At a certain point, it no longer seemed possible that coincidence alone brought so many queer men to Fleet Street to write press gossip. A more thorough analysis of the link between gossip writing and homosexuality was necessary.

I do not wish to paint every gossip writer with the same brush: certainly not everyone who wrote gossip for the press was a homosexual man. The most widely known gossip writers of the period were not avowedly homosexual, and many women also filled the ranks of the Fleet Street gossip mill.[10] The contributions of these figures are clearly established, and many of them have been the subjects of historical research.[11] The role of homosexual men as gossip writers, however, is much less understood.[12] This is less true in the United States, where the contributions of homosexual men have been seen as an important part of the history of celebrity gossip.[13] My history of gossip writing, then, is queer not only in its chosen human subjects but also in its willingness to read against the grain of the established history of gossip writing in Britain, which has been largely blind to the important role of homosexual men in this type of work.[14]

What I am suggesting by focusing on those gossip writers with avowed homosexual inclinations is that queer men occupy a very distinct – and one might even say paradigmatic – relationship to the social 'inside'. Socially marked as abnormal and marginal, the queer gossip writer was also a crucial interlocutor of normative sociability. His sexual proclivity placed him at a remove from the social norms and heterosexual rituals of courtship and marriage that sat at the centre of his work – wedding receptions, child christenings and debutante balls – with which he needed to pretend to be at home, and about which he was seen to be an expert. The gay gossip, then, can be seen as a kind of ideal type of the 'marginally inside' gossip writer.

More fundamentally, gossip writing drew upon concepts and logics with close ties to queer identity before the decriminalisation of homosexual acts: exposure, revelation and self-deception.[15] At its core, gossip writing necessitated knowledge of behaviours that might be marked as socially stigmatised. By the 1930s, the gossip column was only one part of a broader strategy by the editors of popular newspapers to tap into a market demand for sensational revelation of the private details of people's lives.[16] Deborah Cohen has recently argued that popular press 'confession' columns, made popular by the tabloid the *Daily Mirror* in the mid-1930s, were predicated on the idea of exposing hidden secrets in order to unburden one's conscience.[17] The 1930s gossip column, like the confession column, satisfied a popular demand for the revelation of private information. It was a crucial part of the rise of celebrity reporting predicated on revealing the private truths behind the public façade.[18] The gossip column functioned as a space where the 'public face' was revealed to be a social mask necessitated by custom and behavioral protocol, obscuring one's true character beneath falsity and deceit. Homosexual men, as this chapter shows, were well suited to act as commentators on the artifice of public life because the performance of a false identity for public approval was a basic aspect of their social lives. Writing at a moment in which being exposed as a homosexual had serious legal and social repercussions, the gay gossip was uniquely qualified to speak to the social pressures associated with the revelation of private secrets.

## The Edwardian dandy and the origins of celebrity gossip

Celebrity gossip writing began as a dandy's occupation. The fact that dandies were identified with, yet liminally situated in, respectable society made them well suited to the type of class-conscious gossip that characterised the British popular press. The dandy has long been understood to be an observer and satirist of upper-class life who was an important actor in elite social circles, despite his cultivated dislike of the conformity of polite society. The press gossip was a mass-media version of the arch dandy circulating in aristocratic and bohemian circles, a standard figure in British society since the days of Beau Brummell.[19]

If any one figure could be considered responsible for creating the modern celebrity gossip column it would be Fleet Street's legendary bohemian and dandy, Hannen Swaffer. There seems to be a historical consensus that something changed in press gossip in the years around 1910, and that Swaffer was directly responsible, through the creation of the 'Today's Gossip' column in the tabloid the *Daily Sketch*, where he worked as editor after his move from the *Daily Mirror*.[20] Swaffer never penned the column himself, but he was instrumental in determining its form. His friend Edgar Wallace placed the development of personality gossip squarely at his feet: 'Nobody seems to realise that personalities are his invention and that personalities boiled down ... meant intimate gossip.'[21] Swaffer himself was quick to claim ownership over the form. In his memoirs, he told of the moment of its conception, in a meeting with the proprietor of the *Daily Sketch*, Edward Hulton, in 1913: 'what is now called gossip was born in my brain – an attempt to put into print reaction to modern life'.[22]

The column was a form of class-conscious observation conveyed through the eyes of 'Mr Gossip', a man about town, polished and observant, with an encyclopaedic memory of names and faces. Mr Gossip's diaristic social commentary occupied a position somewhere between the flowery diaries of Society life found in nineteenth-century women's magazines and the acid-tongued tabloid gossip that would emerge around the middle of the twentieth century.[23] It appeared in every issue, on or about page three, reliably filled with small paragraphs aimed at lower middle-class women, who most likely would never see the inside of the restaurants and ballrooms about which Mr Gossip seemed to know so much.

Swaffer's dandyism helped to inform the way that journalists and the public at large understood gossip writers in Britain over the next few decades. His highly contrived public persona and exaggeratedly stylised attire and affectations (visual representations of him always caricatured his elaborate, floppy bow ties, protruding cravats and ruffled sleeves) set a standard followed by nearly all the gossip writers who were to follow in his footsteps. The caricatured image that he included on the cover of one of his books (see Figure 7) reveals how he cultivated an image of himself, and was constructed in the popular imagination, as a limp-wristed, fey aesthete with attenuated limbs and arched eyebrows. Cut quite from a similar mould, all of the major gossip columnists of the pre-Second World War period (homosexual or not) – the most famous being Viscount Castlerosse and the Marquess of Donegall – were notoriously dandyish in their demeanour and self-presentation.[24]

The biting tone and dry wit of the dandy often came through in the 'Today's Gossip' column: observational quips animated by the voice of someone who was well versed in the social customs of the rich. Swaffer is best known as a somewhat harsh and unforgiving theatre critic – quick with acerbic insider comments about notable theatrical personalities with whom he had personal relationships – and he worked to make Mr Gossip a reflection of his own style.[25] The gossip writer Patrick Balfour reflected back decades later, pointing to the fact that it was Swaffer who was among the first gossip writers to actually

**7** Caricature of Hannen Swaffer from the cover
of his book *Really Behind the Scenes* (London:
George Newnes, 1929).

'know the world [he] wrote of', and still be willing to offer an objective, even critical point of view, remarking, 'it was only reasonable
to have a social correspondent who moved in the social world. The
newspaper-reading public were out for snobstuff, so let it be authoritative snobstuff!'[26] Swaffer's gossip, and that of the men he hired
to write for his newspapers, sat at that curious threshold between
insider and outsider that has typified mass-media gossip ever since.

The dandyishness of gossip writers was widely recognised, and
commented upon, by the end of the first decade of the twentieth century. Among the most demonstrative of dandy gossip writers in the

Swaffer mould was Philip (Peter) Page, the Oxford-educated socialite hired by Swaffer as the original Mr Gossip for the *Daily Sketch*.[27] Known for his brightly dyed hair and neatly pressed velvet jackets, Page actively cultivated a life of an aesthete, complete with a (most likely fictitious) royal pedigree that he claimed to trace back to Louis XVIII, as well as an Elizabethan manor house in Essex, descriptions of which sound as if they are taken from the pages of *À rebours*, the decadent's handbook of turn-of-the-century aestheticism.[28] Another example of this type of dandy gossip writer can be found in the columnist who was understood to be Page's rival at the *Daily Mirror* in the early 1910s, Randall Charlton. Charlton's obituary in *The Newspaper World* is rather telling, focusing almost exclusively on his aesthetic presentation: 'wherever he went he was observed because of his tall and striking figure.... He possessed a surprisingly graceful appearance, particularly as he developed an exquisite taste in clothes, especially in overcoats, and also in sticks ... Charlton posed as an old-fashioned Bohemian.'[29] Swaffer, a longtime friend of Charlton, wrote of how Charlton's 'flamboyant' dress made him somewhat of a public spectacle, but he admitted to being 'impressed by his elegance' and even admitted that he had taken inspiration from Charlton's dandified appearance.[30]

Though dandyism did not necessarily denote homosexual behaviour, the post-Oscar Wilde associations between dandyism and sexual immorality could lead to a conceptual slippage between the two. As many historians have shown, the trials of Oscar Wilde had, by the early twentieth century, cemented the relationship between dandyism and homosexuality in the public mind.[31] It became increasingly more difficult to put on affected, sartorially fastidious airs without welcoming at least a slight suspicion of homosexual inclinations. This slippage between a dandyish demeanour and homosexuality would inform the popular representation of the gossip columnist for decades to come.

The queering of the dandy gossip writer would be made most evident when the journalist Philip Gibbs created a satirical portrait of Charlton in his 1909 satire of Fleet Street life, *The Street of Adventure*. In what Gibbs later admitted was intended as a 'semi-fictional' portrait of Charlton, he offered a vision of the prototypical gossip writer: 'He was dressed like a dandy of the Georgian period, in a wide-brimmed tall hat, a long frock overcoat tight at the waist, and peg-top trousers, with polished patent boots.' This was not, in any way, an inaccurate representation of Charlton, who was quite the polished dandy, nor of most gossip writers. The trouble came when Gibbs suggested that the character was a sexual deviant. In one passage the fictional version of Charlton asks pleadingly to a fellow journalist: 'I appeal to you. Do you discern any sign of decadence in me?' to which the journalist replies 'Yes ... you are damnably decadent all over, from your golden hair to your effeminate feet!'[32] After the novel's release, Charlton threatened to sue Gibbs for libel for publishing what he called 'damnably incriminating passages' that imputed 'unnatural' desire.[33]

I do not mean to imply that Charlton *was* homosexual simply because he might have been caricatured as such. Charlton's sexuality will have to remain a mystery. But what is interesting is that this suggestion that the dandy gossip writer also engaged in homosexual acts turned out to be quite true by the 1920s. The interwar years saw many young men follow in Swaffer and Charlton's footsteps, presenting themselves in quite the same dandyish way. Unlike their predecessors, however, these men left testimonial evidence of their same-sex desire.

## The Oxford manner

The interwar years were a boom time for press gossip on Fleet Street. What had started as regular features in illustrated newspapers such as the *Daily Sketch* and the *Daily Mirror*, and in weeklies such as the *Tatler*, the *Sketch* and the *Bystander*, had, by the 1920s, spread to most mass-circulation broadsheet newspapers as well. With pseudonyms such as 'The Bachelor' and 'The Rambler', the columnists who proliferated in the wake of 'Mr Gossip' served as the eyes and ears of the public at fashionable West End restaurants and balls, providing their readers with a quick précis of events in columns with evocative titles such as 'Talk of London', 'Echoes of the Town' and 'A Londoner's Diary'. In the two decades after the First World War, a new generation of dandyish would-be writers and journalists flooded into Fleet Street to meet this growing demand for press gossip.

The interwar gossip writer was not unfamiliar with the accusations of 'decadent' behaviour that followed his Edwardian predecessors. Many (if not most) of these young men arrived from the aesthete-havens of Oxford and Cambridge, both of which had earned the reputation of being hotbeds of homosexual experimentation, and were blamed for the production of what some social critics euphemistically decried as 'overcultivated' young men.[34] It was not coincidental that Evelyn Waugh's satire of gossip writing, *Vile Bodies*, focused on an Oxford-educated young man transplanted to London's dizzying social scene.[35] Once on Fleet Street, these young men drew attention to themselves as a somewhat emasculated breed. Swaffer himself, perhaps unhappy at the beast he had unleashed, ridiculed the obviously effeminate taste of the Oxford-educated gossip writer, suggesting 'These young men who come down from Oxford and write gossip ... think knowing Tallulah Bankhead by sight is all there is to learn'.[36] The news mogul Lord Northcliffe weighed in on the matter with the characteristically categorical statement, 'The Oxford manner is the most pernicious taint to a newspaper man'.[37]

The 'taint' that he referred to was a reference to the effeminacy associated with the 'Oxford manner'. Many of these young Oxford men wore their status as 'aesthete' as a badge of pride. Patrick Balfour, an Oxford alumnus who would become one of the *Daily Sketch*'s Mr Gossips in the late 1920s, remarked in a letter to his mother, 'Personally I think that the name "aesthete" should not be a term of opprobrium at all.... I think there is quite as much to be said for the aesthetic point of view as for the dull and hearty.'[38] Gossip writers even brought some of the Oxbridge aestheticism to their columns. One of the more interesting gossip columns in this regard appeared under the pseudonym 'The Bachelor' in the tabloid the *Sunday Graphic*. The author included pieces on 'The Aesthetic Set', and in one revealing paragraph entitled 'Varsity Beauties' he referred to 'the gilded youths who wear bright-coloured shirts and floppy bow ties and the individual at Cambridge who always carries a lily in his hand'.[39]

Some of the gossip writers who would later look for work on Fleet Street sharpened their teeth writing for the Oxford aesthete journal *Isis*. Re-launched in 1919 after a half-decade hiatus by the eventual gossip writer – and defiant homosexual – Beverley Nichols, *Isis* represented much about the cultivated effeminacy of interwar Oxbridge life.[40] The journal had much of the cutting sarcasm and perceptive social commentary that would characterise some of the gossip columns that its authors would produce in the decades to come. Material from *Isis*, some of which was suggestively queer in nature, made it into some of the interwar gossip columns. A small illustration taken from the journal, reproduced in the *Sunday Graphic*'s 'Talk of London' column, shows two elegantly dressed young men, delicately walking arm in arm.[41] A third figure – a small, frail man – looks on aghast, eyes bulging, at the young male couple so intimately walking together. Though this image could be read many ways, it is certainly suggestive of the level to which the aesthete's 'Oxford manner' had infiltrated Britain's gossip columns. The horrified response of the small figure in the cartoon represents quite well the response that many homosexual, Oxford-educated gossip writers received on their arrival in Fleet Street.

Nichols seems to have played a prominent role in convincing many of these young homosexual men to take up gossip writing. Like many of his Oxbridge peers with a penchant for writing, he came to London with dreams of becoming a novelist, and compromised by becoming a journalist, writing gossip columns for the *Sunday Chronicle*, the *Sketch* and the short-lived tabloid the *Looker-On*.[42] By the late 1920s, he was somewhat of an icon of the young man about town, wry and cutting in his wit. His reputation was such that he often felt he needed to protest against his caricatured image as a 'Bright Young Man'.[43] He was apparently of two minds about this, however, as he appeared quite dandyish and urbane – the picture of the Bright Young Man – in his photograph that accompanied the column. He often included stories of a suggestive, even homoerotic, nature, as when he wrote several paragraphs about his extensive experience in the nude steam baths of Berlin, accompanied by a semi-nude photograph of 'fine specimens of young German manhood at a sports gathering'.[44]

Because of his high profile, several homosexual gossip writers mention Nichols as an inspiration for their move towards gossip and social criticism. His autobiographical work *25* was a clever, gossipy bestseller that Balfour cited as part of the motivation behind his turn to gossip writing.[45] Brodrick Haldane also admitted that his quick foray into gossip writing came after reading Nichols's celebrity exposé *Are They the Same at Home?*[46] Godfrey Winn borrowed the most from Nichols, publicly admitting his indebtedness to him, a form of flattery that Nichols himself could have lived without.[47] Nichols's 1927 novel *Crazy Pavements* might also have played a role in recruiting homosexual men to the world of gossip as well, as the story has been interpreted as a homoerotic love story between a gossip writer and his longtime male companion.[48]

The gossip column in the 1920s and 1930s has much to tell the historian – even if obliquely and unwittingly – about the lives of a certain privileged class of homosexual men in interwar Britain. These columns communicated surprising amounts of information about the social activities of notable homosexual men. Figures such as Cecil Beaton, Ivor Novello, Stephen Tennant and Rex Whistler – in part because many of them were friends with gossip writers – became standard figures in gossip columns. When he began writing gossip for the 'Talk of London' column in the *Daily Express*, collaborating with the much older, establishmentarian patrician Colonel Percy Sewell, Tom Driberg emphasised the difference between his paragraphs and those of Sewell: 'mine contained mostly the names of my school and Oxford friends, people of a younger generation than Sewell's.... I recognise as mine some paragraphs about a party attended by the composer Constant Lambert, the artist Oliver Messel, and the writers Peter Quennell and Harold Acton, and by Stephen Tennant, who "wore a football jersey and earrings" and "arrived in an electric brougham."'[49] Eccentric Oxford aesthetes were the bread and butter of his and many of his contemporaries' gossip writing.

Although historians such as Matt Houlbrook have convincingly shown how homosexual men were largely forced to live in silence and shame, constantly under fear of criminal punishment, the visibility and general popularity of this small subset of widely acknowledged homosexual men illustrate the inequity and unevenness in the punishment of homosexual acts.[50] Wealth, acclaim and the support of major newspapermen clearly translated into protection from the punitive arm of the law. Case in point, when Driberg was tried for acts of 'gross indecency' with two young men, it was only his close relationship with the Fleet Street mogul Lord Beaverbrook (who paid for his legal expenses and managed to keep the story out of the newspapers) that saved him from public outing and the repercussions of anti-homosexuality laws.[51] Many scholars have shown how popular newspapers in the post-Second World War period sought to out homosexual men, and call for the punishment of their outlaw sexuality, but in the interwar period the inverse was true, at least in Driberg's case.[52] Although danger lurked around every corner of London's streets, and the repercussions of engaging in homosexual sex could be quite severe, the gossip writer seemed to live quite happily – if still with his guards up – under the noses of his millions of readers.

This is not to say that homosexuality was unproblematic on Fleet Street. For all the well-known debauches of newspapermen, homosexuality was a highly fraught subject, and Fleet Street social life was marred by an often-intense homophobia, which persisted throughout most of the twentieth century. The journalist Peter Wildeblood (who would, during his 1954 trial for engaging in homosexual acts, feel the wrath of the tabloids' commitment to scandalous exposure) remarked, 'I could hardly have chosen a profession in which being a homosexual was more of a handicap than it was in Fleet Street.... Its morality was that of the saloon bar: every sexual excess was talked about and tolerated, provided it was "normal."'[53] So, while it was possible for homosexual men to play a prominent role in journalistic life, it was not without its own pitfalls and social stigmas. On Fleet Street, as elsewhere, one had to be on guard, and remain conscious of how others might interpret particular behaviours. And as it turns out, this skill set – learning the 'appropriate' way to act in particular social settings – was eminently applicable to the task of gossip writing.

## Pose, pose

By the later 1920s, the gossip column was slowly evolving into a meatier read than it had been in the Edwardian years. It became increasingly implicated in a broader culture of celebrity built upon the appeal of discovering what celebrities were 'really like' when not in public. Gossip writers, like candid photographers whose skill at capturing embarrassing behaviour on camera was called upon extensively in the early and mid-1930s, provided testimonial evidence of the less than savoury aspects of celebrity life.[54] Gossip writers chipped away at the manufactured celebrity image.

The aesthetic young gossip writer succeeded as a social commentator precisely because of his ambiguous status in the social world about which he wrote. One had to be at least a bit of an outsider to write good gossip. Most of these men spoke witheringly about the people with whom they were asked to socialise in order to satisfy their editors.[55] The queer gossip writers of the late 1920s evinced a cagey, and at times forensically distant, relationship to the world of London Society. Balfour, in a letter to his mother while still employed as Mr Gossip, wrote of his relationship to his work:

> You must distinguish between the subjective and the objective attitude towards people – that is terribly important ... one regards very few people from a subjective point of view – i.e. as really affecting oneself ... I mean of the people I see in London. The rest one looks upon in quite a different way – detached, one looks on them and enjoys their company and is amused by them – or sometimes merely at them, and they aren't in the least part of oneself, not personally important.[56]

Balfour evinces an almost clinical detachment from the human element in his work. To treat celebrities as specimens – as things to be 'looked at' – was a necessary element of the particular mode of critique implicit in gossip writing.

Maintaining this cold distance from their subjects helped gossip writers to decipher genuine personality from pretence and affectation. It was part of their job, as they construed it, to determine what about a particular personality was 'real' and what was a 'pose'. Press gossip increasingly became preoccupied with questions about what secrets were buried beneath the veneer of social protocol. This kind of gossip writing required the perceptive eye of someone who knew the telltale signs of a social masquerade. Gossip was fundamentally about identifying what kinds of behaviours and 'poses' were required to be a successful social actor. Queer gossip writers seemed particularly preoccupied with these questions, revealing a marked interest in the lies that people tell themselves in the pursuit of public approval.

A common theme among several homosexual gossip writers was the question of the 'masks' that people affected when interacting at social functions. Nichols often expounded on this subject, making the motifs of the mask central to his novelistic send-up of gossip writing, *Crazy Pavements*. One of the main characters in that book, a debauched Bright Young Thing, creates masks of his socialite friends that are meant to represent their more sinister characteristics. Tellingly, he keeps those masks hidden in his closet.[57] Nichols also produced a series of gossip columns in the *Sketch* under the title 'Celebrities in Undress' – later compiled in a volume with the equally telling title *Are They the Same at Home?* – that were very direct in their appeal to the desire of readers to see behind the façade of celebrity life. He made frequent reference to the divide between the public and private self, ironically suggesting that artifice comes naturally: 'Pose, pose – it all comes down to that. I am posing all my life. So are you. Why not admit it? And as one poses, so, to a certain extent, one becomes.'[58] The tropes of the pose and the mask,

which acknowledged the ubiquity of performance and fakery in West
End social life, occurred again and again in his columns. One of his
*Sunday Chronicle* columns announced cheekily, 'If you Imitate Do It
Well', and described the best tactics for pretending to be someone
that you are not.[59]

The subject of the masks that people wear to fit in – the performance of a desired self for public consumption – was central to the
lives of queer men, especially in a moment when homosexual sex
was punishable by law. Masking and its inverse, revelation, were
crucial aspects of queer identity before decriminalisation.[60] Queer
men made such good gossip writers, in part, because they had such
a clear understanding of the fundamental components of effective
gossip: the demands of social protocol, and the exposure and revelation of unspoken secrets. Balfour, for one, stated this quite unequivo-
cally: 'people who lead public lives are fair game for social columns.
Unless they are secretive about their private affairs they must pay
the penalty of publicity.'[61] While libel laws[62] and social etiquette
kept Balfour from espousing some of his more potent criticisms of
notable people (those he saved for his autobiographical works), his
gossip writing was characterised by a cutting attention to unflattering
detail and slightly humiliating social *faux pas*. Identifying the 'dirty
secrets' that lay behind the performed personality of public figures,
which columnists such as Balfour and Nichols made so central to
their gossip writing, was a familiar skill for queer men. For most men
with acknowledged homosexual desires, it was as a matter of course
in their day-to-day lives.

### Godfrey Winn and the 'mask'

The gossip columnist whose public persona relied most heavily on
veiled, yet nonetheless utterly legible, tropes of his homosexuality was
Godfrey Winn, who would become one of the most famous gossip
writers with his column 'Personality Parade' in the *Daily Mirror*.[63]
Hugh Cudlipp, the editor of the *Daily Mirror* who hired Winn, dedicated a chapter of one of his memoirs to Winn – tellingly entitled
'The Fabulous Godfrey Winn' – in which he described Winn's personal presentation in a way that reads like a litany of early twentieth-
century stereotypes of homosexual men.[64] Winn's popularity among
women readers only cemented his reputation as the effeminate coun-
terpoint to the manly Fleet Street journalist. He would later give

up his position at the *Daily Mirror* to write a column for the weekly magazine *Woman's Illustrated*, which was the most glaring testament to the fact that he built his career on appealing to women readers.[65] His gossip columns combined observational commentary on West End fêtes and soirées with a personal, conversational tone designed to appeal to a (mostly female) cross-section of the social spectrum. His close relationship with his mother – with whom he lived (and ate breakfast every morning as one column informed his readers), and who often appeared in photographs included in his column – helped to consolidate his reputation as a 'confirmed bachelor' whose respect for women, and interest in women's issues, was entirely filial or brotherly, never sexual. Whatever the stereotypical codes of his sexual identity might have signified to his contemporaries, it goes without saying that Winn never announced his sexual preference to his reading public, and only barely did so in his meandering and egomaniacally long autobiography.[66]

Winn faced the same kinds of discrimination from some of the more bigoted newspapermen that most homosexual journalists in Britain faced, but that seemed to have no negative effect on his success as a gossip writer. Later in his career, Winn wrote to Driberg of his status as somewhat of a joke among many Fleet Street men, 'Taking the micky out of me is an almost occupational disease among a large section of the members of my own profession: and I have become conditioned to such cracks: and simply carry on.'[67] According to Winn, Cudlipp prefaced his offer of the column by rather indelicately remarking, 'A lot of Fleet Street people regard you as a bit of a sissy, but I am going to prove them wrong.'[68] Cudlipp admitted to his anxiety about his close association with Winn, for fear that it would lead others to label him, in his words, a 'poof'.[69] Whatever Cudlipp's motivations for hiring Winn, it is interesting to note that Winn's reputation *as* a 'sissy' was one of the chief reasons that the editor found him to be an appropriate choice for the author of a gossip column.

Winn's columns, perhaps more than any other gossip writer's of his time, were preoccupied with discussions of the social mask, and of the pretence of public personalities. He worked hard to sell himself as a writer with a proud dedication to identifying, and offering advice to remedy, disingenuousness and self-delusion in everyone from film stars to typists.[70] This was expressed most clearly in his bizarrely earnest investment in 'sincerity', what Cudlipp mockingly referred to as that 'thing ... which he called (with sincerity) "my sincerity"'.[71] In advance of the launch of his column, *Woman's Illustrated* advertised Winn as 'courageously sincere' and claimed that 'sincerity is the only thing that he is a snob about'.[72] And Winn's writing was, if anything, sincere. He prided himself on never telling lies, and offered his readers what he promised was the absolute truth about issues of importance to them. This frankness usually came filtered through some sort of personal revelation, or a private story taken from the life of a prominent celebrity. It was his avowed task to provide insight into the intimate lives of celebrities, unencumbered by the artifice of public life, as well as to open his ears to those who needed to unburden their consciences of unspoken secrets and lies. His dishy books, such as *Scrapbooks of the Stars*, just like his personalised gossip in his *Daily Mirror* and *Woman's Illustrated* columns, were preoccupied with questions about the pressures of public acceptability and the desire to seek public approval and acclaim through acts of deception (deceiving others as much as oneself).

Resorting to the trope of the mask seems to have allowed Winn to assault falsity and disingenuousness, while also analysing its psychological roots. The question of the mask came up quite frequently in his column, and was one of the defining motifs of his gossip writing. Most notably, he discussed the subject in a column for 'Personality Parade' entitled 'A Devil's Mask'. He began with a jab at the artifice of London nightlife:

> It is not often that I find myself in a night club, thank God, but when I do, and look round the room and see the painted faces of the women pretending they are enjoying themselves, and the blank, leathery faces of their escorts drowning self-criticism in drink, I always think of a story I was once told. It is the story of a woman who, during her lifetime, was famous for the beauty of her hair, which she wore in a loose cascade over her shoulders. When the time came for her to die, her husband went to take his last farewell of her after her body had been prepared for the funeral. Can you image what his feelings were when he suddenly realised that the reason why his wife had always worn her hair in this peculiar fashion was not because of its beauty, but because at the back of her head was another face? It was a caricature of the one she had always shown to the world, a ghastly image in which cruelty and fear and self-ish desire had twisted and tortured the features into a devil's mask.[73]

Winn evoked the Wildean surrogate visage – the hideously disfigured face hidden away from view. Like Dorian Gray's shameful picture tucked away in the attic, the woman's second face reveals her truer, uglier nature. The woman's grotesque second face is a rather obvious metaphor for the secret perversion and deviance hidden within. It is symbolic of the lies we all tell ourselves.

Through such parables, Winn exhorted his readers to take an alternative course, to be true to themselves, and not fall prey to the same kinds of affectations that the socialites and celebrities of the West End had made such a part of their public personae. He somewhat patronisingly saw his role as a moral guide, using the social world of celebrities as his map, for his millions of readers. The lies and falsities of the social elite could serve as a warning to those tempted to bury their secrets instead of processing them in a healthier way.

All of Winn's 'sincerity' only worked to highlight, especially in the 20/20 of hindsight, the spectacular silence at the centre of his frank revelations about his personal life and secret desires, i.e., his sexual preference. Clearly not everything could be safely confessed. Some secrets, he acknowledged, were too dangerous to reveal. Occasionally, Winn's sincerity would push him even closer to telling his readers what kinds of secrets lay behind his own mask; never, of course, speaking with too much incriminating honesty. This resulted in strategic omission and euphemism. In one column, he asked his readers:

> If you died to-morrow, would you carry with you to the grave some secret that for the last years of your life has been harrying you like a shadow? I know that it would be so in my own case. But I cannot tell you what my secret is, just as you cannot tell me what yours is, either ... In any case, the human mechanism is such a very complex affair and it has been maintained by scientific pens on many occasions that there is, in fact, no such thing as a completely normal man or woman. Take courage, take comfort from that. And also from the knowledge that in the case of those who appear most normal, most true to type, on the surface, if you could burrow down, you would find strange, unexpected, even tragic secrets.... Remember that other people wear a self-protecting mask as well as yourself.[74]

Historians could read this in many ways, but, given his utter honesty on every topic except one, it seems that the reference to his 'grave secret' denotes his silence about his sexuality. He even evokes a vaguely sexological conception of the complexity of the 'human mechanism'. But to make too much of his sexuality would miss the larger importance of Winn's interest in the 'secret' and the 'mask'. In a broader sense, the question of the 'secret' is situated at the centre of gossip writing in general: what do public figures hide, and what ends up obscured by the masks that they wear?

## Conclusion

Social gossip writing by queer men in interwar Britain evinces an acute awareness of social custom and protocol, in the hypocrisies of the world of the glamorous social elite. Inhabiting the ambiguous space between insider and outsider, the gay gossip came to know the 'centre' better than those who took its customs and mores for granted. Gossip is predicated on navigating the boundaries of the publicly acceptable. Excavating the secrets that celebrities hide involves an acute knowledge of what kinds of information society has a vested interest in suppressing. In this way, gossip writing required its practitioners to have an intimate knowledge of exactly the kinds of hidden personal secrets that would have been very familiar to most men with avowed same-sex desires.

Homosexual men, especially at this historical moment, had an acute knowledge of the desire, and indeed the need, to keep sensitive information from reaching unsympathetic ears. Matters of personal privacy, social deception and self-delusion played an acknowledged and defining role in homosexual identity and social life. It is not difficult to see the relevance of issues about exposing the hidden – outing celebrities' 'private affairs' – to the lives of queer men forced to live at least part of their lives behind a façade. So, while not all gossip writers were homosexual, it certainly helped, it seems, to have intimate knowledge of the very issues – matters of revelation, exposure and masking – that sat at the centre of homosexual identity in the interwar years.

It is tempting to suggest that the gossip column provided (and still provides) a space for the expression of a gay sensibility, whatever that might mean. Gossip has become a part of the broader cultural stereotype of homosexual behaviour and identity, for better or worse, and this chapter has shown how this association has deeper historical links than might at first have been imagined. The fact that so many gossip writers were queer men, whose sexuality was never entirely invisible to their colleagues or their readers, is remarkable, and suggests that gossip really does seem to be a form of knowledge production with close links to male homosexuality. In the period under consideration here, the ubiquity and popularity of the gay gossips (many of whom were not particularly discreet about their sexuality) working for the mass press seems exceptionally notable. In an era defined by the systematic repression of homosexual public life, it is surprising that so many queer men could occupy such a prominent and visible public role.

But can we, or should we, read the work of homosexual men *as homosexual*? Am I merely imputing homosexual meaning when it is not there? It seems to me that this could, in fact, be the case. Perhaps I am just another gay gossip, searching to expose the hidden secrets of historical actors. But then again, what is history, but an elaborated form of gossip?

## Notes

1 Quoted in Val Holley, *Mike Connolly: The Manly Art of Hollywood Gossip* (London: McFarland, 2003), p. 8. See also Daniel Harris, *The Rise and Fall of Gay Culture* (New York: Hyperion, 1997).

2 Patricia Meyer Spacks, *Gossip* (New York: Knopf, 1985). See also Alexander Rysman, 'How gossip became a woman', *Journal of Communication*, 27 (1977), 176–80.

3 Jorg Bergmann, *Discreet Indiscretions: The Social Organization of Gossip* (New York: Aldine De Gruyter, 1993). See also Amy Milne-Smith, 'Club talk: Gossip, masculinity, and the importance of oral communities in late nineteenth-century London', *Gender and History*, 21:1 (2009), 86–106.

4 See Eve Sedgwick, *Epistemology of the Closet* (Berkeley: University of California Press, 1990), p. 247. Gavin Butt has made a similar claim about gossip as a form of queer knowledge, though his study focuses on the idea that gossip is a form of hearsay that is queer in its defiance of a purely true/false dichotomy. See Gavin Butt, *Between You and Me: Queer Disclosures in the New York Art World, 1948–1963* (Durham, NC, and London: Duke University Press, 2005). Michael Warner also claims that gossip is part of the community transactions of homosexual sub-cultures. Michael Warner, *Publics and Counterpublics* (New York: Zone Books, 2005), p. 203.

5 For more on the development of gossip writing in Britain, see Sarah Newman, *The Talk of London: The British Newspaper Gossip Column, 1918–39* (PhD dissertation, Oxford University, forthcoming). See also Roger Wilkes, *Scandal!: A Scurrilous History of Gossip* (London: Atlantic Books, 2002); Andrew Barrow, *Gossip: A History of High Society, 1920–1970* (London: Coward, McCann & Geoghegan, 1979).

6 For contemporary commentary on this, see Jane Soames, *The English*

*Press: Newspapers and News* (London: Stanley Nott, 1936); Aldous Huxley, 'English snobbery', in *The Olive Tree and Other Essays* (London: Chatto & Windus, 1936); Patrick Balfour, *Society Racket: A Critical Survey of Modern Social Life* (London: Long John, 1933). For more on the history of the British fascination with upper-class life, see Martin Weiner, *English Culture and the Decline of the Industrial Spirit, 1850–1980* (Cambridge: Cambridge University Press, 1982); Ross McKibbin, *Classes and Cultures: England 1918–1951* (Oxford: Oxford University Press, 1998); Frank Mort, *Capital Affairs: London and the Making of the Permissive Society* (New Haven: Yale University Press, 2010).

7  See Jack Levin and Arnold Arluke, *Gossip: The Inside Scoop* (London: Plenum Press, 1987), p. 90.

8  See, for example, Tom Driberg, *Ruling Passions* (London: Jonathan Cape, 1977); Patrick Balfour, Balfour of Kinross Papers, National Library of Scotland; John Patrick Douglas Balfour (Lord Kinross), *The Candid Eye* (London: The Richards Press, 1958); Brodrick Haldane, *Time Exposure* (London: Arcadia, 1999); Marie-Jacqueline Lancaster, *Brian Howard: Portrait of a Failure* (London: Anthony Blond, 1968); Beverley Nichols, *All I Could Never Be* (London: Jonathan Cape, 1949), 29; Bryan Connon, *Beverley Nichols: A Life* (London: Constable, 1991); Godfrey Winn, *Infirm Glory: Volume 1 of His Autobiography* (London: Michael Joseph, 1967).

9  It is inaccurate to assert that all were uncomplicatedly 'homosexual' – Patrick Balfour would marry a woman later in life – but all of the figures at the centre of this study were unorthodox in their sexual orientation, and were known to have had sex with men.

10  The heavyweights of the period were undoubtedly Viscount Castlerosse, whose 'Londoner's Log' was the pre-eminent gossip column of the interwar era. The Marquess of Donegall, another leading columnist, contributed pithy social gossip in a variety of newspapers and women's magazines. Lady Eleanor Smith was perhaps the most famous female gossip writer, with her column 'From My Window in Vanity Fair'. Other women gossip writers included Olive Viner, Pamela Murray and Louise Heilgers. See Viscount Castlerosse, *Valentine's Day* (London: Methuen, 1936); Lady Eleanor Smith, *Life's a Circus* (London: Longmans Green, 1939).

11  See Newman, 'The Talk of London'; Leonard Mosley, *Castlerosse* (London: Arthur Barker, 1956); Lord Birkenhead, *Lady Eleanor Smith – A Memoir* (London: Hutchinson, 1953).

12  Roger Wilkes focuses much on Balfour, and acknowledges his homosexuality, but this is not a central piece of his analysis. See Wilkes, *Scandal!*. For a similar treatment of the sexuality of gossip writers, see also D. J. Taylor, *Bright Young People: The Lost Generation of London's Jazz Age* (New York: Farrar, Straus and Giroux, 2009). Adrian Bingham

briefly discusses homosexuality on Fleet Street, but not with regard to gossip writing. See Adrian Bingham, *Family Newspapers?: Sex, Private Life, and the British Popular Press, 1918–1978* (Oxford: Oxford University Press, 2009).

13  In 1920s and 1930s New York, 'Champagne Cholly', the pseudonym of the homosexual gossip writer Maury Paul, wrote spicy gossip about Manhattan café society. See Eve Brown, *Champagne Cholly: The Life and Times of Maury Paul* (New York: Dutton, 1947). In Los Angeles, Mike Connolly dished the dirt on Hollywood stars while simultaneously chronicling the doings of Hollywood's homosexual coterie. Holley, *Mike Connolly*.

14  For more on this notion of the queerness of marginal historical investigation see Richard Meyer, 'At home in marginal domains', *Documents*, 18 (Summer 2000), 19–32.

15  For more on queer life in Britain before decriminalisation, see Matt Houlbrook, *Queer London: Perils and Pleasures in the Sexual Metropolis, 1918–1957* (Chicago: University of Chicago Press, 2005). See also Jeffrey Weeks, *Coming Out: Homosexual Politics in Britain from the Nineteenth Century to the Present* (London: Quartet Books, 1977).

16  This is the subject of Ryan Linkof, *The Public Eye: Celebrity and Photojournalism in the Making of the British Tabloids, 1904–1938* (PhD dissertation, University of Southern California, 2011). See also Chris Horrie, *Tabloid Nation: From the Birth of the Mirror to the Death of the Tabloid* (London: André Deutsch, 2003); Joel H. Weiner, *Papers for the Millions: The New Journalism in Britain, 1850s–1914* (Westport, CT: Greenwood Press, 1988).

17  For more on this, see Deborah Cohen, *Family Secrets: Shame and Privacy in Modern Britain* (Oxford: Oxford University Press, 2013), chapter six.

18  See, in particular, Charles Ponce de Leon, *Self Exposure: Human-Interest Journalism and the Emergence of Celebrity in America, 1890–1940* (Chapel Hill: University of North Carolina Press, 2002).

19  For more on the British dandy and his relationship to High Society, see Leo Braudy, *The Frenzy of Renown: Fame and its History* (Oxford: Oxford University Press, 1986), pp. 401–6; Rhonda Garelick, *Rising Star: Dandyism, Gender and Performance at the Fin de Siècle* (Princeton: Princeton University Press, 1999); Ellen Moers, *The Dandy: Brummell to Beerbohm* (Lincoln: University of Nebraska Press, 1978).

20  The fact that Swaffer's biography was written by Tom Driberg, one of the leading gossip writers of the 1930s and 1940s, who attributed his own career to the work of Swaffer, is a testament to his influence. See Tom Driberg, *Swaff: The Life and Times of Hannen Swaffer* (London: Macdonald, 1974). Swaffer was identified as the originator of press

gossip in, of all places, a parliamentary commission. See House of Commons Parliamentary Papers, *Royal Commission on the Press*, 'Members of the National Union of Journalists before the Committee, taken 19th June and 16th July 1947', 38. For a discussion of Swaffer's role in creating the modern gossip column, see Horrie, *Tabloid Nation*.

21  Hannen Swaffer, *Hannen Swaffer's Who's Who* (London: Hutchinson, 1929), p. 6.

22  Quoted in Driberg, *Swaff*, p. 56.

23  Will Straw's work on the New York tabloid gossip of the 1930s makes a similar claim. Will Straw, 'Squawkies and talkies', *Parallax*, 14 (2008), 26. Late nineteenth-century women's magazines hired gossip writers with some connection to elite sociability, paying them *pro rata* to expose some of the secrets of aristocratic living. It did not take long, however, before the peddler in gossip underwent a sex change. See Balfour, *Society Racket*, pp. 88–9; Laura Smith, 'Society journalism: Its rise and development', *Newspaper Press Directory* (1898), pp. 80–1. For analyses of the cattier gossip of the mid-twentieth century, largely American in derivation, see Neal Gabler, *Winchell: Gossip, Power and the Culture of Celebrity* (New York: Vintage, 1995); Samantha Barbas, *The First Lady of Hollywood: A Biography of Louella Parsons* (Berkeley: University of California Press, 2005).

24  For more on the aesthetic presentation of the gossip writer, see Wilkes, *Scandal!*, p. 149; Mosley, *Castlerosse*, p. 65.

25  See Hannen Swaffer, *Really Behind the Scenes* (London: George Newnes, 1929); Driberg, *Swaff*.

26  Balfour, *Society Racket*, pp. 91–2.

27  For Swaffer's description of him, see Driberg, *Swaff*, p. 61.

28  This description comes from the editor extraordinaire William Comyns Beaumont. See William Comyns Beaumont, *A Rebel in Fleet Street* (London: Hutchinson, 1943), p. 109. *À rebours* is a work by the French author J. K. Huysmans noted for its ties to *fin-de-siècle* aestheticism, and is said to have been the devilish book read by Dorian Gray in Oscar Wilde's *The Picture of Dorian Gray*.

29  *The Newspaper World* (2 January 1932), 4.

30  Driberg, *Swaff*, p. 60.

31  Alan Sinfield, *The Wilde Century: Oscar Wilde, Effeminacy and the Queer Moment* (New York: Columbia University Press, 1994); Ed Cohen, *Talk on the Wilde Side: Towards a Genealogy of the Discourse of Male Homosexuality* (London: Routledge, 1988).

32  Philip Gibbs, *The Street of Adventure*, pp. 5–6.

33  For discussion of the libel case, see Philip Gibbs, *Adventures in Journalism* (London: William Heinemann, 1923), p. 107.

34  See Martin Green, *Children of the Sun: A Narrative of 'Decadence' after*

*1918* (Mount Jackson, VA: Axios Press, 2008). For the longer history of the associations of Oxford and homosexuality, see Linda Dowling, *Hellenism and Homosexuality in Victorian Oxford* (Ithaca: Cornell University Press, 1994).

35  Evelyn Waugh, *Vile Bodies* (New York: Modern Library, 1930).

36  Swaffer, *Hannen Swaffer's Who's Who*, p. 215.

37  That Northcliffe said this is suggested in Gibbs, *Street of Adventure*, p. 11.

38  Balfour, Balfour of Kinross Papers, letter to his mother, 25 February 1927.

39  *Sunday Graphic* (27 January 1929), 13.

40  For more on Nichols and his sexuality, see Connon, *Beverley Nichols*.

41  *Sunday Graphic* (3 February 1929), 13.

42  See Nichols, *All I Could Never Be*; Beverley Nichols, *25: Being the Candid Recollections of His Elders and Betters* (London: Jonathan Cape, 1926), p. 146; Connon, *Beverley Nichols*; Beverley Nichols, *Star Spangled Manner* (London: Jonathan Cape, 1927); Beverley Nichols, *Are They the Same at Home?: Being a Series of Bouquets Diffidently Distributed* (New York: George H. Doran, 1927).

43  See 'Saddled with a Reputation', *Sunday Chronicle* (25 September 1932), 2.

44  These are both included in the same column, *Sunday Chronicle* (11 December 1932), 2.

45  Balfour met Nichols in Paris in the late 1920s, and Nichols apparently encouraged Balfour to take up gossip. In a letter to his mother, Balfour wrote that Nichols 'says that what really pays is writing Gossip! ... Though there is no doubt he has rather a gift for that sort of journalistic stuff, and, more important, the courage of his convictions ... And this will, he says, probably go on for ever, as he can always find enough celebrities to write about. He is terribly good at getting to know the right people.' Patrick Balfour, Balfour of Kinross Papers, National Library of Scotland, letters to mother (1926–32), no date.

46  Haldane, *Time Exposure*, p. 62.

47  Nichols loathed Winn, and thought of his work as derivative of his own. See Connon, *Beverley Nichols*, pp. 164–5.

48  This is suggested in Wilkes, *Scandal!*, p. 14.

49  Driberg, *Ruling Passions*, p. 102.

50  Houlbrook, *Queer London*. See also, Jeffrey Weeks, *Coming Out*.

51  See Driberg, *Ruling Passions*, p. 110; Francis Wheen, *Tom Driberg: His Life and Indiscretions* (London: Chatto and Windus, 1990); Francis Wheen, *Soul of Indiscretion: Tom Driberg – Poet, Philanderer, Legislator, Outlaw* (London: Fourth Estate, 2001).

52  Most famously, the so-called 'Evil Men' series in the Sunday Pictorial sought to out homosexual men in positions of power. See Douglas Warth, 'Evil Men', *Sunday Pictorial* (25 May 1952), 6, 15. For historical

treatments, see Dominic Sandbrook, *Never Had It So Good: A History of Britain from Suez to the Beatles* (London: Abacus Books, 2006), p. 601; Weeks, *Coming Out*, p. 162.

53  Quoted in Bingham, *Family Newspapers?*, p. 27. For a further discussion of homophobia on Fleet Street, see Connon, *Beverley Nichols*, p. 164.

54  For more on this, see Linkof, 'The Public Eye', chapter two.

55  See, for example, Lancaster, *Brian Howard*, p. 319; Nichols, *All I Could Never Be*; Godfrey Winn, *Infirm Glory*; Wheen, *Tom Driberg*, p. 79. Charles Graves, 'Goin' everywhere and doin' everything', *World's Press News* (20 June 1935), 2; Balfour, *Society Racket*, pp. 231–2; Balfour, *The Candid Eye*. The distaste of gossip writing was a common theme in literature written by those who knew the work intimately. See Beverley Nichols, *Crazy Pavements* (London: Jonathan Cape, 1927), pp. 7–8, 11; Waugh, *Vile Bodies*; Gordon West, *Dancing Debutante* (London: John Hamilton, 1936).

56  Balfour, Balfour of Kinross Papers, letter to his mother, n.d.

57  Nichols, *Crazy Pavements*, p. 90.

58  Nichols, *Are They the Same at Home?*, p. 228.

59  *Sunday Chronicle* (15 January 1933), 2.

60  For more on the mask and homosexual identity, see Harris, *Rise and Fall*; B. H. Fussell, 'The masks of Oscar Wilde', *The Sewanee Review*, 80:1 (Winter 1972), 124–39; Martin Meeker, 'Behind the mask of respectability: Reconsidering the Mattachine Society and male homophile practice, 1950s and 1960s', *Journal of the History of Sexuality*, 10:1 (January 2001), 78–116.

61  Balfour, *Society Racket*, pp. 95–6.

62  Libel was an important check on the types of criticisms and revelations that gossip writers could make. Nearly all gossip writers complained that they were shackled by draconian libel laws that kept true revelations from making it to print. The writer Jane Soames criticised social gossip columnists for being cowed by libel law. She remarked that the gossip column 'is the most anodyne reading imaginable: there is never one line which might not be read by the most innocent – the scandals are not mentioned, nor the divorces (except very discreetly, as a fait accompli), nor the bankruptcies.' Soames, *The English Press*, p. 98.

63  Winn compiled highlights from his column in a published volume, Godfrey Winn, *Personality Parade: All of Humanity on a Single Page* (London: Peter Davies, 1937).

64  Hugh Cudlipp, *Publish and Be Damned!: The Astonishing Story of the Daily Mirror* (London: Andrew Dakers, 1953), chapter 15, esp. p. 109.

65  He later published *The Queen's Countrywomen* (London: Hutchinson, 1954), which consolidated his reputation as a friend and confidant of women.

66 Winn, *Infirm Glory*, vol. 1; Godfrey Winn, *Infirm Glory*, vol. 2: *The Growing Years* (London: Pan Books, 1969).
67 Letter marked '1955?', Tom Driberg Papers, Christ Church College, Oxford.
68 Winn, *Infirm Glory*, p. 322.
69 Hugh Cudlipp, *Walking on Water* (London: Bodley Head, 1976), p. 144.
70 See Winn, *Infirm Glory*, p. 321.
71 Cudlipp, *Publish*, p. 110.
72 *Woman's Illustrated* (18 February 1938), 10, 18.
73 Winn, *Personality Parade*, p. 17.
74 *Ibid.*, p. 42.

# 6

# Thinking queer:
# the social and the sexual in interwar Britain
*Matt Houlbrook*

In this chapter I want to argue for the importance of thinking queer in our practice as historians. Engaging with what I see as a persistent tendency in recent work on modern British same-sexualities, I tease out the possibilities opened up by shifting our definition of queer from a position to a process; from a mode of sexual selfhood – however unstable – to a set of critical practices; from something we consider our subjects to be, to something we do. In so doing I draw upon Laura Doan's recent work, particularly the challenging reading of historiographies of sexuality developed in her *Disturbing Practices: History, Sexuality, and Women's Experience of Modern War*. Doan's starting point is Lee Edelman's claim that 'Queerness can never define an identity: it can only disturb one'. Building on this proposition, she foregrounds the analytic distinction between 'queerness-as-being' and 'queerness-as-method' to sketch out the possibilities of a 'critical queer history of sexuality' in reorienting our understanding of past subjectivities and behaviours.[1] Rather than rehearse Doan's theoretical and historiographical positioning, I want to explore what the critical history she envisages might look like. Thinking queer represents my attempt to work through the implications of 'queerness-as-method' – initially as historiographical critique, and then through a more speculative reading of two life-stories as a way of rethinking interwar British society.[2]

My focus is thus twofold. First, thinking queer provides a point of engagement with that burgeoning historiography (including my own work) on male same-sex relations that Chris Waters terms the 'New British Queer History'. This formulation underscores how recent interventions by Harry Cocks, Matt Cook and others have challenged the foundational assumptions of an earlier project of lesbian and gay history conceived largely as an exercise in social historical recovery.[3] At the same time, the queerness Waters claims for this work is unclear. In the texts he discusses, I suggest, queer often works as a catch-all term that sketches out a field coterminous with LGBT or to signal a renewed emphasis on diachronic and synchronic plurality and difference as defining features of sexual subjectivities. It gestures towards a growing attentiveness to differences between then and now and to the constitutive importance of fissures of class, age, race, ethnicity, gender and place in shaping sexual subjectivities. Yet while our conceptual apparatus might have shifted productively, what we do remains constrained within binary notions of sexual difference and normality that efface the complex regimes within which past sexualities were understood, retaining the assumption that historical actors had a sexuality or sexual identity to be apprehended. As such, we remain preoccupied with the quest for a bounded queer subject – an elusive being that, I argue, can never be anything more than chimeric. Thinking queer is something we still find difficult to do.[4]

Second, thinking queer enables a move beyond the thematic constraints of sexuality studies. Following Seth Koven and Stephanie Newell, I explore the capacity of a queer historical practice to elucidate social and cultural formations that engage issues of sex and sexuality occasionally, tangentially and sometimes not at all.[5] What happens when we think queer about subjects that cannot be subsumed into LGBT identity categories? In this sense, my chapter represents a conversation between the project that culminated in *Queer London: Perils and Pleasures in the Sexual Metropolis, 1918–57* (2005) and my current interest in rethinking British modernities. Seeking to move on, I avoided working on histories of sexuality and within queer frameworks for several years. Yet the invitation to present a keynote at the 'Histories of Sexuality' conference in Newcastle, Australia, in 2011 pushed me to return to earlier orientations, highlighting what I am slowly coming to understand as the usefulness of thinking queer as part of a broader cultural historical practice. My current project *The Prince of Tricksters: Cultures of Confidence in Interwar Britain* explores the interrelationship between the social and the subject, tracking the transnational deceptions of a confidence trickster, crime writer and biographer to problematise dominant narratives of the interwar as the 'Long Weekend' or 'morbid age'; as the Great War's traumatic aftershocks or the hesitant emergence of social democracy.[6] It traces how – amid massive social, economic, cultural and political upheaval – confidence and authenticity became increasingly important organising values across social relations and cultural forms. The chameleon-like trickster provides my avatar for a broader reconfiguration of ideas of selfhood in which subjectivity was bound up with the fictional and the dream, and the emergence of mass cultural forms which incited such troubling self-fashionings. Thinking queer, I suggest, allows us to use the conman to disrupt dominant historiographical narratives. Always-already-in-process, the trickster speaks to alternative readings of interwar Britain as provisional and unsettling.

Why think *queer*? What might we gain (or lose) through this problematic? Carla Freccero has recently expressed scepticism about the term's imperial tendency to claim new territories to unsettle. Such claims, Freccero suggests, strip queer of its power to do specific work in sexuality studies: 'I have wanted to preserve sexuality's importance to the notion of queer mostly because there are other quasi concepts that convey the work of denormativization, broadly conceived, for other domains. Queer, to me, is the name of a certain unsettling in relation to heteronormativity.'[7] There is a logic here: reduced to a metaphor queer loses much of the precision that has made it useful. Cognisant of the risks of reorienting queer away from the sexual, however, we should be equally wary of any move that constrains histories of sexuality within narrow boundaries of content. Moreover, queer is an appropriate analytic in the historical contexts to which I turn. That is true in an immediate sense: the life-stories on which I focus are suffused with unruly traces of desires, bodies and couplings. More than this: in thinking queer with this material we are better equipped to consider affinities between the sexual and the social. In the interwar worlds on which I focus class and status were increasingly situated in deceptive practices commonly associated with the fleeting traces of same-sex desire.

We might reduce these arguments to a glib formulation: thinking queer is too useful to be confined to the study of the queer. In the second part of this chapter I tease out this premise by focusing on two lives – the Society beauty Josephine O'Dare, exposed as an adventuress, bankrupt and fraud in 1926; and the petty conman and not-so-petty matricide Sydney Fox. United by their criminality, mobility and celebrity, neither can be easily accommodated within the conventional bounds of a queer history. That is precisely the point. In his encounters with the normalising projects of law and criminology Fox *could* be identified as a 'sodomite' and 'invert', yet simultaneously appeared as a predatory rake exploiting older men and women alike. Characterised as an amoral vamp, O'Dare cultivated a charged public persona while insisting on her chaste respectability. Figured as sites of social and cultural disturbance, their lives suggested the fictive and illusory nature of sexual and social categorisation. Accepting this indeterminacy I seek to understand the practices and processes within which these lives took shape. Following Sharon Marcus, I think queer in order 'to ask what social formations swim into focus once we abandon the preconception of strict divisions between men and women, homosexuality and heterosexuality, same-sex bonds and those of family and marriage'. Building on Marcus, I consider what happens when we also displace the preconception of rigid distinctions between Society and underworld.[8] For it was within the realm of the social rather than the sexual that these lives were understood: not as individual pathologies nor as psychological interiors nor as functions of sexual object choice but through their radical social mobilities. This doubling might seem counterintuitive, but in certain contexts and as a temporary historicising operation perhaps the time has come to both think and *not* think about sex.[9]

So what happens if we follow interwar commentators and treat Fox's and O'Dare's lives as 'irreducibly social' rather than within notions of sexual difference and 'normality'? At its simplest this problematises our understanding of sexology's hegemony. More than this: the mutability of identities disrupted the capacity of institutions to stabilise forms of governance in which the social was articulated as 'a totality, a system, with its own logic' susceptible to classification and management.[10] To put it another way: Fox's and O'Dare's lives were not disruptive because they transgressed emerging taxonomies of sexual behaviour then – we are told – consolidating around binaries of homosexual and heterosexual. Nor were they disruptive because they transgressed boundaries of class and systems of social classification. Neither of these readings can accommodate the inchoate nature of social and sexual boundaries. David Halperin makes the classic statement of Doan's 'queer-as-being': 'Queer is by definition whatever is at odds with the normal, the legitimate, the dominant. There is nothing in particular to which it necessarily refers. It is an identity without an essence. Queer then, demarcates not a positivity but a *positionality vis-à-vis the normative.*'[11]

Yet marking queer as a binarised non-normative, as Elizabeth Stephens suggests, 'leave[s] uninterrogated the concepts and cultural

function of both normativity and normality themselves.'[12] Building
on Stephens's historicisation of the 'normal', I treat the interwar as
a moment at which established structures of class were disrupted
by social and economic change and new mass cultural forms. With
the signifiers of class in flux, the intrigue and danger of O'Dare and
Fox rested in their radical social mobilities. Whether their affinities
were same- or opposite-sex they were situated within a way of seeing
which foregrounded sex's unruly capacities to enable and embody
those mobilities – that brought what we might now term 'queer'
and 'normal' within a common analytic frame. Their participation in
promiscuous or mercenary sex meant O'Dare and Fox were simultaneously figured within attempts to articulate that idealised realm
of companionate domesticity central to postwar reconstruction and
within a broader crisis of social relations. Their lives, I argue, expose
the fictive and insecure nature of the heterosexual/homosexual
binary and the hierarchical organisation of the social in a period
during which we have often assumed they were acquiring hegemonic
status. They prompt us to reconsider what Regina Kunzel describes
as 'falsely even and misleadingly totalizing' accounts of the formation
of sexual modernities. Their lives 'failed to synchronize with dominant notions of sexuality ... which held sexual acts and desires to be
expressions of sexual identity' and confound modes of categorisation
that historians have seen as 'the most distinctive marker of modern
sexuality' and suggest alternative intersecting temporalities.[13]

I think this is what Doan means by a critical queer history. In what
follows I explore how sexual and social lives were apprehended and
understood in interwar Britain. While this is a recognisable historicist
move, I resist the impulse to tease out a 'genealogy of ... homoerotic
desire', insisting on the radical alterity of the sexual past and the opacity of social and sexual classification.[14] Following Joan Scott in using
storytelling as historical critique, I foreground the 'decentering effect'
of Fox and O'Dare's lives to suggest 'epistemological challenges to ...
orthodox categories of current historiography: surprising them, throwing them off their guard'.[15] Scott notes elsewhere that critical history
'ought to make us uncomfortable', historicising social and cultural formations that appear self-evident and outside time. I want this chapter
to make you uncomfortable.[16] We are used to thinking of identity categories (gay and straight, homosexual and heterosexual) as time- and
place-specific; we are too comfortable with this move, finding secu-
rity in pervasive notions of 'queerness-as-being' and almost-familiar

regimes of sexual difference susceptible to the historian's toolkit. In thinking queer I want to unsettle such assumptions – setting aside categorisation, binaries, sexuality and sexual identity, highlighting their limited presence in interwar ways of seeing and being and questioning their utility as historicising operations.

We can clarify these arguments in conversation with Lauren Berlant's question: 'What does it matter who one is?' As historians of sexuality, we know that it *does* matter – the when, how and why of *our* writing shapes our accounts; our politics and fantasies indelibly mark our histories. Yet the question might equally be applied to those at the centre of investigation. Berlant uses it to frame an issue of *Critical Inquiry* that considers the contingent relationship between the case study and the formation of knowledge: it underscores an interest in the ontological effects of reconfiguring the subject of knowledge. While the legitimacy of knowledge is consolidated through its capacity to absorb a case, there remains the possibility that a different subject might 'frustrate the operation of legitimacy of the system that is mobilized by its appearance'.[17] Thinking queer forces us to simultaneously reconfigure and leave uncertain the subjects of historical knowledge (the *who* of our writing) and generates precisely these disruptive effects; it crystallises not a crisis of categorisation but its impossibility; it draws attention to points at which our analytic structures are not quite working. What does it matter whether Fox 'is' homosexual, or a sodomite, or queer, or something or nothing or everything else entirely? It matters a lot: shifting the grounds on which our subjects are defined questions established modes of expert knowledge – the truth-claims of interwar sexology and notions of individuated sexual pathology. Moreover, taking seriously subjects who are neither bounded nor knowable disrupts *both* historically specific ways of knowing about sex *and* the methodologies and theoretical frameworks through which we have sought to understand those past ways of knowing.

## Queer lives?

In *Queer London* I explored the geography, culture and politics of 'queer urban life' between the Great War and the Wolfenden Report. Influenced by queer and feminist theory, I sought to move beyond anachronistic categories of homosexual or gay – to emphasise, in ways then being reiterated by people like Cocks, Cook and Morris

Kaplan, the historical specificity of sexual subjectivities and the irreducible social differences that problematised homogeneous notions
of sexual difference and normality. Part of the 'altericist reaction', I
sought to defamiliarise the past, disrupting equivalences between
then and now around which the recuperative project of gay and lesbian history had developed and questioning the periodisation implicated in the idea of a distinctively 'modern' homosexuality.[18] I would
stand by much of this. At the same time, I now wonder how far this
intervention was the radical historiographical break I then thought.
As its title suggests, *Queer London* tried to move beyond simplistic
exercises in historical recovery. Still, it was underpinned by a notion
of queerness-as-being – of social worlds and subjectivities which
(however differentiated) could be isolated and explored. At its simplest, it was a history of particular urban subcultures at a particular
historical moment, its bounds and organisation increasingly cutting
against the queer approaches I sought to deploy. However unfamiliar
the sexual practices in working-class neighbourhoods, they were contained within a project still recognisably influenced by the identitarian premises of LGBT histories. However much *Queer London* sought
to problematise categories of identity, it remained wedded to binary
understandings of difference – teasing out oppositions between
queer and normal that shadowed and anticipated, even if they did not
map on to, those between homosexual and heterosexual. The result
was an account that flattened the terrain on which sexual subjectivities took shape and never quite managed to problematise the norms
*against* which, I suggested, resistant queer cultures formed. It was an
account that elided the possibility that same-sex intimacies could be
incorporated *within* the bounds of the normal.

   In part, such elisions were the product of my own training as a
social historian. Yet I think they were also symptomatic of the new
queer historiography then emerging. Rather than tease out these tensions, more recent work by Charles Upchurch, Brian Lewis and others
reproduces similar contradictions. These historians have broken new
ground in expanding the terrain on which we operate, exploring shifting formations of 'homosexuality' in realms of family, religion, market
and military. Considering the *fin-de-siècle* 'politics of friendship', Leela
Gandhi's compelling reading of Edward Carpenter 'explore[s] the circuits along which the libidinal economy of late-nineteenth-century
homosexuality came to traverse equally the incongruous circuits
of cross-cultural affinity and same-sex desire' – foregrounding the

'ethico-political ingredients in [Carpenter's] late-Victorian homosexual self-apprehension' animating his anti-imperial politics. At the
same time, there has been little interest in continuing to interrogate the categories around which the field has taken shape. Fixing
binary notions of 'homosexuality' and never taking up the challenge
of thinking queer, such work struggles to move beyond identitarian
traditions. Gandhi acknowledges the limits of 'a generalizable problematic of homo/heterosexual definition', but wants to understand
Carpenter through his 'sexual dissidence', securing his 'homosexuality' against a contemporaneous 'amplification of heteronormativity'.[19] In an otherwise nuanced essay Justin Bengry considers how
the magazine *Men Only* 'assumed and deliberately cultivated a queer
audience segment' in the 1930s. While his title – 'Courting the Pink
Pound' – is ironic, it suggests how Bengry is oriented towards the
assumed existence of an unproblematised queer consumer. This
market segment has a coherent prior existence (queer-as-being) and
so can be cultivated through codes available to journalists and illus-
trators. However suggestive his analysis, I think Bengry is asking the
wrong questions. Thinking queer we might instead consider how
*Men Only* enabled particular identifications for very specific social
worlds – *calling into being* temporary provisional affiliations – in a
critical practice that suspends both our own categories of sexual identity and the notion of identity itself.[20]

What do I mean? Consider the photograph taken by the
Metropolitan Police after raiding a party in Fitzroy Square in 1927.
One woman and five men sit side-by-side on a sofa in a room richly
decorated in an Oriental style. The men wear shirt, tie and waistcoat,
though their faces suggest lipstick and rouge. A younger man in
a dressing gown stands behind them; another man leans on the
sofa, dressed to perform a Salome dance and naked above the waist.
In *Queer London* I used this image to illustrate the formation of
vibrant queer worlds around unstable boundaries between public
and private. Isolating the man in the foreground, whose gaze con-
fronts that of the police photographer, I highlighted the gendering
of desire in working-class cultures and the resistant moments at
which men met the state. Refusing to engage in a ritual of recognition and stressing the photograph's alterity, this nonetheless constrained it within a gaze defined by presentist preoccupations. We
might read the nuances of self-presentation and interior design
against accompanying statements. Yet the men remain inscrutable

and unknowable once we step outside its frame.[21] Neither can we attribute the photograph's evidentiary power to its capacity to fix the men within coherent contradistinctions between difference and normality. We might read it as part of a disciplinary process that sought to establish the bounds of the normal. Yet the photograph's power was breaking down even at its moment of stabilisation. In court, defence counsel attacked the 'unexpected police procedure of taking photographs of male dancers in "fancy dress"' since 'it was improper to take photographs of persons found on raided premises unless they faithfully portrayed the actual positions of the individuals at the time of the raid'. Highlighting the photograph's constructedness rendered it untrustworthy. Passed to the judges, the images were unviewable and indecipherable: 'Mr Justice Sankey declined to look at them, and after examining one and observing "Is he a man?" Mr Justice Avory handed them back.' Ruled admissible after this brief non-viewing, Avory deliberately effaced the photograph's contradictory production: 'there was no sinister motive in posing them for the purpose. It was merely done to show the costumes in which these people were found, and it was essential to prove that they were assembling for the purpose of carrying on abominable offences.' Yet it was impossible to stabilise connections between image, 'acts' and 'identity' that were themselves indeterminate. The enigmatic photograph cannot easily be made complicit with the work we want it to do.[22]

We might stop here – thinking queer having rendered our subjects indecipherable. That is what Scott Herring does, 'embracing mystification' and seeking the 'undoing of gay and lesbian history' in his reading of late-modern slumming narratives. Uninterested in the traces of modern sexual communities, Herring 'cancel[s] out a hermeneutics of sexual suspicion by concentrating on its embedded inverse – a suspicion of sexual hermeneutics'. *Queering the Underworld* 'makes nothing more – and nothing less – than trouble'. Writers refuse to identify sexually; they shake off teleologies into which they have been enlisted and question the formation of homosexual categories for which their work has provided evidence. Look closer, and the subjects of historical knowledge only dissolve further from view. Yet despite their affinities, in thinking queer I would resist the nihilism of Herring's 'underworld unknowing'. He is right to suggest 'you will find no there there' if you are looking for recognisable regimes of sexual difference and normality.[23] Yet we are well beyond that point. Unexpected and often unimaginable, there is a there to trace in interwar subjectivities and social worlds. It consists in structured processes of becoming rather than structured positions – ways of seeing and being sexually that were overdetermined by class and social mobilities.

To make this argument I focus on two lives defined by their spectacular mobilities. Sydney Fox and Josephine O'Dare were born around 1900. Both from rural working-class families, they were further united by the bewildering performances through which they claimed the status of metropolitan Society. In London's West End, Fox moved with the mien of the Right Honourable gentleman. In everyday interaction such privileging secured social position and material reward, not least through fraud and forgery. From humble beginnings O'Dare rose to prominence: cultivating friendships with older men, insinuating herself into networks of female sociability and securing credit from upscale shops. Eventually her image appeared on the cover of the patrician *Bystander* and her Mayfair salon became the talk of the tabloids. Yet mobility was never one-dimensional. Regularly falling foul of the law, the parvenu trickster and vamp were put in their place (and prison) through sensational trials and rhetorics of revelatory exposure. Refashioned as confessing ex-crooks, Fox and O'Dare traded on personal notoriety and demand for the 'inside story', securing lucrative access to emerging modes of cultural production and selling their stories to the press.

I make no systematic claims about the law's importance as a site at which sexuality was constituted and contested, focusing upon these flashpoints simply because they generate rich sources to think queer with and because they are symptomatic of a particular moment. Fox and O'Dare might be considered what the poet James Laver called 'people of the aftermath' – archetypal figures like the flapper or unemployed ex-serviceman.[24] Historians have highlighted the proliferation of narratives of mobility after the Great War. Often focused around axes of gender or race, the trickster's or vamp's classed deceptions were equally prominent, often considered an outcome of postwar modernities.[25] In part, consciousness of such deceptions reflected the shifting concerns of the state and the news value of crime. Yet Fox's and O'Dare's mobilities were underpinned by specific social, economic and cultural circumstances: the penetration of consumer markets by transnational capital; the growth of mass consumption; the transformation of the West End into a demotic heterosocial space; the movement of mass populations through war and Empire. At

the same time, war, taxation and the consolidation of new forms of
social democracy challenged established social elites. Encapsulating
these trajectories, O'Dare and Fox moved in worlds characterised
by uncertainty. In a marketplace still governed by notions of trust
and deference, for example, West End outfitters extended credit to
the well-mannered customer, whether known, credibly introduced or
insistent on their privilege. Yet increasingly the penurious aristocrat
and silken-tongued stranger problematised that market and highlighted its expediences.[26] Lawrence Napper reminds us, 'it is easy to
forget ... quite how much of the fabric of British life was unfamiliar,
in doubt, or (at the very least) *in the process of establishing itself* during
the interwar period'.[27]

## Sydney Fox

Sydney Fox murdered his mother. He was executed for it – aged
thirty-one – in 1930. A former bank clerk and manservant, in and out
of prison since 1919, and desperate for money, he insured Rosaline's
life for £3,000 then suffocated her in the Hotel Metropole in Margate.
Introducing the *Notable British Trials* volume on the 'Mystery of Room
66', the writer F. Tennyson Jesse reflected:

> Vulgar as the crime was ... there was a flavour of the monstrous and hor-
> rible about it which appealed to the imagination. Matricide is something
> uncommon, but even apart from this obvious truth, there was some-
> thing so peculiar, not only about the character of the son, but about that
> of the mother, that the case remains to a certain extent mysterious ...[28]

While the case was driven by advances in forensic science, observers
were absorbed by the peculiarities of Fox's character and the difficulties of situating him within modes of social and psychological
classification. After the trial, all newspapers rehearsed his biography.
His execution, commented the *Daily Mail*, 'closes a long career of
crime ... [for] since the age of 13 [he] has almost without interruption
preyed upon society, though given repeated chances of return to an
honest life'.[29]

As Tennyson Jesse entered the debate over the making of a matricide she turned to emerging forms of criminological and sexological
knowledge. Self-consciously modern, this aligned her with progressive trajectories of penal reform that sought the origins of criminality
through scrutiny of the psychological and social subject: 'Fox was an

invert, and it is a curious thing ... that he was vain of his inversion. He could not bear even his own counsel to think that he had ever gone with a woman save for the money he might get from her. He took a pride in the fact that his pleasure lay entirely with his own sex.'[30] Tennyson Jesse fixes Fox within an essentialised 'inversion' that (borrowing from Havelock Ellis) is initially predicated upon the innateness, exclusivity and orientation of desire and the isolation of sexuality as an interiorised domain of personhood. Yet the coherence of her positioning is immediately compromised; the category of inversion breaks down as it is secured. Desire exceeds its bounds. Rather than stable orientation towards same or opposite-sexed bodies, it is defined by motive force – mercenary or pleasure-seeking or misplaced vanity – in a consumerist economy of desire. The elaboration of this definition moved between registers and inscribed sex simultaneously within sexological, social, gendered and moral classifications: arrested in 1919 Fox possessed 'rouge and a scented body of papier poudre'; he was 'particular friend' of 'officers placed more highly than he'; 'JD Cassels ... was certainly being kind when he said that accused "from his youth has known no other companion but his mother"'.[31]

Tennyson Jesse was the only commentator to engage in this process of identification. In doing so she drew together competing narratives, trying yet failing to hold them together within homogeneous categories of difference. During the trial journalists scrutinised Fox's body and behaviour for clues as to his character and occasionally fixated upon apparent transgressions of gender. The *Daily Mail* described 'dark hair inclined to curl and crinkle and a well-formed but effeminate mouth and chin'.[32] Shane Leslie remembered the 'angel-faced page-boy' who stole from his aristocratic grandfather: a policeman 'revealed to me a career squalid and terrifying ... [Fox] had lived a life with men of wealth who should have known better. He showed me his photograph in female dress with his beautiful eyes upturned to heaven.'[33] Personal accounts placed Fox in proximity to overlapping homosocial worlds. He would enjoy 'a drink and a run around the West End' with friends, visiting Rayner's Bar in Piccadilly then spending the night at the Turkish Baths.[34] In the Trocadero's Long Bar he met the 'inveterate picker up' Duggie Fairby – one of those 'impulsive friendships [that] tended to burst into bloom' around closing time. Fairby thought Fox a 'charmer' and told how he had 'got to know a presentable young man, bought him a good suit, dropped him and left him to his own devices'.[35]

There is an easy reading of these accounts – overdetermined by what we *think* we know about past sexualities and glimpses of something we *think* we recognise. It reiterates the emerging claims of sexology and repeats the process of identification in which Tennyson Jesse engaged. It opposes queer-as-being to a coherent norm. Yet Fox both eluded classification and called attention to its epistemological and ontological impossibility. An effeminate invert? Inspector Hambrook described 'a crafty professional criminal' – 'Sturdily built and physically strong ... with a quiet and convincing manner of speech'. This 'mask of innocence' was unsettling, but concealed a 'steely ... coldness [that] reflected an absolute contempt of his fellow mortals' rather than aberrant desires and emotional excess.[36] Contradictory descriptions render any easy reading of Fox precarious. Such unknowability is bracing. It is tempting to see Tennyson Jesse as the prescient 'modern' commentator. Fixating on the apparent familiarity of her designation, she *can* be subsumed into a genealogy of present identity categories. Yet the regime of knowledge she deployed had almost no purchase among interwar commentators. Fox was situated within ways of seeing which confound our expectations, abrade binary regimes of difference and normality and underscore the ineffable difference of the sexual past. To put it differently: the internal tensions of Tennyson Jesse's account should be taken seriously as a sign of multiple sexual modernities – consumerist, sexological, moral and social – rather than the contested emergence of modern (homo) sexuality. Kunzel reminds us: the 'homo/heterosexual binary was not only "stunningly recent" ... but ... also remarkably uneven and considerably less hegemonic and less coherent than historians have often assumed'.[37]

We can develop this argument by considering how the identification of an 'invert' dissolved through the conflicted processes of scientific knowledge. Fox regularly met medical professionals: he was referred for pre-sentencing report on five occasions after 1917. While this archive provides striking evidence of progressive penal practice, it is equally striking how Prison Medical Officers operated within a field of vision that effaced any possibility of sexual categorisation. They remained preoccupied with isolating the social and psychological effects of Fox's epilepsy – for which he claimed to have been discharged from the army and appealed for mitigation of sentence – and its relationship to character and self-control. While criminologists hypothesised links between epilepsy, crime and sexual immorality,

the central question for Medical Officers was that of criminal responsibility. Rather than symptom of sexual pathology, 'epileptic psycho-
ses' were considered temporary effects of an 'organic brain disease'
which 'may lead to anti-social behaviour'.[38]

The most detailed report came after Fox was examined by the notable psychiatrist and criminologist William Norwood East in 1922.
Then Senior Medical Officer at Brixton, East later became Head of
the Prison Medical Service and a driving force in progressive penal
policy, overseeing official studies of adolescent criminality, sexual
offences and the psychological treatment of crime.[39] His report
described Fox's offence (a confidence trick at the Hotel Belgravia)
then set out a biography under headings 'family' and 'personal history': military service; work in advertising; 'very bad' fits in school
and army; hospital treatment; 18s weekly wages and 8s pension.
Fox – living with his mother – attributed his lapse to the desire 'for
a change to break the monotony of being alone at the flat' while she
was away. Assessing the causes of criminality against the preoccupations of interwar criminology, East's questions narrowed: 'Does not
go in for betting – does not get drunk. Not mixed up with any girl,
shuns female society.'[40] Unremarked, such questions did not betray
an impulse to classify sexually. Instead they suggested how sex was
integrated into a precarious economy of character and control in
which youths were forever vulnerable to the temptations of pleasure.
Equivalent to gambling and alcohol as an indulgence of unregulated
desire, sex was disruptive and potentially dangerous. With desire
and consumerism entwined, youths might be seduced into crime to
impress girls. 'Shunning female society' did not mark Fox as transgressive, or speak to a notion of 'sexuality' as an interiorised domain
of personhood, or situate him within a binary of 'heterosexuality'
and 'homosexuality' – ideas that animated East's work in the late
1930s.[41] Instead it implicitly linked him to an undefined incoherent
normal. Under 'Condition on admission', East noted: 'Talks quietly
and rationally, memory, attention, perception, judgement and rea-
soning appear normal. Seems to have started a determined practice
of leading a criminal life and to follow his inclinations instead of his
social and moral obligations. No feeblemindedness.'[42]

'Normal' signalled East's appraisal of Fox's psychological processes
as typical and healthy. In 1939 he would define 'mental abnormality' as a 'complete lack of moral sense and attempt at self-discipline
in all fields of activity'.[43] Yet here his subject was rendered both

psychologically normal and dangerously criminal. East's report evinced the impossibility of classification. An early navigation of the imperatives of sexological knowledge, it prioritised personal responsibility and character's physiological and psychological foundations. If the urge to categorise was weak and unpredictable its diagnostic technologies were compromised. In 1930 Inspector Hambrook observed of East's 'case paper': 'the majority of the particulars ... – supplied it is assumed by Fox – are lies'. Whatever the claims of modern 'science', one falsehood could derail its operations.[44]

Here thinking queer – suspending both contemporary identity categories and binary understandings of difference and normality – opens up new ways of making sense of the porousness of interwar understandings of sexual and social behaviour. We might extend this analysis to newspaper and archival versions of Fox's life. Eliding social mobilities with troubling accounts of sexual meetings and desires, narratives like 'My Life Story', published in the *News of the World* in 1930, were overdetermined by class rather than sex and confound any notion of sexuality as a domain of personhood. Its narrator is an amorphous presence inscribed variously in psychological notions of the self-within, social and environmental circumstances and generic conventions of popular life-writing. The episodic narrative is driven by desire: unfixed and mobile in expressions and objects and shaped through historically specific contexts of wartime hedonism and postwar consumerism. Working at Cox's Bank, Fox is entranced by the officers he sees: 'These boys on leave filled every minute with gaiety and gave me the fever badly ... I went here, there and everywhere with them, spending more money than I ought to have done but "keeping my end up".'[45] Rephrasing East's emphasis on the disruptive power of unregulated instinct, this 'fever' overwhelms the realities of social position and possibility of self-control.

'My Life Story' is insistently sexualised. Yet it short-circuits binary oppositions and abrades coherent understandings of morality and transgression. Fox breathlessly describes his dalliances with West End performers like Billie Carleton in terms that invite both pleasurable identification and scandalised distance. Yet he is penitent in confessing his adulterous relationship with the older Mrs Morse. Exceeding the bounds of morality, unbridled passion threatened the sanctity of companionate marriage then invested with such resonance as the bedrock of postwar reconstruction. Morse would later describe Fox – corespondent in her husband's divorce suit – as a 'very nice boyfriend'.[46] Yet his desires were dangerously inscrutable. At a Southsea hotel 'Fox conceived a most diabolical plan plot to murder her. He made love to her, and she, not suspecting that his protestations of affection were only the fair mask of a foul mind, fell into the trap. She became infatuated with him' and named him beneficiary of her will.[47] Fox's appearance as a predatory rake exposed the incoherence of sexual classification and the limited resonance of the sexual modernity Tennyson Jesse sought to mobilise. His seductive charms drew men and women; they enabled his hedonism and propelled his fall from grace. An editorial in the *News of the World* framed his life-story: 'It is his defence that the circumstances, the gay life of the West End, an attempt to keep pace with wealthy associates and the patronage of pretty women lured him from honest rectitude to the ways and means of easy money not countenanced by the law.'[48] Desire is both aspirational and erotic. It animates a drive towards the sensory pleasures of metropolitan consumption as much as towards same- or opposite-sexed bodies. It is cause and consequence of a man's criminality.[49]

Desire is shaped, moreover, by an account in which same and opposite-sex attractions are equally compelling. Fox's 'wealthy associates' were key presences in the *News of the World*. Serving in the Royal Army Ordnance Corps he meets 'Colonel — ... commandant at a big auxiliary hospital in the North'.

> For some reason he took a great liking to me. I was young and filled with a stupid desire to move among those whose station in life was far above my own. This man took me to places that I had never been to before ... He introduced me to a number of titled and other people whose names are well known to the general public, among them the late Lord Lathom one of the finest and kindliest of men. This was my first peep behind the scenes of theatrical life, for Lord Lathom appeared to know everybody connected with the stage. In turn I was introduced to a number of beautiful actresses, and cultivated expensive habits. It was nothing for me to entertain one or other of our younger stage stars in those days, and night after night I was at gay parties with some of the most beautiful girls in the profession. I was seeing life at its fullest then, and it was all made possible by the money sent to me by my friend, Colonel —.[50]

Patronage secures entry into the glittering world of Society and theatre. Like Noel Coward, Fox comes under the wing of the flamboyant Lord Lathom and is drawn into the social whirl around his Mayfair flat and Lancashire estate.[51] Why? The generosity of his patrons is acknowledged; indeed, it is crucial in staging Fox's status claims. Yet left unremarked it suggests the absence of any reflexive understanding of the diagnostic weight Tennyson Jesse would later place upon it. Social mobility is animated by the 'great liking' between men. Yet the nature of that emotional bond is unstated and ambiguous – 'for some reason' – rather than specific and dangerous.

To indulge his 'stupid desire' for social mobility Fox claimed the privileges of social leadership through dress, demeanour and story-telling. A shop assistant described the Honourable Sydney Granville Lane-Fox as 'well-educated and of gentlemanly appearance'.[52] Roles and names proliferated: a businessman, Royal Flying Corps officer, man-about-town. Such claims were the material basis of Fox's mobilities. Unable to manage on a clerk's wages, he relied on the generosity of wealthier friends, borrowing money, accepting treats and being introduced to sources of credit. Eventually he fell back on crime. The *Daily Mail* reflected: 'He posed as an Old Etonian, and the public school manner was apparently so natural to him that no one challenged his claim.' Elusive and amorphous, Fox's 'natural' capacity for reinvention defied attempts to place him within a coherent regime of social classification.[53]

This preoccupation with Fox's mobilities extended across newspapers and police files. Fox first came to official notice in November 1916 – arrested, though not prosecuted, for stealing and forging cheques at Cox's Bank. Arrested in September 1919:

> Police searched his address and from correspondence and enquiries made Fox was suspected of being a Sodomite. He had been associating with an Army Officer, Brigadier General Holland, and other officers. The officer mentioned was removed from the Army last year, in connection with his conduct with Fox and another cadet ...
>
> It is quite evident from correspondence found in possession of Fox that he has been associating with Sodomites up to the time of his arrest. Among the letters found are some from the notorious Sodomite, Gerald Hamilton ... it is quite clear that Fox and Hamilton are very intimate.[54]

Fox is 'suspected of being' and 'associated with' sodomites. Yet knowledge of his *sexual* 'conduct' and 'intimacy' with Holland and Hamilton remains opaque; the notion of the 'sodomite' as a sexual *being* collapses. Instead the report foregrounds particular social connections and a troubling undefinable mobility. Immortalised in

Christopher Isherwood's *Mr Norris Changes Trains* (1935), Hamilton himself defied national borders, moving within the 'rarefied atmosphere of court circles' and 'Bohemian and fashionable circles' while being 'privileged to meet ... many ... famous crooks'.[55] Isherwood thought him 'deeply dishonest', a cynical adventurer recently released from internment for his pro-German sentiments and links to the Irish nationalist Roger Casement.[56] For police, such acquaintances evinced Fox's bewildering ability to move between putatively discrete social worlds: 'Although he was only a bank clerk it is known he was associating and dining at Hotels with officers of high rank in the Army and Navy.' Fox was arrested again in November having obtained £323 from Grindlay's Bank by forgery.[57] Inspector Goodwillie concluded, 'There is every reason to believe that most of this money was spent by him whilst associated with men of a higher social standard than himself, but who like Fox are addicted to Sodomistic practices'. This final clause was removed from the composite criminal record submitted to the Director of Public Prosecutions in 1930. Rather than solidifying, sexual practices were being *unthought* in official narratives of Fox's life.[58] Rather than diagnostic key to the 'truth' of the self, sex was both outcome and origin of social mobilities that could not be fixed. Rather than a function of sexual identity, sodomistic practices were subsumed into ways of seeing that emphasised processes of becoming: imprecise, mobile and fleeting in ways that shaped and shadowed the indeterminacy of modern consumerist identities.

There was much of Fox in E. H. W. Meyerstein's story 'Bolland', written in 1920 but unpublished until 1958. A fellow of Magdalen College, Oxford, Meyerstein regularly visited London's courts and watched Fox's murder trial closely. Perhaps he knew him: writing to a friend in 1931 Meyerstein commented enigmatically: 'snub-nosed English murderer is the best. What on earth does he mean by that? He cannot tell you.'[59] Meyerstein's narrative follows Reginald Bolland's metropolitan misadventures to consider the 'development of a weak nature under adverse circumstances'.[60] Arriving in London, Bolland has a series of chance meetings: the prostitute Georgette, drug dealer Roderick Ames and mysterious Mr Castle. Cultivating older male admirers, he enters a glittering social realm. Ames attempts to seduce him; Castle questions him on the 'modern' view which 'does not rule out passion in friendships between men'; Arthur Jacoby, the writer to whom he becomes secretary, declares his love.[61] Bolland is on the make. Mercenary and manipulative, he revels in ensnaring

Jacoby while keeping him at arm's length. Social power is attributed to physical beauty:

> The trouble with me has always been that I am attractive ... I draw people to me, they like to catch hold of my arm and put their mouths close to mine when speaking ...
>     Now attractiveness has its dangers, and if there is any moral in what I am writing ... it is that an attractive person is greatly to be pitied, for he does himself a great deal of harm by simply being what he is. No one has ever accused me of malice or threats, but it has been said to my face that I lead people on and land them in tight corners ...[62]

Meyerstein never fixes the 'truth' of Bolland's conduct. Insistently revealing its conditions of production, the first-person narrative disrupts chronology and identification. Bolland thinks it 'extraordinary how I have been able to remember details and the *concocted order of events*'.[63] The story anticipates an unstated catastrophe that has already happened. Bolland denies the 'reputation of a young blackmailer' and that there 'was indecency in ... any of my letters'. Yet denial signals previously absent possibilities.[64] While characters and couplings are animated by same- and opposite-sex desire, desire never stabilises around a recognisable homosexual/heterosexual binary. It remains uncontainable, coalescing temporarily around consumerist pleasures and social opportunities before being reconfigured elsewhere. After sleeping with Dorothy – 'whore' and confidante – Bolland reflects on his 'great desire to see a man'.

> I am like that. When I am with a woman, I yearn for a man's company and his sharp direct common sense. When I am with men, I say to myself, 'Oh you are bores, all of you, deadly creatures of fact. Give me a woman any day.' For a woman is light and airy, and charms you with her colour ... and movement ... This is only the instinct for variety, planted in everybody, but with me it is acute, and I am really unhappy unless I am switched off ... from sex to sex pretty constantly.[65]

Even after losing his virginity to Georgette, sexuality remains illegible:

> I was only a little flushed when I reached home, full of beneficent intentions towards the world and good hopes for the future. There was only one disadvantage; I had lost the card which until now I took for the ace of trumps, my bodily innocence ... The looking-glass showed no difference in my face. I expected a knowing look to appear in my eyes in the course of the next few days, but no; I gave up watching for it after three weeks.[66]

The feared knowingness never appears in Bolland's mirror; sexuality and sexual difference never appear in Meyerstein's narrative. Bolland's manuscript is unfinished. Any hope of closure is preempted by his mysterious death. Though the story seems remarkably frank, all we ultimately see are Bolland's performative status claims. Like Fox, these mobilities mean he eludes classification and reveals its impossibility. When Bolland and Dorothy discuss the importance of being 'true to type' he asks 'what am I then?' Dorothy replies, 'Oh, you're a joy-boy.'[67]

## Josephine O'Dare

Perhaps Josephine O'Dare was a 'joy-girl'. Portrayed as a ruthless adventuress, she and Fox existed within a common analytic frame overdetermined by the intersections of sex and social mobilities. By 1925 O'Dare was at Society's heart: social and geographical mobility collapsed in carefully staged dramas of her climb from 'Pig feeding on a Hereford farm to the glories of Mayfair'.[68] Moving to London, O'Dare claimed the privileges of elite sociability through elaborate narratives of aristocratic origin. She established a productive relationship with the press, aligning herself with the rhythms of patrician life through interviews and alluring studio portraits.[69] Her fall was equally spectacular: declared bankrupt in July 1926, the 'pretty Society girl' was sensationally caught up in a huge forgery ring alongside her former lover. Tried and imprisoned the following summer, her first-person life-stories appeared in *Reynold's* and the *People*.[70]

For most observers O'Dare embodied the sexualised vamp of popular entertainment. Of 'prepossessing appearance, coy demeanour and invariably fashionably dressed', she was 'as callous in the treatment of her victims ... as she is immoral and unscrupulous'.[71] Social mobilities were situated in her capacity to incite male desire. Just as Fox relied on male patronage, O'Dare cultivated 'lucrative semi-liaisons' and succeeded 'because she was countenanced by some wealthy and influential men whom her feminine wiles had ... ensnared' – the Earl of March and the solicitor Edwin Docker. The *People* invited readers to:

> imagine a slim dark woman of rather petite figure, with a small round face and fine dark eyes possessing an almost Oriental lustre ... and an enchanting little trick she has of seeming to lend her whole attention and interest to whomever she is conversing with ... [O'Dare has]

social tact amounted to genius ... when talking to an intellectual man she would seem the incarnation of rogueish understanding. Should she find it worth her while ... to receive the timid advances of some wealthy young fool attracted by her beauty, she would be half-reserved, half-flirtatious – the most desirable woman in the world.[72]

Orientalised and eroticised, elusive and amorphous, consisting entirely in surfaces and mirrors: these motifs coalesced in descriptions of O'Dare's 'personal charm' and 'winning personality' – terms that evinced an understanding of deceptive femininity as constitutive of disruptive mobilities and questioning of the possibility of social classification.[73]

If O'Dare was desired, so she was also a *desiring* subject – a social climber with 'absurdly extravagant tastes', driven into crime and dressmaking debts rumoured at 'over a thousand a year'.[74] The disruptive social and psychological effects of mass culture were seen as most problematic for young women. Impressionable and irrational, female consumers were considered particularly susceptible to the distractions of films and novels which fuelled unregulated fantasy and undisciplined desire and overwhelmed self-control. Yet advertising traded in these possibilities for personal transformation, selling cosmetics as mechanisms through which to achieve the illusion of fashionable femininity and suggesting that social identities might be secured through careful engagement with consumer culture rather than authentic and stable. O'Dare thus became a limit case for thinking about the everyday. Exceeding the bounds of the cautionary tale that framed them, O'Dare's life-stories reproduced an erotics of social mobility in which such pleasures were both celebrated and denied.[75]

In this context, O'Dare's conviction was narrated as a moment at which the lowborn vamp was put in her place. The *New York Times* promised to unravel the 'tangled threads which moved Josephine's life from labourer's cottage to Mayfair mansion flat, from country manor to forger's den, from Hereford to London, and London to Paris'.[76] Yet irreconcilable versions of O'Dare's life proliferated and the intermingling of 'fact' and 'fiction' rendered identity's 'truth' unknowable. The 'threads' of O'Dare's lives were irrevocably tangled and 'Trixie the land "grub," poor but pretty Trixie, the jolly country hostess – Teresa, the "innocent" in town ... Josephine, the sensation of a London season' coexisted.[77] These radical social mobilities highlighted a porousness of social worlds which cohered in the recurrent image of the 'Thieves' Kitchen in Mayfair'. Inspector Yarndell told the court, 'While she was entertaining in a perfect manner members of the highest aristocracy in the land in one part of her house, the lower part of the establishment was nothing more than a thieves' kitchen, the resort of convicted criminals and forgers.'[78] Defined by a notional social and spatial incongruity, this juxtaposition was illustrated in a syndicated report in the United States. Divided by an indistinct horizontal line, the elegant sociability of O'Dare's drawing room is nonetheless contained within the same silhouetted frame as the conspiratorial criminality below. Rather than bounded and discrete, underworld and overworld collapse. The chimeric O'Dare exists simultaneously within putatively discrete social worlds, her mobility drawing attention to the porousness of hierarchy and the impossibility of social classification.[79]

O'Dare's relationship with the press suggests complicity in her sexualisation: allusive and suggestive, life-stories like 'Men Who Have Pursued Me' anticipated the kiss-and-tell stories and cheque book journalism of the 1950s.[80] At the same time, O'Dare used the press to refute pejorative versions of her life. The *People's* 'My Wasted Years' admitted her ambition, desire for wealth and deceptions yet rejected allegations of sexual immorality and blackmail: she was 'a girl who loved money yet never sold herself for it'; 'I do not care for the kisses of men'; 'I have never lived with any man in my life. I have never had a lover.'[81] O'Dare attacked Society's corruption, echoing Evelyn Waugh's recent *Vile Bodies* (1930) and aligning herself with middlebrow respectability. At country house parties she found 'relations between the sexes ... so loose and lax that I felt revolted'.[82] Above all, O'Dare lamented her failure to find love: 'I had met the only man whom I have ever really loved, and the only man whom I would ever have married. But it was just not to be ... if it could have been so, then I should have been the happiest girl in the world.'[83]

Addressing the Interdepartmental Committee on Abortion in 1937 the feminist Stella Browne remarked, 'I know it is a dreadful confession, but I have never met the normal woman. I have seen a lot about her in print, and heard a lot ... but I have never met her.' Browne was reacting to the emergence of complex mechanisms for identifying, isolating and maintaining the normal after the Great War.[84] In Charlotte Haldane's *Motherhood and Its Enemies* (1927), such preoccupations informed an elaborate typology:

one can discern today the following types of female psychology: there is the ordinary normal woman who, on attaining maturity, mates and bears children. There is the fundamentally normal type, who for some reason fails to mate or to bear, and in whom the frustrated instincts seek satisfaction in a less straightforward manner. There is the woman unwilling to bear children, largely a product of civilization, who, whether she be deified or prostituted, is prepared to gratify masculine desire, provided that she may avoid childbearing and may cultivate or express her own 'personality.' There is the amateur prostitute. We have also to remember the very large number of women who, owing to the present organization of society, play an increasing part in it, and who, through ill-health or undernourishment chiefly caused by their economic situation, have failed to develop a normal sex-life. Finally, there are the women whose psychology is in greater or less degree masculine, and in whom there is a strong latent or expressed antagonism to the prescribed activities of femininity.

The detail of Haldane's schema is striking. So is the elasticity and incoherence of the 'normal' she unsuccessfully tries to fix. It is articulated through competing registers of the commonsensical and the moral, in realms of gender and sexual behaviour, as product of particular social and economic circumstances and individuated psychopathology. Each of the positions Haldane seeks to isolate bleeds into the next such that their existence as discrete 'types' (let alone *psychological* types) is insecure. This polyvalent typology marks a refusal of what could be termed 'heterosexuality' as a mode of categorisation of different-sex relations and the absence of binaries of normal and non-normative.[85]

Thinking queer, we might set O'Dare against Haldane's typology. With one exception (the 'ordinary normal woman') O'Dare was everywoman. Narratives of her life moved across each position Haldane sought to establish as bounded and distinct – suggesting both the fictive nature of this mode of categorisation and the impossibility of categorisation itself. Dismissed as a duplicitous vamp, O'Dare's self-fashionings nonetheless reflected the imperatives of mass culture and the precepts of fashionable femininity. Positioned beyond reproductive domesticity and modern love, she refused alignment with the 'amateur', reiterated respectable moralities and claimed the possibilities of romantic fulfilment. This sexual subject remained elusive. In a confidential report, Inspector Yarndell described his courtroom meeting with Louis Millett, O'Dare's wealthy lover: '[H]e voluntarily approached me and said that "O'Dare" was a woman more to be pitied than blamed and that so far as her moral character was concerned she was virgo intacta and even went so far as to suggest a medical establishment to establish this.'[86] Yarndell had 'no faith in Millett', describing him as 'the suave and slimey type', yet was forced to confront the difficulty of placing O'Dare within coherent systems of classification. Moral and scientific regimes of knowledge intersected and conflicted:

> [O'Dare] stated that she had never been the mistress of any man, but this … is as untrue as it is absurd. She has, in fact, cohabited with a number of men, among whom are … [William George] Davis, Guy Hart … and Louis Millett whose signed statement that he lived with her as Mrs Millett at three different addresses in London (where on more than one occasion they have been seen in bed together) is in our possession. I am told, on good authority however, that O'Dare represents one of those unusual cases infrequently met where it is difficult to definitely say whether or not she is 'virgo intacta'.[87]

Claim and counterclaim rendered O'Dare unknowable. Mayfair gossip was parsed as 'facts' that allowed O'Dare's claimed chastity to be deemed 'absurd'; Millet's 'signed statement' attesting to their cohabitation was elided with an unattributed claim that he and O'Dare had been seen in bed; O'Dare's body refused to be legible to medical scrutiny. Established on unidentified 'good authority', her elastic hymen made it impossible to establish the embodied fact of sexual immorality. This 'strange, imperious and beautiful vampire' retained an 'intriguing air of mystery' that we should accept on its own terms.[88] As Doan suggests, 'the distinctive calibrations of [past] hetero-relations are lost if we assume an equivalence to a later formulation that sexologists, psychologists, and eventually the general public would locate predominantly within a binary logic of normal and abnormal'.[89]

## Plausibility and parasexuality

There is one term that recurs around the lives upon which this chapter has focused: it is the characterisation of O'Dare and Fox as *plausible*. E. H. W. Meyerstein described Fox's voice as of the 'acquired genteel type' yet still considered his 'personality … as expressed by the word "plausible"'.[90] Plausibility provided a way of making sense of the social mobilities in which Fox and O'Dare consisted. It was a containing term – a term that denoted a distrust of surfaces, a radical uncertainty of identification and the impossibility of classification itself. While apparently convincing, the plausible rogue was never quite what they seemed. Figured as a site of profound social and cultural disturbance, plausibility invoked and evoked the trickster's dangerous charms, the vamp's seductive allure and the mobilities such practices enabled. Thinking queer, we might draw attention to the points of convergence between the social and the sexual – formations that, I argue, possessed close affinity between the wars. Akin to Peter Bailey's notion of parasexuality, plausibility can be understood as 'a new form of open yet licit sexuality'. Rather than 'another exclusive territory' (queer-as-being), the identifications it enabled consisted in 'an extensive ensemble of sites, practices and occasions that mediate across the frontiers of the putative public/private divide' and were embodied in 'enhanced yet distanced' modes of self-fashioning. Plausibility, in this reading, crystallises the social practices and cultural forms animating O'Dare's and Fox's lives.[91]

Let me be clear: plausibility did not signal a move across boundaries between real and fake. Neither did it signal a kind of passing in which the deceptive subject successfully masqueraded as something they were not. No – plausibility gestured towards the fictive and incoherent nature of systems of social and sexual classification and identification. It resonates with Neil Bartlett's notion of forgery: 'to make a copy, a fake which, when detected, alarmingly reveals that a fake has just as much life, as much validity, as the real thing'. Thinking queer we might consider how plausibility's operations exceeded and disrupted systematic forms of knowledge and drew attention to the absence of fixed boundaries and oppositions that included those between fake and real. Despite the rhetoric of exposure within which O'Dare's and Fox's trials were figured, the fluidity of identification made it impossible to establish coherence and certainty. Society beauty and gentleman: each demonstrated the precarious and problematic nature of status claims and exposed class and character as arbitrary and attainable.[92] Rather than working with established associations between queerness, alterity and transgression, my approach highlights the 'elasticity, mobility and plasticity of norms and institutions'.[93] Close attention to competing regimes of state, culture and market underscores the definitional uncertainty and constructedness of emerging forms of governance that cannot be subsumed under sprawling notions of 'heteronormativity'. More than this, O'Dare and Fox were defined by mobilities that rendered them unknowable (hence threatening and intriguing) to contemporaries and revealed the indeterminacy of identity within broader crises of social relations. The moment we embark on the task of locating the 'real' biographical individual we are doomed to failure; the moment we attempt to isolate the 'sexuality' of past actors we reiterate inappropriate restrictive binaries. Far better to explore the possibilities of a critical historical practice that accepts 'an irreducible dimension of opacity' and considers the particular forms, practices and processes that animated their mobilities and which generate new ways of thinking about interwar Britain. This is what I mean by thinking queer.[94]

## Notes

1 Lee Edelman, *No Future: Queer Theory and the Death Drive* (Durham, NC: Duke University Press, 2004), p. 17; Laura Doan, *Disturbing Practices: History, Sexuality and Women's Experience of Modern War, 1914–1918* (Chicago: University of Chicago Press, 2013).

2 On queer theory see Donald Hall, *Queer Theories* (Houndmills, Basingstoke: Palgrave Macmillan, 2003); Annamarie Jagose, *Queer Theory: An Introduction* (New York: New York University Press, 2006).

3 Different versions of this project include Jeffrey Weeks, *Coming Out: Homosexual Politics in Britain from the Nineteenth Century to the Present* (London: Quartet Books, 1990); Hugh David, *On Queer Street: A Social History of British Homosexuality, 1895–1995* (London: HarperCollins, 1997).

4 Chris Waters, 'Distance and desire in the new British queer history', *GLQ*, 14:1 (2007), 139–55. Waters discusses H. G. Cocks, *Nameless Offences: Homosexual Desire in the Nineteenth Century* (London: I. B. Tauris, 2003); Matt Cook, *London and the Culture of Homosexuality, 1885–1914* (Cambridge: Cambridge University Press, 2003); Matt Houlbrook, *Queer London: Perils and Pleasures in the Sexual Metropolis, 1918–57* (Chicago: University of Chicago Press, 2005); Morris Kaplan, *Sodom on the Thames: Sex, Love and Scandal in Wilde Times* (Ithaca: Cornell University Press, 2005).

5 Seth Koven, *Slumming: Social and Sexual Politics in Victorian London* (Princeton: Princeton University Press, 2004); Stephanie Newell, *The Forger's Tale: The Search for Odeziaku* (Athens: Ohio University Press, 2006); James Vernon, 'For some queer reason: The trials and tribulations of Colonel Barker's masquerade in interwar London', *Signs*, 26:1

(2000), 37–62; Patrick O'Malley, 'Epistemology of the cloister: Victorian England's queer Catholicism', *GLQ*, 15:4 (2009), 535–64.

6 Robert Graves and Alan Hodge, *The Long Week-End: A Social History of Great Britain, 1918–39* (London: Penguin, 1971); Richard Overy, *The Morbid Age: Britain and the Crisis of Civilization, 1919–39* (London: Penguin, 2010); Susan Kingsley Kent, *Aftershocks: Politics and Trauma in Britain, 1918–31* (Houndmills, Basingstoke: Palgrave Macmillan, 2009).

7 Carla Freccero, 'Queer times', *South Atlantic Quarterly*, 106:3 (2007), 485.

8 Sharon Marcus, *Between Women: Friendship, Desire and Marriage in Victorian England* (Princeton: Princeton University Press, 2007), p. 13.

9 My formulation reworks Gayle Rubin's 'Thinking sex: Notes for a radical theory of the politics of sexuality', in Carole Vance (ed.), *Pleasure and Danger: Exploring Female Sexuality* (London: Routledge, 1984), p. 267.

10 James Vernon, *Hunger: A Modern History* (Cambridge, MA: Harvard University Press, 2007), p. 13.

11 David Halperin, *Saint Foucault: Towards a Gay Hagiography* (Oxford: Oxford University Press, 1995), p. 62.

12 Elizabeth Stephens, 'Sex as a normalising technology: Early twentieth-century public sex education campaigns', *Psychology and Sexuality*, 1:3 (2010), 263.

13 Regina Kunzel, *Criminal Intimacy: Prison and the Uneven History of Modern American Sexuality* (Chicago: University of Chicago Press, 2008), pp. 2, 4, 6.

14 Valerie Traub, *The Renaissance of Lesbianism in Early Modern England* (Cambridge: Cambridge University Press, 2002), p. 13. See also Halperin, *How to Do the History of Homosexuality* (Chicago: University of Chicago Press, 2002). Alternative versions of 'queer time' foreground the anachronism necessary to 'porous, permeable pasts and futures'. See Carla Freccero, *Queer/Early/Modern* (Durham, NC: Duke University Press, 2006), p. 69.

15 Joan Scott, 'Storytelling', *History and Theory*, 50:2 (2011), 205.

16 Scott, 'History-writing as critique', in Keith Jenkins, Sue Morgan and Alan Munslow (eds), *Manifestos for History* (London: Routledge, 2007), pp. 34–5. See Claire Potter, 'Queer Hoover: Sex, lies, and political history', *Journal of the History of Sexuality*, 15:3 (2006), 355–81; Shruti Kapila, 'Masculinity and madness: Princely personhood and colonial sciences of the mind in western India, 1871–1940', *Past and Present*, 187:1 (2005), 121–56.

17 Lauren Berlant, 'What does it matter who one is?', *Critical Inquiry*, 34:1 (2007), 1–4.

18 Freccero, 'Queer times', 487.

19 Leela Gandhi, *Affective Communities: Anticolonial Thought, Fin-de-Siècle*

*Radicalism and the Politics of Friendship* (Durham, NC: Duke University Press, 2006), pp. 11, 35, 47, 49; Sean Brady, *Masculinity and Male Homosexuality in Britain, 1861–1913* (Houndmills, Basingstoke: Palgrave Macmillan, 2005); Charles Upchurch, *Before Wilde: Sex between Men in Britain's Age of Reform* (Berkeley: University of California Press, 2009); Emma Vickers, 'Queer sex in the metropolis? Place, subjectivity and the Second World War', *Feminist Review*, 96 (2010), 58–73; Timothy Jones, 'The stained glass closet: Celibacy and homosexuality in the Church of England to 1955', *Journal of the History of Sexuality*, 20:1 (2011), 132–52; Brian Lewis, 'The queer life and afterlife of Roger Casement', *Journal of the History of Sexuality*, 14:4 (2005), 363–82.

20 Justin Bengry, 'Courting the pink pound: *Men Only* and the queer consumer, 1935–39', *History Workshop Journal*, 68 (2009), 123. Compelling recent queer work includes Christopher Reed, 'Design for (queer) living: Sexual identity, performance, and decor in British *Vogue*, 1922–1926', *GLQ*, 12:3 (2006), 385; Jane Shaw, *Octavia, Daughter of God: The Story of a Female Messiah and Her Followers* (London: Jonathan Cape, 2011); Cocks, 'The discovery of Sodom, 1851', *Representations*, 112:1 (2010), 1–26; Richard Hornsey, *The Spiv and the Architect: Unruly Life in Postwar London* (Minneapolis: University of Minnesota Press, 2010); Elizabeth Darling, 'Finella, Mansfield Forbes, Raymond McGrath and modernist architecture in Britain', *Journal of British Studies*, 50:1 (2011), 125–55.

21 Houlbrook, *Queer London*, pp. 131–3.

22 'Photographs taken by the police', *Reynold's* (27 March 1927); 'Police photographs', *Reynold's* (3 April 1927); National Archives (hereafter TNA), CRIM/1/387, Result of Final Appeal, 28 March 1927.

23 Scott Herring, *Queering the Underworld: Slumming, Literature and the Undoing of Lesbian and Gay History* (Chicago: University of Chicago Press, 2007), pp. 14, 21, 147.

24 Ronald Blythe, *The Great Illusion: England in the Twenties and Thirties* (London: Phoenix, 2001), p. 15.

25 Vernon, 'Some queer reason'; Lucy Bland, 'White women and men of colour: Miscegenation fears in Britain after the Great War', *Gender and History*, 17:1 (2005), 29–61; Alison Oram, *'Her Husband was a Woman!' Women's Gender Crossing and Modern British Popular Culture* (London: Routledge, 2007); Angus McLaren, 'Smoke and mirrors: Willy Clarkson and the role of disguises in interwar England', *Journal of Social History*, 40:3 (2007), 597–618.

26 John Goodwin, *Sidelights on Criminal Matters* (London: Hutchinson, 1923), p. 127.

27 Lawrence Napper, *British Cinema and Middlebrow Culture in the Interwar Years* (Exeter: University of Exeter Press, 2009), pp. 7–8. This resonates with recent work on sexualities: Paul Deslandes, 'Curing mind and

body in the heart of the Canadian Rockies: Empire, sexual scandal and the reclamation of masculinity, 1880s–1920s', *Gender and History*, 21:2 (2009), 358–79; Kate Fisher, *Birth Control, Sex and Marriage in Britain, 1918–60* (Oxford: Oxford University Press, 2006).

28  F. Tennyson Jesse, *The Trial of Sidney [sic] Harry Fox* (Edinburgh: William Hodge, 1934), p. 1. Tennyson Jesse's other work included *The Trial of Madeleine Smith* (Edinburgh: William Hodge, 1927) and *Murder and Its Motives* (London: William Heinemann, 1924).

29  'A revolting crime', *Daily Mail* (22 March 1930); 'Vanity of "Lord Fauntleroy"', *Sunday Dispatch* (23 March 1930). For forensic evidence see 'The room 66 mystery', *East Kent Times* (1 February 1930).

30  Jesse, *Trial*, p. 3.

31  *Ibid.*, pp. 7–8.

32  'Fox on Trial for Mother's Murder', *Daily Mail* (13 March 1930).

33  Shane Leslie, *The Film of Memory* (London: Michael Joseph, 1938), p. 107.

34  TNA, MEPO/3/862, Item 56, Charles Campbell, 18 November 1929; Item 59, Alfred Lupson, 26 November 1929.

35  Emlyn Williams, *Emlyn: An Early Autobiography 1927–1935* (London: Penguin, 1973), pp. 151–2, 204.

36  Walter Hambrook, *Hambrook of the Yard* (London: Robert Hale, 1937), pp. 213–14.

37  Kunzel, *Criminal Intimacy*, p. 237.

38  See William Norwood East and W. H. Hubert, *Report on the Psychological Treatment of Crime* (London: HMSO, 1939), pp. 5–6, 33, 87; East, *Medical Aspects of Crime* (London: J&A Churchill, 1936), pp. 340, 382. On Fox see TNA, HO/144/17767, W. K. Watson, 24 December 1919; 394847/1, Sydney Fox, 3 November 1919.

39  East stressed the importance of social *and* psychological knowledge in understanding crime: 'personality' reflected complex interactions between unconscious, emotions and environment. East, *An Introduction to Forensic Psychiatry in the Criminal Courts* (London: J&A Churchill, 1927); East, *The Adolescent Criminal: A Medic-Sociological Study of 4000 Male Adolescents* (London: J&A Churchill, 1942); East, *Society and the Criminal* (London: HMSO, 1949); East, *Sexual Offenders* (London: Deslile, 1955).

40  TNA, MEPO/3/862, Minute 44l, 10 April 1922.

41  East, *Psychological Treatment of Crime*, p. 165.

42  TNA, MEPO/3/862, Minute 44l, 10 April 1922. This echoed the emphasis on the 'inherited instincts and their associated emotions' in East, *The Relation of the Skull and Brain to Crime* (London: Oliver and Boyd, 1928), pp. 26–7.

43  East, *Psychological Treatment of Crime*, p. 35.

44  TNA, MEPO/3/862, Minute 44b, CI Hambrook, 31 March 1930.

45  'My life story', *News of the World* (30 March 1930).

46  'Sydney Fox executed', *Illustrated Police News* (17 April 1930).

47  Hambrook, *Hambrook of the Yard*, p. 41.

48  'My life story', *News of the World* (30 March 1930).

49  Anna Clark, *Desire: A History of European Sexuality* (London and New York: Routledge, 2008), p. 10.

50  'My life story', *News of the World* (23 March 1930).

51  Richard Huggett, *Binkie Beaumont: Eminence Grise of the West End Theatre: 1933–1973*, (London: Hodder and Stoughton, 1989); Philip Hoare, *Noel Coward: A Biography* (London: Sinclair Stevenson, 1995).

52  TNA, MEPO/3/862, Item 4, PS Goodwillie, 4 September 1919.

53  'Fox's shudder', *Daily Mail* (22 March 1930).

54  TNA, MEPO/3/862, Report respecting a case of forgery, 4 September 1919; CI Hawkins, 17 September 1919.

55  Gerald Hamilton, *Mr Norris and I: An Autobiographical Sketch* (London: Allen Wingate, 1956), pp. 44, 46–7; Christopher Isherwood, *Mr Norris Changes Trains* (London: Vintage, 1999).

56  Isherwood, *Christopher and His Kind* (Minneapolis: University of Minnesota Press, 2001), p. 76. Hamilton elaborated his claims in three autobiographies: Hamilton, *As Young as Sophocles* (London: Martin Secker & Warburg, 1937); Hamilton, *Mr Norris and I*; Hamilton, *The Way It Was With Me* (London: Leslie Frewin, 1969).

57  TNA, DPP/1/90, Antecedents, 1929.

58  TNA, MEPO/3/862, Item 4, Report respecting a case of forgery, 4 September 1919; Inspector Goodwillie, 6 November 1919; TNA, DPP/1/90, Antecedents, 1929.

59  Rowland Watson (ed.), *Some Letters of EHW Meyerstein* (London: Neville Spearman, 1959), p. 131.

60  E. H. W. Meyerstein, *Bolland and Other Stories* (London: Neville Spearman, 1958), p. xv.

61  *Ibid.*, pp. 34, 52–3; 64, 67.

62  *Ibid.*, pp. 75–6.

63  *Ibid.*, pp. 50.

64  *Ibid.*, pp. 25–6.

65  *Ibid.*, p. 87.

66  *Ibid.*, p. 38.

67  *Ibid.*, pp. 80–1.

68  'My partnership with Josephine O'Dare', *World's Pictorial News* (5 June 1927).

69  'The adorable swindler unmasked', *People* (5 June 1927); 'Miss Josephine O'Dare', *Bystander* (9 December 1925).

70  'Secret of society girl's wealth', *Reynold's* (19 December 1926). George

Dilnot, *Getting Rich Quick* (London: Geoffrey Bliss, 1935), chapter XIV, is a longer biography. For O'Dare's trial see e.g. 'Notorious crook gang unmasked', *Reynold's* (5 June 1927).

71  TNA, MEPO/3/441, Trixie Skyrme, May 1926.

72  'The adorable swindler unmasked', *People* (5 June 1927).

73  'The O'Dare case', *Daily Telegraph* (2 June 1927); Bechhofer Roberts, *Sir Travers Humphreys* (London: John Lane, 1936), pp. 218–19.

74  TNA, MEPO/3/441, Trixie Skyrme, May 1926.

75  Matt Houlbrook, '"A pin to see the peepshow": Culture, fiction and selfhood in Edith Thompson's letters, 1921–22', *Past and Present*, 207:1 (2010), 215–49.

76  'The adorable swindler unmasked', *People* (5 June 1927).

77  *Ibid.*

78  'London's cleverest criminal gang sentenced', *Daily Express* (2 June 1927).

79  'London's "Miss Jekyll and Hyde"', *San Mateo Times* (9 July 1927).

80  'Men who have pursued me', *People* (27 July 1930).

81  'Happiness always eluded me', *People* (24 August 1930); 'My wasted years', *People* (6 July 1930).

82  'What I saw at a country house party', *People* (10 August 1930).

83  'Happiness always eluded me!', *People* (24 August 1930).

84  TNA, MH/71/23, Minutes of Evidence at Eighth Meeting of the Interdepartmental Committee on Abortion: Stella Browne, 17 November 1937.

85  Charlotte Haldane, *Motherhood and Its Enemies* (London, Chatto and Windus, 1927), p. 134.

86  TNA, MEPO/3/441, Minute 26a Inspector Yarndell, 29 March 1927.

87  *Ibid.*, Minute 31a Inspector Yarndell, 22 June 1927.

88  'Country girl who duped Mayfair', *Sunday News* (5 June 1927).

89  Laura Doan, 'Sex education and the Great War soldier: A queer analysis of the practice of "hetero" sex', *Journal of British Studies*, 51:3 (July 2012), 641–63.

90  Jesse, *Trial*, p. 40. See 'A cunning and plausible young man', *Hants Chronicle* (3 March 1928); TNA, MEPO/3/441, Trixie Skyrme, May 1926.

91  Peter Bailey, 'Parasexuality and glamour: The Victorian barmaid as cultural prototype', *Gender and History*, 2:2 (1990), 148, 152.

92  Neil Bartlett, *Who Was That Man? A Present for Mr Oscar Wilde* (London: Serpent's Tail, 1988), p. 169.

93  Marcus, *Between Women*, pp. 21–2.

94  Kaplan, *Sodom on the Thames*, p. 270.

# 7

# 'I conformed; I got married. It seemed like a good idea at the time': domesticity in postwar lesbian oral history

*Amy Tooth Murphy*

Since the end of the twentieth century research on postwar British lesbian life and culture has commonly focused on themes such as socialising and the creation of networks, especially the lesbian bar scene and lesbian social organisations. Research into the history of *Arena Three*, the first lesbian magazine in Britain, for example, has provided evidence of the ways in which more geographically isolated women sought out connections and means of self-identification.[1] This focus is hardly surprising since the postwar period saw the most widespread creation of such lesbian communities in Britain to date. Although lesbians had of course formed social spaces previously, these were, for the most part, isolated nuclei – notably a tiny number of bohemian bars in London where lesbians drank alongside artists and prostitutes.[2]

The postwar period, in contrast, brought the emergence of coherent and extended networks that achieved the sizeable ideological leap of extending beyond urban centres. The bar scene grew in number and in visibility, particularly after the release in 1968 of *The Killing of Sister George*, which introduced the hitherto merely subculturally famous Gateways nightclub to mainstream cinema audiences across the country.[3] Elsewhere the media brought the theme of lesbianism – albeit often negatively – into the average home.[4] This general increase in visibility was aided in no small part by the efforts of the board of *Arena Three*, fronted by the indomitable Esme Langley. From the outset Langley et al. made explicit their aims to increase public awareness and knowledge of lesbianism. They pursued this agenda vigorously by engaging with the media head-on, all the while continuing to faithfully produce their monthly magazine for subscribers both across the UK and overseas.[5] When *Arena Three* eventually folded in 1971 they had so successfully aided the formation of communities, both physical and conceptual, that *Sappho* magazine and its various satellite social groups were able to step in to cater for the increasing demand.

Thanks to the groundbreaking work of historians such as Emily Hamer, Rebecca Jennings and Alison Oram, scholars of lesbian history now have a much more vivid picture of postwar lesbians' lives 'out and about'. Crucially this research has highlighted the great significance of this new availability of social spaces. In being able to formulate their own public spaces and their own networks within them, lesbians were able to conceptualise and configure their identities from an informed contextual position that had previously been unavailable.

Though 'private' in the sense of controlled access, all these means of interaction focus on lesbian lives in public spaces.[6] In contrast, the role played by domestic space remains comparatively absent from research. We still know little about how lesbian women lived their lives behind the closed doors of the home. Rebecca Jennings devotes a chapter of her book *Tomboys and Bachelor Girls* to lesbian domesticity but ultimately concludes, 'The narrative of domestic aspiration which contemporary cultural media ascribed to women in the postwar period is ... largely absent from lesbian accounts of their lives'. Note here that Jennings refers to 'domestic aspiration'. Her analysis is therefore intrinsically bound to the grand narrative of the reinforcement of the gender binary and gender-specific roles that followed the Second World War. By adopting this discourse of the domestic space as one that was complicit in perpetuating both feminine conformity and a narrowly defined scope for female 'achievement', Jennings necessarily perpetuates this binary framework of gender-appropriate space.

The historiography of postwar lesbian life, based as it is on documenting a drive to widen networks, formulate communities and increase independence and mobility, creates a hierarchical approach to public and private space and is therefore ultimately tied to the postwar heteronormative discourse of a return to gender appropriateness. Clearly the image of lesbians in public and community spaces is an important picture to reveal. Lesbians' desire to create coherent social spaces was a challenge to both homophobic and androcentric attitudes towards public space. It is hardly necessary here to state the role played by lesbians throughout the second half of the twentieth century in forwarding feminist agendas of female agency.

However, focusing so resolutely on this aspect of lesbian life has led to domestic life being obscured in the process. While it is true that 'domestic aspiration' for women formed a central component of postwar heteronormative discourse, it is also true that conceiving of domesticity as singularly heteronormative and restrictive for women risks the erasure of a multiplicity of lived lesbian experiences. After all, lesbians who frequented bars or who were aware of the existence of *Arena Three* still made up an extremely small number.[7] As lesbians formed new social worlds and communities it is important to remember that they did so within the wider context of their everyday lives. The importance of the home and the creation of domestic space must not be understated. Where did these women return to after work or when the bar closed? When their copy of *Arena Three* arrived in the post what lay beyond the doormat where it landed?

This chapter aims to open a small window on to the previously obscured area of postwar lesbian domesticity. In doing so it seeks to open debate into how we can situate and contextualise this fundamental facet of daily life within the existing, primarily public, historiography of postwar lesbian experience, ultimately providing a more complete and fully rounded picture of that experience. In order to delve beyond public spaces into the innately intimate and private space of the home I will draw primarily on testimonies garnered through a series of oral history interviews I conducted with self-identifying lesbian women born before 1955 and living in Britain.[8] Oral history as a discipline allows us to examine the minutiae of individual lives. Detailed investigation of how individuals construct their narratives can be hugely revealing as to how they understand their past. In making a tentative step into lesbians' experiences of domesticity in postwar Britain I am in no way attempting to present a big picture. Rather, through detailed textual analysis of a small number of case studies, I hope to demonstrate the various ways in which lesbian women have incorporated their experiences of hetero- and homo-domesticity into the overall narratives of their lives.

Roughly speaking, narrators fall into two camps: those who had previously been in heterosexual marriages before coming out (either having been unaware of their lesbian sexuality or having been consciously in the closet) and those who had experience only of same-sex relationships.[9] For the purposes of my analysis I draw a distinction between what can usefully be termed hetero-domesticity and homo-domesticity. By hetero-domesticity I imply marriage and its concomitant associations, a heterosexual relationship situated within and operating from a shared home. Similarly, homo-domesticity implies a committed and long-term same-sex relationship also situated within a shared home. It may seem obvious to state but, to date, the historiography of twentieth-century British lesbianism has mainly focused on women who were identifiably or visibly 'lesbian'. This visibility is of course how these women's lives have come to be included in documentation. However, it is vital that we attempt also to recover the experiences of those women who were obscured. Great numbers of women were entirely invisible as lesbians, being completely closeted or, indeed, not even being 'visible' to themselves, as yet unaware of their lesbian sexuality. But these women's stories are no less valid. In fact their stories are crucial in demonstrating the ways in which women transitioned into lesbian lives at different phases of life and by different paths. Therefore I will deal here with women who were actively lesbian as well as those who, for various reasons, did not come to live lesbian lives until later.

A comparison of the ways in which the aforementioned loosely defined groups narrate their recollections of domestic life reveals some intriguing differences. In some narratives of previously married women the spectre of hetero-domesticity can loom large, constituting an oppressive and restrictive institution at odds with self-expression and self-fulfilment. A number of my narrators reject their previously married lives as alien, a rupture in the narrative composition of their life-stories. For some women unencumbered by personal experience of hetero-domesticity, homo-domesticity constitutes a declaration of the normality of lesbian relationships. Analysis of case studies from across this range of experience reveals the impact of available models of hetero-domesticity on the ways in which narrators envisioned and created domestic spaces to foster and live out lesbian relationships. A relatively high percentage of my narrators explicitly referenced the lack of alternative models of domesticity. Within this cultural context it appears that women who did not have to reconcile previous experiences of hetero-domesticity with their lesbian selves and within their same-sex relationships were able to construct homo-domestic spaces in a less complicated fashion, seemingly mirroring heteronormativity. These women were unfettered by the tensions between a heterosexual life and a new homosexual life. For those women coming from a heterosexual past their narratives reflect a necessary process of working through change and transition, and a willingness to construct their new lesbian lives as different and distinct.

If we return to consider Rebecca Jennings's phrase 'domestic aspiration', clearly all of my narrators were creating their domestic lives, be they hetero- or homo-, within the context of a mainstream culture that ascribed value to a woman's ability to 'succeed' within the primacy of her domestic role as housewife and mother.[10] Therefore it is no surprise that so many of my narrators should make reference to such a model. Oftentimes this was in relation to direct personal experience. However, in some cases narrators spoke about perceptions they had held about what hetero-domestic life would be like. Formed at a very young age, these ideas strongly shaped these women's fervent wish to avoid marriage and everything that they were sure would come with it. Jean, Penelope and Nina's testimonies all demonstrate this anti-marriage ideology.[11]

Although Jean had no idea she was a lesbian until her late twenties she rejected heteronormative expectations from adolescence. Her attitude to men and dating was one of indifference. She recalls that even though all her friends were getting engaged and married she had no desire to join in: 'There, there always was this, the kind've, "oh, y'know, where's your boyfriend, have you got a boyfriend?" and all that kind've thing. And I used to never bother.'[12]

Jean did eventually date men, but their enthusiasm and persistence were always quashed by her apathy and refusal to see such relationships as anything other than friendship: 'I did go out with a guy [...] And I went out wi' him, and stayed at his flat and things like that. Em, not an, nothing involved, we were just great friends. Em ... an' he was one of the nicest chaps as well. But I just, knew that I didnae want, I didnae want that.' Jean never defines exactly what 'that' is, but within our interview it is implied that a definition is unnecessary. 'That' simply stands for the all-encompassing and interwoven responsibilities, roles and expectations that make up what it was to be a married woman. She elaborates slightly on what she perceived married life would hold when recalling another eager male suitor:

> And then I was going out with a guy from Caithness, [...] and he got quite serious but I couldnae cope wi' that. But, we were, again we were just great friends ultimately. He was wanting to get married and have six kids and I thought 'No, no, no, not for me, man!' [...] Em, and after that, [Puffs] ... Just kind've drifted really. But I just knew I, I was not wanting to get married and all that kind've involvement.

Note that once again she leaves a shorthand, 'all that kind've involvement', perhaps to stand for what I have here termed hetero-domesticity. Note also that it was not a realisation of her lesbianism that drove this rejection of heteronormative life and aspiration, but something much more vague; just an awareness that she did not want the model that mainstream culture had to offer.

Penelope and Nina speak evocatively about the restrictiveness they imagined would come with hetero-domesticity. Penelope, like Jean, was not aware of her sexual attraction to women when she decided she did not want to get married:

> P: I looked at all my friends as they were leaving college and they were all pairing up as if there was no tomorrow [...] [A]ll I knew was that I didn't want to do that. I just knew I didn't want to be getting married and, em, I knew that wasn't for me.
> ATM: What was it that motivated that feeling?
> P: Just a feeling that you would be dying inside if you followed that path. [Pause] I didn't know what the alternative was but I knew that I would die inside if that happened. And that I would probably be intolerable to live with. Because I'd be so angry, at being forced into doing it.

Despite the lack of any alternative models of living Penelope was clearly and resolutely unwilling to succumb to what she saw as the monolithic model of heteronormative conformity laid out for her.

Nina's story is somewhat different in that she recalls being aware of her attraction to other women from about the age of fifteen and embarked on her first lesbian relationship at the age of eighteen. Another marked difference is that, alongside a rejection of hetero-normative expectations of married life, Nina observed tangible possible alternatives presented to her at the girls' grammar school she attended. In the following excerpts she contrasts positive lesbian relationships between her teachers with what she perceived as the negative model of hetero-domesticity provided by her parents:

> [T]he staff were very kindly. And there were a fair number of lesbians on the staff. [...] Well History and Geography lived together. [...] The staff there were generally good role models. Because they were independent women, educated. Science and Maths definitely were [in a same-sex relationship]. And they kept a kind of eye on me. Y'know, they must have known what I was gonna be. And, um, were kind've quite tender with me, in that they looked after me.
>
> Cos, y'know, my parents' marriage, eh, I think I decided quite early on I wasn't going to marry. It seemed like a dire ... I felt women lost

their profession, and their individuality, y'know. And if I'd married into my contemporary ... group, y'know, male group, um, I would've spent the rest of my life bringing up kids; y'know, washing somebody else's dirty socks as well as my own, um, and had no profession of my own. Y'know, the woman came last in the family, so the kids would have new clothes but the mother wouldn't. So, and none of that would've suited me, and I wouldn't have been suited to it either. Y'know. I didn't have a, a model of good parenting so it wouldn't have been a good idea. Whereas the, the relationships amongst my teachers were, they treated each other with mutual respect. And they both had careers. Y'know. That seemed very enviable. And something I wanted for myself.

It is clear that one of the main motivating factors for Nina's rejection of hetero-domesticity was so as not to sacrifice a sense of self and self-fulfilment that she expected would disappear with marriage. Although she does talk about the positive relationships exhibited by her teachers, the aspects she focuses on are 'mutual respect' and that each woman was able to retain her career. She does not make explicit reference to any of these relationships as sexual. This is all suggestive of the idea that Nina saw more to draw her to same-sex relationship models than merely her sexual identity as a lesbian. For Nina same-sex relationships represented an alternative to the drudgery of married life and the dissolution of a woman in that role. Lesbian relationships offered emancipation extending far beyond the purely sexual.

Despite each being at a different stage in determining their lesbian sexuality, Jean, Penelope and Nina were all assured from an early age that the dominant cultural model of married life could only be stifling and suffocating. It was not overtly the desire for other women that motivated them. Rather it was the perceived oppressiveness of the institution of marriage itself. Lesbian desire came later, and fitted with an already crystallised decision to live life out from under the yoke of hetero-domesticity.

However, not all of my narrators were able to go against the grain so determinedly. For some women I interviewed the pressure to conform to social expectation was overwhelming, overcoming feelings of uncertainty, discomfort or even acknowledged same-sex desire. Such was the case for Linda, Mira, Laura and Hazel, each previously married.[13] In Linda's case the marriage lasted nearly thirty years. In Hazel's case she lived with her husband for only six months. No matter the length of time, each woman's testimony demonstrates the long-term impact that marriage and hetero-domesticity had on her and her self-identification as a lesbian. In the following excerpt Linda seeks to explain the socio-cultural context of conformity and situate herself as having to exist firmly within it: 'Well it was the social norm. You never thought of anything else ... that, that was the norm: you had a boyfriend, you got married, you had children.'

Linda alludes to this socio-cultural context at various points in her narrative, along with a refrain that the 1950s world she grew up in was 'traditional', with social convention instilling obedience. A crucial side-effect of this 'traditional' dominant discourse was that Linda could not conceive of any alternatives to married heterosexual life: 'I didn't have, I didn't understand. And it sounds stupid ... but I just had no ... no concept of lesbianism, as it would relate to me. [...] There was no role model ... There was no role model because people weren't open, in the way they are nowadays.'

However, other previously married women were all too aware of their lesbianism when they entered hetero-domestic life. For closeted women, the expectation to marry provided camouflage from the rest of the world as well as a hiding place from their own troubling thoughts and emotions. Mira was aware of her attraction to girls from a young age but soon learned to keep her feelings hidden for fear of censure: 'I think fear was the, the biggest thing ... Eh, because, eh, it was such a no-no. [...] But the, the, this fear of being shunned and, thought of until you almost thought of yourself as something unworthy, and ought not to have been born type of thing. Eh, just kept you, eh, very much closeted.' Her response to this extreme fear and internalised homophobia was to seek refuge and cover behind convention: 'I tried my hardest to conform, being sure I would ... I'd grow out of it. [...] I conformed; I got married. It seemed like a good idea at the time.'

The veil of pretended heterosexuality did not last long. Mira got married when she was twenty-one and was divorced by the time she was twenty-five. However, this did not immediately precipitate her transition into an active lesbian life. This was rather slower in coming, such was the force of the homophobic and heteronormative discourses she felt acting upon her. In fact she did not have a lesbian relationship until she was thirty-four. For the interim nine years following her divorce she lived a sexually inactive life, albeit protesting her heterosexuality. Laura's account bears obvious parallels:

I had to prove I wasn't. Rather than accept you might be. I mean it's a
different time. You had to prove that clearly you weren't. Um, which
meant just doing what everybody else did and going out with boys and
stuff like that. It was never very ... wonderful. But this is what everybody
did, and the reason it didn't work was ... you might say to yourself, 'It's
my fault', y'know, 'There's something wrong with me. None of this is
working.' And that was, when I got married I thought, 'Well ... we, we
seem to get along. So ...' – I don't know where I got that from because
we didn't!

These excerpts all demonstrate how each woman seeks to convey
to me, the interviewer, the dominant socio-cultural mechanisms that
propelled their journey into conformity and married life. Graham
Dawson's concept of 'composure' is now widely referenced by oral
historians to describe what happens when a person constructs
their oral history narrative within an interview.[14] It can be usefully
employed here to provide a framework within which to analyse the
narrative strategies demonstrated in these three women's recollections of hetero-domesticity. To briefly outline the usage of Dawson's
theory, its meaning is two fold. Firstly, during the interview process a narrator 'composes' her narrative. This highlights the act of
creation that narrators are involved in when giving their testimonies.
Dawson then invokes a second definition: that the narrator becomes
'composed', i.e. self-possessed and collected, through achieving the
articulation of a coherent life-story, and by extension a projected self,
with which she feels comfortable. Ultimately the test of the success
of a composure project is that the narrator is able to locate her experience within an overarching narrative that 'makes sense' to both narrator and audience. In the case of the above excerpts, each woman's
composure project relied in that moment upon her being able to
adequately convey to me the extent of the pressure to conform being
perpetuated at a deep and omnipresent socio-cultural level.

Achieving composure can be a tenuous and fragile process.
Dawson's theory posits that the narrator and the narrative are equally
dependent on the success of both forms of 'composure'. If either
or both of these facets is absent or flawed the narrative coherency
is threatened, as is the self presented through it.[15] This can result
in 'discomposure' when, for example, irreconcilable contradictions
appear in the narrative. Similarly, the narrative may simply break
down with the flow faltering and the narrative becoming incoherent. Narrators' responses to such discomposure can vary widely,

from becoming anxious, angry or uncooperative to attempting to re-impose order, perhaps by drawing on established tropes or cultural grand narratives.[16]

In dealing with the concept of composure and discomposure I wish to focus on what I term 'narrative rupture' – that is, where something at odds with the bulk of the narrative intrudes and disrupts both the narrative and the self the narrator is seeking to portray. Throughout the interviews ruptures occurred across a variety of topics but none was so prevalent and as pronounced as the often unwelcome intrusion of the theme of marriage. For women such as Mira and Laura the issue of their previous heterosexual marriages clashed with the testimony and the self they were composing, jarring the narrative. For these women, marriage presented a significant inherent barrier to the construction of a fully composed self.

In looking back at her short-lived marriage Mira is able to reflect from the standpoint of her present-day self, a confident, out lesbian: 'I shouldn't have got married in the first place. Quite happy to hold my hands up to that.' Taken along with her assessment of her heteronormative conformity, this suggests that Mira has integrated and explained her marriage within her metanarrative. However, there is a refrain in her testimony that serves to potentially undermine this apparent composure. Moving on to discuss the transformational period in her mid-thirties when she began her first lesbian relationship she remarks, 'Maybe I'm not the best subject here because none of me really starts till I was thirty-four'. With one seemingly minor sentence Mira effectively draws a distinction between two selves: the lesbian self she identifies with and recognises at the time of the interview, and an almost spectral image, hollow and faintly drawn. The 'me' she refers to is everything that the conforming Mira was not. The newly acknowledged and active lesbian self that emerged in that crucial life phase renders her conforming self unrecognisable and alien. As such she also deems it irrelevant to the life-story that she is constructing and conveying. By dissolving the heteronormative and conforming Mira and rejecting her place within the overarching narrative she also nullifies her marriage, her husband and their hetero-domestic life together. Ultimately Mira opts to cancel out her previous hetero-domestic life lest its impact threaten the composure of a coherent narrative which for her has become contingent on a composed lesbian self.

Laura similarly adopts a strategy of disassociation in her pursuit of composure. Like Mira she posits two distinct selves, one in the present and one, now unrecognisable, in the past. Laura married her husband in 1970 having met him at university in the late 1960s. Problems appear in her testimony when she attempts to negotiate a period of her life that is seemingly at odds with the general narrative trajectory: 'It was a weird relationship. Looking back on it, it doesn't seem possible. Y'know, ye kinda look back on things and ye think, "Was that me?" S'pose it was, but, em ... [pause] Just seems like another world totally.' Note the similarity to Mira's narrative as Laura refers to the 'me' she is attempting to convey at the centre of her account. She reluctantly acknowledges that the person she is referring to was in fact 'her'. But she effectively rejects this segment of her narrative as 'another world totally'. In attempting to relate this previous part of her life and this previous self she struggles to situate them both within the framework through which she understands her current identity position. Ultimately it 'doesn't seem possible'.

Therefore Laura is forced to grapple with the contradictions this life phase presents. Branching out from a discussion of her sexuality she also demonstrates that she and her husband were wholly incompatible in other areas of their lives. She paints a picture of his demanding personality repressing her development in much the same way that his heterosexual presence repressed the development of her lesbian identity:

> I don't think he was very happy with [pause] my political ... – in fact I know he was unhappy. [...] But ... he was quite demanding and I ended up, y'know, spending more time with him and doing what he wanted than studying, so I, I ended up with a Third.
> When I got married I thought [...], 'it'll be alright.' And it just wasn't. [pause] And part of it was to do with ... just had totally different views on everything. An' he was a bit of a bully. He liked his own way, and didn't like my friends, and didn't like this, and didn't like my politics, an' blah de blah de blah.

Any audience to Laura's narrative would not be at a loss to understand why the marriage did not work. Laura provides plenty of evidence to this end. However, by comparison she spends little time attempting to explain how she came to be married in the first place. Perhaps seeking to draw a tangible thread through to the present day she relates a recent anecdote: 'As my sister said to me the other day, "I don't know why you married him". An' I don't either. Maybe it was because I felt

so unconfident about things. Difficult to know really. Um, but I did.'
Finding no solid or satisfactory answer Laura is left only with the bald
fact of her marriage. In both Laura's and Mira's cases former hetero-
domesticity poses a threat to the continuity of their narrative trajectories and their presentation of themselves as out and 'composed'
lesbian women. In order to overcome this obstacle both women opt
to distance themselves from that which they no longer recognise or
cannot explain within the context of their narrative arc.

Moving from Laura's and Mira's narratives which bear obvious
parallels, Hazel's narrative stands out in the interview set for a variety
of reasons, many of which are directly or indirectly linked to a fundamental rejection of domesticity as a lifestyle choice. Hazel recalls
being acutely aware of her sexual attraction to other girls as a young
teenager and began having sexual relationships with other women
at the age of eighteen. She made her career in the Royal Navy, travelling the world and gathering a wealth of anecdotes along the way. An
accomplished storyteller and performer, she revels in a Jack-the-lad
persona cultivated to regale her audience with tales of sexual frisson,
liaisons, a string of sexual conquests and an altogether good time
had by all courtesy of the WRNS. Throughout this depiction she
posits herself as an active and virile figure, possessing full agency
over her sexual self and being comfortable with, even rejoicing in her
lesbianism.

However, the intrusion of her marriage to a merchant seaman at
the age of nineteen constitutes a stark rupture in this narrative of
sexual empowerment and assumed dominance. This is true not only
of the narrative in analytical terms or for Hazel in her composure
project, but also for me, the audience. Swept along by her vibrant and
engaging storytelling, I was jarred and even shocked by the revelation that she had previously been married. When it does emerge, the
effect of her hetero-domestic past is pronounced, manifesting in her
initial failure to make chronological space for it in the narrative. The
following excerpt sees Hazel in full flow, immersed in one of her
typically extensive and rollicking tales, in this instance recalling early
encounters with women. She is so caught up in this narrative track
that she completely forgets about her marriage, skipping over it. To
her amusement she catches herself and has to retrace her steps to fill
in the omission. I have included a sizeable chunk of the transcript
here in order to convey a sense of the narrative flow and also to give a
flavour of Hazel's usual narrative style and persona:

I think I was waitin' for my Naval interview or somethn', I cannae mind. But I got work at this, eh, office. And there was a girl there who ... I don't know to this day how anything happened because, ken? ... And we ... like ... clicked. Not at all intellectually the same, nothing. I wouldn't look at her now but, ken what I mean, that's just when you're younger that you see different things I s'pose. And ... we got closer and then we ended up, y'know, embracing and kissing, and I ended up living in there with her parents in her house. They didn't know anything, it was 19 [coughs] when I was about eighteen I suppose, whatever. An' it was never mentioned. But this happened. And that was my first encounter. And it was, it was very interesting and it was fine. Very enjoyable. But that didn't last long because it was, y'know, wasn't right for me. And then, I met a straight woman, and eh, [all laugh] I tried to de ... develop something but she wouldn't have it. She wanted my company but she didn't want any knickety-knackety, no-no-no! [all laugh] So that was alright. I only took her to the pictures once, I said, 'Bugger me, I'm nae takin' you oot again, if that's a' I'm getting!' [all laugh] So, that was another little, just a little adventure. But in the back of my mind ... Och, I've missed oot a bit! [Laughs] This guy, I went to the dances in Inverurie as I was eighteen, seventeen, eighteen. I met this guy, Jack. And we ended up getting married would you believe it?

Oral historians and academics working in communication studies have discussed how people employ common life-stage markers around which to orientate their narratives. It has been argued that women typically use domestic markers, such as births, marriages and deaths, which emphasise relationships, family and community. Men, on the other hand, may tend to use more individualistic markers, such as career progression or other personal achievements.[17] Using this set of criteria, Hazel's narrative more accurately conforms to a 'male' format. Positioning herself fixedly at the centre of her narrative she focuses on individual achievement and advancement in her career, always uses 'I' and never 'we', and generally tells a story of an active self, master of her own destiny.[18] Crucially, Hazel does not recount a single sexual relationship in terms of domesticity or 'partnership'. In this her interview is unique within the set.

Given this tendency towards a 'male' narrative structure Hazel's initial omission of her marriage may be partially explainable as a formulaic trope. Also one might argue that a woman being interviewed about her lesbian identity may not pay much heed to a heterosexual marriage. However, despite some narrators' problems in contextualising their marriages within their narratives, all previously married narrators chose to relate the experience as part of a trajectory of a sexual life.[19] Therefore it can be argued that Hazel's omission, apparently caused by a temporary 'amnesia' about her married life, stems from her marriage's function as a site of narrative rupture. In structural terms the emergence of the marriage threatens and destabilises Hazel's 'male' narrative of her individual and independent agency. Furthermore, it quite clearly destabilises her depiction of herself as a self-aware and active lesbian.

Having broached the subject Hazel then attempts to explain the inherent contradictions it presents, since she was aware of her lesbianism and was even engaging in sexual relationships with women while simultaneously getting engaged:

And that's the hard bit. People always say, 'Why the hell'd ye get ...?, I says, 'I can't honestly tell you. It was like fashionable I suppose. He was ... experienced, he was out and about. But I never let him touch me until we were married. Oh Christ, I wish I had done because I would a' never got married, it was such a horrendous experience for me. Y'know, the virgin, the virgin Mary, the virgin Hazel. And that's, that's how it was. I'd never, I'd been strictly brought up and that was it. And how Jack st ... stood with it I don't know, because he was a sailor. Y'know. He had a good free life. I knew he was! a drinker, a womaniser. [...] But I mean, we werenae compatible really. However, so, that didn't work and in the background was this bubbling thing about going into the Navy.

What little Hazel offers in the way of explanation is in fact reminiscent of the fleeting and vague answers proffered by Mira and Laura. 'Fashionable' seems like a curiously casual word to apply to a decision to get married and serves to underscore the inadequacy of the explanation. I would suggest that 'fashionable' might be taken to imply 'expected'. Again, this would link Hazel's account to both Mira's and Laura's.

One of the most striking features of the above excerpt is the abrupt shift in tone that signals the narrative rupture. This is more difficult to convey in written text as opposed to hearing the original recording. Hazel's normally jocular delivery gives way to a muted and serious tone as she seeks to portray her deeply unpleasant experience of heterosexual sex. She also draws a stark contrast between her and her husband. Jack is depicted as extremely sexually experienced whereas she describes herself as painfully naive and unprepared for her conjugal duties. However, Hazel has previously detailed sexual encounters she had with women that took place around the same time. While naive and passive in heterosexuality she is confident and active in her lesbian encounters. The two Hazels, by force of chronology, coexist side by side.

Clearly Hazel's brief spell of hetero-domesticity was an unpleasant one. The extreme lack of agency she conveys is diametrically opposed to her general narrative arc of independence and liberation. Her overwhelmingly negative experience of marriage rears its head at several points in the interview and in each case is accompanied by the same abrupt shift in tone and she is at pains to move the focus back to the composed lesbian self she seeks to portray. As I have said, this self is predicated largely upon a knowingly comical Jack-the-Lad or Lothario persona. Interestingly some parallels can be drawn between this Hazel and the references she makes to her husband. I want to make clear that she certainly never seeks to portray herself negatively as a womaniser or drunkard, etc. But the 'good free life' that she says he lived seems akin to the life she would soon pursue. In particular she would go on to be sexually experienced with women in the same way Jack was when they married. Her narrative is scattered with references to liaisons with 'hot lookin' blondes', 'bold little critters', 'wee smashers', 'pieces' and 'buxom lasses'. This 'good free life' that Jack possesses is explainable by the fact that he is a sailor. At the end of the section above Hazel links herself explicitly to this by turning to her decision to enter the Navy. In doing this she simultaneously reasserts control over her testimony by returning to the main narrative trajectory. This deft piece of manoeuvring allows Hazel to overthrow the rupture that so threatened her narrative.

So far marriage has been seen to feature significantly, either as a key life phase that has to be worked around or as a resounding cultural trope that narrators have had to work to exclude from their lives' trajectories. As such an overtly present theme its overwhelmingly negative impact is keenly felt, predominantly hindering and constraining narrators' composure projects and their attempts to articulate cogent lesbian selves. But what about those women for whom hetero-domesticity was never in the picture? Some narrators depict a world of exclusively lesbian sexuality, seemingly unaffected by the forces of a dominant discourse that so fiercely imposed marital aspiration on others. This lack of hetero-domestic infiltration enabled some women to more easily use their domestic lives as cornerstones of their narratives.

Jane and Betty provide two of the most fully composed and coherent narratives in my interview sample.[20] Their interviews are flowing, substantial, articulate and generally thematically and structurally sound. They both employ a generally chronological framework, often describing their lives in terms of a series of phases or eras. Both women also share in common the fact that they realised their sexuality at a young age: early childhood for Betty and around age nineteen for Jane. They were also active in that sexuality in adolescence or early adulthood. Betty met her first partner when she was in the sixth form and their relationship developed while she was at college (c. 1955). Jane discovered her sexuality when she met her long-term partner and a relationship developed in their first year of university (1963). Betty, in reference to this early realisation, describes herself as a 'cradle lesbian' while Jane calls herself a 'kosher lesbian', having never had a relationship with a man. Therefore both women come from a background of establishing primary sexual relationships with women from the outset. Unlike Mira and Laura, Jane and Betty were able to reconcile their feelings with their actions early in their sexual development. They are also able, in the present, to trace a narrative trajectory uninterrupted by seismic shifts in lifestyle.

Both women tend to break their lives down into temporal chunks generally delineated by identifying characteristics such as where they were living and what job they were doing. But, more importantly, these delineations also take into account the primary sexual relationship in their lives. In Jane's case she was with the same woman for several decades and she usually relates episodes in her life in terms of 'we' as much as 'I'. In Betty's case, she had a series of partners, often long-term, and these various relationships punctuate the narrative. In this sense both women fall under what has been termed a typically 'female' communication style, positing their domestic lives and their primary relationships as relational benchmarks for composition. It seems provocatively ironic that those women who have no experience of a heterosexual or hetero-domestic lifestyle should most succinctly demonstrate such gender essentialist narrative strategies. However, this phenomenon is provocative for the reason that it is more complicated than it at first appears and demands some unpacking.

I would argue that the very fact that these women have not experienced hetero-domestic relationships can be seen as an aid to their construction of their narratives around domestic markers. For some women hetero-domesticity directly inhibits the composure project by destabilising the unified self that a narrator must attempt to present.

Betty and Jane face no such obstacle. Having avoided hetero-domestic scenarios, their domestic anecdotes are unencumbered by unavoidable comparisons. Therefore their experiences of hetero-domesticity and long-term lesbian relationships are relayed from a position of relative narrative freedom. This in turn enables them to employ their experiences of sexual and domestic relationships as uncomplicated testimonies to their identity as lesbian women, thus forming cornerstones in their composure projects.

However, another layer of analysis can be posited which complicates the picture, challenging this concept of relative narrative freedom. Jane demonstrates a sophisticated ability to reflect on her life-story when she remarks that her relationship with her long-term partner was 'entirely constructed in, in heteronormative terms'. Situating her experience within the context of postwar lesbian life she raises a now familiar refrain: '[T]hat's because there weren't any other models. [...] For women who were born in the first half of the century, there were no models. They did not know what a lesbian should look like, or ought to be like, or talk like, or act like.'

As has been touched upon, narrators rely on available narrative tropes in relaying their experiences. If, as Jane suggests, heteronormative models were necessarily employed in order to conceptualise and live out lesbian relationships, it stands to reason that they would appear strongly in these narratives in the form of archetypal modes. In this case the influence of culturally ingrained heteronormative models can be seen to undermine the concept of 'unencumbered' homo-domestic narratives. Although neither woman needs to incorporate comparisons to personal prior experience of heterosexual relationships, their narratives must be understood as being formed in the context of a society that resolutely employs heteronormative standards as dominant and monolithic.

Jane's narrative style is defined by its sophisticated level of complexity and coherence, suggestive of someone who lives comfortably within her composed story. However, her concession that she and her partner's relationship did emulate heteronormative models runs counter to her construction of herself as an enlightened and educated feminist lesbian. The contradiction brings with it the potential to disrupt her composure project. But, as an accomplished narrator, Jane adroitly dodges that bullet. By devoting a significant yet subtly embedded proportion of her narrative to metanarrative reflection and commentary, from her position as informed and omniscient present-day narrator, she is able to deal with these potentially disruptive issues by seemingly anticipating them and dealing with them as they appear. This ultimately leads to a more fully composed narrative. The following excerpt demonstrates this sophisticated narration style:

> It's odd isn't it? Because the other thing that was happening ... was that ... apart from the fact that I'd fallen in love with another woman, everything else that I'd ever been taught I did and believed. So I thought you met somebody and you stayed with them for the rest of your life. So, weirdly, in spite of all the opposition and all the secrecy, and all the trauma [...] [A]t the same time I completely bought into the love, y'know, the love that lasts forever, the romantic, the marriage, I mean I, I thought of myself as married. I thought that I had actually done what my parents wanted me to do, which was to find the right person for me and marry them. And I was going to stay with them for the rest of my life. And the only thing that was sad was that I couldn't tell them, because it wasn't a man. ... So oddly, in spite of all the difficulties, I don't think I ever thought that we wouldn't be together for the rest of our lives. Um, and uh, I can remember saying things like, y'know, after we'd graduated and were living in a little house, cos my partner was, um, doing doctoral research, and I was training to be a teacher and then getting a job, so we went on living in Oxford for a bit. And I can remember, one night, saying, y'know, 'We are hard up, we're very poor now' [...] 'But you know eventually we will be better off than all our friends because we're not gonna have children.' And so I remember that because it tells me that I believed it was forever. It never crossed my mind that it wasn't. *In spite* of all the difficulties. And they were huge. So, really very odd that, isn't it?

If we turn to consider Betty's interview, she too presents as a confident and comfortable narrator with a well-composed narrative. Her testimony of lifelong lesbianism assists her in her presentation of herself as an informed narrator, someone who can speak from a position of experience and knowledge, both about herself and about wider social attitudes to lesbianism. From a starting point of early childhood signs of otherness in both her gender and her sexuality Betty goes on to construct a narrative which positions lesbianism at its core. As her narrative moves from adolescence to adulthood she uses this thematic focus to place emphasis on sexual relationships. Often she uses these relationships as situational markers for life phases. When college ended Betty and her partner entered the 'adult' world of shared domesticity:

> When I left college I, we got a, I got a job down in Sussex. We got a cottage, we moved in together. [...] [I]n a very remote cottage, in the middle of a wood. And I did teach for a while. [...] And, um, we had an acre of ground and we had a sort of smallholding and sold vegetables for a while when I stopped teaching. And we didn't know any other lesbians, whatsoever, in the whole world.

Note how 'I' and 'we' are almost interchangeable, another typically 'female' narration style.[21] Betty paints a picture of a shared life where what 'I' is doing is dictated by what 'we' do and vice versa.

As she traces her way through her past via her committed relationships, so intrinsic is Betty's use of 'we' as opposed to 'I' that the listener must be sensitively attuned to mark the transitions from one relationship to the next:

> [On meeting other lesbians and breaking into a lesbian 'scene'] Um, and really what happened was, in the, uh, mid 60s, we actually met some other lesbians [...] And we sort of then got into a little bit of a lesbian scene. [...] So we got to know some Americans. And we had – by that time I had found myself a new partner – we had a couple of other people we knew. We lived in Chichester by then. [...] And there was this women's group [...] We didn't really like it very much. But we actually met some other people who didn't like it either. So we kind of let that go but, and through them we met a couple there who we still know.

This is only a small chunk of an excerpt that ranges over several years, going into some detail about how Betty's lesbian world expanded. One of the most striking features is that frequent use of the word 'we', even more so than in the previous excerpt. It is clear from this just how strongly Betty employs significant relationships in order to orientate her narrative. But note the unusual feature in that it is not always clear just who 'we' is. There are, in fact, at least three different 'wes' in this short extract. The first transition is noted, albeit in an aside, but the second one passes unacknowledged. I interviewed Betty along with her current partner, Val. When Betty says, 'we met a couple there who we still know', confusingly the 'we' she is referring to is actually herself and Val, not herself and the partner she was actually with then. Through Betty's deft manipulation of the word 'we' Val is granted a part of a shared history. This technique or verbal slip, whichever you deem it to be, is actually very effective in giving the narrative a smooth and flowing feel, as Betty transitions from one life phase to the next. It also foregrounds the significance of partners in Betty's construction of herself and the paths she has taken in her life. Clearly for Betty these paths have been taken in solidarity and companionship with other women:

> [W]e've got a terrific social life. And it's all through who we are [being lesbians]. And it's been an absolute joy. I mean, I regard it as a, a complete blessing in life actually. Having had this, it's brought me wonderful friends and relationships worldwide. It's been amazing. So I have absolutely no regrets whatsoever.

For Betty being a lesbian is very much about the social and romantic relationships you find and foster. This recurring theme provides an excellent framework for a well-composed narrative in which partnerships give meaning to both life and sexual identity. The search for and attainment of these bonds gives Betty the hook for her narrative of self-recognition and identity formation.

Both Jane and Betty convey testimonies hinged upon lifelong lesbian identities, narrating life stories with centrally important committed homo-domestic partnerships. In this sense both narratives conform to a traditional 'female' narration style. This may seem on the one hand to be conforming to gender essentialist concepts, regarding not only narration but also priorities, aspirations and value systems. However, the fact that these narratives are built around lesbian relationships challenges this conventionality and lends these testimonies radical potential. This is especially true considering that these relationships were lived out against a socio-cultural backdrop of moral censure and widespread public disapproval. Although Jane acknowledges the adoption of heteronormative relationship models, the fact that the relationship existed and survived against this backdrop is proof that heteronormative expectation and pressure were not enough to undo it. Using the tools available to them she and her partner constructed a rich and full personal life bringing them both fulfilment and pleasure.

The testimonies featured here are only tiny snippets of lengthy interviews in which these narrators reflected on their lives as a whole. Domesticity was only one of a wide range of themes that emerged, one piece of the intricate jigsaw that makes up a life. And of course each woman's story is much more complex than I can possibly do justice to here. I have merely skimmed the surface of the range of ways in which narrators chose to deal with domesticity in their testimonies. I do hope, however, that it is clear that lesbian women's experiences of both hetero- and homo-domesticity can, with greater attention, lend insights to significantly enrich our knowledge of lesbian identities in postwar Britain. As has been seen, histories of domestic life are less easily brought to light and lend themselves less comfortably to a unified picture than, for example, formalised organisations and social groups. I would argue that the fact that we are, as yet, without an established discourse of lesbian experiences of domestic life in this period is self-perpetuating in inhibiting women from recounting their experiences of this integral facet of life. By widening our scope to incorporate these experiences more directly, we will, in the process, provide a space for such narratives to flourish.

## Notes

1 Key texts include Emily Hamer, *Britannia's Glory: A History of Twentieth-Century Lesbians* (London: Cassell, 1996); Rebecca Jennings, *A Lesbian History of Britain: Love and Sex between Women Since 1500* (Oxford: Greenwood World Publishing, 2007) and *Tomboys and Bachelor Girls: A Lesbian History of Post-War Britain, 1945–1971* (Manchester: Manchester University Press, 2007); and Alison Oram, 'Little by little? *Arena Three* and lesbian politics in the 1960s', in Marcus Collins (ed.), *The Permissive Society and its Enemies: Sixties British Culture* (London: Rivers Oram Press, 2007).
2 See Jennings, *A Lesbian History of Britain* and *Tomboys*, for chapters on the development of the lesbian bar scene.
3 Jill Gardiner, *From the Closet to the Screen: Women at the Gateways Club, 1945–85* (London: Pandora, 2003), pp. 133–53.
4 *Ibid.*, pp. 89–114.
5 See Jennings, *Tomboys*, pp. 134–72, for a detailed history of *Arena Three*.
6 Despite the relatively heightened profile of lesbianism as a real and lived lifestyle, it likely goes without saying that lesbian sexuality was in no way mainstreamed. Women wishing to socialise as lesbians were generally able to do so only in demarcated spaces, such as the aforementioned Gateways and other lesbian bars and clubs, or at lesbian social groups and clubs advertised via *Arena Three*. Similarly, *Arena Three* remained a subscription-only publication for the majority of its existence, switching to general distribution only in 1969.
7 Jennings reports around six hundred *Arena Three* subscribers in 1971.
8 These interviews were not explicitly about domestic life but were originally conducted as part of a larger project about lesbian life and lesbian literature in the postwar period. Therefore a range of themes such as work, home, family, relationships, coming out etc. were addressed.

In keeping with ethical good practice only first names are used and where other people are referred to names have been changed. Over the course of the project I interviewed a total of seventeen women from across Britain. Recruitment was, for the most part, via the 'snowballing' method whereby existing participants suggest friends and acquaintances to be involved in the research. This is a particularly useful method for hard-to-reach and minority groups such as this. It also helps to establish trust and rapport between narrator and researcher. At the time of writing, all interview recordings and transcripts remain solely in my possession. It is envisaged that either or both will eventually be housed in an appropriate archive so that the full richness of these narratives can be available to other researchers. However, there are no concrete plans as yet.

9   The use of the word 'narrator' as opposed to 'interviewee' is a methodological and theoretical position advocated by, amongst others, feminist oral historians as a way in which to privilege the authority of the information provider within the oral history interview dynamic.

10  Jennings, *Tomboys*, pp. 78–9.

11  Born in 1943, 1945 and 1933 respectively.

12  I have attempted at all times to retain the original speech patterns and dialects of each narrator, as far as clarity will allow. Punctuation has been used to convey the pacing and emphasis of the speech pattern as opposed to attempting to impose written English punctuation standards.

13  Born 1950, 1948, 1947 and 1939 respectively.

14  Graham Dawson, *Soldier Heroes: British Adventure, Empire and the Imagining of Masculinities* (London: Routledge, 1994). Also see Lynn Abrams, *Oral History Theory* (London: Routledge, 2010) on composure and related theoretical and methodological strategies.

15  *Ibid.*, pp. 22–3.

16  Some examples of discomposure and its manifestations can be found in Alistair Thomson, *Anzac Memories: Living with the Legend* (Oxford: Oxford University Press, 1994) and Penny Summerfield, 'Dis/composing the subject: Intersubjectivities in oral history', in Tess Cosslett, Celia Lury and Penny Summerfield (eds), *Feminism and Autobiography* (London: Routledge, 2000).

17  Kristina Minister, 'A feminist frame for the oral history interview', in Sherna Berger Gluck and Daphne Patai (eds), *Women's Words: The Feminist Practice of Oral History* (London: Routledge, 1991). See also Mary Gergen, 'Life stories: Pieces of a dream', in George C. Rosenwald and Richard L. Ochberg (eds), *Storied Lives: The Cultural Politics of Self-Understanding* (New Haven: Yale University Press, 1992). Also Abrams, *Oral History Theory*, pp. 44–5 and pp. 119–21, where Abrams recaps

some of the work done in this area and points out some of the objections raised against this kind of essentialist coding. Clearly much more work still needs to be done.

18  Minister, 'A feminist frame'.
19  Indeed for some narrators their experience of heterosexual marriage fits comfortably into a narrative of self-discovery.
20  Born 1945 and 1936 respectively.
21  As defined in Minister, 'A feminist frame'.

# 8

# The homosexual as a social being in Britain, 1945–1968[1]

*Chris Waters*

In Britain in the two decades after the end of the Second World War the social world of the male homosexual achieved a visibility it hitherto had not enjoyed, for the first time becoming the object of social scientific investigation. This chapter is concerned with the various professional practices through which that world was rendered increasingly legible between 1945 and 1968. It will address a series of questions pertaining to a crucial shift in focus that took place in these years, a shift from what many increasingly believed to be a narrow interest in the psychological anatomy of the individual to a much broader interest in the social dynamics of the group and in the larger social world the homosexual inhabited. When, exactly, did homosexuality first come to be viewed as a broad social phenomenon and how did this help to undermine – or at least to supplement – older understandings of homosexuality as an individual, psychosexual pathology? When, and why, did British doctors, psychiatrists, sexologists, social commentators and social scientists come explicitly to observe an important social dimension to homosexuality and begin to write about homosexuality as a *social problem*, amenable to social solutions? In this respect, how and when did the homosexual become the object of new practices of social management? How did the homosexual subsequently also come to be conceptualised not only as a 'social problem' but as a member of a 'minority', enjoying a distinctive 'way of life' that could now be dissected and mapped with some precision?[2] More generally, how can we understand the transformation that took place, especially in educated circles in Britain, from the view of the homosexual as an atomised and anatomised – and often pathological – case study to an actor in a complex social world, to an individual whose behaviour was as much rooted in society as it was in biology or the psychodynamics of the family? In short, what processes were at work by which the homosexual was constituted as a social being?

This chapter will argue that the process of uncovering, dissecting and mapping the social world of the male homosexual and his relations with the broader society took place relatively late in Britain, that it had scarcely begun before the advent of the Second World War, and that it led to any significant, published studies only in the 1950s and 1960s. The focus is largely on the male homosexual, given that the investigative practices and discursive strategies under scrutiny here can only fleetingly be seen to incorporate studies of lesbianism a little later. Furthermore, it will also be suggested that, as significant as these early postwar studies were, the extensive paradigm shift in sociological practice that characterised the 1970s, coupled with the advent of a more radical gay liberation movement in that decade, either rendered these slightly earlier works wholly problematic or tended to marginalise them or to overlook them entirely, erasing a crucial period in queer British history that needs to be re-examined and recuperated.

To say that the male homosexual in Britain had a relatively invisible social presence prior to 1945 is also to say much about the relative invisibility of the social sciences in Britain before the Second World War. To be sure, as we all know, there is a long history of social investigation in Britain, stretching back as far as Edwin Chadwick's *Report on the Sanitary Condition of the Labouring Population of Great Britain* in 1842 and Henry Mayhew's *London Labour and the London Poor* (1851–62). Nevertheless, the formal discipline of sociology came relatively late to Britain. While a chair in sociology had been established at the London School of Economics in 1907, there were no academic positions in sociology at Oxford until 1955 and Cambridge until 1962.[3] But, as Mike Savage has recently suggested, the formal establishment of social scientific investigative practices in Britain grew exponentially with the advent of the postwar welfare state. Savage notes what he terms 'the remarkable new role for social scientific research' in the 1950s and 1960s and explores the ways in which new investigative practices 'mined down to reveal mundane, ordinary life, in miniature', practices that were central to 'a broader process of building a modern, rational, post-imperial nation'.[4] Writing in 2004, the sociologist A. H. Halsey waxed lyrical about those earlier postwar years: 'My contemporaries and I were activists, full of enthusiasm for the reform of British society in the direction of the welfare state' –

reform that was in part to be brought about through the practices of modern social science.[5] And it was in that state that the homosexual emerged in the social sphere in Britain, initially as one of a number of problems of management – or, to use the language of the day, as a 'social problem' to be studied and dealt with accordingly – and shortly thereafter as a member of a 'minority group', itself open to the investigative practices on which Savage has focused.

Obviously the male homosexual had a rich social existence prior to 1945, an existence mapped extensively in recent years by a number of historians.[6] But in virtually all of the published *scholarly* writing that appeared before 1945 the homosexual merely had an atomised, psychological selfhood; the object of medical and psychiatric investigation, the male homosexual was rendered clinically knowable as a case study, the heightened interest in the individual and the ætiology of his desires coming at the expense of any interest in his social being. There were certainly a number of moments when the queer social world erupted into public view, such as during the trials of Oscar Wilde in the 1890s. Indeed, revelations concerning the existence of an entire homosexual underground were so startling at this time precisely because so little was known about it. Nevertheless, that world had not yet become the object of serious investigation. Even Havelock Ellis, who pioneered the study of homosexuality in Britain, retained and advanced the formal apparatus of the individual case study, which largely precluded any broader investigation of homosexuality as a social phenomenon.[7]

Certainly between the wars trial reports in the tabloid press continued to offer glimpses into an underground world of 'sexual deviants'. And certainly amateur observers bemoaned the lack of focus on the social life of the homosexual and set out to remedy the perceived defect. As Taylor Croft wrote, lamenting the near-exclusive interest in the individual as a case study, 'Even such handbooks as [Iwan] Bloch's *Sexual Life of Our Time*, treat these matters simply from the pathological and not from the practical point of view. They give cases of abnormal persons, tracing their lives from childhood, but they do not show these people in relation to the rest of mankind, they do not expose their organised activities in a modern city'.[8] Croft began to map the urban 'organised activities' of London's homosexual underground, but few followed in his footsteps. Even in the United States prior to 1945 there was little writing in the sociology of sex, according to Edward Sagarin, the 1950s American sociologist and homophile activist. This was in part because of the prevailing biological and psychological orientations dominant with respect to sexuality at the time – unlike prostitution, which was often seen to result from social conditions that could increasingly be studied with a degree of sociological precision.[9]

In Britain, prior to 1945, in the space not occupied by a social science that scarcely existed, any encounter with the social life of the male homosexual came largely through the accounts offered of it by the tabloid press. While interwar expertise focused first and foremost on the individual, especially on the 'homosexual offender', battling over the various biological or psychological roots of his 'condition', it was largely the tabloids that explored the social world in which the homosexual moved, rendering it intelligible in particular ways via a unique 'tabloid discourse' of homosexuality.[10] Centring on trial reportage between the wars and increasingly on investigative reportage after the war, the popular press presented the homosexual as a social being – not as a technical 'social problem' to be dissected with the dispassionate tools of modern social science, or as a member of a distinctive minority, subject to the sociological investigation of the group, but as a social menace, a member of a disreputable underground. Trading in an older language of sexual danger and moral panic that persisted well into the 1960s, the tabloids mapped the social realm of the homosexual, albeit within a very different set of cultural referents from those that were central to the investigative strategies of postwar social science. This would begin to change in the 1950s when, as Adrian Bingham has noted, tabloids sometimes sponsored and published progressive surveys of sexual life and attitudes in Britain.[11] Nevertheless, in terms of any explicit coverage of homosexuality, the general representational strategies deployed by the popular press remained at odds with the new understandings of the homosexual as a social being that were coming to the fore in the social sciences.

Fixed in the public imagination as disreputable and threatening, the social realm of the homosexual had been rendered such an abject space that few homosexuals who began to argue for legal and social recognition wished to be identified with it. When 'Anomaly' published his classic study, *The Invert and His Social Adjustment*, in 1927, he offered some passing references to the social life of the homosexual. Most of all, however, he offered a conduct manual that instructed his readers how to behave, how to be discreet, how to be respectable – and, most of all, how to avoid the social realm entirely.[12] Advocates of reform, like 'Anomaly', eagerly detached the individual from his social world, rendering him as the anomalous object of sympathy, a character worthy of pity and toleration; focusing on the dilemmas of the individual, they did not call loudly for further investigation into the social life of the homosexual. Moreover, such practices often persisted long into the postwar years. Even in the 1960s the focus of the newly established Homosexual Law Reform Society usually remained on the plight of the individual homosexual and the need for tolerance, understanding and legal reform; discussion of the underground, social world of the homosexual was generally avoided. The image of the isolated, solitary homosexual as a 'sad young man', to borrow from the work of Richard Dyer – divorced from any broader social life, given its negative connotations – remained a strategically useful image in the emancipatory politics of the period, cultivated by any number of homosexual law reformers.[13] In this context activists' ambivalence about focusing in any detail on the social realm of homosexuality paralleled academic writing that focused primarily on the psychosexual dynamics of the individual homosexual, largely ignoring his broader social world.

## Homosexuality as a social problem

It was the veritable explosion of the human sciences during and after the war that would slowly but dramatically shift the representational strategies through which homosexuality was rendered intelligible in Britain. The administrative support given to those sciences during the war would continue after the war when new investigations would be funded into various 'social problems' that were perceived to result from the social changes unleashed by the war itself, homosexuality amongst them. Moreover, building a 'New Jerusalem' in the wake of the Labour Party's 1945 electoral victory required new expertise; the collectivist current in British society unleashed by the war was now harnessed to securing the peace. A new age required new therapeutic approaches to the problems of modern society, and to the relationship between the individual and society.[14] As John Bowlby, author of the important 1953 study *Child Care and the Growth of Love*, wrote eagerly in 1946, calling for a new social psychology that would address any number of perceived social ills, 'the hope for the future lies in a far more profound understanding of the emotional forces', along with the 'development of scientific social techniques for modifying them'.[15] Or, as Richard Hornsey has put it recently, social psychology was called upon after the war to address a cast of problematic figures who seemed dangerously out of place in the ordered, rational postwar landscape.[16]

Most of all, in the aftermath of the war, the human sciences were called upon to deal with a number of so-called 'social problems', the declining birth-rate, divorce, anti-Semitism, race relations, juvenile delinquency and homosexuality amongst them. In the context of a series of broad anxieties about family breakdown, demographic decline and an exponential rise in the number of prosecutions for homosexual offences, numerous moral issues came to the fore. This culminated in a series of debates about 'vice', especially in London around the time of the coronation in 1953.[17] As one doctor, Fraser Mackenzie, wrote in 1947, 'the problem presented by recent changes in moral standards exceeds, in its possible effects on the well-being of the nation, that of any other problem awaiting solution'. In general, he argued, 'there has been a lowering of the standards of honesty, an increase in juvenile delinquency, the loosening of family ties [and] greater promiscuity'.[18] Mackenzie, like others at the time, argued that aberrant behaviours resulted from social failures, thereby necessitating investigation and the application of a unique battery of problem-solving techniques.

Such logic drove homosexuality firmly into the orbit of social investigation. Nowhere can the shift be seen more clearly than at the first ever British conference on 'The Social Aspects of Homosexuality', organised in 1947 by the Royal Medical Society. There Dr E. A. Bennett, of London's West End Hospital for Nervous Diseases, noted, 'It will hardly be disputed that our knowledge of homosexuality as a social phenomenon is fragmentary'.[19] Bennett called for detailed studies of the social stigma that surrounded homosexuality and that influenced homosexual behaviour, while Hermann Mannheim, the émigré Reader in Criminology at the University of London, commented on the need to study 'social and anti-social homosexual groups' and the various responses of society towards them. He, like others at the conference, also conceived of homosexuality as a '*social* problem'.[20] So did Lord Hailsham, who, with respect to homosexuality, wrote in 1955, 'In so far as active homosexuality is a problem ..., it is a problem of social environment and not of congenital make-up'; as such, he insisted, it is 'within the field of social science'.[21] For Hailsham, as for others after the war, the unalterable, congenital invert of the past was now less the focus of attention than the more modern homo-sexual, the product of a complex array of psycho-social factors that required investigation. While the participants in the 1947 conference might not have shared Hailsham's belief that homosexuality must 'be treated as a socially undesirable activity', and while they were less apt to argue that homosexual activity resulted from the break-down of social mores, they too argued that the homosexual was made rather than born.[22] The tools of the human sciences were thus to be turned to focus on the social production of homosexuality – and, for Hailsham and those who shared his sentiments, used to help solve what they perceived to be one of the great social problems of the postwar years.

Social problems seemed ubiquitous after the war, although the term itself was seldom deployed in Britain before the war. Certainly in the nineteenth century writers discussed the 'social question' and indeed, in a general sense, '*the* social problem' (in the singular), or the general state of society in the wake of industrialisation and the corresponding social upheavals that resulted therefrom. In the 1930s, responding to the publication of the report of the Mental Deficiency Committee (the Wood Report of 1929), the Eugenics Society consid-ered the 'social problem group' and focused on the social costs of low intelligence. According to the General-secretary of the Society, C. P. Blacker, some of the conditions characteristic of the social problem group were medico-psychological in origin and others were socio-logical.[23] As Gillian Swanson has suggested, the Eugenics Society was engaged in a series of 'experiments in knowledge' that made a 'distinctive contribution to modernising the conceptual resources of those forms of social planning designed in the pursuit of national improvement'.[24] Those experiments, she argues, helped inform the beginnings of interdisciplinary investigations into a range of social problems. Moreover, the conceptual apparatus developed by Blacker and his colleagues – especially with respect to mapping the medico-psychological and sociological bases of different behaviours – would be deployed especially after 1945 in the heightened study of any number of presumed disruptive actors in the expanded domain of the social.

In 1953 the American journal *Social Problems* was established, grounded in the belief – shared by many in Britain – that the 'knowl-edge gained from social science research is basic to wise formulation of policy', that the careful study of social problems was required for 'sound social action'.[25] For some two decades the journal remained in the forefront of investigations into homosexuality as a social phenomenon, consolidating the social problem paradigm that already had a long history in the United States, its modern origins to be found earlier in the twentieth century in an emergent social science that demanded discrete problems with their own specific procedures for solution.[26] More recently we have come to understand 'social problems' as 'the activities of individuals or groups making assertions about perceived social conditions which they consider unwanted, unjust, immoral and thus about which something should be done'. [27] This particular understanding of the concept has informed more recent work on the phenomenon of the social problem in Britain, especially John Hill's classic study of the 'social problem film', a study that focuses in part on the ways in which some of the films of Basil Dearden in the 1950s and early 1960s constituted the very problems they claimed to dissect: *Violent Playground* (1958, juvenile delinquency); *Sapphire* (1959, race relations); and *Victim* (1961, homosexuality).[28]

While *Victim* took for granted that homosexuality was a social problem that needed to be explored calmly and dispassionately, it was a decade or more earlier, in the wake of the social dislocations associated with the war and the various anxieties to which they gave rise, that homosexuality was first constituted as a particular problem 'about which something should be done'. As Kenneth Soddy, physician to the Department of Psychological Medicine at University College London Hospital wrote in 1954, 'In settled times, homosexuality does not greatly trouble the community. But social disturbance – and particularly a war – is apt to cause variations in social and sexual practices which engender attacks of acute public anxiety.'[29] As a troubling social presence, homosexuality was configured by Soddy and others in the late 1940s and early 1950s as a social problem in ways that it had not been earlier. Indeed, what is most striking is not only the proliferation of discourse about social problems after the war in general but the ways in which homosexuality was firmly inscribed in this discourse. This had certainly not been the case before the war, a time when homosexuality was rarely studied as a social phenomenon or imagined as a social problem. As early as 1914, the British Society for the Study of Sex Psychology claimed that it would study the 'problems' of sex psychology in terms of their sociological aspects, although no such formal studies ever materialised.[30] Around the same time, it translated the 1903 edition of a German pamphlet by Magnus Hirschfeld that cannot at all be fitted into the social problem paradigm as *The Social Problem of Sexual Inversion*, despite the fact that its German title – *Was soll das Volk vom dritten Geschlect wissen?* – might better be translated as 'What should the people know about the third sex?'[31] In short, despite occasional references to homosexuality as a social problem before the war, it was only after the war that the concept flourished as an important means for rendering homosexuality amenable to the investigative practices of postwar social science.

Social problems demand solutions, and before that investigation, and the speakers at the 1947 Royal Medical Society conference discussed the need for the kinds of broad studies of attitudes and behaviour that were to be found in the United States but that appeared to be lacking in Britain. One cited the importance of Katharine Bement Davis's *Factors in the Sex Life of Twenty-Two Hundred Women*, published by the Bureau of Social Hygiene in 1929; another spoke approvingly of Joseph Fishman's *Sex in Prison*, published in Britain in 1935.[32] Moreover, it was in the context of this perceived deficit in British social science investigations into matters of sexuality that the two Kinsey reports hit readers in Britain like a bombshell, reports that themselves moved radically from the realm of the psychological to the sociological. Their appearance led to further soul-searching about why no similar studies had been undertaken in Britain. At the time the second report appeared in 1953, broadsheets such as *The Times*, the *Observer* and the *Guardian* were all engaged in a shared campaign against the sensational coverage of homosexuality that had proliferated in the tabloids in recent years. Contributing to the conceptualisation of homosexuality as a social problem, they too viewed it as a phenomenon that required scientific investigation, calling for the kind of 'sober' and 'rational' discussion they deemed characteristic of Kinsey's work.[33] As *The Sunday Times* claimed in an editorial in 1953, 'A Social Problem', serious investigation was required in the struggle to reduce the overall incidence of homosexuality in society, given that, as the paper suggested, 'in public terms, a society with a high or growing proportion of unnaturalness is a weakened and perhaps a decadent society'.[34]

Casting homosexuality as a social problem in these terms, the human sciences were enjoined to explore those social influences that contributed to homosexuality in various social milieux. This gave rise to a number of studies in the later 1940s and 1950s that charted the effects of single-sex institutions, especially prisons, on the presumed growth of homosexuality in society, or that focused on homosexuality in particular contexts, such as that of Oxford undergraduate culture.[35] All of these works were concerned with the social production of homosexuality, with those social conditions that exacerbated homosexual tendencies in individuals and thereby contributed to the perceived social problem. In pursuing such avenues of enquiry, however, they also began to focus on the social contexts of homosexuality and, invariably, on the group life of the homosexual, shifting the focus away from the more narrow social problem paradigm, as we shall see in the next section. But the primary aim of these works was still to link observation with the development of practical solutions to the 'problem', which, in the case of *The Sunday Times* led back from society to the family. Five weeks after the newspaper constituted homosexuality as a social problem on its editorial pages, the paper published 'Mothers and Sons', a lengthy reflection from the wife of a businessman in the Midlands who spoke of the obligations of the family to the preservation of social cohesion and morality. One 'of the main causes of sexual inversion is an unhealthy relationship between mother and son', she noted, a point echoed by a huge number of subsequent letter writers, all engaged in a litany of maternal self-flagellation.[36] For such writers the postwar social problem of homosexuality could be localised in the social unit of the family, which now needed to be the focus of social policy. As the progressive sex reformers Kenneth Walker and Peter Fletcher noted in 1955, the problem of the homosexual was both broadly social and the result of specific interpersonal relationships. 'In our experience', they wrote, echoing those mothers who wrote to *The Sunday Times*, 'the most potent factor of all in the causation of homosexuality is an over-prolongation of female influence on a boy's life.' The social problem of homosexuality was, for them, 'a symptom of arrested personal development' – albeit one that could 'be understood only by reference to the social climate in which it flourishes'.[37]

This, then, was the social problem of homosexuality in early postwar Britain, a problem in the apparent rise in the incidence of homosexuality – in need of containment and reduction – brought about by a complex series of factors, all related to a perceived breakdown in the various operations of society. As one writer noted in a 1947 forum on 'The Sociological Aspects of Homosexuality', the phenomenon was 'the outcome of environmental and social disharmonies. It is produced *in* society and *by* society.'[38] Aside from an

emphasis placed on various single-sex institutions, its precise location was, however, often only vaguely specified, although maternal
failure was ubiquitous in such writings. This certainly complicates
any straightforward story of a shift from a focus on the psychopathology of the individual to a broader focus on the individual in a larger
social setting, a shift from the practices of psychiatry to those of sociology. While new calls were being made for the social investigation of
homosexuality, they were part of a growing awareness of the various
ways in which the individual was embedded in a complex web of both
narrow family dynamics and broader social practices, now requiring
the attention of both the psychiatrist and the sociologist. Moreover,
by the 1950s, progressive psychiatrists and psychoanalysts – medical
professionals who themselves cautiously began to champion homosexual law reform – were themselves more and more apt to comment
on the social life of the homosexual and the broader social context
in which homosexuality flourished than had been the case between
the wars. Although in the 1930s he had been a pioneer in the clinical
assessment and treatment of the individual homosexual, the psychoanalyst Edward Glover increasingly focused not on the social problem
of homosexuality but on the problems faced by the homosexual in
society, which, he noted, often resulted from what would soon come
to be known as homophobia.[39] In short, the problem for him was
not homosexuality per se but social attitudes towards homosexuality.
Glover and his progressive colleagues increasingly no longer viewed
homosexuality as a menace to society, as a social problem; nevertheless, they – along with a growing number of social scientists and
early postwar homosexual rights activists – certainly believed that the
social life of the homosexual merited further attention.

## From social problem to social group

While at the Royal Medical Society in 1947 calls were made for empirical studies of the 'social aspects of homosexuality' to rival those
being produced in the United States, work in Britain was given a
particular boost by the presence of central European émigrés in the
social sciences. Karl Mannheim (1893–1947) settled in Britain in 1933
and had turned his attention to the application of the social sciences
to social reconstruction before his untimely death shortly after the
end of the war. The Polish émigré Leon Radzinowicz (1906–99) was
the founding director of the Institute of Criminology at the University

of Cambridge and co-author of a major report on *Sexual Offences* published there in 1957. Hermann Mannheim (1889–1974) moved from Germany to England in 1934, spoke at the Royal Medical Society conference in 1947, and in 1950 was one of the co-founders, along with the psychoanalyist Edward Glover and Emanuel Miller, of the *British Journal of Delinquency*. And it was in the pages of that journal in 1954 that Gerrit Theodore Kempe (1911–79), a professor of criminology at the University of Utrecht, offered a very early analysis of the homosexual as a member of a minority social group, subject to the investigative procedures of sociology as much as members of any other social group.

Kempe's article marked something of a watershed in writing published in Britain about homosexuality. It broke with the normative assumptions of the social problem paradigm and focused explicitly on a relatively new object of investigation, one that had not received serious academic attention before the war: the homosexual group. The article's importance led to its appearance, in slightly different form, both in the *International Journal of Sexology* and in *One*, the American homophile journal, contributing to the practices of international cross-fertilisation in the social sciences, an important, albeit seldom studied, feature of this period.[40] To be sure, in the United States Donald Webster Cory (pseudonym of the sociologist Edward Sagarin) had already focused on the social and cultural structures of what he termed the 'homosexual minority' in his path-breaking 1951 study, *The Homosexual in America*. But the book was not published in Britain until 1953 – and then by a small press, Peter Nevill – and was rarely cited in the UK before the 1960s, even though it exerted a powerful influence in 1953 on Antony Grey, later secretary of the Homosexual Law Reform Society.[41] Likewise, in an important 1956 study of the social organisation of a homosexual community in Canada, summarised in the American journal *Social Problems*, two sociologists argued that the social and legal hostility to homosexuality 'produced a complex structure of concealed social relations' that now merited rigorous 'sociological investigation'. A product of the Chicago School of urban sociology's interest in sexual variation, this study broke new ground in terms of the object of its investigation. Again, however, this was a North American work and while such investigations were more and more ubiquitous in the United States they were far from the radar screens of the British sociological establishment.[42]

Although doctors, psychiatrists and criminologists had all called for investigations into the social aspects of homosexuality at the Royal Medical Society conference in 1947, it was Kempe who both offered a new framework in which such work could be undertaken and further specified the new object of investigation: the homosexual 'minority group'. As he put it, 'Though the homophiles do not form a community as is often supposed, they are a *group*, the members of which feel themselves strongly and *permanently* linked together by the circumstances that they are all predominantly attracted to persons of their own sex.' There was amongst them, he continued, a 'consciousness' of belonging together, even if the group was heterogeneous and one could not speak of a cohesive 'group ideology'. Furthermore, he insisted, their status was that of a 'minority group', in constant tension with the heterosexual majority in society.[43] The investigative framework put forward by Kempe was not unlike that being deployed by British students of race relations in the 1950s, individuals who also constituted social problems by positing the existence of in-groups and out-groups, minority groups and majority groups. Both for race relations writers and for Kempe the aim of social science was to understand the logic of these groups, thereby contributing to social cohesion by providing the knowledge that might bring the groups together on terms of mutual understanding.[44] As Kempe noted, homosexual members of the minority group were constantly made aware of the unwillingness of the majority to accept them, often making them aggressive and hostile to the majority. What was needed, he argued, was 'real understanding' between the groups, something that the existing sciences seemed quite incapable of providing: 'Homophile man has created a scientific problem with which psychology, psychopathology, biology and sociology are dealing with equal zeal. Up till now the results of these efforts have been so alarmingly small.'[45]

Kempe's call for 'understanding' amongst individuals who inhabited different social worlds staked out a new position increasingly shared by a number of reformist psychiatrists and doctors who, as we have seen, recognised that many of the personal problems experienced by the homosexual were often a result of social marginalisation, that the so-called 'problem' of homosexuality was one of social attitudes and dysfunctional group relations. As the homosexual law reformer Antony Grey wrote in a letter to *The Sunday Times* in 1954, responding to that paper's editorial of the previous November,

'A social problem', if society were to frown less on homosexuality, then the marginalisation experienced by the homosexual would itself decline, reducing 'his incidence as a social problem'. In short, improved social health would result from policies derived from the careful study of homosexual group dynamics and the responses of society to them.[46] Whether or not one accepts the functionalist logic central to this particular paradigm, it was a paradigm that informed much liberal opinion in Britain in the 1950s. It was particularly influential with progressive sex educators at the time, individuals who were more attuned to the social dimensions of sexual behaviour than were the conservative psychiatrists and doctors who continued to treat homosexuality as an illness. Writing in the same year as Kempe, for example, Eustace Chesser differentiated between a psychological approach to homosexuality that isolated it as a personal deviation in the sexual sphere and a 'moral and ethical' approach, one more concerned with the social life of the male homosexual and his larger relationship with society. Given that the homosexual was perceived as 'society's outcast, its pariah', he wrote, it was now 'essential to deal with the public attitude, for it is this that must be changed if we are to have any solution to the problem'.[47]

By the mid-1950s, then, the social problem paradigm was already giving way to a more expansive, and often more value neutral, call for the study of the homosexual as a social being. Now firmly embedded in an expanded notion of the social, the homosexual had assumed a social form and come to merit social investigation. Attention thus began to be paid to the homosexual as a member of a minority social group, to use Kempe's formulation, and to that group's relationship with the broader society in which it operated. New arenas were being opened for investigation – not only those specific elements of the social world that were believed to constitute the homosexual but, in the less judgemental work of writers like Kempe, the actual world *of* the homosexual itself. Moreover, the investigations of the Wolfenden Committee, appointed by the Home Office in 1954 to investigate prostitution and homosexuality, took place against the backdrop of this new interest by postwar 'experts' in the social domain. Most of all, those investigations gave official sanction to the kind of work for which Kempe was calling.

While the role played by the Wolfenden Committee's recommendations in contributing to the decriminalisation of homosexuality in Britain is well known, Jeffrey Weeks and other scholars have come to understand the more complex ways in which the work of the Committee must be viewed as part of a broader search for 'a more effective regulation of sexual deviance'.[48] But the work of the Committee was as much about defining who a homosexual was as what should be done about the problem of homosexuality. And, as Frank Mort has shown, this task required a deep engagement with the actual social world the homosexual inhabited. One of the unintended consequences of the investigations undertaken by the Committee, then, was the contribution they made to rendering the social life of the homosexual increasingly visible. Committee members compiled a dossier of official information about sex in London, documenting where men met, how they recognised one another, what they did. The published report of the Committee in 1957 provided a geography of homosexual acts and a typology of those who committed them, all part of an exercise in the techniques of productive surveillance associated with the exercise of modern state power.[49] It documented homosexual experience, and, while it often relied on medical and psychiatric expertise to explain the ætiology and behavioural practices of the individual, it also engaged in the mapping of social types – the rent boy, the guardsman, the respectable gentleman – and their perambulations around the city. In short, the work of the Wolfenden Committee gave particular form to the social life of the homosexual, constituting the homosexual as an actor in the social world. This served as a catalyst for the acquisition of further knowledge about that life. It also legitimated social scientific investigations into that life and made government agency and philanthropic body funding of such investigations acceptable in ways that had hitherto not been the case.

Despite the calls made for the investigation into homosexuality as a social phenomenon, prior to the publication of the Wolfenden Report there was very little work undertaken in Britain along the lines called for. One of the first forays into the sociology of homosexual life was made by Mass Observation in a brief, five-page appendix to what has been called Britain's 'Little Kinsey'. This was the first major survey of sexual attitudes carried out in Britain, paid for by the *Sunday Pictorial* and in part published by that paper, indicative, as Adrian Bingham suggests, of the ways in which certain newspapers began to use 'the prestige of social science to legitimize "modern", more explicit styles of writing about sex for a mass-market family audience'.[50] For the survey, a number of mass-observers collected material on 'homosexual cliques', and in the appendix, 'Homosexual

Groups' – itself a telling title, given that such phenomena had not
been the subject of serious investigation before the war – charted the
lives of a small group of friends who 'only move in "queer" circles'.[51]
Gone was the heavy-handed, sensationalist rhetoric that characterised much investigative reporting on the topic of homosexuality in
the tabloids. Voyeuristic strategies of shedding the spotlight of publicity on the darkest corners of vice and depravity found no place
in 'Little Kinsey'. Indeed, the report's restrained matter-of-factness
marks a radical rupture with such discursive strategies. What we
have instead is a narrative of everyday ordinariness, a story of John, a
receptionist in a London hotel (age thirty), and Michael (age twenty-
eight), a private secretary to a prominent public figure, who have lived
together for some eight years. We see the world in which they move,
their friends, the parties they hold, the sexual partners they have,
their weekend outings to Brighton. To be sure there is a fascination
with forms of behavioural campiness: in Brighton, for example, we
learn that 'Michael was rather carried away by the environment in
this "queers" bar and was given to draping himself over the staircase
railings, smiling around the room, speaking loudly and [exhibiting]
exaggerated gestures and mannerisms'.[52] But there is also a pulling
back from attempts to render these men threatening and deviant,
as was the case in the tabloids, along with the invocation of various
similarities to heterosexual behavioural norms. While complaining
that the 'isolationist manner' in which homosexual groups often
seemed to function contributed to society's ignorance of, and hostility
towards, homosexuality, the report's authors argued that social tolerance would result from greater knowledge of such groups, anticipating Kempe's 1954 template for the study of homosexual groups and
their relationship with the broader society. In this respect, the report
also attempted to foster such tolerance through its own discursive
practices of normalisation.[53]

'Little Kinsey' was certainly no professional, sociological study.
Indeed, it must be seen as part of a tradition of gentlemanly, amateur social investigation which Mike Savage claims still prevailed in
Britain into the 1950s.[54] Its observations of the homosexual group
were bracketed, ghettoised, relegated to an appendix and never sys-
tematically analysed. On some level this confirms Liz Stanley's conclusions that the report's authors came close to capturing difference,
fragmentation and complexity but lacked a firm analytic framework
for making sense of it.[55] Nevertheless, the work did mark a radical

break both from contemporary tabloid sensationalism and more elite, still hegemonic, discourses that focused narrowly on individual psychopathology. And in its foray into the social world of homosexuality, 'Little Kinsey' worked within a much more progressive, emergent framework than the social problem paradigm, one that at least implicitly constituted social groups in opposition to each other and called for greater understanding and tolerance between them. It also contributed to thinking about sexual attitudes and behaviour in socio-cultural, rather than psychological, terms, and in so doing contributed both to a conceptual framework and an investigative practice that was carried much further in the work of Michael Schofield. It is in his work that we can further chart the intellectual shifts that were taking place in the 1950s and 1960s as a once hegemonic focus on the psychological make-up of the male homosexual was increasingly supplemented by a series of investigative practices into the social world in which he moved.

Writing under the pseudonym Gordon Westwood, Schofield published his first study, *Society and the Homosexual*, in 1952, at a time when the social investigation of homosexuality in Britain was still in its infancy and no full-length study of the phenomenon had yet appeared in print. His publisher, Victor Gollancz, felt that the book's credibility needed to be secured by a preface from an important medical expert in the field, indicative of the continuing discursive importance of medical accounts of the aetiology of individual homosexual behaviour. Schofield turned to Edward Glover to provide that credibility, the psychoanalyst he had first encountered in a futile attempt to eradicate his own homosexual impulses back at the outset of the war.[56] Glover obliged, itself indicative not only of his own, hesitant turn to the social but of the increasing fusion of the tools of psychiatry and sociology in the context of understanding homosexuality as a social phenomenon.

On one level Schofield's work in the 1950s would have been immediately recognisable to any educated person at least vaguely aware of the latest, progressive thinking in the realm of psychiatry: 'the causes of homosexuality are rooted in emotional conflicts acquired in early childhood', he wrote in a book explicitly indebted to psychoanalysis in general and the work of Glover in particular, focusing as it did extensively on the causes of, and possible treatments for, homosexuality.[57] Schofield had received his degree in psychology, not sociology; moreover, as he later noted, he 'grew up with psychological language' and, when he undertook his research for the book in the Cambridge University Library in the later 1940s, the 'psychological language' of the homosexual was largely all that was available to him. Nevertheless, it was a language he was already beginning to question, finding it inadequate for addressing the issues with which he was now concerned.[58] In short, the book moved uneasily between different registers, something that can be evidenced in the awkward phrasing of its own prefatory blurb: 'This is not a medical treatise', it began, 'but an attempt to evaluate the social implications of homosexuality.' Having rescued the study in advance for a newer kind of investigative practice, the blurb immediately and firmly reinscribed the work in a hegemonic medical discourse: 'In order to understand the development of this abnormality, it has been necessary to draw upon the papers of practicing psychiatrists.'[59] Glover, in his preface, saw no contradiction in all of this, praising Schofield for 'setting homosexuality in proper perspective as a social as well as a sexual manifestation'.[60] But Schofield struggled at times, working within an older model of disease, or at least mental aberration, yet attempting to fit this into a newer 'social problem' paradigm: homosexuality, he wrote, was a social problem in so far as the 'disease' (again, note the slippage here) 'is the outcome of constitutional factors aggravated by environment and social disharmonies. It is produced *in* society *by* society.'[61]

These slippages – these movements between different methodological registers and conceptual frameworks – were widespread in the 1950s and were as characteristic of Donald J. West's classic 1955 account of homosexuality as they were of Schofield's 1952 study.[62] In some respects both works are dominated by a psychodynamic narrative of individual development that their authors struggled to work within and move beyond. The actual lived society of the homosexual is given short shrift in West's study and is only slightly more the object of focus in Schofield's earlier work, for Schofield devoted a mere thirty pages to what he termed the various 'levels of homosexual society'. And yet it is here, where he discussed 'street corners', 'the queer bars' and the 'exclusive clubs' – along with those 'outsiders' who 'do not know the logic of the street corners, cannot afford to become members of the exclusive clubs and don't know where the queer bars are or don't care to enter them'[63] – that Schofield avoided the language of both psychological disorder and social problem and discovered a number of men who, he observed, 'if not completely adjusted to their situation, at least have recognized it and given up any serious attempt to alter it'.[64] It is these men – some of whom Schofield knew personally – to whom he gave social form, constituting a genealogy of social types, of actors in the social realm. Those actors are also given a voice in Schofield's work; his subjects are complicit in their own mapping, in this respect not dissimilar from those homosexuals shortly to be interviewed by the Wolfenden Committee. Moreover, as Richard Hornsey has recently argued, Schofield's 1952 study is suggestive of an 'uneasy collusion' between professionals 'and certain groups of bourgeois queer men'.[65] Schofield himself might well be considered a bourgeois queer professional who, working closely with his friends and informants, articulated a particular image of respectable homosexuality. In this respect, the turn to the social in early postwar writing about homosexuality was as much a product of the desires of queer men to explore and legitimate the actual world they inhabited as it was of the experts to map its contours. In addition, while Schofield's 1952 study 'offered its readers a panoramic tour through a range of metropolitan queer spaces', as Hornsey claims, it codified those spaces in particular ways, carving out a realm of respectability intended to assuage the anxieties of those who still held to the belief that homosexuality was a social problem.[66]

Schofield's second major study of the subject, published eight years later in 1960 as *A Minority: A Report on the Life of the Male Homosexual in Great Britain*, relied even more than did his previous book on the testimony of his subjects. It also operated more centrally within a 'minority studies' paradigm, delving deeply into the social world of the homosexual and giving much shorter shrift to the language of psychopathology that had characterised his earlier work. Moreover, by the time it appeared, the calls that had been made in 1947 for the formal social investigation into homosexuality in Britain no longer fell on deaf ears. Unlike the United States, no British funding body had previously sponsored any social investigations of homosexuality, although the legitimacy conferred on the topic by the work of the Wolfenden Committee, along with the rise of the sexual survey in the popular press in the wake of the Kinsey reports, meant that funds were increasingly forthcoming. The Home Office supported Richard Hauser's work, published as *The Homosexual Society* in 1962, while Schofield's second study was funded by the British Social Biology Council, chaired at the time by Kenneth Walker, the eminent sexologist and first chairman of the Homosexual Law Reform Society.[67]

*A Minority* was similar to Schofield's earlier work in so far as it was presented to its readers as a scientific account of an understudied problem. But it differed given that its starting point was not the individual life of the solitary homosexual but the group life of a minority, a life meticulously reconstructed through a quantitative sampling of the lives of over one hundred self-confessed gay men – a much more formal work of professional sociology than his earlier study. Schofield claimed that most works by doctors, psychiatrists or criminologists took as their subjects the individual prisoner or the patient, while he aimed for a comprehensive picture of the ordinary and everyday, of those who had evaded the clutches of the law and medicine, situating their lives in the broadest possible context: 'If the purpose of research', he wrote, 'is to lead to social action, the homosexual must be studied in the wide context of the whole community.'[68] In this respect Schofield's work was absolutely central to what Mike Savage has identified as the key practice of British sociology after the war, a focus 'on eliciting accounts from which sociologists could unravel how people's ordinary situations shaped their lives, actions, thoughts, and endeavours'.[69] It also drew from and developed further those attempts made in the 1950s to conceptualise the homosexual as a member of a minority group, attempts that had been evident in the work of Donald Webster Cory in the United States a decade earlier but only slowly entered the conceptual repertoire of British social investigation. While throughout the 1950s the term 'minority' had been applied in Britain to ethnic, racial and religious criteria, Schofield was the first boldly to consolidate its use in the study of the social life of the homosexual.

Two years later the social investigation of the homosexual as a member of a distinctive minority was continued in the work of Richard Hauser, an Austrian sociologist who had come to Britain in 1957 with the intention of 'investigating several neglected social problems in Britain, one of which was homosexuality'.[70] In many respects *The Homosexual Society*, commissioned by the Home Office Research Department, was a throwback to an earlier era, Hauser arguing that psychological immaturity was characteristic of the homosexual, an individual who needed to be urged to develop more socially useful roles. Like earlier postwar thinkers, he also argued that homosexuality could be 'environmentally produced' and that consequently 'there is a great need to understand the issues primarily in order to contain the evil' and 'handle it properly when it occurs'.[71] For this he was roundly attacked by increasingly vocal advocates of homosexual law reform. And yet, like Schofield, Hauser was interested in the social life of the homosexual and was the first in Britain to conceptualise and explore that life in terms of subcultural theory, understanding a subculture to be 'a section of a major culture (or of a minority culture) which has its own particular way of life, its rites and taboos, its common interests and enemies, its "secrets" and often its free masonry or loyalty between members'.[72] He was also interested in mapping the various social types he discovered in that subculture – forty-six in all – and while both contemporary writers and subsequent sociologists often found these of 'dubious value', his survey relied on, and gave voice to, the evidence of hundreds of men, which, taken together, offered the most detailed depiction of the social life of the male homosexual published in Britain to date.[73]

By the time that Hauser's *The Homosexual Society* and Schofield's *A Minority* appeared in print – the very time that Britain was entering its 'permissive' moment – research that led to social action was increasingly called for by a reformist state. It was also much more generously funded than it had been in the 1940s and early 1950s. Schofield himself realised the growing importance of sociological investigation for these endeavours and called for greater precision in the studies being undertaken 'because people with power and authority are making more and more use of them and the results are going to impinge upon our lives'.[74] It was in this context that his third – and final – study of homosexuality, *Sociological Aspects of Homosexuality*, was published, in 1965, also funded by the Home Office in the lead-up to the penultimate parliamentary debates that resulted in the partial decriminalisation of male homosexuality in 1967. Schofield still claimed that the difficulties of undertaking sociological research into homosexuality in Britain were enormous, in large part because of a continuing 'tendency to see homosexuality only in medical terms, as a sickness or as a mental disorder, while ignoring the more important social aspects'.[75] Certainly by this time, however, Schofield had severed his reliance on those discourses that had pathologised the homosexual. Again, to borrow from Savage's characterisation of the new sociological studies that appeared in the 1960s, any 'overt psychologizing has given way to the language of social relationships, roles, networks, and norms, the evidence for which is extracted from people's own accounts'.[76]

Not only did it mark a radical break from his earlier interest in the psychology of sexual deviation, but Schofield's work in the mid-1960s is also suggestive of the distance that had been travelled since the social problem paradigm first opened up the world of homosexuality for social investigation after the war. While in *A Minority* he had still thought of homosexuals as a potential social problem in so far as social hostility expressed towards them tended to drive them 'away from community-integration into secret minority groups' that threatened social cohesion, the rhetoric of the homosexual potentially being a social problem was wholly lacking in the later study.[77] Any social problem that existed was now seen by Schofield to be manufactured by society as a result of processes of social labelling: 'it is important to realize that as society is condemning the homosexual, simultaneously it is creating a social problem'.[78] While in 1952 Schofield had very few works of sociology upon which he could draw for guidance, by the mid-1960s he was influenced by Erving Goffman and Howard Becker, borrowing from the latter's 1963 study, *Outsiders: Studies in the Sociology of Deviance*, the notion that deviance was only that which society labelled as such: the deviance, he argued, 'is not necessarily a quality of the homosexual act'.[79] Even the term 'minority' was used less in 1965, Schofield adopting the more recent language of the subculture that had found its way into British studies of homosexuality through Hauser's 1962 study. By this time, more enamoured of the new work on labelling theory and the sociology of deviance, Schofield had moved far from the social problem paradigm that was ubiquitous when he published his first book in 1952.

By the later 1960s Schofield was not alone in disentangling his interests in the structure and organisation of gay lives in Britain from the psychological discourses of homosexual selfhood that were so ubiquitous in the world in which he received his education in the 1940s. For him – and for an increasingly vocal number of gay activists – it was clear that the tools of psychiatry no longer seemed appropriate to the study of homosexuality. In 1964, the secretary of the Homosexual Law Reform Society, Antony Grey, had penned a review of two recently published books by fairly liberal psychiatrists – Ismond Rosen's edited collection of essays *The Pathology and Treatment of Sexual Deviation*, and Anthony Storr's Penguin paperback *Sexual Deviation*. There, echoing a number of Schofield's concerns, Grey bemoaned the continued medicalisation of homosexuality and the lack of attention still being paid to the social sphere. Even though he praised Storr for including a section in his book on sociology, he noted

that 'the really important problem of how to improve society's attitudes towards the sexually deviant is virtually ignored'.[80] Meanwhile,
those still deeply committed to the study of homosexuality as an
individual deviation from the norm were actively hostile to the new
attempts to inscribe the homosexual in the social. In a review of
Schofield's *Sociological Aspects of Homosexuality*, Irving Bieber, one of
the American psychoanalysts most associated with the still prevalent
view of homosexuality as a treatable condition, roundly condemned
the study. Faulting his research methods, Bieber insisted that when
'Mr. Schofield attempts to fit various interesting pieces of his investigation into a coherent statement about homosexuality, the work misfires'. And he added that Schofield wrongly viewed homosexuality as
'non-pathological' and had implied in his work that psychiatrists who
did view it as such were primarily influenced by 'prevailing social
attitudes', an implication that Bieber firmly rejected.[81] Bieber's, however, was increasingly a voice in the wilderness.

Throughout the 1960s, new currents of social activism, coupled
with the anti-psychiatry movement of that decade, fuelled the rejection of psychiatry as a social analytic, leading Britain's Gay Liberation
Front (GLF) to publish in 1972 its 'Interim statement of the counter
psychiatry group', a pamphlet that pilloried psychiatrists, disputed
their knowledge claims, and accused them of attempting blatantly
to lend scientific credibility to widespread public hostility towards
homosexuals. Attacking what it deemed the continuing pathologisation of homosexuality, the GLF reified the lived experience of gay
men and lesbians themselves in the face of psychiatric expertise.[82]
It was that lived experience that had already been rendered increasingly visible through the varied practices of post-war social investigation in Britain; it was also a heightened interest in lived experience
more generally that was central to the new social history that now
flourished in the 1960s and 1970s, especially in the new universities. Moreover, in 1971, a year before the appearance of the GLF's
diatribe against psychiatry, Charlotte Wolff – herself a practising
psychiatrist – published her seminal study, *Love between Women*. She,
too, was indebted to those newer practices – both in her focus on the
ways in which individual lives were moulded by group membership
and in her reliance on oral testimony to reconstruct collective behaviour.[83] Even H. Montgomery Hyde, in the first published history of
homosexuality in Britain (1970), was indebted to the social turn of the
1960s and borrowed extensively from the work of Michael Schofield

in the survey of contemporary gay life that opened his book.[84] The turn to the social was now commonplace and the homosexual had come to acquire the status of a social being.

## Goodbye to all that

This chapter has only scratched the surface of the emergence and con-solidation of a number of new discourses of homosexuality as a social practice in postwar Britain; it has only offered an overview of those shifts in the material practices of research through which the homo-sexual was rendered knowable as a social object. Certainly by the end of the 1960s a radical shift in the object and methods of investigation had taken place, both fulfilling and moving beyond the agenda set forth by the speakers at the 1947 conference of the Royal Medical Society on 'The Social Aspects of Homosexuality'. Jeffrey Escoffier, the American critic, has commented perceptively on the similarly important shifts that were taking place at roughly the same time in the United States. In 1969, he argued, in the year of the Stonewall riots in New York City, 'the psychiatric discourse on homosexuality was hegemonic'. And yet throughout the 1950s and 1960s a new, counter-discourse emerged, shaped by a body of literature that began to map the social dimen-sions of what was coming to be known as gay life. This, according to Escoffier, 'initiated a process that potentially disrupted the hegemony of the psychiatric discourse of individual pathology'.[85] The story of this shift has not been told in detail, either for the United States or for Britain. And yet by the end of the 1960s it is indeed clear that in both countries a significant space had been carved out in which the study of homosexuality as a social phenomenon could now flourish, in part the result of a radical change in the intellectual climate that generated increasing attacks on the science of the individual.

It was in this context that the British sociologist Mary McIntosh published her often-cited 1968 article, 'The homosexual role' – in the American journal Social Problems. Celebrated as an ur-text in Britain, taken up by gay activists, other sociologists and historians, its impor-tance, according to Jeffrey Weeks, was that it asked an entirely new question – not the question posed from the late nineteenth century onwards, not 'what are the causes of homosexuality, but rather, why are we so concerned with seeing homosexuality as a condition that has causes?'[86] Weeks suggests that her question opened up a new research agenda by positing homosexuals as a social category rather than as a medical or psychiatric one. It certainly created opportunities for historians, encouraging them to study the mechanisms by which various homosexual identities and roles emerged and to delineate those historical and social forms in which homosexuality came to be organised. Two seminal works from the 1970s have been hugely influential in that project, and indeed on our own practices today – Weeks's *Coming Out*, published in 1977, and Kenneth Plummer's *Sexual Stigma*, published two years earlier. Both authors have admitted their own profound debts to McIntosh – and more broadly to the new constructionist strains of sociology that, in the realm of sexuality, were pioneered in the United States by John Gagnon and William Simon. As Weeks and his colleague Janet Holland wrote with respect to Gagnon and Simon's 1973 work, *Sexual Conduct*, it 'was for many of us a revelation. It made the now widely accepted, but then revelatory observation that sex, far from being the most natural thing about us, was to an extraordinary degree subject to socio-cultural moulding.'[87]

Celebrating the intellectual moment of 1968 and the new sociological practices that congealed around that time, both Plummer and Weeks tended to overlook or denigrate those earlier contributions that rendered the social domain of homosexuality visible in Britain. In *Sexual Stigma*, for example, Plummer called for a serious sociology of sexuality which, he argued, would be hampered 'if it remained on the Schofield and Kinsey level of social book-keeping'.[88] A few years later Plummer praised the importance of Schofield's work in the 1960s, and even McIntosh had, in a footnote to her 1968 article, acknowledged the work of Donald Webster Cory and Evelyn Hooker in the United States and Michael Schofield in Britain, which she characterised as marking an 'interesting beginning', full of 'valuable descriptive material'.[89] Nevertheless, amidst the new, radical climate of the 1970s, dominated by impatience with the cautious earnestness of earlier reformers, the desire to move beyond the various intellectual frameworks in which they operated was great. Certainly few of the writers discussed in this chapter, with the possible exception of Schofield by the time of his later work, shared the agenda that drove the very different concerns that inspired the work produced in and after the 1970s.[90] But while it is indeed easy to dismiss the work of earlier post-war writers, it was then that a space was first carved out for the study of homosexuality as a broad social phenomenon rather than merely as an individual psychological aberration; it was then that the homosexual in Britain first assumed social form.

## Notes

1 A longer version of this chapter was first published in the *Journal of British Studies*, 51:3 (July 2012), © 2012 by North American Conference on British Studies. I would like to thank the University of Chicago Press for permitting me to publish my material in this volume. The chapter grew out of a symposium I co-organised with Joanne Meyerowitz at Yale University in 2008, 'Social Science and the Construction of Modern Sexuality', and I am grateful to Joanne and the other symposium participants for helping me frame these ideas. Earlier versions of this chapter were presented in 2010 at a symposium on homosexuality in postwar Europe at the Center for European Studies, Harvard University; at the Simpson Center, University of Washington; and at the conference 'British Queer History' at McGill University. I would like to thank Judith Surkis, Jordanna Bailkin and Brian Lewis, respectively, for their kind invitations to share my work at these venues and for their helpful comments. Finally, I want to thank Deborah Cohen, Laura Doan, Steve Epstein and Matt Houlbrook for their keen insights and advice.

2 The term is borrowed from the title of Peter Wildeblood's study of 'the underworld in our midst'. Wildeblood, *A Way of Life* (London: Weidenfeld and Nicolson, 1956), dust jacket.

3 See the essays in Martin Bulmer (ed.), *Essays on the History of British Sociological Research* (Cambridge: Cambridge University Press, 1985), especially chapter 1, Bulmer, 'The development of sociology and of empirical social research in Britain'.

4 Mike Savage, *Identities and Social Change in Britain since 1940: The Politics of Method* (Oxford: Oxford University Press, 2010), p. vii.

5 A. H. Halsey, *A History of Sociology in Britain: Science, Literature and Society* (Oxford: Oxford University Press, 2004), p. vi.

6 See Sean Brady, *Masculinity and Male Homosexuality in Britain, 1861–1913* (Houndmills, Basingstoke: Palgrave Macmillan, 2005); H. G. Cocks, *Nameless Offences: Homosexual Desire in the Nineteenth Century* (London: I. B. Tauris, 2003); Matt Cook, *London and the Culture of Homosexuality, 1885–1914* (Cambridge: Cambridge University Press, 2003); Matt Houlbrook, *Queer London: Perils and Pleasures in the Sexual Metropolis, 1918–1957* (Chicago: University of Chicago Press, 2005); Morris B. Kaplan, *Sodom on the Thames: Sex, Love, and Scandal in Wilde Times* (Ithaca: Cornell University Press, 2005); Charles Upchurch, *Before Wilde: Sex between Men in Britain's Age of Reform* (Berkeley: University of California Press, 2009). For an assessment of the recent literature, see Chris Waters, 'Distance and desire in the new British queer history', *GLQ: A Journal of Lesbian and Gay Studies*, 14:1 (2008), 139–55.

7 Havelock Ellis and John Addington Symonds, *Sexual Inversion: A*

*Critical Edition*, ed. Ivan Crozier (Houndmills, Basingstoke: Palgrave Macmillan, 2008).

8 Taylor Croft, *The Cloven Hoof: A Study in Contemporary London Vices* (London: D. Archer, 1932), p. 12. Taylor Croft was an interwar pen name of the novelist and travel writer Rupert Croft-Cooke (1903–79), himself arrested on charges of gross indecency in 1952, about which he wrote in *The Verdict of You All* (London: Secker and Warburg, 1955). My thanks to Matt Houlbrook for this reference.

9 Edward Sagarin, 'Sex research and sociology: retrospective and prospective', in J. M. Henslin (ed.), *Studies in the Sociology of Sex* (New York: Appleton-Century-Crofts, 1971), pp. 377–408. For recent histories of sociological investigations of sexuality, some of which dispute Sagarin's claims, see the articles in 'Sex and sociology: sociological studies of sexuality, 1910–1978', a special issue of *Qualitative Sociology*, 26:4 (2003), 429–555. Writing under the pseudonym Donald Webster Cory, Sagarin had published a hugely important work that offered a pioneering study of the social dimensions of homosexuality in 1951, *The Homosexual in America: A Subjective Approach*.

10 See Chris Waters, 'Disorders of the mind, disorders of the body social: Peter Wildeblood and the making of the modern homosexual', in Becky Conekin, Frank Mort and Chris Waters (eds), *Moments of Modernity: Reconstructing Britain 1945–1964* (London: Rivers Oram Press, 1999), pp. 134–51.

11 Adrian Bingham, '"The K-Bomb": social surveys, the popular press, and British sexual culture in the 1940s and 1950s', *Journal of British Studies*, 50:1 (2011), 2, 6. See also Bingham, *Family Newspapers? Sex, Private Life and the British Popular Press, 1918–1978* (Oxford: Oxford University Press, 2009).

12 'Anomaly' [Harry Baldwin], *The Invert and His Social Adjustment* (London: Baillière, Tindall, 1927). The book was reprinted with a sequel in 1948.

13 Richard Dyer, 'Coming out as going in: the image of the homosexual as a sad young man', in his *The Matter of Images: Essays on Representation* (London: Routledge, 1993), pp. 73–92.

14 See Mathew Thomson, *Psychological Subjects: Identity, Culture and Health in Twentieth-Century Britain* (Oxford: Oxford University Press, 2006), esp. p. 234.

15 John Bowlby, 'Psychology and democracy', *Political Quarterly*, 17:1 (1946), 76.

16 Richard Hornsey, *The Spiv and the Architect: Unruly Life in Postwar London* (Minneapolis: University of Minnesota Press, 2010), p. 26.

17 See Frank Mort, *Capital Affairs: London and the Making of the Permissive Society* (New Haven: Yale University Press, 2010), pp. 41–8.

18  Fraser Mackenzie, *Social Health and Morals: An Analysis and a Plan* (London: Victor Gollancz, 1947), pp. 13, 15.

19  Dr E. A. Bennett, in 'Discussion on the social aspects of homosexuality', *Proceedings of the Royal Society of Medicine*, 40:10 (1947), 585. See also the papers in 'The social problem of homosexuality', *The Medical Press*, 218 (1947), 207–23.

20  'Discussion on the social aspects of homosexuality', pp. 586–7, 589. See also D. Stanley-Jones, 'Sexual inversion and the English Law', *Medical Practitioner*, 215 (1946), 391–6; 'Sexual inversion: an ethical study', *The Lancet*, 252 (March 1947), pp. 366–9. See also 'The sociological aspects of homosexuality', *Medico-Legal Journal*, 15:1 (1947), 11–23.

21  Viscount Hailsham, QC, 'Homosexuality and society', in J. Tudor Rees and Harley V. Usill (eds), *They Stand Apart: A Critical Survey of the Problems of Homosexuality* (London: Heinemann, 1955), pp. 21, 24.

22  *Ibid.*, p. 31.

23  C. P. Blacker (ed.), *A Social Problem Group?* (London: Oxford University Press, 1937), p. 4. For a discussion, see Greta Jones, *Social Hygiene in Twentieth-Century Britain* (London: Croom Helm, 1986), chapter 5.

24  Gillian Swanson, 'Serenity, self-regard and the genetic sequence: social psychiatry and preventive eugenics in Britain, 1930s-1950s', *New Formations*, 60 (Spring 2007), 50–1.

25  Ernest W. Burgess, 'The aims of the Society for the Study of Social Problems', *Social Problems*, 1:1 (1953), 2–3.

26  See Hillel Schwartz, 'On the origin of the phrase "social problems"', *Social Problems*, 44:2 (1997), 276–96, esp. 281–2.

27  Malcolm Spector and John I. Kitsuse, *Constructing Social Problems* (New Brunswick, NJ: Transaction Publishers, 2001 [1977]), p. xi.

28  John Hill, *Sex, Class and Realism: British Cinema 1956–1963* (London: British Film Institute, 1986), esp. chapters 4–5.

29  Kenneth Soddy, 'Homosexuality', *The Lancet*, 264 (11 September 1954), 541.

30  British Society for the Study of Sex Psychology, *Policy & Principles. General Aims*, publication no. 1 (London, 1914), p. 1.

31  British Society for the Study of Sex Psychology, *The Social Problem of Sexual Inversion*, publication no. 2 (London, c. 1914).

32  'Discussion on the social aspects of homosexuality', pp. 585, 587.

33  Editorial, *Observer* (8 November 1953), p. 6.

34  'A social problem', *The Sunday Times* (1 November 1953), p. 6.

35  For examples, see W. Calder, 'The sexual offender: a prison medical officer's viewpoint', *British Journal of Criminology*, 6:1 (1955), 26–40; Anon., 'Prison and after: the experiences of a former homosexual', *Howard Journal*, 9:2 (1955), 118–24; S. J. Spencer, 'Homosexuality among Oxford undergraduates', *Journal of Mental Science*, 105 (1959), 393–405.

36 'Mothers and sons', *The Sunday Times* (6 December 1953), p. 6.
37 Kenneth Walker and Peter Fletcher, *Sex and Society: A Psychological Study of Sexual Behaviour in a Competitive Culture* (London: Penguin, 1955), pp. 173, 177.
38 John Charlsley Mackwood, 'Male homosexuality', in 'The sociological aspects of homosexuality', *Medico-Legal Journal*, 15:1 (1947), 14.
39 Edward Glover, *The Problem of Homosexuality* (London: Institute for the Study and Treatment of Delinquency, 1957).
40 G. Th. Kempe, 'The homosexual in society', *British Journal of Delinquency*, 5:1 (1954), 4–20; Kempe, 'The homophiles in society', *International Journal of Sexology*, 7:5 (1954), 217–19; Kempe, 'The homophile in society', *One*, 3:3 (1955), 8–15.
41 Antony Grey, *Quest for Justice: Towards Homosexual Emancipation* (London: Sinclair-Stevenson, 1992), pp. 3, 288.
42 Maurice Leznoff and William A. Westley, 'The homosexual community', *Social Problems*, 3:4 (1956), 257.
43 Kempe, 'Homophiles in society', 217.
44 For the 'race relations' paradigm in Britain, see Chris Waters, '"Dark strangers" in our midst: discourses of race and nation in Britain, 1947–1963', *Journal of British Studies*, 36:2 (1997), 207–38. Michael Schofield admitted his own debts to that paradigm in *A Minority: A Report on the Life of the Male Homosexual in Great Britain* (London: Longmans, 1960), esp. pp. 189–91. For a comprehensive set of foundational texts in the sociology of homosexuality, see Ken Plummer (ed.), *Sexualities: Critical Concepts in Sociology*, vol. I, *Making a Sociology of Sexualities* (London: Routledge, 2002), esp. chapter 7.
45 Kempe, 'Homophiles in society', 219.
46 Antony Grey, letter to *The Sunday Times* (2 April 1954), reprinted in Grey, *Quest for Justice*, pp. 279–82.
47 Eustace Chesser, 'Society and the homosexual', *International Journal of Sexology*, 7:4 (1954), 214.
48 Jeffrey Weeks, *Sex, Politics, and Society: The Regulation of Sexuality since 1800* (London: Longman, 1981), p. 242.
49 *Report of the Committee on Homosexual Offences and Prostitution* (London, 1957). For an elaboration of these points, see Frank Mort, 'Mapping sexual London: The Wolfenden Committee on Homosexual Offences and Prostitution', *New Formations*, 37 (Spring 1999), 92–113; Mort, *Capital Affairs*, pp. 151–72. See also Houlbrook, *Queer London*, pp. 254–61.
50 Bingham, '"The K-Bomb"', 158; see also 165.
51 Liz Stanley, *Sex Surveyed, 1949–1994: From Mass Observation's 'Little Kinsey' to the National Survey and the Hite Reports* (London: Taylor and Francis, 1995), p. 70. See also Liz Stanley, 'Mass Observation's "Little

Kinsey" and the British sex survey tradition', in Jeffrey Weeks and Janet Holland (eds), *Sexual Cultures: Communities, Values and Intimacy* (New York: St Martin's Press, 1996), pp. 97–113.

52  Stanley, *Sex Surveyed*, p. 203.

53  *Ibid.*, p. 200. For a contemporary commentary and summary, see Leonard England, 'A British sex survey', *International Journal of Sexology*, 3:3 (1950), 148–54.

54  Savage, *Identities and Social Change*, pp. 19–20, 94.

55  Stanley, 'Mass Observation's "Little Kinsey"', p. 124.

56  Author's interview with Michael Schofield, 21 August 2000.

57  Gordon Westwood [Michael Schofield], *Society and the Homosexual* (London: Victor Gollancz, 1952), p. 68.

58  Interview with Schofield.

59  Westwood [Schofield], *Society and the Homosexual*, p. 4.

60  *Ibid.*, p. 2.

61  *Ibid.*, p. 181.

62  D. J. West, *Homosexuality* (London: Duckworth, 1955).

63  Westwood [Schofield], *Society and the Homosexual*, p. 136.

64  *Ibid.*

65  Hornsey, *The Spiv and the Architect*, p. 28; see also pp. 117–19, 131–5.

66  *Ibid.*, p. 134.

67  Schofield later wrote that he was more apt to receive funding for his work when he said he was undertaking a British Kinsey report; see his comments in Peter M. Nardi and Beth E. Schneider (eds), 'Kinsey: a 50th anniversary symposium', *Sexualities*, 1:1 (1998), 83–106.

68  Westwood [Schofield], *A Minority*, p. 1; see also p. 197.

69  Savage, *Identities and Social Change*, p. 236. Schofield himself also wrote about the new practices, and how to undertake them, in his *Social Research* (London: Heinemann, 1969).

70  Grey, *Quest for Justice*, p. 50.

71  Richard Hauser, *The Homosexual Society* (London: Bodley Head, 1962), p. 23.

72  *Ibid.*, p. 95.

73  Kenneth Plummer found 'dubious value' in Hauser's classifications, roundly condemning his book: Plummer, *Sexual Stigma: An Interactionist Account* (London: Routledge and Kegan Paul, 1975), p. 97. At the time, D. J. West both condemned his sampling methods and his classifications, but praised him for his reproduction of the candid views expressed by the men he interviewed: West, 'Which homosexual society?', *Man and Society*, 2:1 (1962), 32.

74  Schofield, *Social Research*, p. 119.

75  Michael Schofield, *Sociological Aspects of Homosexuality: A Comparative Study of Three Types of Homosexuals* (London: Longmans, Green & Co.,

1965), p. 147. For a slightly earlier discussion of the problems faced by the social sciences in the study of homosexuality in Britain, see Gordon Westwood [Michael Schofield], 'Problems of research into sexual deviations', *Man and Society*, 1:1 (1961), 29–32.

76  Savage, *Identities and Social Change*, p. 97.

77  Westwood [Schofield], *A Minority*, p. 195.

78  Schofield, *Sociological Aspects*, p. 188.

79  *Ibid.*, p. 211.

80  Antony Grey, 'Doctors' dilemmas', *Man and Society*, 7 (1964), 29.

81  Irving Bieber, review of Schofield, *Sociological Aspects of Homosexuality*, in *Archives of General Psychiatry*, 15:2 (1966), 214–15.

82  'Interim statement of the counter psychiatry group of the Gay Liberation Front' (London, 1972), mimeographed leaflet in the Chesterman Papers, Hall-Carpenter Archives, London School of Economics.

83  Charlotte Wolff, *Love between Women* (London: Duckworth, 1971), esp. chapter 8. See also Rebecca Jennings, *Tomboys and Bachelor Girls: A Lesbian History of Post-War Britain* (Manchester: Manchester University Press, 2007), chapter 5.

84  H. Montgomery Hyde, *The Other Love: An Historical and Contemporary Survey of Homosexuality in Britain* (London: Heinemann, 1970), esp. chapter 1.

85  Jeffrey Escoffier, *American Homo: Community and Perversity* (Berkeley: University of California Press, 1998), p. 82.

86  Jeffrey Weeks, 'Mary McIntosh and the "homosexual role"', in his *Making Sexual History* (Cambridge: Polity Press, 2000), p. 54. McIntosh's article first appeared in *Social Problems*, 16:2 (1968), 182–92. For the article and her subsequent reflections on it, see Kenneth Plummer (ed.), *The Making of the Modern Homosexual* (London: Hutchison, 1981), pp. 30–49.

87  Jeffrey Weeks and Janet Holland, 'Introduction', in Weeks and Holland (eds), *Sexual Cultures*, p. 4.

88  Plummer, *Sexual Stigma*, p. 199; see also p. 3 and p. vii where, despite his criticisms, he thanked Schofield for kindling his interest in sex research.

89  McIntosh, 'Homosexual role', p. 190, n. 30; Plummer, *Making of the Modern Homosexual*, p. 18.

90  For his recent reflections on the transformative ambitions of the more radical 1970s moment, see Jeffrey Weeks, 'Making the human gesture: History, sexuality and social justice', *History Workshop Journal*, 70 (Autumn 2010), 5–20.

# 9

# Mr Grey goes to Washington: the homophile internationalism of Britain's Homosexual Law Reform Society

*David Minto*

Towards the end of 1967, soon after Westminster partially decriminalised gay sex in England and Wales, Britain's leading lobbyist went on holiday. First, Antony Grey headed to Amsterdam, where he recuperated in the apartment of a prominent member of the Dutch homophile movement. Then he flew across the Atlantic and began what he later described as 'the most hectic four weeks of my life'.[1] Following law reform at home, Grey was embarking on a transcontinental lecture tour of the United States: a victory lap of sorts, but one to a country where gay sex remained illegal almost everywhere, much to the chagrin of its homophile activists.

The trip had been more than a year in the planning, although US homophiles had mooted bringing over Grey, the secretary of Britain's Homosexual Law Reform Society (HLRS), long before that. Dorr Legg, a co-founder of Los Angeles group ONE, had eventually sealed the deal by waiting until the Sexual Offences Bill cleared Parliament and by bankrolling the venture. With sodomy laws still on the books in all but one state, Legg envisioned Grey's visit as not only enabling strategic discussions and solidarities but also directly advancing campaign goals, arguing that 'the public support on every sort of level which could be achieved by throwing a spotlight on law reform efforts in the two English speaking nations [is] hardly to be estimated'.[2] Afterwards, he was even more emphatic in suggesting that Grey's tour had reached millions through newspaper columns, radio and TV programmes, and face-to-face encounters. 'As a result,' Legg told ONE members, 'countless men and women have now been made a little more ready to listen to reason concerning homosexuality, a little less rigid and fearful than they once were. This is how the successful law reform campaign was conducted in England; this is about the way it must also be conducted in the U.S.'[3]

Grey's analysis, however, was less enthusiastic. Privately, he fretted that his US tour had had little impact; publicly, he did not hesitate to criticise the US homophile movement itself. 'There is an unfortunate tendency', he wrote in HLRS's newsletter, 'on the part of some of these groups to spend their time and energy criticizing their colleagues (rivals?) in "the movement" instead of drawing the general public's attention to the undoubtedly greater discrimination against known or suspected homosexuals that exists in American public and business life compared to British.' Grey admired the dedication of homophile leaders, and even ambivalently admitted that the militancy of some activists was 'at once startling and salutary to those who are perhaps too accustomed to a different style of public discourse'.[4] Yet in the months that followed the tour, Grey glibly told numerous correspondents (including some US ones) that he was glad that the homophile movement, as he saw it, remained foreign to Britain. Indeed, Legg even reported to ONE members that homophile infighting had led Grey to question whether 'law reform in England would ever have succeeded if there had been such a thing as a Homophile Movement'.[5] In fact, a homophile-type organization for lesbians had existed in Britain since 1963 with the foundation of the Minorities Research Group, which also cultivated links with homophile women across the Atlantic. That Grey overlooked this speaks to the male domination of both US homophile activism and British debate over homosexuality in this period, a dynamic that had been reinforced in Britain by criminalization of same-sex intimacy only between men.

Despite Grey's criticisms, the realisation of HLRS's US expedition in itself suggests the importance of international affiliations to postwar homophiles, reformers and their allies, and the limitations of movement histories that adopt too rigid a local or national focus. Recent scholarship has begun instructively to position Western homophile activism in a more international setting, examining cross-border ties that potentially shaped identity as well as politics.[6] In a particularly helpful article for thinking about transnationalism,[7] Leila J. Rupp explores how one umbrella group, the International Committee for Sexual Equality (ICSE), 'elaborated a homophile identity that crossed nationality' in the 1940s and 1950s. Positioning ICSE as the 'middle link in a chain of transnational activism' stretching from Magnus Hirschfeld to gay liberation, Rupp describes the committee's efforts to bring together European and American homophiles for discussions and social events, to lobby supranational organisations beyond national governments and to exploit cultures of tourism and pen-pal networks. Rupp argues not only that the ICSE had international ambitions but also that the group was held together by a proud transnationalism recognising sexual identity as a bond that united individuals across national divides. Cultivating such solidarity was important in overcoming recent wartime hostilities, but nevertheless took courage in a persecutory Cold War environment of imagined homosexual conspiracies. ICSE's very existence then suggests that in the history of homosexual activism 'there is more connection across time and space than first meets the eye'.[8]

Yet the double-meaning of Rupp's title – the *persistence* of transnational organising – invokes the difficulties as well as successes of homophile cross-border connections, and if we shift our focus from the Netherlands-based ICSE to Britain's HLRS we find that sometimes the former outweighed the latter. Tensions could stem from not only the practical problems of languages and distance but also the persistence – and perhaps entrenchment – of national frames in the postwar period, fostering distinct organising traditions and political cultures, and supporting different regulatory and constitutional regimes. Even ICSE's transnationalism appears to have rested on a particular brand of Dutch internationalism, its vice-president stating in 1957, 'it is commensurate with Dutch mentality to open the doors to all countries of the world'.[9] By contrast, HLRS refused officially to affiliate with ICSE, a stance reflecting the fact that (despite its many homosexual subscribers) it did not consider itself a homophile group, but rather a 'broadly-based national organization supported by many eminent people' who recognised a need for law reform while differing 'profoundly ... as to the medical nature, sinfulness or desirability of homosexual behaviour'.[10] That said, the man at HLRS's centre – Antony Grey – was gay and during the 1960s became enmeshed in North American, European and Commonwealth homophile networks, leaving a trail of correspondence evidencing both attachment and conflict. Rather than simply representing the opposite pole to the culture of transnationalism and internationalism realised by ICSE, the case of HLRS may help further to elucidate that culture's possibilities and limitations.

This chapter, then, explores a British variant on homophile internationalism before and immediately after the 1967 Sexual Offences Act by mapping Grey's cross-border connections while noting strain against transnational solidarity. In charge of HLRS's day-to-day operation during this period, Grey authored and received much of the correspondence on which this chapter is based, although his work more generally depended on HLRS's Executive Committee, office staff, affiliated professionals, honorary trustees and volunteers. Born in 1927, Grey became active in HLRS soon after its foundation in 1958 but was not always liked by fellow campaigners, and it is worth noting from the outset the frequently pompous and officious tone of his writing, products in part of a mid-century Cambridge education, training at the Bar, religious faith that fostered reverence for the Church and a lobbying career for British steel interests that habituated him to sweet-talking those in power. Yet while Grey assumed the role of gatekeeper at HLRS as the conduit between its grassroots supporters and high-level committees, it seems more valuable to reflect on how his perspectives and actions were shaped by his environment, rather than attributing agency or blame to personality alone. Here comparative analysis and the examination of transnational currents can be particularly helpful. Whether we view Grey's positions as accurate readings of the world around him, or indeed as policy successes or failures, they tell us something about the pressures and resources of the political space he occupied, and the incentives to reach abroad, together with the complexities of doing so.

When in December 1962 Antony Grey was appointed acting secretary of HLRS and its sister society, the social welfare-oriented Albany Trust, he took the helm of an organisation that was self-consciously distinct from homophile groups in Europe and the United States. Grey's immediate predecessors in the post were John and Venetia Newall, a wealthy heterosexual couple who, seeking a philanthropic cause, had agreed to take the society's reins for a couple of years. Its Honorary Committee comprised prominent churchmen, doctors, politicians, academics and lawyers, while the small decision-making Executive Committee included the *New Statesman* journalist and social commentator C. R. Hewitt and the archaeologist Jacquetta Hawkes. Headed by this ostensibly heterosexual collection of the great and the good, HLRS sought to gain standing in the British debate over decriminalising homosexual intimacy between men by assuming a posture of objectivity that it deemed incompatible with self-interested homophiles elsewhere. Therefore, when Danish magazine *Eos* and other foreign homophile publications asked to reprint material from HLRS's journal, the Executive Committee 'agreed that it could only do the Society harm to be associated with these organisations', and withheld permission.[11] When in the same year ONE contacted European groups about its first proposed homophile 'cruise' through the continent – receiving enthusiastic replies from Denmark, France, the Netherlands and Switzerland – Venetia Newall responded that she and her husband would be abroad at the time of the trip, so that 'there would be little point in your troubling to call'.[12]

But behind the scenes at least one volunteer was forging connections with homophiles overseas. In 1960 Edgar Wright took his first trip to Amsterdam, where he visited the main clubhouse of the Dutch homophile group COC, one of almost six thousand international visitors that year.[13] An article Wright drafted shortly after his trip indicates the impression it made on him. 'Men. Dancing together,' he began. 'Women dancing together is OK: we're used to that. But *men*. Dancing *together!*' With around three thousand members spread across the Netherlands and operating with the approval of the police, the self-run COC, Wright argued, made homosexuality respectable by taking it off the streets. Professionals were on hand for those who needed legal, religious or psychiatric advice. More than that, however, the COC realised a vision of society in which gay men could 'meet their own kind freely and socially as people rather than sordidly and furtively as criminals'. Plus, they could dance, a sight that Wright wrote 'astonishes an Englishman'. Inspired, Edgar Wright began further to flesh out an alternative persona, the work name of Antony Grey – the Englishman who returned from Amsterdam and wondered: 'why not?'[14]

Grey's article apparently remained unpublished, but his enthusiasm for the COC exerted some limited influence on HLRS's leadership. Grey told the Newalls that the Dutch homophiles proposed that HLRS should affiliate with their international wing, the ICSE, but as he suspected this step was overruled.[15] Information, however, could be exchanged informally, and in fact HLRS already had a presence in the US homophile press, appealing for donations soon after its foundation. Abroad, there was confusion over whether HLRS was a homophile group and about its relationship with the Albany Trust, which increasingly became the title organisation. But while lonely gay men and women from across the world who sought social contacts through HLRS would continue to be disappointed, Grey told the COC that its work in the Netherlands 'has many important lessons for us in England'.[16] Preparing for a meeting with the Home Secretary, the Newalls mooted the idea of a 'carefully supervised social centre' that might promote social adaptation 'along the lines successfully instituted in Holland', but then questioned whether to mention this at all 'as the idea is superficially most unattractive to heterosexuals'.[17] In the event, Grey reported that the HLRS deputation did indeed relay 'how it was almost impossible to do constructive social work of the kind you are able to achieve in Holland while the English law remains unchanged'. Grey thought this made quite an impression on the Home Secretary, but the risks involved in introducing gay men to each other persisted and in effect took practical plans for a club off HLRS's agenda.[18]

Yet within the confines of the law, a change of tone accompanied the Newalls' departure at the end of 1962 when Grey offered his services as secretary and the Executive Committee (with a reluctance due apparently to his sexuality) appointed him on a probationary basis. A major watershed occurred soon after when the *Observer* – at which Grey took sub-editing shifts – ran a report on the COC. Headlined 'A Club for Homosexuals', the story was sensational to some precisely because it eschewed sensationalism, and for years afterwards British men and women wrote to HLRS asking for the address of the Dutch club. This, safely beyond Britain's borders, Grey happily provided, sometimes also including a copy of the letter the *Observer* printed the same day in which he argued it was 'high time that we followed the lead of countries such as Holland'.[19] Assisting ordinary Britons to picture what this might mean, Grey subsequently facilitated contact between the COC and the documentary filmmaker Bryan Magee. The result was that in 1964 British television viewers saw scenes of Dutchmen dancing. Perhaps, like Grey, they found the sight astonishing, yet there it was, happening across a slender stretch of the North Sea. This vision, however, also affected the terms of reaction, solidifying the line between law reform and social acceptance so that years later Grey would say of HLRS's chief supporter in the House of Lords, 'he always foams at the mouth re "Dutch clubs"!'[20]

With friends like these, HLRS's organisational culture would continue to retard public affiliation with European homophiles, and, while Grey maintained his own ties, irritation and wariness surfaced on occasion in private too. Before accepting the HLRS secretaryship, Grey had seriously considered moving to the Netherlands and had been offered a board position with the ICSE. By the early 1960s, however, ICSE was all but defunct, and Grey's efforts to help resurrect its newsletter were frustrated to the extent that he said of Dutch homophile problems, 'I fear there is something about the fraternity which makes it extremely difficult to organise constructive team-work!'[21] Meanwhile, although HLRS's journal became more like other homophile publications, with increased content by and about homosexuals, foreign homophiles did not always appreciate the change. A year after Grey took over, Marc Daniel from the French group Arcadie commented that HLRS materials were 'not especially appealing to foreign readers' given 'the complete absence … of references and data on non-British laws, homosexual organizations, and magazines and life'.[22] This critique was somewhat unfair as the current Autumn 1963 issue included an interview with the COC founder Bob Angelo, although even here edits dampened down an earlier draft's call for British activists to form a group based on Dutch and US homophile organisations.[23] In a terse reply to Daniel, Grey indicated that HLRS was no 'brother-organization', as the Frenchman had put it, and that the law would have to be reformed before any 'broader effort on behalf of the homosexual community'.[24]

Despite these misgivings, Grey's continuing participation in the European homophile scene suggested compensations in finding a peer group of sorts, and as the British law reform effort gathered pace he further recognised both practical and abstract benefits to his involvement. Beyond occasional meetings and correspondence with European homophiles, Grey became more assiduous in publicising the law and social conditions of other countries, in 1965 running an article by a Copenhagen contact on the repeal of Denmark's 'Ugly Law' and a year later publishing a version of a talk he invited Daniel himself to give for the Albany Trust.[25] Leaflet swaps with the COC evolved into a scheme whereby British visitors to the Dutch club were handed information on the trust when presenting their passport for admission.[26] Meanwhile, in the rare emergency situations that came to Grey's attention, the European homophile network could be tapped for assistance. In one instance, Grey appealed to the COC after an HLRS supporter sought legal help for a friend who had been imprisoned in West Germany.[27] In another case, Grey secured Arcadie's assistance for a British man who had been arrested in Paris but remained bewildered as to the details of the charge.[28] While there were particular schemes and specific examples of co-operation, however, Grey in part viewed the advantage of a European connection as more diffusely cultural, edging Britons closer to enlightened

Continental mores. In a striking 1965 letter to Daniel, Grey postulated that the 'main tragedy of the Common Market negotiations was of course psychological – it would have been the one thing which might possibly have dragged the British into the mainstream of 20th century life!'[29] Through personal relationships and light institutional association with European homophiles, perhaps Grey and HLRS would succeed where politicians continued to fail.

Such ambitions of transnational cordiality, however, gave Grey pause when it came to US homophile organisations, some of which were confronting hostile opposition with increasing assertiveness. In contrast to the Newalls, Grey steadily cultivated transatlantic contacts, but, while by the mid-1960s he was corresponding with homophiles across the United States, he was also attuned to the movement's factionalism. Epistolary exchanges, in any case, were not necessarily straightforward transmissions of candid perspectives. Sometimes flattering US homophiles, Grey could dismiss their work to their rivals, doing both at the same time when he told the leader of a New York-based group that he hoped their new journal 'will be a superior production to the others of the genre that have previously appeared in the States'.[30] Particular dialogues often amounted to only a handful of letters and were typically general in nature, although the network also enabled Grey to source specific materials and information, as when he asked a Chicago lawyer about the practical effects that had followed Illinois's 1962 repeal of its sodomy statute.[31] But US homophiles tracking law reform prospects in Britain could reach a pitch of excitement that discomforted Grey and that he tried to temper. In late 1965 the Miami homophile Richard Inman enthused that on the back of European official reports 'we of the Homophile Civil Rights Movement in the US could tear down the fences of organized resistance to sexual law reform, in only a very few years'. Far more reserved in tone, Grey cautioned, 'What is needed is a slow, steady reiteration of common sense based upon authoritative views such as those of the Wolfenden Committee and the churches.'[32]

If keeping US homophiles in check across the Atlantic was one thing, coping with their visits was another, especially when Grey put himself at personal inconvenience to make them feel at home. In 1964 when ONE's first overseas tour party descended on London at the same time as the New York-based social reformer Alfred Gross, Grey joked to another US homophile that he didn't know if he should 'dread an encounter between these two transatlantic manifestations – or whether it might be rather fun to promote it!'[33] Although Grey accommodated ONE's request for a social gathering in a private residence by opening up his own apartment, his acid pen subsequently judged Gross to be a 'very self-centred and cantankerous old man', while the ONE crowd fared little better, as 'really quite something: mostly over fifty and distinctly bizarre!' Nevertheless, Grey thought that they had enjoyed the 'hectic tea party' and left 'with quite warm feelings towards the Albany Trust, so I feel it was a good bit of public relations work'.[34] The impression was confirmed when a ONE member wrote to say he hoped their organisations would 'continue to cement bonds of friendship and cooperation'.[35]

Yet the contrast between Grey's description of 'public relations work' and the homophile visitor's appeal to 'friendship and cooperation' seems telling, the difference between felt solidarity and an act of diplomacy that consciously sought benefits, mitigated liabilities and gave Grey a sense of self-importance. A year after the visit and a disastrous split within ONE produced what Grey called a 'very public washing of dirty laundry', and he wrote a series of letters to both parties posing as a 'quite disinterested' outsider. 'To foreign eyes,' Grey lamented, 'neither side looks entirely dignified (which is always a desirable public posture to maintain).'[36] Assuming the position of peacemaker, Grey's intervention may have signalled a growing investment in the US homophile movement, but it also betrayed fears – however alarmist – that this foreign public spat portrayed homosexuals in general as 'schizophrenic' and 'unfit for freedom' with potential repercussions in Britain.[37] Indeed, months later Grey articulated the dangers of homophile internationalism for HLRS even more strongly in arguing that an eccentric British clergyman – allegedly aiming to lead a world homophile movement on the back of a conference on religion and homosexuality – risked raising in Parliament 'a great outcry about "the homintern" and perhaps irreparable damage would be done to our prospects of the Bill'.[38] Firing off a telegram to ONE headed 'VERY PERTURBED RE LONDON CLERGY CONSULTATION', Grey urged Legg to intervene with a US homophile from another group who despite his warnings remained committed to the venture.[39]

Following the Labour Party's March 1966 election victory, however, HLRS faced the likelihood of not only law reform success but de facto obsolescence, and two key institutional incentives thus rose to the fore to promote transatlantic ties: expertise for repurposing and money to fund more ambitious social projects. Ironically enough, the aforementioned Anglo-American consultation on religion and homosexuality tantalised Grey on both scores after he successfully displaced the rogue reverend to organise and chair the conference himself. With Grey in charge, the private meeting was firmly weighted towards the participation of sympathetic British religious leaders rather than the take-off of homophile internationalism, but it nevertheless brought to London the likes of the charismatic US clergyman Ted McIlvenna, who embodied the potential power of coalitions between pastors and homophiles, and the San Francisco activist Don Lucas, whose interest in social welfare projects matched Grey's own. These men, together with the Kinsey Institute's John Gagnon, not only commanded respect for their expertise but were evidently well connected to US charitable foundations and other funding streams. Characterising the conference as 'at once encouraging and dismaying because it indicates how much there is still to be done and how little we have to do it with', Grey nevertheless told an Albany Trust psychologist, 'I am *hoping* that it may even get us a little bit of material, in addition to moral, support from the States.'[40] Even before the consultation, Grey had been scoping out US financial opportunities, hoping to go beyond the steady trickle of transatlantic donations by working with a former participant at ONE to launch a US 'Albany Foundation' that would target substantial stateside resources. In the end, this particular project failed to get off the ground, but Grey remained confident that 'it is not impossible to devise ways in which American funds can be charitably distributed abroad – after all Rockefeller, Kellogg and co. manage to do it'.[41]

It was in this context that Grey started seriously to contemplate taking a transatlantic trip himself following a 'totally unexpected' offer Legg had made at the height of the ONE split that took the stakes of Anglo-American homophile diplomacy to a whole new level. ONE's invitation to bring over the HLRS secretary at a time of intense US homophile interest in Westminster could be read as an attempt to outdo rival movement factions as well as to promote law reform in the United States, and Grey remained hesitant about committing to Legg. In the summer of 1966, however, the pair met both in London and at an Amsterdam homophile conference, and afterwards Grey confided to Arcadie's Daniel that he found Legg 'capable and sincere', while Legg joked he had 'many times laughed in trying to picture what manner of horns and hoofs picture of me you must have had'.[42] Even at this point, Grey could write to a US contact that friendliness didn't mean 'I am ready to identify myself or the Albany Trust with any of the so called homophile organisations in the States, other than to maintain amicable correspondence from time to time', but negotiations over the format and itinerary of a possible trip did step up a gear.[43] Although Grey continued to stress the desirability of US homophile unity, the most important item was that ONE should fund the expedition, a point he periodically reconfirmed. Legg, in response, informed Grey that his people had approved the financial outlay on condition 'that there be NO joint arrangements with other homophile organizations', and stressed that jealousies within the movement meant that 'the slightest hint to anyone of your possible coming to US could spike the whole thing before it started'.[44]

Once the Sexual Offences Act passed in the summer of 1967, Grey took the final steps to cross the Atlantic in person, but emphasised aims that had as much to do with the survival of his organisation as with promoting transnational solidarity. Checking ONE's commitment to pay, Grey highlighted the parlous state of the society's finances and expressed a desire to meet with charitable foundations that might look favourably on the social mission of the Albany Trust. 'It would be a tragedy,' he wrote, 'if the work we are trying to do here should have to fold up now that this very partial and tentative law reform has been achieved.'[45] Law reform, indeed, suddenly seemed an anti-climax and Grey, on holiday in Amsterdam, confessed he felt 'deflated and depressed'.[46]

Legg reassured him that ONE would cover all the transatlantic travel and living costs for the engagements it scheduled and looked forward to discussing 'concrete proposals' for the trust's future. He also, however, clarified rules of engagement, and these did not bode well for homophile togetherness. While Grey forwarded lists of those he wanted to meet and contemplated a week's extension to take in Washington, DC, Legg continued to emphasise homophile divisions that Grey hoped could be overcome. Jetting down to Richard Inman in Florida was out, Legg confirmed, since 'many people feel that Inman is dynamite and sets things back with his unshakable tenacity'.[47] Legg did schedule a New York dinner for key East Coast homophile activists, but continued to warn that other groups would not hesitate to take credit for ONE's hard work. Furthermore, there were troubling signs of non-cooperation. Domestic, let alone transnational, solidarity, could not be considered a given. 'You speak of the need for harmony', Legg wrote, ominously. 'I agree, but easier said than done.'[48]

Grey arrived in New York on 23 October 1967 and embarked on a whirlwind itinerary of media appearances, public meetings and private consultations with homophiles, clergy and professionals in New York, Detroit, Chicago, Bloomington, Los Angeles, San Francisco and – in the event – Washington, DC. During this time he contested the airwaves with the psychoanalyst Irving Bieber, discussed opportunities with *Harper's* and *Playboy*, toured the Kinsey Institute, met prominent ACLU lawyers, questioned UCLA students about their sexual attitudes and, of course, lectured at ONE's Californian clubhouse. Less formal activities included nights at a gay-themed off-Broadway play and a tour of LA go-go boy bars, fulfilling Grey's wry hope 'that in addition to the public persona there will be occasional opportunities for private relaxation with consenting adult friends!'[49] His first engagement, however, was a sparsely attended press conference, for which Grey's prepared notes gave no indication of his links to the US homophile movement and instead spotlighted the international co-operation he anticipated fostering among professionals and research workers.[50] Indeed, throughout the trip Grey presented himself – in public at least – as an adviser with the authority of experience, rather than a self-invested activist forging transnational bonds with US compatriots. At the press conference, Grey did stress that reforming sex laws was not enough in itself, and argued that society must help homosexuals to accept themselves. But asked by a radio reporter the inevitable follow-up question – was he a homosexual? – Grey pleaded the Fifth and refused to incriminate himself.[51]

This perhaps was not just continued deference to British lobbying decorum, but an acknowledgement of the potential hazards posed by crossing borders. Throughout Grey's tenure as secretary, HLRS supporters had frequently written for advice on foreign travel and emigration, and their concerns were not merely academic. Shortly before his US trip, at the beginning of 1967, Grey had asked a Chicago lawyer affiliated with ONE about the best course of action for an Englishman who had been convicted of importuning and now wished to emigrate to the United States.[52] A further letter reached him a few months later from a man in Canada 'having to fight a great medico-legal battle' to take up a US job offer. Grey advised him that it was unlikely he had been blacklisted for an earlier suicide attempt and treatment in London, but noted that a recent ruling in the US *Boutillier* case found that 'all homosexuals are "psychopathic" personalities and that any positive evidence of a homosexual identification is therefore held to bar aliens from entering the U.S.A.'[53] Grey's public self-presentation therefore took no chances. Asked again on a TV show whether he was homosexual, Grey reportedly replied to the African-American interviewer Louis Lomax, 'Surely, Mr. Lomax, of all people you should know that one does not need to be a Negro to have an interest in civil rights.'[54]

Grey's restrained approach sat uneasily with ONE's combative promotion of his trip and the tumultuous US homophile scene. ONE touted the coup of securing the man who had been 'in the very thick of the battle' to reform England's 'barbarous' law as proof not only that it was dedicated to achieving 'full citizenship and rights for homosexuals', but that it was the 'most respected and active' US homophile group.[55] Despite this boastfulness, Legg urged other homophile leaders to attend the New York 'harmony dinner' at the start of Grey's visit. A number of East Coast activists showed up – and this proved to be an explosive mix.

According to Legg's self-serving account, trouble started when the campaigner Barbara Gittings attempted to record Grey's address to the group, prompting Legg to insist that ONE's financial investment gave it sole rights to publish Grey's speeches. Legg reported that Gittings fought back, loudly berating ONE for 'how it was wrecking the movement', with other homophiles stirring the pot. Thus, when Grey eventually delivered his scheduled talk, he pointedly remarked that the US homophile movement seemed to have 'many prima donnas all singing arias from different operas at the same time'. With leaders like these, Grey later asked Legg rhetorically, 'how soon do you think you are going to achieve law reforms?'[56]

Personal animosities between US homophiles mirrored political differences, and while Grey called for unity he also backed particular types of public action. Recognising that US activists faced circumstances different from those faced by English reformers, Grey nevertheless stressed the same need for 'long and patient laboring at the creation of a climate favorable to law reform' through alliances with professionals and clergy, and the avoidance of flashy statements.[57] As Legg told it, Grey exacted revenge on Gittings at the harmony dinner by 'stating his total disagreement with Barbara's widely publicized picketing activities' – a reference to the small but public homophile protests she and fellow activist Frank Kameny had led in Washington and Philadelphia since 1965.[58] Legg himself was no fan of these public actions, and the emphasis in his account was doubtless coloured by his own politics. However, the *San Francisco Chronicle*'s report on Grey's final public lecture gave a clear indication of the British reformer's overall political message, with a photo of Grey captioned 'No waving banners', and text that relayed his stress on educating the public 'very slowly'.[59]

Yet Grey also received advice as well as dispensing it during his tour, and San Francisco was not the final leg, for in California it became clear that a week's extension was feasible on the back of lecture earnings.[60] Mr Grey, therefore, did indeed have the chance to go to Washington, where he spent a couple of days with Frank Kameny – the homophile movement's banner-waver-in-chief. Given Grey's public objections to these tactics, it may seem puzzling that Kameny also became one of the three men to whom Grey, decades later, dedicated his 1992 book on the British law reform campaign.[61] This was not, however, simply a retrospective gesture recognising the importance of Kameny's brand of protest after the event; Grey learned of the Washington activist's work long before meeting him and, although the handful of letters the two men exchanged in the years before the 1967 tour paled in comparison to the volume of correspondence traded with Legg, the relationship nevertheless had an unmatched intensity. These exchanges, unique in tone and content, offer an alternative if more obscure trajectory to Grey's US visit.

Kameny had first made contact with HLRS in May 1964 with a missive that was characteristically incisive and blunt in its dissection of British law reform efforts. He introduced himself as the president of the Mattachine Society of Washington and as a man who had 'appeared in that capacity and as a homosexual, on both radio and television'. Indeed, Kameny was the nearest thing the homophile movement had to a public figure after contesting his expulsion from federal government employment due to his homosexuality and appearing before Congress to demand the right of his homophile group to assemble. These experiences led to familiarity with US legal procedure and, although Kameny claimed no expertise in English law, he found himself exasperated by the sheer vagueness of the term 'gross indecency', which had been used to prosecute an open-ended range of male homosexual practices since its introduction through the 1885 Labouchère Amendment. Shouldn't this legally imprecise offence be challenged through the courts? In the United States, such obscurity would leave a law vulnerable to being voided. Furthermore, what counted as 'indecency' could obviously be debated. Kameny cited recent headway made in cases contesting the US Civil Service Commission's ban on 'immoral conduct' in part on the grounds that 'homosexual acts are NOT immoral'. He understood that the English legal system was 'a very much more conservative one than ours'. Nevertheless, he would await HLRS's reaction to his suggestion.[62]

The curveball was hardly likely to make HLRS abandon its cautious agitation of MPs, but, in describing an alternative strategy to parliamentary lobbying, it also forced Grey to write a searching reply that most other homophile letters simply did not require. On this occasion, Grey explained that public and government attitudes in Britain still lagged behind the Wolfenden recommendations, and that a challenge for vagueness stood little chance of success, since, once Parliament had passed a law, 'its interpretation is entirely a matter for the Judges; and they are usually not slow to write in details'. Nevertheless, Grey said he would review the matter with legal advisers, praised what he had heard of Kameny's Washington campaigns and urged him to keep in touch.[63]

Kameny's next letter, over a year later, was on the surface little more than a thank you note for the parliamentary transcripts Grey had sent him, but it also relayed what to English eyes was perhaps as startling as Dutchmen dancing: the advent of the first group protest by a handful of homosexuals outside the White House. The initial picket, reflected Kameny, had been little more than a test run. The second, however, 'was shown on television newscasts all over the country', and Reuters had promised to link it to the legislative debate in Britain. 'Did they?' he wanted to know.[64]

But before Grey had a chance to reply, Kameny fired off a further, even more extraordinary letter. He had now read the parliamentary reports Grey had sent him, and was incensed by the comments of the MP Cyril Osborne. However, Kameny did not merely express his anger to Grey but also wrote directly to Osborne 'as a homosexual American citizen – or, more important in this context, as a homosexual human being', tearing into the MP's contention that sodomy should remain illegal because the majority considered it wrong. Then he went considerably further. Condemning Osborne's willingness to see homosexuals imprisoned, he called him 'a profoundly immoral, fundamentally evil, and callously viciously cruel person'. In fact, in the 'short step between prison cells for homosexuals and gas ovens for Jews', there appeared to be 'amazingly little difference between Osborne and Hitler'.[65]

Although probably not privy to the ferocity of this invective, Grey was told by Kameny that he had taken 'the strongest possible exception' to Osborne. Far from objecting to the hinted assertiveness of the foreign intervention, Grey instead moved to harness it. Dismissing Osborne as a 'national joke', Grey suggested that the MP was 'really not worth wasting breath on', yet more serious opponents to the reform bill did exist, and he hoped that in due course Kameny would engage them. Even more surprising was Grey's claim that he would 'personally like to see a British equivalent of the Mattachine Society acting as a "ginger group"' to make the public more aware that Wolfenden was 'a very moderate compromise'. A scrawled addendum on the typed letter qualified this desire by noting its potential to lead to a 'hysterical "heterosexual backlash"'. Nevertheless, Grey hoped that Kameny would write an article for HLRS's journal 'to make British readers more aware of what you regard as the legitimate objectives of a reforming campaign to be, and how our own discussions strike you as an American citizen'.[66] The magazine was the voice of a charitable body rather than of a homophile group, Grey told him, so it would be inappropriate to advocate the formation of activist organizations. But, he continued, 'I do think you could express surprise from your own standpoint ... that such a movement does not exist, and that you might point to some of the things it could usefully do.'[67]

That Grey came close here in the mid-1960s to backing the rise of a British homophile movement by proxy suggests the heady nature of the exchange with Kameny, easier to read as a forum in which Grey confronted and thought beyond (however fleetingly) HLRS's organisational constraints than as a diplomatic attempt to curry favour with an important US activist. In contrast to the gruesome details of the ONE fight taking place at this moment, the conversation probed both philosophical and practical dimensions of the Anglo-American struggle. Across the Atlantic, Grey perceived a 'great and growing consciousness of Civil Rights as a burning political issue' that was hardly visible in Britain. The welfare state, he argued, had led to the widespread delusion that his country did not have underprivileged minorities. 'I therefore feel,' he confided to Kameny, 'that in the "Civil Rights" field, as in the organization of a "self-conscious" homophile movement, we are many years behind you, even though we may achieve a measure of legal reform before you do'.[68]

With the interlocutors now dead and limited documentary sources, it is difficult to assess the ironies or goodwill Barbara Gittings sought to convey when at the end of Grey's US tour – and thus three weeks after the harmony dinner – she wrote to Kameny, 'Hope your visit with Antony Grey is proving highly productive!'[69] Upon meeting Kameny, Grey noted in his diary the activist's dominant personality and obsessive recollection of his homophile activities, leaving the British reformer to retire to bed early in the morning, exhausted.[70] Over a year later Kameny recalled of the encounter that it was on the questions of self-representation and militancy 'that Anthony Grey and I, though in full agreement on fundamentals, found ourselves to differ most'.[71] Yet a letter from Grey soon after his return to Britain tells its own tale. Inviting Kameny to become a member of a UK Human Rights Year working group, Grey described how he attended the first meeting at the House of Commons intending to keep quiet, but, as discussion turned to which minority problems the group should address, decided to speak up. Citing his 'special interest' in homosexuality, Grey told his colleagues they should 'consider discrimination against homosexuals as a group or class'. To his surprise, his fellow committee members were enthusiastic. One MP even suggested that Grey write round each government department to ask whether they would employ someone they thought to be homosexual. And so here Grey was asking Kameny for advice on a project that at least bore superficial resemblance to the Washington activist's own work in challenging the US civil service's employment discrimination. In contrast to his usual sign-off of 'Yours sincerely', the note ended 'Yours ever'.[72]

Disentangling the varied and sometimes contradictory threads that had trailed for years across the Atlantic and knotted together during Grey's US tour would be a futile task if by doing so one sought to locate the single line that mattered. After arriving back in Britain, Grey's default refrain was that '[h]aving met the leading personalities in most of the American groups I am quite glad we do not have a "homophile" movement in England', and he even advised a critical funder of ONE – the transsexual millionaire Reed Erickson – that the main US moves to be made at a federal level should not be trusted to the homophiles.[73] This somewhat Judas-like kiss may have been a desperate attempt to offer instead his own expertise in a formal capacity or at least to divert some of Erickson's philanthropic resources to the struggling Albany Trust. It was not, however, the whole story. Perhaps US activists were wasting their energy squabbling and perhaps HLRS lobbying would not have succeeded in such circumstances, but following his trip Grey also recognised that most US homophile groups viewed Wolfenden-style legislative reform as a low priority, favouring instead social education, protests against policing and even entertainment for members. Indeed, the cumulative impact on Grey of his dinner dates, drinks parties, theatre trips, visits to homophile clubs and nights in San Francisco bathhouses may very well have been as great as political discussion. If Grey had found homophile divisions frustrating, he also now better understood the empowering social and organisational infrastructure informing Legg's perception that in England 'the law change was a gift handed down, as it were, from on high to the homophiles' and Kameny's critique that the 'Albany Trust (whatever its members may be in private life) tends to act more *for* the homosexual than *as* homosexuals'.[74] Six months before his trip, during the final parliamentary push, Grey had confided to Legg his 'rather paranoid feeling of isolation', referring to it as an 'occupational hazard'.[75] From now on, Grey would find it even harder to overlook the constraints on his position as a man enmeshed in international homophile circles from which those 'on high' in his organisation kept their distance.

This tension became most dramatically evident in disagreements about what HLRS and the Albany Trust should do in the wake of law reform, and in particular whether to support a COC-style social organisation. 'Everyone here is now loudly demanding a "club",' wrote Grey to a US correspondent ahead of his trip, 'quite oblivious of the 20 years work and effort which has gone into creating the one in Amsterdam'.[76] Grey expressed personal sympathy with Manchester supporters who had mooted the idea even before the Sexual Offences Bill passed, but warned that '[p]remature action might bring about the "back-lash" which could destroy a great deal of our preparatory work'.[77] There were indeed strong countervailing forces attached to HLRS, and during the final law reform drive Grey apparently received a 'hysterical telephone call' from Lord Arran, the main sponsor of the Sexual Offences Bill in the House of Lords, 'saying that he did not want to think that anything he was doing might lead to the

appearance of "Dutch Clubs" in London'.[78] Obsequiously, and in a
nationalistic tone of voice, Grey had attempted to appease the peer on
this 'and other shenanigans', confirming that he had 'endeavoured to
damp down the ardour of the handful of our supporters who ... wish
such foreign institutions to flourish upon our native soil'.[79] Yet after
law reform, the Manchester group pushed forward anyway and Grey
became more involved, on his return from the States even putting in
the legwork to bring over COC representatives for a weekend as con-
sultants.[80] A private initiative that had at least a passing resemblance
to a homophile organization, the club project remained separate from
HLRS and the Albany Trust, but Grey was offered a position as a vice-
president and accepted. He did not, however, retain the role for long.
When in the spring of 1968 Arran and his House of Commons counterpart, Leo Abse, got wind of the Manchester venture, the game was
up, and in May his Executive Committee called an emergency meeting that effectively forced Grey to choose: homophile social club or
Albany Trust. Grey wrote to Amsterdam that the committee had acted
'in a very cowardly manner' and indicated that he and other staff were
considering their positions, since it was 'extremely difficult to do our
work when the necessary support and understanding is lacking'.[81]
In the end, however, he stayed. Complaining to Legg that 'our "grass
roots" are tending to wither because there is too big a credibility gap
between what is practical and what most of the rank and file appear
to expect', he nevertheless rounded on the 'naivety and lack of sophis-
tication of the embryonic British "homophile movement"', concluding, 'God forbid that any of these projects ever get themselves off the
ground'.[82] Through the end of the 1960s the fallout continued, Grey
writing to Kameny in September 1969 that some of the Manchester
group 'seem to have a certain animus against me, because they quite
wrongly imagine that I was the main nigger in the woodpile in with-
drawing Albany Trust support'.[83]

If one wonders what Kameny – whom Legg characterised as the US
homophile movement's Stokely Carmichael[84] – made of the casually
used racial slur and implicit Uncle Tomism of the metaphor, Grey by
this point took the line: 'Ardent admirer though I am of the Kameny
approach, it simply won't work here.'[85] While Kameny started to
reach beyond Grey in connecting Manchester homophiles and
Scottish activists to the US movement, Grey insisted that in Britain
the arbitrary powers of regulatory authorities, an absence of civil
rights culture and a lack of minority consciousness militated against

both Dutch homophile clubs and US homophile activism. Kameny, emphasising public visibility and legal rights, advised British activists to work through the courts, and suggested bringing test cases against recent police crackdowns on commercial venues, joking that he would have to 'come over there, dance at a club, get arrested, and appeal the matter up to the Queen'.[86] Grey, who was forwarded this correspondence, once again stressed Britain's 'utterly different' and 'generally much more adverse' legal system – a claim that among other things signalled the distinction between the United Kingdom's parliamentary sovereignty and US judicial review, through which the Supreme Court could overturn laws deemed unconstitutional. According to Grey, the only realistic way to move forward in Britain was 'sustained public education and work through professional people, social workers etc. from the top'. The country, he argued, had neither the political environment nor human resources for homophile activism. Indeed, the Manchester club debacle had even jeopardised the Albany Trust's existing social programmes, including its counselling efforts directed at 'lonely, isolated, and inadequate people' as casework poured in.[87]

The transnational unity that Rupp argues ICSE both promoted and was sustained by appears here, in the case of HLRS's homophile internationalism, strained to the limit. The vicissitudes of personality played their part, as did Grey's position as a kind of gatekeeper for organised gay politics in Britain and his desire not to be sidelined by either his own institution or other activists. Yet, while these particular dynamics may be unique, they suggest at least two general points that merit attention from further work on cross-border aspects of the homophile movement. First, that even when international exchanges appear to sustain transnational solidarity, local and national frames will likely continue to be of crucial importance, especially given the small-scale community and jurisdictional basis of much homophile activism, and an international communications network that tended to support only periodic interaction. And second, that cosmopolitanism in forging international links did not necessarily translate into what might be considered vanguardist, radical or even progressive politics along the lines of the proud identity that Rupp argues ICSE ultimately fostered. Grey, challenged by Kameny, remained cautious; taking his reform message to the United States, he publicly supported a relatively conservative stance that, next to more militant attitudes, could be considered reactionary.

Local, national and comparative frameworks therefore

remain important – not least in attempting to test Grey's policy claims – but British queer history still has much to gain from the transnational turn. In the case of HLRS we could certainly move beyond the social and political pulls of the COC, ONE and Kameny to consider cross-border flows of capital (although Grey apparently met little success tapping US foundations), social contact (with hundreds of ordinary men and women across the world corresponding with Grey, though without being put in touch with each other), information (the circulation of ideas, texts and knowledge perhaps more important to the Albany Trust's social work than to HLRS's politics), and people (foreign visitors regularly dropping by HLRS's office and its personnel sometimes travelling abroad). In terms of homophile internationalism alone, there is much still to say about HLRS's links with other European and US homophile groups, and its direct influence on reformers in New Zealand, South Africa and beyond.

Furthermore, transnational feelings of homophile kinship and solidarity, while difficult to pin down, surely played a part in moving someone even as cautious and guarded as Grey. In the same letter as he vehemently rejected Kameny's methods, Grey concluded that 'a Kameny visit would be a real tonic', and by the beginning of the 1970s Grey needed it. While Kameny's correspondence started to acquire an unfamiliar levity, enthusing that the US homophile movement had grown incredibly since a riot at the Stonewall Inn, Grey was once again struck by how 'totally different' the US scene appeared, and revealed that his doctor had warned him 'to take things more easily or else ...'.[88] When Kameny wrote back excitedly with news of New York City's first gay pride parade ('A great day!!!'), the reply came from one of Grey's colleagues, for the man himself was taking 'a much needed rest'.[89] Yet Grey would soon return to the political field as an early participant in London's Gay Liberation Front. Born directly from the experience of British activists in its New York counterpart, this radical group was another transatlantic phenomenon in the transnational story of gay movement politics. Grey was not a natural fit for this anti-establishment scene and seems to have been distrusted by fellow activists. After a year, he left the group, accepting an invitation to lead the Albany Trust. Yet, before he did so, he helped to initiate an action that would have taken some of his old US homophile contacts by surprise: the London Gay Liberation Front's first public demonstration.[90] Whatever the caveats, this confrontational mode clearly represented an ideological journey for Grey – one even more striking than, though perhaps related to, the distance travelled on his Washington trip.

## Notes

1  Antony Grey, *Quest for Justice: Towards Homosexual Emancipation* (London: Sinclair-Stevenson, 1992), p. 142.
2  Hall Carpenter Archives (hereafter HCA), London, Albany Trust Papers (hereafter ATP), 14/145, Dorr Legg to Antony Grey, 7 July 1966.
3  *ONE Confidential* (December 1967), 13.
4  *Spectrum* (November 1967), 2.
5  *ONE Confidential* (November 1967), 6.
6  See in particular Leila J. Rupp, 'The persistence of transnational organizing: The case of the homophile movement', *American Historical Review*, 116:4 (2011), 1014–39; Julian Jackson, *Living in Arcadia: Homosexuality, Politics, and Morality in France from the Liberation to AIDS* (Chicago: University of Chicago Press, 2009); David S. Churchill, 'Transnationalism and homophile political culture in the postwar decades', *GLQ*, 15:1 (2008), 31–66.
7  In this chapter, I take 'transnational' to signal a transgression of national integrity through, for example, hybrid identities or deterritorialised networks. The term therefore is qualitatively distinct from 'international', which tends to reify nations (and in particular nation states) even as it denotes interaction between them.
8  Rupp, 'The persistence of transnational organizing', 1017, 1034, 1018.
9  1957 interview quoted in *ibid.*, 1018.
10 HCA, ATP, 6/3, Grey to President of the Philadelphia Janus Society, 19 February 1964; 6/1, Grey to Marc Daniel, 29 October 1963.
11 HCA, Antony Grey Papers (hereafter AGP), 1/2(a), Draft Executive Committee minutes for 5 July 1961.
12 *ONE Magazine* (August 1961), 30–1.
13 HCA, ATP, 7/3(a), Bob Angelo to Grey (as Edgar Wright), 13 January 1961.
14 Antony Grey, 'Why not?' (1960), in Antony Grey, *Speaking Out: Writings on Sex, Law, Politics, and Society, 1954–1995* (London: Cassell, 1997), pp. 61–3.
15 HCA, ATP, 7/3(a), Grey to Walter Jacobs, 10 January 1961.
16 HCA, ATP, 7/3(a), Grey to Bob Angelo, 10 January 1961.
17 HCA, AGP, 1/2(a), Draft Executive Committee minutes for 1 March 1961; memo 'General Considerations for Discussion: 20th June, 1961'.
18 HCA, ATP, 7/3(a), Grey to Bob Angelo, 26 March 1962.
19 Roy Perrott, 'A Club for Homosexuals', *Observer* (13 January 1963), p. 28; Antony Grey, letter, *Observer* (13 January 1963), p. 31.

20  HCA, ATP, 6/21, Grey to Allan Horsfall, 28 March 1968.
21  HCA, ATP, 7/3(b), Grey to Henri Methorst, 3 July 1964.
22  HCA, ATP, 7/20(a), Marc Daniel to Albany Trust, 24 October 1963.
23  HCA, ATP, 7/3(a), draft interview, April 1963.
24  HCA, ATP, 7/20(a), Grey to Marc Daniel, 29 October 1963.
25  In 1961 the Danish Parliament explicitly made it a criminal offence to receive sexual favours from a person of the same sex under twenty-one years old in return for payment. A section of the press objected that the measure promoted blackmail and would affect relationships beyond prostitution, dubbing it the 'Ugly Law'.
26  HCA, ATP, 7/3(b), Grey to Jan de Groot, 25 June 1965.
27  HCA, ATP, 6/5, Grey to Henri Methorst, 9 September 1964.
28  HCA, ATP, 6/14, Grey to Marc Daniel, 26 October 1966.
29  HCA, ATP, 6/7, Grey to Marc Daniel, 8 April 1965.
30  HCA, ATP, 6/5, Grey to Curtis Dewees, 2 November 1964.
31  ONE National Gay & Lesbian Archives, Los Angeles, One Incorporated Records, 26, Grey to Paul Goldman, 4 March 1966.
32  HCA, ATP, 14/145, Richard Inman to Grey, 17 December 1965; Grey to Inman, 25 February 1966.
33  HCA, ATP, 7/15, Grey to Curtis Dewees, 6 October 1964.
34  HCA, ATP, 6/5, Grey to Rodney Riggall, 8 November 1964.
35  HCA, ATP, 14/145, Monwell Boyfrank to Grey, 18 November 1964.
36  HCA, ATP, 14/145, Grey to Don Slater, 24 February 1966.
37  HCA, ATP, 14/145, Grey to William Glover, 20 August 1965; Grey to Don Slater, 29 December 1965.
38  HCA, ATP, 14/77, Grey to Richard Inman, 18 May 1966.
39  ONE National Gay & Lesbian Archives, Los Angeles, One Incorporated Records, 26, telegram by Grey to Dorr Legg, 1 July 1966.
40  HCA, ATP, 6/13, Grey to Rodney Riggall, 6 September 1966; Grey to Eva Bene, 30 August 1966.
41  HCA, ATP, 6/14, Grey to Rodney Riggall, 18 October 1966.
42  HCA, ATP, 6/13, Grey to Marc Daniel (as Michel Duchein), 13 July 1966; 14/145, Dorr Legg to Grey, 27 July 1966.
43  HCA, ATP, 6/14, Grey to Rodney Riggall, 18 October 1966.
44  HCA, ATP, 14/145, Dorr Legg to Grey, 6 August 1966.
45  HCA, ATP, 7/36, Grey to Dorr Legg, 1 August 1967.
46  ONE National Gay & Lesbian Archives, Los Angeles, One Incorporated Records, 26, Grey to Dorr Legg, 15 August 1967.
47  HCA, ATP, 7/36, Dorr Legg to Grey, 11 August 1967.
48  HCA, ATP, 7/36, Dorr Legg to Grey, 17 October 1967.
49  ONE National Gay & Lesbian Archives, Los Angeles, One Incorporated Records, 26, Grey to Dorr Legg, 15 August 1967.
50  HCA, ATP, 12/17, Grey notes 'Press Conference 24/10/67'.

51  Grey, *Quest for Justice*, p. 170.
52  HCA, ATP, 6/15, Grey to Paul Goldman, 11 January 1967.
53  HCA, ATP, 6/18, Grey to Eva Bene, 1 August 1967; HCA, ATP, letter 244 by Grey, 1 August 1967.
54  *ONE Confidential* (December 1967), 8–9.
55  HCA, ATP, 14/145, circular by ONE board of directors to ONE members, October 1967.
56  *ONE Confidential* (November 1967), 7–8.
57  *ONE Confidential* (December 1967), 13.
58  *ONE Confidential* (November 1967), 9.
59  'Word From Britain on Sex Laws', *San Francisco Chronicle* (9 November 1967).
60  Library of Congress (hereafter LC), Washington, DC, Frank Kameny Papers (hereafter FKP), 4, Grey to Kameny, 8 November 1967.
61  For the fullest account to date of Kameny's story, see David K. Johnson, *The Lavender Scare: The Cold War Persecution of Gays and Lesbians in the Federal Government* (Chicago: University of Chicago Press, 2004).
62  LC, FKP, 4, Kameny to Grey, 31 May 1964.
63  LC, FKP, 4, Grey to Kameny, 11 June 1964.
64  LC, FKP, 4, Kameny to Grey, 7 June 1965.
65  LC, FKP, 4, Kameny to Grey, 20 June 1965; Kameny to Cyril Osborne, 20 June 1965.
66  LC, FKP, 4, Grey to Kameny, 29 June 1965.
67  LC, FKP, 4, Grey to Kameny, 20 August 1965.
68  LC, FKP, 4, Kameny to Grey, 25 July 1965; Grey to Kameny, 20 August 1965.
69  LC, FKP, 3, Barbara Gittings to Kameny, 15 November 1967.
70  Antony Grey, *Personal Tapestry* (London: One Roof Press, 2008), Appendix: 'My American Trip (October–November 1967)', p. 186.
71  HCA, ATP, 7/42(b), Kameny to Ian Dunn, 1 February 1969.
72  LC, FKP, 4, Grey to Kameny, 28 November 1967.
73  HCA, ATP, 7/20(b), Grey to Marc Daniel, 23 November 1967; 7/42(a), Grey to Reed Erickson, 24 November 1967.
74  HCA, ATP, 7/42, Dorr Legg to Grey, 7 December 1967; 7/42(b), Kameny to Ian Dunn, 1 February 1969.
75  HCA, ATP, 14/145, Grey to Dorr Legg, 13 April 1967.
76  HCA, ATP, 6/19, Grey to Alfred Gross, 1 September 1967.
77  HCA, ATP, 6/17, Grey to Allan Horsfall, 19 June 1967.
78  HCA, ATP, 6/16, Grey to Benno Premsala, 28 March 1967.
79  HCA, ATP, 6/17, Grey to Lord Arran, 11 May 1967.
80  HCA, ATP, 6/21, Grey to Jan de Groot, 4 April 1968.
81  HCA, ATP, 6/22, Grey to Jan de Groot, 22 May 1968.
82  HCA, ATP, 7/42(b), Grey to Dorr Legg, 15 July 1968.

83  HCA, ATP, 7/42(b), Grey to Kameny, 18 September 1969.

84  HCA, ATP, 7/42(b), Dorr Legg to Grey, 7 December 1967.

85  HCA, ATP, 7/42(b), Grey to Kameny, 18 September 1969.

86  HCA, ATP, 7/42(b), Kameny to Ian Dunn, 17 June 1969.

87  HCA, ATP, 7/42(b), Grey to Kameny, 18 September 1969.

88  HCA, ATP, 7/42(b), Grey to Kameny, 18 September 1969; LC, FKP, 4,
    Grey to Kameny, 30 April 1970; Kameny to Grey, 6 May 1970; Grey to
    Kameny, 12 May 1970.

89  LC, FKP, 4, Kameny to Grey, 3 July 1970; Avril Fox to Kameny, 8 July
    1970.

90  Grey, *Quest for Justice*, pp. 175–9; Jeffrey Weeks, *Coming Out:
    Homosexual Politics in Britain, from the Nineteenth Century to the Present*
    (London: Quartet Books, 1977), pp. 189–90.

# 10

# Films and Filming:
# the making of a queer marketplace in pre-decriminalisation Britain

*Justin Bengry*

In 1966 David McGillivray contacted the *Films and Filming* editor Peter Baker asking for the opportunity to write for the magazine. He wanted to be a film critic. McGillivray was just eighteen years old and had no idea that, besides being an established and respected film publication, *Films and Filming* was also well known among queer men for its homosexually themed articles, advertising and contact ads. According to McGillivray, 'It was my friends who knew all about it because they said things like "Well, there's always men on the cover". And I hadn't noticed. I was very, very green.'[1] McGillivray's confusion, however, illuminates *Films and Filming*'s strength. The magazine in fact succeeded as a mainstream and internationally respected film title for decades because its queer content remained unnoticed by many. But among those who knew and could decode the magazine's multiple voices, *Films and Filming* acknowledged Britain's pre-decriminalisation homosexual community and actively courted a nascent queer market segment.

Long before homosexual activity between consenting men was partially decriminalised in Britain in 1967, *Films and Filming* included articles and images, erotically charged commercial advertisements and same-sex contact ads that established its queer leanings. Published and edited by homosexual men and assembled by a largely queer staff, *Films and Filming* had producers who deliberately coded the magazine for men like themselves, with little or no interest in lesbians. Throughout its life, *Films and Filming*'s articles on censorship of homosexual themes in film, references to sexually ambiguous male actors like Rock Hudson and Dirk Bogarde, humour, sexual innuendo and homoerotic photo spreads all reinforced for many that *Films and Filming* was queer. From its initial issues in 1954, *Films and Filming* sought what we would today call the pink pound, or Britain's queer market segment. Commercial advertisements promoted queer-friendly and queer-owned businesses; the first issues included ads for Vince Man's Shop, the notorious Soho men's boutique. Discreet 'bachelor' ads from men looking for same-sex partners began appearing in the mid-1950s. These were soon a key feature of the publication's pre-decriminalisation years, later becoming more explicit adverts for sexual partners and queer prostitutes. By the 1960s, some readers were so sure of the magazine's queer audience, they even sought to buy or sell homoerotic magazines and films through its classified ads. Advertisers and readers both recognised that the tone and focus of much of the magazine's visual, editorial and feature content spoke directly to queer men as one of the magazine's intended audiences. Readers too actively participated in the magazine's queer project, submitting and responding to personal contact ads that confirmed their place among *Films and Filming*'s growing and lucrative readership.

But *Films and Filming* was also an important mainstream film publication, widely respected and universally available. Barry Pattison, who worked at *Films and Filming* from 1961 to 1963, was drawn to the magazine first as a reader and then as a contributor because of its importance as a film journal. It was, he recalls, 'the first [film magazine] in English where fifties and sixties films were discussed by their intended audience, who had a different take on cinema to the prevailing views put forward by older press critics'.[2] He was struck so strongly by the magazine, in fact, that more than fifty years later he even remembers the film appearing on the cover of the first issue he bought upon arriving in London from Australia in 1959 – *The Letter that was Never Sent*. Despite its camp innuendo and queer references, throughout the 1950s and 1960s *Films and Filming* remained an internationally respected and successful film journal.

This commercial double life was key to both the magazine's financial success and its appeal to many queer men. The editor Robin Bean once explained his motivation to the *Films and Filming* contributor Michael Armstrong: 'Gay men who were in the closet, especially those who still lived at home with their parents or were married, could openly sit on the tube or a bus or in school or the office and be viewed reading the magazine without fear of anyone suspecting they were gay.'[3] This strategy allowed *Films and Filming* to appeal successfully to both mainstream and queer markets without alienating either. Queer codes and innuendo were subtle enough to be overlooked or misread by mainstream readers, while at the same time they offered validation and expression of homosexual interests and desires. *Films and Filming* successfully navigated this line for almost two decades.

*Films and Filming*, then, is significant for at least two reasons. First, it was the only mainstream, pre-decriminalisation, mass-circulation publication in Britain to remain successful while actively courting a queer market segment. There were, to be sure, underground titles that explicitly targeted queer consumers throughout the twentieth century. And there were pre-decriminalisation mainstream titles that temporarily explored the opportunities offered by appealing to a queer market segment. The former never achieved success on the scale or international scope of *Films and Filming*; this wasn't their goal. And the latter were only temporary anomalies in an otherwise orthodox market-positioning strategy. Publications that dabbled in the queer market eventually folded, returned to an exclusively mainstream appeal or chose to pursue another target market instead. Second, *Films and Filming* is important because it affords us the opportunity to discuss the role and significance of mass-circulation publications to queer history. Not only was the magazine itself a consumer good, which could survive only with sufficient sales and support from several groups of consumers, but it was also a venue through which advertisers seeking the pink pound could be sure to access this nascent target market. Why and how did *Films and Filming* seek the marginalised queer consumer? What appeal or utility would homosexuals find in a film magazine? And why did this strategy finally collapse after two decades?

Though it was among the best known and longest running pre-decriminalisation publications to engage actively with the queer male market, *Films and Filming* was not the first publication to court the pink pound, garner a significant homosexual readership or print homosexually coded commercial or contact ads. While not yet extensive, there is a growing literature both on pre-gay-liberation homophile publications and also on mainstream publications that cultivated queer audiences. Julian Jackson's study of *Arcadie* (1954–82) in France and Hubert Kennedy's study of the trilingual Swiss journal *Der Kreis* (1932–67) both illuminate the histories of these important homophile publications.[4] In the US, numerous scholars, including Martin Meeker, Rodger Streitmatter and Manuela Soares, have identified the significance of *One Magazine* (1953–72), *The Mattachine*

*Review* (1955–66), *The Ladder* (1956–70) and other publications to twentieth-century American queer communities.[5] And in Britain, Rebecca Jennings's work on *Arena Three* (1963–72) traces the history of this UK lesbian publication and the women who founded it.[6]

But underground or marginal social and activist publications were not the only materials that pre-liberation homosexuals read. Nor were they the only publications that actively sought queer readers. Some mainstream publications sought queer consumers for other reasons, namely as a potential market. Laurel Brake and Matt Cook have uncovered this as early as the late nineteenth century in arts publications like *The Artist and Journal of Home Culture* (1880–1902) and *The Studio: An Illustrated Magazine of Fine and Applied Arts* (1893–94) whose coded text and imagery emphasising male beauty and classical allusions appear directed at what Brake calls a 'pink market niche'.[7] And through the Edwardian and interwar periods, some early men's magazines such as *The Modern Man* (1908–15) and *Men Only* (est. 1935) also walked a fine line, seeking homosexual consumers without alienating mainstream readers.[8] But in each of these cases, the publication's appeal to queer consumers was only temporary. The magazine folded, new editors redirected priorities or wartime economic conditions shifted interests to other more lucrative markets. More typically, however, magazines' treatments of homosexuality mirror what Kenon Breazeale finds in the US men's magazine *Esquire* (est. 1933). Elements of the magazine all worked together, according to Breazeale, to reinforce a heteronormative male reader, unblemished by what the editor Arnold Gingrich called any 'whiff of lavender'.[9]

In tandem with some publishers' and editors' courting of homosexual readers, and in spite of others' desires to eschew them, queer men long used the classified columns of magazines and newspapers to make contact with one another. Advertisements offered privacy and anonymity to men who chose not to disclose their names. But, appearing in even national newspapers, they were also highly public and accessible. They advertised men's interest in same-sex companionship when other opportunities for contact among queer men were largely restricted to urban centres and actively discouraged by laws and policing that continued to proscribe homosexual activity. The historian Harry Cocks, for example, has uncovered a remarkable history of same-sex personal advertisements appearing in mainstream magazines and newspapers including *Link* and even the *Daily Express* from the first decades of the twentieth century.[10] In the second half of the twentieth century, anxiety over the content of queer ads extended still further. With their suspect codes and transgressive sexuality, queer personal ads appearing in even mainstream publications now met the ire of government officials and parliamentarians. In a letter to Sir John Wolfenden, Chair of the Departmental Committee on Homosexual Offences and Prostitution, one committee member wondered in 1956 whether legal reform might actually encourage 'More adverts for male "companions"' and cited the appearance of such ads in *Filmgoers Weekly, New Statesman* 'and even *The Times* (and the *Church Times*!)'.[11]

To what extent producers of the *New Statesman* (or the *Church Times*) realised the uses for which queer men employed their publications is difficult to determine. Too often historians can only speculate as to the explicit intentions of producers who left little or no record of magazines' consumer acquisition strategies. And rarely if ever do readers leave behind detailed records to illuminate their reception of publications. Analysis of *Films and Filming*, however, is supported by first-hand testimony from both producers and consumers, unique among pre-decriminalisation publications. Ample oral histories and reminiscences from *Films and Filming*'s editors and contributors leave no doubt as to producers' market strategies and awareness of their consequences. Further, evidence from readers testifies to the magazine's reception by queer men. *Films and Filming*, then, which included not only content and imagery but also advertising and contact ads directed at queer consumers, is likely unique, certainly remarkable and undoubtedly a powerful source for uncovering the entwined history of homosexuality and consumerism.

The publisher Philip Dosse's series of seven arts titles put out by his firm Hansom Books began in January 1950 with the publication of *Dance and Dancers*.[12] The series then grew to include *Music and Musicians* (1952) and *Plays and Players* (1953). *Films and Filming* appeared next in October 1954. This was followed by *Books and Bookmen* (1955), *Records and Recording* (1957) and finally *Art and Artists* (1966).[13] Positioned upmarket of fan magazines, but more intellectually accessible than the British Film Institute's *Sight and Sound, Films and Filming* was widely available in mainstream bookshops and newsagents in Britain and abroad. Priced at two shillings in the late 1950s and only three shillings a decade later, it remained affordable to a broad range of readers.

The dance expert Peter Brinson was first to edit *Films and Filming*, but was soon replaced by Peter Baker, who would remain at its helm throughout much of the 1950s and 1960s.[14] Baker's assistant, Robin Bean, played a pivotal role in the magazine as its last editor under publisher Philip Dosse from 1968, though his influence on the magazine extended further back into its 1960s heyday. Described as a 'cheeseparing eccentric', Dosse himself remained an enigmatic figure throughout his tenure as publisher, largely unknown even to some editors and most contributors to his magazines.[15] Many contributors worked from home, interacting only with editorial staff in the final days before going to print. And even among the core staff, interactions with Dosse were few, with day-to-day operations being undertaken by senior editors. But it was Dosse, most contributors agree, whose vision guided *Films and Filming* to seek a queer audience.

While *Films and Filming* was respected and well known throughout the 1950s and 1960s, and remained among the most successful of Dosse's titles (reportedly covering the costs of his other magazines), Hansom Books was always in a precarious financial position. Stanley Stewart, personal assistant to Dosse in 1959, experienced the already uncertain finances of Hansom Books in those early days. In the short time he worked for Dosse, the operation moved three times in two years, presumably to lower overheads.[16] Barry Pattison, who wrote for *Films and Filming* from 1961 to 1963, describes the operation as being run on a shoestring out of a Belgravia basement a few years later. He even heard of staff members having to buy their own paper clips. And when he parted ways from Dosse's empire in 1963, his last cheque was for only half the agreed amount.[17]

In response to Philip Dosse's financial straits, editorial decisions were consciously based in part on accessing a potential homosexual market. Dosse recognised that a nascent market of culturally literate and cosmopolitan queer men with disposable incomes was appearing in Britain and abroad. Titles like *Films and Filming* spoke specifically to this market, even while maintaining mainstream credibility and availability. Although Dosse did not take an active role in the day-to-day running of all his magazines – David McGillivray describes him as more *éminence grise* – he nonetheless exerted influence over each, especially *Films and Filming*, by recommending specific editorial decisions. Contributors remember him being responsible for encouraging the magazine's most explicit homoerotic content precisely to court queer consumers. Dosse would suggest particular articles, remembered McGillivray, to allow editors to 'get more dolly boys on the cover'.[18] This made good financial sense, ensuring that *Films and Filming* remained Dosse's most popular and successful title. Likely part of this same strategy, Barry Pattison remembers, 'Having Alain Delon (*Plein Soleil*) on the cover with his shirt off was said to have produced an increase in sales and having Charlton Heston taking his pants off (*Big Country*) sent them soaring.'[19] But this strategy to appeal to queer men was not supported by Dosse's last *Films and Filming* editor. Michael Armstrong recalls conflict between Dosse, who sought bolder homosexual content, and the editor Robin Bean, who preferred initially to keep both the magazine's and his own homosexual inclinations less pronounced.[20]

*Films and Filming* nonetheless long remained among the most respected English-language film publications. Its significance and market penetration by the 1960s are hard to exaggerate. On staff were leading critics like Raymond Durgnat and Gordon Gow, and articles appeared from world-famous critics, directors and actors like Ingmar Bergman and Kenneth Tynan, Boris Karloff and even Lillian Gish.[21] It even penetrated popular consciousness and was referenced in films and theatre in its own right. In *The Swimmer* (1968) starring Burt Lancaster, Janet Rule's character Shirley Abbot is seen lounging by the pool reading a copy. And in the British stage production of Woody Allen's *Play It Again Sam* (1969), Dudley Moore's character Allan Felix is a reviewer for *Films and Filming*.[22]

By the 1970s, however, the decline had begun, but the magazine still managed to maintain relevance by gaining exclusive access to film sets and printing stills that appeared nowhere else. Its photo spreads at this time were, remembers David McGillivray, internationally renowned. And the magazine's leading critics still secured interviews with cinema's most influential personalities.[23] A secretive man, the editor Robin Bean it seems was remarkably well connected. Though by this time he had little interest in the magazine's written content, he regularly secured unique set photos for the magazine and exclusive interviews and write-ups with emerging, and handsome, actors. It was under the later years of Bean's editorship that the magazine's queer focus became strongest and least coded. While queer personal ads disappeared shortly before decriminalisation, the 1970s saw *Films and Filming* break more taboos than ever before, but at the cost of alienating key audiences.

How did readers identify *Films and Filming* as a potentially queer publication? Ostensibly reporting on the world of actors and cinema, *Films and Filming* deliberately appealed to its queer market through its editorials, features and strategically selected film stills. Besides reviews and editorials that appealed to interests in queer film and law reform, editors and producers also used articles to discuss hand-some rising actors and thereby justify a healthy dose of male flesh as well. In May 1955, for instance, Clayton Cole spent an entire article evaluating the recent crop of actors to appear in film.[24] So dedicated was Cole that he even developed a taxonomy to categorise the flood of young men in Hollywood. On the one hand, he relayed to read-ers, was the 'Wilson group', discoveries of the beefcake talent agent Henry Wilson, including Tab Hunter, Rock Hudson, Robert Wagner and others. These were 'glamour boys moulded from prime qual-ity beef-cake with no nonsense about Art and Cause'. Then there were the 'Brando boys', men like Montgomery Clift, James Dean and Paul Newman, influenced by the style and success of Marlon Brando. These blue-jean-clad, bare-chested men were 'ardent, sensi-tive and dedicated ... loathe[d] glamour as artificial' and sought films with messages. In the competition between 'Beauty and Blue-Jeans' among film's young leading men, only one thing was certain, accord-ing to Cole: the man who makes us forget Brando will come out the winner. But something else was certain too. Amid film stills of James Dean and Tab Hunter, references to sexually ambiguous actors and an extensive even excessive discussion of emerging Hollywood heart-throbs, the article was rife with information, coded references and subcultural cues that would appeal to *Film and Filming*'s queer audi-ences without alienating mainstream film enthusiasts. Throughout the magazine's run, this kind of fixation on male actors, bordering on salivation, would only become less circumspect.

Rarely missing the opportunity to de-contextualise film stills and print a naked torso or steamy glance between two men, producers offered mild homoerotica even in the 1950s and 1960s when such material remained largely inaccessible. Editors, for example, used a photo spread on Michael Cacoyannis's *Our Last Spring* (1960) to exhibit a queer sensibility through image selection. Amid other stills that inevitably displayed chiselled, brooding Greek youths, some are more suggestive, including images of covert glances among men, a bevy of bare-chested youths at the beach and one image that seems to fulfil no other purpose than to highlight the bottom of one young man pulling himself up after stumbling into a creek.[25] In the same issue, one article stands out in particular. 'The Money in Muscles' described at length a 'Beefcake Invasion' among recent Italian-made films.[26] The article alerted readers to the production and expected release of a range of historical films that emphasised the male body. These 'Italian spectacles', referring to both the film epics themselves and their historical 'musclemen', were 'fabulous – as at least one American "muscle boy" has discovered'. The so-called 'muscle boy' was the heartthrob bodybuilder and actor Steve Reeves, whose break-out role as Hercules was featured in the article and accompanied by a loin-cloth-clad photo still. This so-called invasion of beefcake described and pictured in the article would have immediately resonated with many of *Films and Filming*'s homosexual readers, particularly those already familiar with the language of beefcake in underground and homoerotic physique publications.

*Films and Filming*'s queer market strategy did not rely only on homoerotic spectacle – the money in muscles – to speak to queer men. Articles featured political and social concerns as well. Articles on censorship and homosexuality in film appeared regularly, further signalling to other readers the magazine's position on a divisive issue. In 1958, the same year that the Lord Chamberlain relaxed his ban on homosexuality on the British stage, Denis Duperley and Geoff Donaldson asked in *Films and Filming* whether, in the era of the Wolfenden Report of 1957, which had suggested that the government should decriminalise male homosexual acts, the British Board of Film Censors (BBFC), as it was then called, was ready to finally approve 'films making an honest drama of homosexuality'.[27] Highlighting what they saw as the board's taboo of the subject 'unless ... cloaked with the delicacy of Minnelli's *Tea and Sympathy*, or the obscurity of Hitchcock's *Rope* or Ray's *Rebel Without a Cause*', neither was optimistic. They further wondered whether progressive and homosexually themed films like the Danish *Bundfald* (*The Dregs*) or the German *Anders als du und ich* (released in English as *The Third Sex*) would even be permitted in the UK. Articles such as this opened dialogue on the subject of homosexuality in film at a key moment in Britain and also signalled to queer readers the magazine's own progressive stance on the subject.

Perhaps Duperley's and Donaldson's concerns were not so far off the mark. While there is no record of *Bundfald* being submitted to the BBFC for certification, *The Third Sex* was. Neither Duperley nor Donaldson realised that it had already been rejected for public exhibition almost six months before their call for it to be shown.[28] The BBFC found fault not just with the theme of homosexuality, too openly presented for its standards, but also with its visual representation in the film, noting especially 'scenes in which boys are shown wrestling in scanty clothing … and elderly men dressed as women'. The board, however, was less concerned with expressions of explicit homosexuality: 'The seduction scene is frank but probably would not have been unacceptable for an "X" certificate.' Claiming it would have considered passing a film that treated the subject of homosexuality seriously and with decency, the board concluded that *The Third Sex* had done neither.[29] And when the board viewed the film a second time, it reiterated these points, demanding that homosexuality 'should be conveyed by inference rather than by direct observation or dialogue'.[30] In 1958 the BBFC was not yet ready for the kind of open treatment of homosexuality that Duperley and Donaldson advocated in *Films and Filming*. A full year later, referencing the May 1958 article, a *Films and Filming* review of *The Third Sex* further berated the BBFC for its attitude to the film, suggesting that the real reason for the board's refusal to certify the film was 'that the film does not condemn or pity homosexuality'.[31] The reviewer then condemned the BBFC, concluding that *The Third Sex*, though flawed and perhaps soon forgotten as a film, 'will be long remembered as a piece of British censorship bigotry'.

With a queer market segment having been identified by *Films and Filming*'s publisher and editors, advertisers soon cottoned on to the potential of this group. From its very first issues, the magazine also included ads from Vince Man's Shop, which appealed to homosexual men with coded language and suggestive images that many would have readily recognised.[32] Unsurprisingly, the aesthetic of these ads – male models posed in revealing swimwear and tight garments – bore a striking resemblance to the physique photography Bill Green (aka Vince) had produced during his period as a beefcake photographer in the late 1940s and early 1950s. It was also not unlike other images of men selected from film stills that appeared in *Films and Filming*. This aesthetic, already coded as queer by virtue of its appearance in physique magazines and erotic photo prints, immediately spoke to homosexual consumers of both *Films and Filming* and Vince's menswear lines with a familiar visual and erotic language. Over time, his ads promoted a range of queer-coded styles while becoming increasingly charged and homoerotic.

Like Vince's earlier erotic physique photography, his ad images were to be looked upon, to be desired and then to instigate the purchase of more images. In April 1955, Vince's ad for 'Capri style jeans' focused as much on the model as the product. The model was posed looking away from the viewer, inviting unselfconscious gazes at his bum, which was deliberately placed at the very centre of the advertisement.[33] Besides the jeans, the ad also advertised the new 1955 leisurewear catalogue, sent on request, presumably showing more of the model in less. The queer journalist and playwright Peter Burton even claimed that Vince's 'catalogue of swim- and underwear could *almost* be classified as an early gay magazine'.[34] The next month's ad showed the catalogue itself, which indeed offered more flesh than earlier images, displaying the model in '2-way stretch swim briefs'.[35] Again looking away, and dressed only in the zebra-print briefs, the model's body is the attraction in the ad. Well-built and muscular, he showed remarkable resemblance to the physical culture enthusiasts Vince had photographed only a few years earlier.

By June of 1958, subtlety was gone. Again advertising the 'famous Vince 2-way stretch brief', the ad was now almost entirely taken up by two pictures cropped to show only the models.[36] Displaying the carefully cultivated bodies of physical culture, the men wore only the small briefs Vince was known for. The images were also positioned to have the two models looking at each other, now the objects of each other's gazes, offering potential sexual tension between the men within the ad itself. Another year later, Vince's ad for the 'New Striped Swimbrief' showed a model more like a homoerotic physique print than ever before. Here Vince's brief left none of the model's anatomy to the imagination, his genitals easily discernible beneath the fabric of the brief swimming costume.[37]

In addition to retail advertisements like Vince's, other businesses catering to homosexuals could be found advertising among the classifieds in *Films and Filming*, further reinforcing recognition of the magazine as an access point for queer consumers. On several occasions adverts ran for a bed and breakfast in Brighton. The bachelor apartment was in Hove just two minutes from the seafront and cost one guinea a night.[38] Nothing in the text of the ad immediately divulged any queer associations. But those interested were asked to write to Filk'n Casuals or 31 Bond Street, Brighton. Filk'n Casuals, named for Phil and Ken, known to clients and friends as Auntie Rose and Auntie Esmé, was the most notorious men's outfitters outside of London. Catering, like Vince, especially to homosexual men, Rose and Esmé designed shirts, swimming trunks, briefs and other articles of clothing whose flamboyance, cut and colour often cast into suspicion the sexuality of those who wore them. Brighton couple Bob and Harry even recalled Rose and Esmé's B&B ads appearing across Hansom Books's other titles. Auntie Rose 'advertised in the gay books you know which was very rare then', Harry remembered. 'Plays, Players and Theatre, Players and, Players and Theatregoers or something', added Bob helpfully.[39] But Filk'n's was not the only ad directed at queer customers of the holiday trade. In the same column, 'a charming country house, near sea, Lisbon' was offered for ten guineas a week 'For the Unconventionals'.[40] Suggesting unconventional clients with unconventional lifestyles, and placed within the context of a magazine with a known and established homosexual audience, the Lisbon accommodation was very likely a queer-friendly business, perhaps queer-owned, but certainly tapping into the market in international leisure and travel among homosexuals.

In addition to bricks and mortar businesses, individuals used *Films and Filming*'s classified ads to sell products and advertise casual employment. These ads too extended beyond widespread appeals to a general audience, and some, again, focused specifically on the queer audience they knew could be found there. Even if in the 1960s erotic and queer beefcake magazines existed largely underground, tellingly, homoerotica could also be bought in the classified ads of *Films and Filming*. In one issue, an ad requested 'A. M. G. 8mm Films new or used'.[41] Likely referring to materials produced by the Athletic Model Guild, Bob Mizer's California beefcake production company, the client was in luck: conveniently, just a few ads below, C. Baxter offered a 'Large Quantity of A. M. G. and similar material for disposal'. *Films and Filming*'s small ads were in some issues a veritable queer marketplace – one that extended beyond consumer goods.

The back pages of *Films and Filming* were used for more than the sales of homoerotic goods, rental of vacation properties and advertisements for queer-friendly businesses. The Market Place section became most renowned among queer men for its personal contact ads.[42] Advertisements offered privacy and anonymity to men who chose not to disclose their identities. But, appearing even in national newspapers and magazines, they exploited the distribution channels that mass-circulation publications relied upon. Liverpool-born Frank Birkhill, who later worked at London's Toynbee Hall, remembered such adverts in the personal columns of London newspapers in the 1930s and 1940s. Widely available in mainstream publications, he remembered ads codedly seeking a 'secretary, or ... travelling companion', but which were nonetheless still clear to men looking for other homosexual men. Related Birkhill, 'I found a few people like that.'[43]

*Films and Filming* offered another generation of men like Birkhill similar opportunities in the 1950s as it became the best-known publication among queer consumers for personal ads. Throughout the 1950s and 1960s an increasing number of same-sex personal ads suggests the stability, even the growth, of the magazine's queer market segment. In these personal ads we find the voices of that audience using the magazine for its own purposes. The earliest ads, in which men indicated 'special interests' of art, ballet and music in their search for like-minded male companions, were soon replaced by terms like 'bachelor', and references to interest in 'physiques'. By May 1958, ads were becoming increasingly suggestive: 'Young man, 28, seeks position that is "different." Anything interesting considered.'[44] Indeed, by the late 1950s and throughout the 1960s most of the magazine's Market Place section comprised ads from men, carefully coded to suggest homosexual desires, seeking same-sex companionship. Commenting on *Films and Filming*, John Stamford of Brighton, founder of the physique magazine *Spartacus* and ultimately the *Spartacus International Gay Guide*, remembered the classified section growing from just a few adverts to one and a half pages of them by the mid-1960s.[45] Over the course of these two decades, *Films and Filming* became a feature of mid-century queer commercial and social life.

Michael O'Sullivan, who would later work for *Films and Filming* managing subscriptions in the mid-1970s, remembers getting his first copies of the magazine aged sixteen in 1962. He made sure to get copies monthly after that, soon recognising the magazine's queer slant and opportunities to make contact with other men. O'Sullivan even sent in an ad himself at seventeen while still living with his parents in Ireland. Replies arrived from all over the world including Hollywood, Malta, Australia and England. He even made a few lifelong friends from the experience. And when O'Sullivan moved to London in 1965 aged eighteen, as a young gay man he again turned to the correspondence ads of *Films and Filming*, knowing he could use its contact ads to find friends and shared accommodation in the city. 'It did have a considerable influence on my life', he remembers.[46]

The magazine's queer network even extended internationally. In May 1965 Peter Bonsall-Boone, who would gain notoriety with his partner seven years later for Australia's first homosexual TV kiss, was already familiar enough with the British magazine *Films and Filming* to place a personal ad knowing it would reach its intended audience.[47] His ad described himself as an 'active young bachelor' from Victoria, Australia, 'interested in most things'. This included finding similar young men. Two 'bachelors' living in Ealing placed an ad in the same issue. Not surprisingly their interests included cinema – and also wrestling. They sought 'male friends', aged 25 to 30, who were encouraged to respond with photos. This last condition was declared 'essential'. A 'Young, Versatile Ex-Matelot', a 'Presentable young designer', an 'Unconventional Bachelor' and 'A Nice warm, sensitive male', among others, all sought the same thing in the back pages of *Films and Filming*. Indeed, most of the magazine's Market Place section by this time comprised ads from men, carefully coded and suggestive of homosexual inclinations, seeking same-sex companionship. Still others, like that of a 'gay and versatile' young man who sought 'interesting, remunerative' work, were less circumspect – 'anything legal considered', he added.[48]

The language used by men in *Films and Filming*'s contact ads is also significant. Besides giving insights into the desires of Britain's pre-decriminalisation queer community, ad posters' use of particular vocabulary charts a linguistic history of British homosexuality. Terms like 'sensitive', 'artistic' and 'unconventional' had held queer associations since the early decades of the twentieth century, particularly when used to describe a 'bachelor'. It is remarkable that they continued to hold currency for British homosexuals even after the Second World War. More remarkable, however, was the appearance of new terms of identification that appeared in *Films and Filming*.

The term 'gay', for instance, imported from the United States, was largely unknown in mainstream British English until the late 1960s with the Stonewall Riots in 1969. The sociologist and historian Jeffrey Weeks has written, in fact, that 'gay' was only widely adopted in Britain with the organisation of the Gay Liberation Front in 1970.[49] Among queer men and others in the know, however, it was used to reference homosexuality even in the UK for at least the previous two decades.[50] *Films and Filming* editors and readers appear to have known and exploited the word's ambiguities. A still from the 1958 film *Bachelor of Hearts* showing Hardy Kruger on the ground appearing to peer up the shorts of a fellow rugby player is suggestively captioned 'Gay Time'. And among many others to use the term, '2 gay bachelors, early 20s' posted a contact ad in 1964 seeking other males between eighteen and thirty. Their special interests: 'physiques'.[51]

Terminologies for sexual preference also appear in the contact ads. Even though 'passive' had long been used to identify the receiving partner in homosexual penetrative sex, it is unclear exactly when the term 'active' came to be used as a term of self-designation identifying the penetrating partner.[52] Still, men like Peter Bonsall-Boone regularly identified themselves as 'active' in their ads, suggesting an understanding of this term's use, and a particular sexual preference to be advertised. Similarly, 'versatile' offers several interesting sexual connotations in the magazine. It may be unclear today how either the 'versatile ex-Matelot' or the 'gay and versatile' young man who advertised in *Films and Filming* in May 1965 intended readers to understand the term, but it was suggestive. They may have intended it in its current usage, which describes homosexual men who perform either the active or passive sexual role. Or they could have meant to identify themselves as being interested in both male and female sexual partners, a more bisexual use of the term that was in use by the late 1950s.[53] Either way, the term held definite sexual connotations that made clear the posters' interest in homosexual activity.

By the December 1966 issue, published just months before the new Sexual Offences Act legalised consensual homosexual acts between men aged twenty-one and over conducted in private, the contact ads were gone but the magazine's other queer elements all remained.[54] The Filk'ns were still advertising their Brighton bachelor rental apartment, now costing two guineas.[55] Also appearing was a far less subtle advertisement. A small business-card-sized advert promoted the drag artist Mr Jean Fredericks, diva/satirist. The two advertised LPs – 'recitals are a drag' and 'cum camp-us' – highlighted the camp, and potentially queer, performance. The first was described as 'Castratically funny with super "high camp"', while the second was from an 'outrageous cabaret in a West End camp site'. Label Eyemark Records no doubt expected that its placement of this ad in *Films and Filming* would find a market with the magazine's queer readers, who continued to be attracted to other elements in *Films and Filming*. Amid ample male flesh on display in this issue's film stills – George

(Jerzy) Zelnik as Rameses XIII in *The Pharaoh*, Jacques Perrin as Daniel in *The Sleeping Car Murders* and Guy Stockwell with other cast members of *Beau Geste* – *Films and Filming* kept queer interest high. Images of Lawrence Harvey and Lionel Jeffries appeared in camp splendour as Francis and Farquhar listening to the Bolshoi Ballet in a still from *The Spy With the Cold Nose*. And amid films being shown at the National Film Theatre following screenings at the Venice Film Festival, *Films and Filming*'s recommendation of one stands out. A still from *Winter Kept Us Warm* (1965) showing two young men in a tender, and possibly naked, embrace, appears directly alongside the article's title, 'The Best of the Fest'.[56] The homoerotic subtext went beyond the selection of the suggestive image. The film itself – in 1966 the first English-language Canadian film to go to Cannes – was itself a story of a romantic friendship with homosexual undertones between two University of Toronto students.

After the passage of the 1967 Sexual Offences Act, *Films and Filming*'s open engagement with the politics of queer film and the censorship of homosexuality continued unabated. Looking forward to a 'Homo breakthrough' after the partial decriminalisation of male homosexual acts, the journal opined, 'Maybe at last homosexuality is going to be given genuine adult treatment in the cinema.'[57] Contemporary films were in fact starting to normalise homosexuality as a natural part of society, 'accepting that homosexuality is no more of a disease than greed or generosity and maybe far less socially disruptive than adultery'. And with word of potential productions in the works for films about teenage homosexuals, an elderly queer couple and homosexually themed plays, *Films and Filming*'s writers were confident that matters were finally improving.

Through the 1950s and 1960s, *Film and Filming*'s homosexual readers could unselfconsciously buy the magazine for both accurate and engaging film commentary but also coded erotic possibilities. It would not remain so veiled, however, and after the 1967 reform of the laws on homosexuality, when Robin Bean took over the reins as editor in 1968, the magazine changed substantially. He had little concern with the magazine's articles; as a photographer he was most interested in its visual content. Through his contacts, Bean had exclusive access to film sets, and secured stills and photos that appeared nowhere else. And *Films and Filming*'s critics continued to secure interviews with major film personalities.[58] But under Robin

Bean's editorship, and the influence of inexperienced sub-editors and contributors, the magazine also became infamous for more explicit homoerotic imagery. Many film enthusiasts began to lose interest, and the publication's sales sagged through the 1970s. No longer satisfied with bare chests, decontextualised gazes and suggestive poses, the magazine now included increasing amounts of nudity, including full-frontal male nudity on some covers. Film buffs, like Barry Pattison, stopped buying the publication because it was no longer relevant to their interests. 'This was not a deliberate choice or a discussed decision', he recalled. 'There was just no longer anything of interest to us in it.'[59] And David McGillivray remembers colleagues at *Films and Filming* who would no longer even be seen reading the magazine in public. They would hide it in the *Guardian*.[60] One even grumbled, 'I don't know why they don't call it *Queers and Queering* and have done with it.'[61]

*Films and Filming* may also have been a victim of the liberalisation that followed legal reform. Men seeking specifically queer or erotic magazines found them increasingly available elsewhere in the 1970s with the emergence of titles like *Jeremy* and *Gay News*. At the same time, as male nudity abounded and reviews of pornography appeared in *Films and Filming*, the quality of its film content diminished precipitously. In its final years the magazine alienated three key markets that had made it both respected and successful. Film buffs lost interest as the strength of its cinema commentary waned. Gay men interested in *Film and Filming*'s erotic content no longer needed the magazine. Finally, its readership of discreet or closeted gay men who had been a mainstay of the magazine's readership in the 1950s and 1960s could no longer read *Films and Filming* at the office or on the Tube, as Robin Bean had once claimed. It was simply too compromising. So, in its final decade the magazine became increasingly irrelevant.

Debt also plagued Hansom Books throughout the 1970s. Philip Dosse had managed to keep the entire operation going for years on the back of *Films and Filming* and his own determination, but in the end it proved impossible even for him. He had founded Hansom Books with only £100 of initial capital. Later, the entire enterprise was increasingly financed with his own bank overdraft. Beginning at some £4,000 during Hansom Books's early operations in the 1950s, his debt grew to £20,311 by 1966, and then £206,722 by 1979.[62] By August 1980 he was forced to close the magazines. In tears he told his staff, 'I can't pay you. The company is finished.' With mounting debts, Philip Dosse killed himself aged fifty-six in September.[63] Hansom Books and the magazines he founded soon folded. *Films and Filming*, the most successful of his titles, was resurrected in 1981, but never resembled its former self. It was neither an important publication nor a queer one, positioned instead as a glossy magazine reporting on popular films and celebrities. It too finally collapsed in March 1990.

*Films and Filming* illuminates an important intersection between homosexuality and commerce that appeared in the postwar period. The film magazine attracted a queer audience segment and in so doing also cultivated a space where advertisers and consumers could interact based on the shared knowledge of queer codes, subcultural experiences and desires. The appearance of queer commercial and personal adverts in *Films and Filming* reflects an integral relationship between the experience of pre-decriminalisation homosexuality and the semi-private but also public world of mass consumerism. *Films and Filming* was widely circulated, affordable, available internationally and accessible to virtually anyone. These were important characteristics in a time when few homosexual publications existed, and those that did were often banned, confiscated or, if imported from abroad, withheld at Customs. Even those published domestically might still be largely inaccessible, or available only at small booksellers, behind-the-counter at some Soho bookshops or traded among like-minded friends. At a time when queer publications were suppressed, it was precisely because of the widespread and public accessibility of commercially available publications like *Films and Filming* that homosexuals used them to encode ads for specialised services and private desires. And *Films and Filming*, though not entirely unique, was the most accessible and successful of these titles with the longest-running campaign to court queer consumers alongside its mainstream audience.

Mainstream publications often sought multiple audiences, including homosexuals, as part of deliberate marketing and distribution strategies.[64] Titles could also be co-opted and utilised by homosexuals to give voice to a range of commercial endeavours and personal desires. In some cases these illustrate an active subversion of the tenor of the publication, while in others producers and editors were complicit in this venture. In each case, however, the relationship between public media and private experience is significant. It demonstrates the important and dynamic symbiosis between homosexuality and commercial enterprise that was a feature of queer experience, social history and sexual opportunity through the entirety of the twentieth century.

Across three decades, *Films and Filming* offered discussions and reflections of desires and experiences available almost nowhere else, and became a key feature in the sexual development of many queer men. The director Ron Peck identified *Films and Filming* as one 'signal' from the outside world that entered his childhood home in Merton Park, London. Long before meeting a girlfriend who finally encouraged him to experiment sexually with other men, Peck's desires were aroused by *Films and Filming*:

> I can remember questions being asked at home when one particular issue came through the letterbox, wrapped up in the *Merton and Morden Borough News*. 'It was a serious film magazine', I said, though it very soon became a magazine I couldn't take to school. It directed my attention to films of special interest that never hit the review column of the *Daily Express* or the round up of new films on the BBC.[65]

In *Films and Filming* Peck encountered Warhol's *Flesh* (1968) and Joe Dallesandro's body. 'I never had any sex education at school', Peck continues. Everything he learned about sex came from that girlfriend, cinema and *Films and Filming*.

## Notes

1  David McGillivray, interview with Justin Bengry, 2 April 2010.
2  Barry Pattison, personal correspondence, 11 September 2010.
3  Michael Armstrong, personal correspondence, 13 October 2010.
4  Julian Jackson, *Living in Arcadia: Homosexuality, Politics, and Morality in France from the Liberation to AIDS* (Chicago: University of Chicago Press, 2009); Hubert Kennedy, *The Ideal Gay Man: The Story of* Der Kreis (Binghamton, NY: The Haworth Press, 1999).
5  See Martin Meeker, *Contacts Desired: Gay and Lesbian Communications and Community, 1940s-1970s* (Chicago: University of Chicago Press, 2005); Manuela Soares, 'The purloined *Ladder*: Its place in lesbian history', in Sonya L. Jones (ed.), *Gay and Lesbian Literature since WWII: History and Memory* (Binghamton, NY: The Haworth Press, 1998), pp. 27–49; Rodger Streitmatter, *Unspeakable: The Rise of the Gay and Lesbian Press in America* (Boston: Faber and Faber, 1995).
6  Rebecca Jennings, *Tomboys and Bachelor Girls: A Lesbian History of Post-War Britain* (Manchester: Manchester University Press, 2007). Also see

Emily Hamer, *Britannia's Glory: A History of Twentieth-Century Lesbians* (London: Cassell, 1996).

7  *The Artist and Journal of Home Culture* was a 6d monthly journal that ran from 1880 to 1902. See Laurel Brake, '"Gay discourse" and *The Artist and Journal of Home Culture*', in Laurel Brake, Bill Bell and David Finkelstein (eds), *Nineteenth-Century Media and the Construction of Identities* (Basingstoke: Palgrave, 2000), pp. 271–94; Matt Cook, *London and the Culture of Homosexuality, 1885–1914* (Cambridge: Cambridge University Press, 2003), pp. 127–9.

8  Justin Bengry, 'Courting the pink pound: *Men Only* and the queer consumer, 1935–1939', *History Workshop Journal*, 68 (2009), 122–48. Also see Brent Shannon, *The Cut of His Coat: Men, Dress, and Consumer Culture in Britain, 1860–1914* (Athens: Ohio University Press, 2006). On *Men Only* also see Jill Greenfield, Sean O'Connell and Chris Reid, 'Fashioning masculinity: *Men Only*, consumption and the development of marketing in the 1930s', *Twentieth-Century British History*, 10:4 (1999), 457–76; Jill Greenfield, Sean O'Connell and Chris Reid, 'Gender, consumer culture and the middle-class male, 1918–1939', in Alan Kidd and David Nichols (eds), *Gender, Civic Culture and Consumerism: Middle-Class Identity in Britain, 1800–1940* (Manchester: Manchester University Press, 1999), pp. 185–90.

9  Kenon Breazeale, 'In spite of women: *Esquire* magazine and the construction of the male consumer', *Signs*, 20:1 (1994), 1–22.

10  Adverts for same-sex companionship, holidays and contacts, which often requested physical descriptions and photographs, appeared, for example, in the *Daily Express* as early as the mid-1920s. H. G. Cocks, '"Sporty girls" and "artistic" boys: friendship, illicit sex, and the British "companionship" advertisement, 1913–1928', *Journal of the History of Sexuality*, 11:3 (2002), 465 n. 33. Also see H. G. Cocks, *Classified: The Secret History of the Personal Column* (London: Random House, 2009).

11  National Archives, HO 345/3, letter to Sir John Wolfenden, Chair, Departmental Committee on Homosexual Offences and Prostitution, 1 May 1956.

12  According to David McGillivray's short history of *Films and Filming*, which appeared in its final March 1990 issue, Philip Dosse began Hansom Books in 1952 with only £100 of capital. But since *Dance and Dancers* was in fact printed from January 1950, the earlier date seems more likely. David McGillivray, 'Goodbye To All That', *Films and Filming* (March 1990), 4–5.

13  Little has been written of the history of *Films and Filming*. Two short articles have appeared in the UK queer and film press. On its deliberate appeal to queer consumers, rise and ultimate decline see Haydon Bridge [David McGillivray], 'Seeks Similar', *QX International* (30 June

2004), n.p., and McGillivray, 'Goodbye To All That'. Haydon Bridge is
the pseudonym of film critic and screenwriter David McGillivray, who
wrote for *Films and Filming* for twenty-five years beginning in 1966.
David McGillivray, personal correspondence, 5 November 2009. A more
extensive discussion appears in Italian. See Mauro Giori, '"Una rivista
equilibrata per spettatori intelligenti": Appunti per una storia di *Films
and Filming* (1954–1990)' ['"A sensible magazine for intelligent filmgoers": Notes for a history of *Films and Filming* (1954–1990)'], *Paragrafo*, V
(2009), 57–88. Also see Anthony Slide (ed.), *International Film, Radio,
and Television Journals* (London: Greenwood Press, 1985), pp. 163–5.

14   Ken Robinson, 'Brinson, Peter Neilson (1920–1995)', *Oxford Dictionary
     of National Biography* (Oxford University Press, September 2004), www.
     oxforddnb.com/view/article/59783, accessed 16 September 2010.

15   Peter Roberts (ed.), *The Best of* Plays and Players, *1953–1968* (London:
     Methuen, 1987), p. 7.

16   Stanley Stewart, personal correspondence, 18 September 2010.

17   Barry Pattison, personal correspondence, 14 September 2010.

18   David McGillivray, interview with Justin Bengry, 2 April 2010.

19   Barry Pattison, personal correspondence, 11 September 2010. Charlton
     Heston appeared on the August 1958 cover, while Alain Delon appeared
     in October 1960.

20   Michael Armstrong, personal correspondence, 13 October 2010.

21   Slide, *International Film, Radio, and Television Journals*, pp. 163–5.

22   Barry Pattison, personal correspondence, 14 September 2010.

23   McGillivray, 'Goodbye To All That', 5.

24   Clayton Cole, 'The Brando Boys', *Films and Filming* (May 1955), 9.

25   'Our Last Spring', *Films and Filming* (July 1960), 18–19.

26   John Francis Lane, 'The Money in Muscles', *Films and Filming* (July
     1960), 9, 33.

27   Denis Duperley and Geoff Donaldson, 'Will Britain See These Films?',
     *Films and Filming* (May 1958), 31.

28   British Board of Film Classification Archives, London, Reference
     AFF060493, *The Third Sex*, rejected 9 December 1957.

29   London Metropolitan Archives (hereafter LMA), GLC/DG/EL/01/194,
     'Extract from letter (24.4.58) from the British Board of Film Censors'.

30   LMA, GLC/DG/EL/01/194, 'Extract from letter (12.1.59) from the British
     Board of Film Censors'.

31   P. G. B., '*The Third Sex* [Review]', *Films and Filming* (May 1959),
     22–3.

32   On photographer-turned-boutique-owner Bill Green (Vince) and his
     influence on the development of Swinging London's Carnaby Street
     revolution in menswear see Justin Bengry, 'Peacock revolution: main-
     streaming queer styles in post-war Britain, 1945–1967', *Socialist History*,

36 (2010), 55–68; Shaun Cole, *'Don We Now Our Gay Apparel': Gay Men's Dress in the Twentieth Century* (London: Berg, 2000).

33 *Films and Filming* (April 1955), inside back cover.

34 Peter Burton, *Parallel Lives* (London: Gay Men's Press, 1985), p. 30. Italics original.

35 *Films and Filming* (May 1955), 4.

36 *Films and Filming* (June 1958), 36.

37 *Films and Filming* (July 1959), 2. A similar ad from Vince in April 1956 showed a young Sean Connery modelling the 'New Vince Capri Shirt', as well as very slim and very short 'Jean Shorts' that left little doubt that Mr Connery dressed to the left.

38 *Films and Filming* (October 1961), 6.

39 Brighton Ourstory, Bob and Harry, interviewed by Tom Sargant, 10 May 1991. Ads for the Brighton B&B also ran in *Plays and Players* and *Art and Artists*.

40 *Films and Filming* (October 1961), 6.

41 *Films and Filming* (December 1965), inside back cover.

42 See Bridge, 'Seeks Similar', for an overview and examples of ads from *Films and Filming*. Bridge attributes to *Films and Filming* the first examples of modern gay contact ads. H. G. Cocks, *Classified: The Secret History of the Personal Column*, however, shows such ads appearing across publications throughout the century in a variety of publications.

43 British Library, Hall-Carpenter Oral History Project, C456/49, Frank Birkhill.

44 Quoted in Bridge, 'Seeks Similar'.

45 Brighton Ourstory, John Stamford, interviewed by Tom Sargant, 10 February 1991.

46 Michael O'Sullivan, personal correspondence, 16 September 2010.

47 By the early 1970s Peter Bonsall-Boone would become secretary of the Campaign Against Moral Persecution (CAMP), Australia's first gay activist organization.

48 For these ads and others see *Films and Filming* (May 1965), 35, 59.

49 According to the Gay Liberation Front (GLF) 'queer', the more usual British term, was also the 'definition of the oppressor' symbolising 'accepted oppression', which is why the GLF chose to use 'gay', a term chosen by homosexuals to indicate the 'new mood among gay men and women'. Jeffrey Weeks, *Coming Out: Homosexual Politics in Britain from the Nineteenth Century to the Present* (London: Quartet Books, 1977), p. 190.

50 'Gay' was used for homosexual in the US from 1945 and in the UK from c. 1955. It had migrated to Australia in the term 'gay boy' by 1951. Eric Partridge, *A Dictionary of Slang and Unconventional English* (1984), 8th edn (London: Routledge, 2002), p. 450.

51  *Films and Filming* (October 1964), 42.
52  'passive, adj. and n.', *OED Online*, draft revision September 2010 (Oxford University Press), http://dictionary.oed.com/, accessed 20 September 2010.
53  'versatile, a.', *OED Online*, second edition 1989 (Oxford University Press), http://dictionary.oed.com/, accessed 20 September 2010.
54  It is unclear why queer personal ads were discontinued, or who was responsible for the decision. According to contributor Michael Armstrong (personal correspondence, 18 October 2010), Robin Bean 'objected violently to the inclusion of gay ads' in *Films* and *Filming*. Another contributor, David McGillivray, noted their occasional disappearance even before the final removal and wondered if authorities had warned Philip Dosse about them, particularly once rent boys began to advertise their services there (Bridge, 'Seeks Similar').
55  'Film market place', *Films* and *Filming* (December 1966), inside back cover.
56  'The best of the fest', *Films and Filming* (December 1966), 39.
57  'Homo breakthrough', *Films and Filming* (November 1967), 38.
58  McGillivray, 'Goodbye To All That', 5.
59  Barry Pattison, personal correspondence, 14 September 2010.
60  David McGillivray, interview with Justin Bengry, 2 April 2010.
61  McGillivray, 'Goodbye To All That', 4–5. In a later interview with Justin Bengry (2 April 2010) McGillivray attributes the quote to Allen Eyles, a long-time contributor to *Films and Filming*, who became editor on its re-launch under new publishers after the suicide of Philip Dosse.
62  These figures are all taken from the Official Receiver's 1981 report of his investigations into the insolvency of Hansom Books. See McGillivray, 'Goodbye To All That', 5.
63  'Arts Publisher Found Dead', *Guardian* (9 September 1980), p. 26.
64  See Bengry, 'Courting the pink pound', 122–48.
65  *Strip Jack Naked: Nighthawks II*, dir. Ron Peck, 1991.

# 11

# The cultural politics of gay pornography in 1970s Britain

*Paul R. Deslandes*

The 1950s and early 1960s ushered in a flourishing market in homoerotic images in the form of British and imported American physique magazines, ostensibly about the promotion of health and fitness but very clearly geared to queer audiences. In many of the editorial introductions to these new publications, the focus on the admiration of the male physique was readily apparent. John Barrington, one of the more prominent figures in the physique photography movement who began taking (and selling) pictures of male nudes in 1948, highlighted this point in his *Male Model Monthly*, which was first published in November 1954.[1] The magazine was a new kind of venture (really the first of its kind in Britain), he asserted, intended to bring 'to the discerning public each month the pick of the world's finest male physiques, photographed by the world's finest camera-artists'. In selling this new venture to his readers (and presumably averting the prying eye of censors) Barrington sought to establish, most prominently, the artistic and aesthetic, not the erotic or masturbatory, significance of his publication by emphasising the quality of the model's physical development, the aesthetic impact of the photographer's vision and the pose of the athlete. The photographs produced in *Male Model Monthly*, especially when paired with statues from antiquity, were thus intended to remind readers, to borrow from Michelangelo (as Barrington did) that 'the highest object for art is man'. Barrington did not, however, entirely discount the possibility of multiple forms of pleasure in introducing his magazine, a point reflected in his contention that 'Art-students and artists, students of photography, connoisseurs, and perspicacious physical-culturists will all find pleasure, instruction, and inspiration in our illustrations.'[2] Such an admission undoubtedly functioned both as a wink and a specialised form of coded language to queer men who found, in the pages of Barrington's magazine, great erotic potential. It also serves as a reminder that the 1950s were full of surreptitious opportunities, especially in London's thriving and diverse sexual landscape.[3]

While scholars like Frank Mort have recently pointed to the existence of this highly variegated and commercialised sexual landscape in the decade of the Teddy Boy and the Suez Crisis and, in the process, rightly questioned the somewhat triumphalist and whiggish narrative of 1960s 'permissiveness', no one can deny that the visual, material and literary culture of queerness, embodied in the form of the physique magazine and other products, expanded dramatically in the years following the passage of the 1967 Sexual Offences Act.[4] As a new gay culture and politics took hold in the late 1960s and 1970s, the growing sense that same-sex-desiring men needed to produce images and articulations of beauty and desire that were not just potentially transgressive or culturally queer but definitively gay (celebrating, in part, the new identities that came to be associated with the pleasure of looking, touching and engaging in sexual contact with other male bodies) seemed a more pressing part of a post-1967 'gay agenda' in Britain. In London, this was especially evident in the emergence of new bookstores in the 1970s (such as the Man-to-Man Shop, Zipper, Stud and Incognito) that catered to the interests of an explicitly gay clientele by providing access to a broad range of fiction and non-fiction, erotica and, most importantly for the purposes of this chapter, magazines.[5] These developments resulted in the creation of a new kind of self-confidently gay and assertive entrepreneur who sought both to make money from a burgeoning community of gay men and to provide them with an invaluable service.[6]

One prominent figure in this period was Alan Purnell: publisher, editor, photographer and filmmaker. In 1974 he founded a new monthly publication titled *Him Exclusive*, which was, first and foremost, a pornographic magazine intended to provide pleasure and information to a self-identified gay audience. In a pointed editorial introduction to the first issue, Purnell noted, 'we are hoping that we have produced the first gay magazine in Britain to have all the elements it needs for success'. Purnell was not content, however, merely to highlight the gayness of *Him Exclusive* or the fact that the magazine was 'completely run by gay people'. He also sought to emphasise the importance of looking, of viewing the fully naked male body, sizing up its aesthetic value and, most importantly, displaying it as an object of desire and titillation: 'Naturally, a gay magazine stands or falls by the photographs it prints, and this is why we are offering more than any previous gay publication for photographs and models.' Finally, Purnell addressed issues of distribution and access and, by extension, questions about the important role of the printed word in gay male culture in the 1970s by reminding readers of the magazine's specific goals: 'We want to make HIM available in every town in the country.'[7]

*Him Exclusive* (1974–76) and its successors *Him International* (1976–78) and *Him Monthly* (1978–83) were part of a new breed of gay magazine that appeared in the wake of the Sexual Offences Act of 1967, the internationally significant Stonewall Riots in New York City in 1969 and the emergence, in 1970, of the London-based Gay Liberation Front. They were not the first, being preceded by *Spartacus, Jeremy* and *Jeffrey* and coexisting with Alex McKenna's *Zipper*, but their boldness and assertiveness represented a politicised departure from both the illicit photographs and postcards of the nineteenth and early twentieth centuries and their somewhat coy physique-oriented predecessors.[8] Instead, this new type of magazine emphasised erotic pleasure, the articulation of a specifically gay identity and a public kind of 'coming out', entirely in keeping with a prevailing political ethos of the day. These publications also both rejected earlier attitudes about pornography as a kind of 'lonely indulgence'[9] and embraced a form of genre mixing that linked the pleasures of viewing nude men and the provision of no-nonsense sexual education with a new kind of sex-positive and informed gay identity.[10] The men who consti-tuted *Him*'s audience were thus encouraged to see, to borrow from a 1981 political manifesto by the American journalist and book editor Michael Denneny, 'gay pornography' as 'by and large a positive fulfil-ment that counteracts the nightmarish fears of our adolescent years and, as such, is politically progressive'.[11]

In narrating the particular developments associated with the pub-lication of *Him Exclusive, Him International* and *Him Monthly* and highlighting the cultural work that pornography did for gay men in the 1970s, this chapter is divided into three discrete, but interrelated, sections. The first of these focuses on the magazines themselves by examining the distinctively gay aesthetic presented in their pages, analysing not only body ideals or desirable masculine types but also the political functions served, in gay pornographic literature, by artic-ulations of desire and celebrations of both male physical beauty and the marketplace of body-oriented products. It was these politically charged articulations of desire that led to the intense scrutiny that queer pornography generated over the course of the decade. Focusing on both the prosecution of gay-oriented booksellers and publishers by legal officials in the mid-1970s and critiques of pornography that were generated by members of the gay left, the second part of this chapter illuminates public perceptions of the naked, queer male body and the possibilities (both positive and negative) it was thought to present as an erotic object and an article of consumption. In so doing, it reveals, most notably, how various agents of the state, charged with enforcing British censorship laws, sought to police not only the boundaries of propriety but also the expression of queer political sensibilities and subjectivities. In its final section, this chapter focuses on evidence collected by the 1977 Committee on Obscenity and Film Censorship to illustrate how gay men conceptualised the place of pornography in their lives and its role in the broader struggle for the freedom, in the words of Sean Barker, an Emmanuel College, Cambridge, man, 'to create beauty in any form, ... to be obscene and excite lust, ... to witness obscenity and to be excited by it, ... to speak truth and ... to lie beautifully'.[12]

## The aesthetics of *Him*

From the very beginning, the publishers of *Him Exclusive* sought to link the aesthetic celebration and eroticisation of men with a new kind of political assertiveness. In the context of Purnell's bold editorial position that *Him* was a magazine by gays for gays, photographic collections and features in the magazine assumed entirely new meanings. The 'Colin Clarke Portfolio', which first appeared in the magazine's second issue in 1975, introduced photographs of fit young men with the following statement: 'What a piece of work is Man. A complex being, beautifully fashioned and superb in design. My portfolio will be an attempt to capture the Masculinity and moods of Manhood.'[13] While statements of this sort may have harkened back to the language of the physique periodical, the unabashed nudity and posterior eroticism of the models, coupled with the magazine's assertion of gayness, meant that the significance of this new kind of aesthetic celebration remained entirely unambiguous (see Figure 8).

Celebrations of the beautiful man carried over from the pages of the magazine into other areas of London's commercial gay culture. In June of 1975, *Him Exclusive* sponsored a Mr Playguy contest at the Fulham Town Hall. When announced in the 'Man Talk' section of the magazine, the event was lauded as an opportunity to 'see some great bodies!' and the 'most enjoyable gay night of 1975', effectively linking the pleasures of viewing hunky men with an increasingly commercialised, vocal and 'out' gay identity in the British metropolis.[14] A print advertisement for the event indicated that this was far removed, in terms of its celebration of sexuality, from the physique and male beauty contests of the early to mid-twentieth century (see Figure 9). Readers of *Him* were asked, in the first line of the advert, 'Who is the most Desirable Man in Britain?' Lest anyone forget what qualities were being judged at the event, the copywriter then queried, 'Who has the right combination of face, physique, and sex appeal to take the First Prize?' While Jean Fredericks, 'the best-loved drag personality in England', was scheduled to host the contest, readers who worried that participation in the event might compromise newfound claims to gay masculinity were placated with two simple statements: 'this will not be a drag ball as such, so no dresses required! It will be a very Butch evening.'[15] In so doing, it used a bit of humour to separate post-Stonewall gay men from the queans and fairies of the pre-Second World War period[16] and ensured that the act of sizing up and judging the aesthetic qualities of other men was confirmed as a thoroughly masculine, as well as a gay, prerogative.

The political implications of viewing and celebrating the aesthetically appealing male face and body continued as the magazine underwent title changes through the latter part of the 1970s and the early 1980s. As Alan Purnell began to undertake new entrepreneurial ventures that catered to the desires of gay men for more images and material that celebrated gay sexuality, the magazine began to address not only portrayals of men in print pornography but also in gay films. When Purnell introduced his 1977 film *Hard Dollar Hustler* to readers of *Him International* he began with a bit of boasting which he undoubtedly hoped would help to secure his position as a gay pioneer in 1970s Britain: 'When you've made the first full-length, sound, gay film in Britain you feel the need to boast a little.' While Purnell questioned, in this article, whether or not the current version of the film would be screened in Britain as a result of obscenity laws, he nonetheless used this opportunity to reflect on the significance of gay entrepreneurial efforts: 'To make an hour of gay film is quite a job, it requires lots of people and organization on a scale hitherto undreamed of by us.'[17] The plot line of the film revolved around a young man's sexual awakening by focusing on both his fantasies and

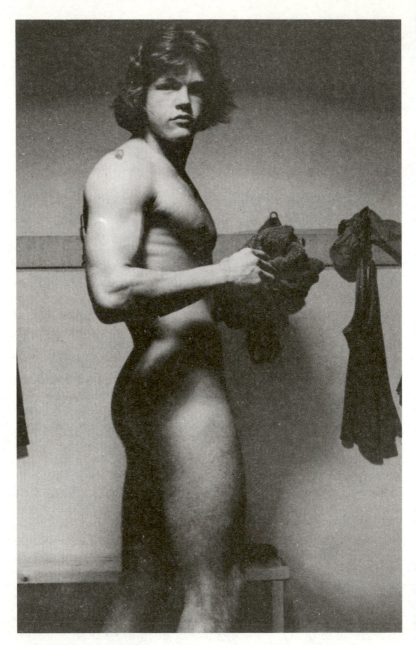

**8** 'The Colin Clarke Portfolio', *Him Exclusive*, 2 (1975), 26–7.

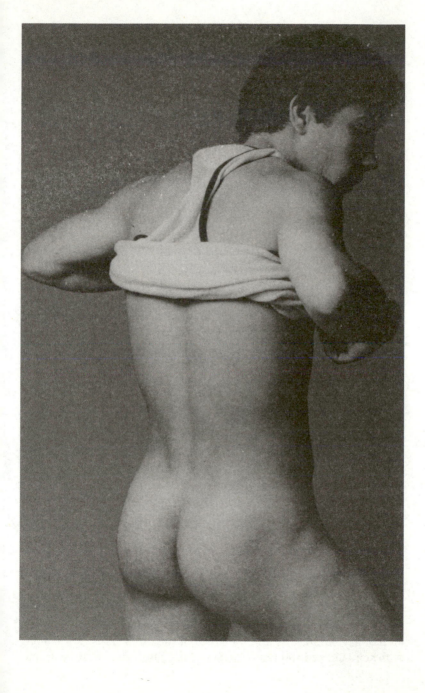

**9** Advertisement for the Mr Playguy Contest, *Him Exclusive*, 5 (1975), 47.

his first sexual experiences with a burly, leather-clad man ('peeking with steely eyes out from under a motorcycle cap') who picks him up in Holland Walk (a London cruising area). Purnell utilises his discussion of gay filmmaking and rehearsal of the film's flimsy story, along with semi-clothed and nude images of the film's star, to showcase his contributions to the visual and material culture of gay London *and* link the pleasures of viewing with increasingly public portrayals of gay sexuality and sociability.

Within Purnell's synopsis of his film are also several hints about the aesthetic that was celebrated in *Him Exclusive* and its successors. For *Him*'s publishers and editors, the aesthetic that was most often revered in their photographic features, erotic fiction and discussion of a fledgling gay cinema was that of the muscled, hairy and, not infrequently, rough man. In the magazine's first editorial, this aesthetic was identified as catering 'to the tastes of the majority' for 'the American "hunky" type masculine model, which has been neglected so much in recent times over here' (see Figure 10).[18] This American aesthetic undoubtedly derived from the physique magazines that travelled across the Atlantic throughout the 1950s and 1960s and reflected the growing cultural influence of the United States in Europe.[19] It also, however, highlighted the extent to which the thriving (and arguably freer) gay culture of cities like New York and San Francisco influenced British men in this period and signposted a new kind of sexual and political assertiveness that reminded readers that they too could revel in the sexuality of 'real men' while celebrating their identities boldly and openly.

The hunky aesthetic extolled by *Him* contributors also entailed the valorisation of the athletic body and the development of a finely tuned physique as well as the celebration of particular styles of clothing. In different photographic essays, sporting men were frequently highlighted in an effort to assert the masculine nature of the magazine and titillate readers who found, in the pages of *Him*, numerous opportunities to fantasise about footballers, swimmers and bodybuilders.[20] This was a perspective summarised by one reader who placed a personal advertisement in 1975: 'London: Wanted: Muscles, masculinity, and moustaches. I'm 26, non camp, interested in body building. Photo please.'[21] *Him* was thus in the business of peddling a particularly appealing and sellable brand of manliness. As Geoff Stout (acting editor of *Him International* while Alan Purnell travelled to the United States in 1976) summed it up, 'The style of *HIM* is geared to the man with emphasis on leather and denim. Him Exclusive models tend to be active, butch, masculine, and hunky. *HIM* is not a particularly soft approach, nor do we intend it to be. It is direct in its appearance, and is intended to tantalize and stimulate the minds of men who are definitely men.'[22]

**10** Cover for *Him Exclusive* (Special Edition), 8 (September 1975).

It is important to note that this predilection for hunks was often racially coded as a desire for the white male body. Occasionally, the editors strayed from a largely white vision of masculine beauty by including black models in the pages of *Him* or by running photo essays on the Notting Hill Carnival. In nearly all cases, however, the tendency was more towards fetishising non-white men for a largely white audience rather than addressing serious issues connected to racism in the gay community or dealing explicitly with the desires or demands of men of Asian, African or Caribbean extraction.[23] In describing the Carnival (an event that began in 1964 to celebrate West Indian culture in London), *Him Exclusive* highlighted distinctions between native Britons and 'Blacks': 'The British find it hard to really let their hair down, and it is left to the Black population to lead the way for us.' The desire to document the Carnival from a male-loving perspective led to the production of a photographic spread in the magazine in which the black male body figured prominently: 'We think we found some very exciting sights, in spite of the fact that chill weather robbed us of the acres of flesh we may have hoped for.'[24] This tendency toward sexualising (and in the process trivialising) the black male body was also highly evident in a *Him Exclusive* article that appeared in 1976 on one man's sexual escapades during a vacation in Mombasa, Kenya. In recounting one experience for his readers, the author writes of a tryst with Peter, 'a broad-shouldered hunk' whose 'skin was black as midnight': 'As soon as we were alone, he put his huge arms around me and, still grinning, kissed me full on the mouth. I was enveloped in that heady, musky black-man scent, and as he ran his hands up and down my body, squeezing my buttocks, I felt almost like a teenager again, dwarfed by his magnificent bulk.'[25] Despite the efforts of authors of other features in the magazine, particularly in later issues, to be more sensitive to racial matters, this tendency remained painfully apparent throughout the 1970s.[26]

While the magazine could, then, occasionally cater to aesthetic tastes that either departed from prevailing white ideals or ran towards younger, softer and more androgynous 'blonds in their late teens' (as Alan Cartwright from Salisbury noted in 1975),[27] most readers seem to have been wholly satisfied with the hyper-masculine vision of male beauty purveyed in the pages of *Him*. Some chose to affirm the magazine's vision by expressing their views or articulating their own desires in letters to the editor and personal classified advertisements, effectively participating in a conversation about what they found attractive and why.[28] By engaging in a sort of aesthetic dialogue with their audience through these different forms of correspondence, the publishers of and contributors to pornographic magazines like *Him* reminded their audience, in both explicit and implicit ways, that openly expressing preferences about the appealing male face and body was, in fact, a specific prerogative of modern gay men. John from Liverpool noted, in a letter from 1975, his appreciation for a 'mag not entirely devoted to pretty teens and twenties' and urged the magazine to consider giving more space to the 'maturer physique of the thirties and even forty-year olds'. George from West Yorkshire echoed some of these concerns in another letter from the same 1975 issue that congratulated the magazine for catering to 'guys who enjoy the more rugged muscular type of model'. He ended by urging the editors to ignore the calls of readers 'who demand the more pretty younger type – there are already more than enough magazines for them'.[29] In another 1975 letter in which R. M. from Bristol asked the editor of *Him Exclusive* to publish images of 'blokes pissing themselves', the author expressed a preference for the uniformed aesthetic and martial masculinity that seemed to be so very popular among the magazine's readers: 'I've had dozens of sailors, soldiers, and particularly guardsmen. It's the virile fitness of these blokes that makes them so good in tight uniforms.'[30] Perspectives of this sort also permeated the classified advertisements that routinely appeared in the magazine throughout the 1970s. In a 1976 issue of *Him International*, for example, an Oxford student expressed his aesthetic demands (and desires for companionship) with the following words: 'Good looking, well-made, easy-going, versatile. Seeking handsome, hairy, athletic type, 21-35.'[31]

*Him*'s images and discussions of aesthetic types were not simply representations of masculine attractiveness. Rather, they were intended to complement the political, social, cultural and artistic concerns of gay men and were thus interspersed in issues of the magazine from the 1970s 'with as many of the intimate questions regarding homosexuality as we can, in an adult and no nonsense way'.[32] These included features on fellatio and anal sex but also articles on the arrest of men for 'cottaging' and the status of gay cinema in Britain.[33] One reader in his sixties (V. R. from Sussex) commented on the importance of these articles in differentiating Purnell's fundamentally British venture from its American counterparts: 'The photographs are beautiful and the articles are obviously written by intelligent people – not like some of the crude American mags.'[34] Bold, informed and intelligent discussions of masculine physical attributes, men's ability to attract other men and gay sexuality opened the magazine up, as we shall see, to potential legal prosecution. It also pointed to the ways in which this publication's editors identified explicit celebrations of male beauty and same-sex intimacy and eroticism as a component of the larger political process that the Gay Liberation Front articulated earlier in the decade by asserting that 'Gay is Good'.[35]

Introduced in the first issue were a variety of other items that indicated that the magazine was as much about providing lifestyle advice and articulating a new kind of gay sexual subjectivity as it was about titillating readers with images of hunky men. Among the more interesting features in this first number were 'Seduction: The Gentle Gay Art' and 'Could You Have a Sexier Body?'[36] This merger of lifestyle features with explicit sexuality continued throughout the 1970s and reflected the perspective that sexuality and personal subjectivities were increasingly indistinguishable for a growing number of self-identified homosexual men. Discussions of fashion, the emerging gym culture in London and even sporting activities were almost always peppered with explicit sexual references and reminders that gay identities in the 1970s were, at least partially, contingent on participating in a thriving (and largely urban) consumer culture that had been around in an earlier period but was now more explicit, more open and more highly sexualised than it had ever been.[37] As we have already seen, denim and leather were products with particular appeal to the readers of *Him* in the 1970s. One author highlighted his own fetish for this particular style of dress in a 1975 article titled 'The Lure of Denim': 'A well-packed crotch beneath naturally faded tight jeans is an almost unbeatable show-stopper as far as I'm concerned.'[38] Other seemingly mundane entries on the revival of the 1950s T-shirt look popularised by James Dean and Marlon Brando (reflecting another form of creeping Americanisation that is inescapable in dissecting 1970s gay culture in Britain) functioned, for example, as an opportunity to remind readers that fashion choices could reflect broader social changes or highlight personal liberation: 'When underwear is liberated and becomes standard overwear it retains its sexual symbolism.'[39]

## Policing gay culture and pornography in the 1970s

While layout, content, tone and aesthetic perspective must be considered, as I have indicated here, in thinking about the cultural impact of pornography in the 1970s, *Him Exclusive*, especially, but also its successors *Him International* and *Him Monthly*, generated considerable political controversy around issues of censorship in the mid-to-late 1970s; an era, as Matt Cook has noted, in which 'the acceptance of sexual difference in British society continued to be highly contingent'.[40] The nude images and explicit discussions of sexuality in Purnell's *Him* ventures, and magazines intended for gay audiences more generally, were subject to regulation under various laws relating to the postal service and the Obscene Publications Acts of 1959 and 1964, which defined obscenity, rather vaguely and subjectively, as materials that 'tend to deprave and corrupt persons'[41] and provided for legal actions against both producers and purveyors of pornography. Following as they did in the wake of the so-called permissive 1960s, the early 1970s witnessed renewed discussions of obscenity, nudity and the objectification of the human body in Parliament, in the press and in a variety of other settings, including the radical publication *Gay Left: A Gay Socialist Journal*.

A new kind of gay press emerged between 1967 and 1972, spurred on, in part, by increased calls for detailed and explicit information about gay sexuality and gay culture. The demand for newspapers and magazines dealing with these issues seems to have been quite extensive, even in a climate where subscribers knew that publications of this sort were likely to be monitored by the police and other government officials. Requests for information about gay material were routinely sent to the Albany Trust, a counselling and research organisation for homosexual men and women. In September 1969, for example, one Hampshire man wrote to the Trust with the following plea: 'Could you kindly give me any information regarding magazines and other publications for male homosexuals, or where such information could be obtained – indeed, any information would be appreciated.'[42] While this correspondent was directed to send an inquiry to the editor of the soon-to-be-published magazine *Jeremy*, the Trust could just as easily have instructed him to write to several other periodicals that were appearing on the scene in the heady days of the late 1960s.

Among the publications that caught the attention of many readers and, ultimately, the law and earned opprobrium from a variety of purity reformers in the early 1970s was the magazine *Spartacus* (founded 1969), billed as the first British magazine exclusively 'for homosexuals, about homosexuals, by homosexuals'[43] and described by its proprietor and editor as 'a genuine and responsible homosexual publication'.[44] While the magazine owed much, aesthetically, to its physique pictorial predecessors, it nonetheless dealt with issues of gay desire and gay sexuality in a far more open manner than anything that had preceded it and was the first magazine in Britain to publish a 'full frontal of a nude male'.[45] As such, it was subject to significant scrutiny from the very beginning. Indeed, careful monitoring led to the prosecution of the magazine's owner and editor, John David Stamford, in 1971 for violating Section 11 of the 1953 Post Office Act which stated: 'A person shall not send or attempt to send or procure to be sent a post packet which encloses any indecent or obscene print, painting, photograph, lithograph engraving, cinematograph film, book, card or written communication or any indecent or obscene article.'[46] While Stamford's lawyer defended him by saying that his actions were no different from sending 'a pin-up picture of a girl to a heterosexual male',[47] this tendency towards scrutiny inaugurated a period of careful monitoring that continued into the 1980s.[48] Adding to this tendency were of course the efforts of individuals like the Christian reformer and notorious homophobe Francis Pakenham, Earl of Longford. In 1972, Lord Longford published his privately commissioned report (drafted by fifty-two commissioners appointed by himself) which found that pornography leads to 'deviant obsessions and actions' and called for a more expansive definition of obscenity, defining it as anything that might 'outrage contemporary standards of decency or humanity accepted by the public at large'.[49] Running through the report were assumptions about homosexuality that John Chesterman of the Gay Liberation Front labelled as an 'incitement to discrimination' and likened to 'the language of witch-hunts'.[50]

It was precisely this cultural climate that increasingly vocal and politicised gay entrepreneurs encountered as they sought to expand the market for gay images beyond the pictorial physique and American-inspired beefcake magazines of the 1950s and 1960s. Many producers of gay-themed publications in the early to mid-1970s were clearly responding to perceptions of homosexuality as a perversion (or as the Longford Report characterised it, according to Chesterman, 'something of itself pornographic')[51] by providing a moralising public directly with what they most feared: bold, assertive and explicit images of the male body that detailed genitalia and were accompanied by uninhibited discussions of gay sexuality. The confrontational nature and stance of *Him Exclusive* led, almost inevitably, to public scrutiny by purity campaigners like Mary Whitehouse (for whom, as Jeffrey Weeks has noted, pornography became a 'canker at the heart of respectability')[52] and legal action by the police and the Director of Public Prosecutions (who had broad powers in interpreting the Obscene Publications Acts of 1959 and 1964). Indeed, this is precisely what happened in 1975 and 1976, as the DPP began to monitor and prosecute publications like *Gay Circle* for running suggestive and openly sexual classified advertisements that allegedly had the potential to 'corrupt public morals', or magazines with explicitly sexual images and articles, a tendency that Michael De-la-Noy (an author and one-time Director of the Albany Trust) condemned in a '*Guardian* Miscellany' column.[53]

On 19 August 1975, Scotland Yard's Obscene Publications squad (also known as the Dirty Squad) seized 16,500 copies of the September issue of *Him Exclusive*, as part of a vigorous anti-porn round-up in the years between 1973 and 1977.[54] The offence related to several unspecified articles (undoubtedly ones dealing with sexual practices and techniques) as well as personal advertisements that were scheduled to appear in just a few weeks' time. In a revised version of issue 8 from September 1975 that the editors prepared after the raid, they detailed the events surrounding the seizure and noted, in their introduction, 'We strongly object to submitting to censorship in this form, but it was a choice between watering down the magazine or not having a magazine at all.' In concluding this opening salvo in what was to become a protracted battle, the editors appealed for funds by noting, in no uncertain terms, what was at stake: 'So far, this action by the Police has cost us almost £20,000. We are determined to spend our last penny in defending the homosexual cause against this blatant persecution, and your support and help would be appreciated.'[55] In the next issue, as the editors waited to hear about the fate of their magazines (were they to be destroyed or returned to their rightful owners?), Alan Purnell let it be known how serious this case was. In concluding his 'Editorial Perks' for the November 1975 number he urged readers to 'Keep *putting the Sex back into Homosexual*', a reminder that the highly eroticised images of the male face and body that had become standard fare in *Him Exclusive* (along with the explicit discussions of sexual techniques and gay fashion) should be seen as a central, not peripheral, concern to modern men with gay subjectivities and to the rapidly evolving homosexual movement.[56]

As the controversy unfolded throughout the autumn of 1975 and the early winter of 1976, readers began to weigh in with letters to the editor. D. W. of Chelsea provided readers of *Him Exclusive* with a copy of a letter that he wrote to the Home Secretary, Roy Jenkins, in late August 1975 and the response that he received from a Home Office official, assigned to deal with what must have been an unpleasant task. In explaining why he was writing to *Him Exclusive* at this particular moment, D. W. pointedly expressed his concerns: 'I think that what is really required, however, is a highly organized national campaign for the complete repeal of the Acts I mention to effectively combat and, I trust, eventually to crush those interfering and repressive factions (the Mary Whitehouse / Lord Longford / Raymond Blackburn / Festival of Light factions) who would have us see and hear and do only what they approve. We all know that they are minority factions but we also know that they are highly organized and militant factions.' Sentiments of this sort are echoed in the actual letter D. W. wrote to Jenkins. With specific reference to what he labelled the 'bigoted opinions' of 'vociferous minority groups' he tried to convey the subjective nature of the very concept of obscenity itself: 'What is obscene to one person is nothing of the kind to another. I, personally, find boxing obscene but pornography wholesome.'[57] By repositioning pornography as a wholesome form of entertainment, D. W. sought both to counter claims of religiously inspired opponents and to elevate in value publications like *Him Exclusive*, which he viewed as symbols of civilisation, not moral degeneration.

By early 1976, the legal situation for the publisher and editor remained uncertain. The court seemed to be dragging its feet in adjudicating this particular case for reasons that were not entirely clear – though, according to Purnell, this was a kind of 'pointless persecution with nuisance value only'. For the editor, the actions of the police constituted discrimination, pure and simple. The fuss was created, he asserted, merely as a result of the magazine's homosexual content. He maintained, however, that *Him Exclusive* would remain at the forefront of the battle for equality: 'It is the policy of this magazine to press the boundaries forward gradually, until we have the same freedom of expression that "straight" magazines enjoy.'[58] This pushing of boundaries would, in fact, prove to be the magazine's downfall in this particular case.[59]

During the spring of 1976, a London magistrate determined that *Him Exclusive* was indeed obscene and ordered that copies be destroyed. Not surprisingly, the reactions of the magazine's editors were especially strong. Alan Purnell labelled the judgement 'reactionary and unenlightened' and indicated that many people who observed the court proceedings called its actions 'harassment of homosexuals'. Of particular concern to the magistrate were images of male genitalia, articles on anal sex (in issue 4) and, curiously, 'Living Together' (in issue 6) and the suggestive personal advertisements that appeared with increasing frequency on the final pages of each number. In issuing his decision, the magistrate ordered the seized copies of the magazine to be burned with the following rhetorical flourish: 'the incinerator is the best place for [them]'.[60] This action did not signal the end of the magazine or its particularly confrontational approach to articulating gay aesthetics and identities. Still, the next issue of *Him* contained some significant changes. While it continued to be edited by Alan Purnell, the magazine was no longer published by Incognito (the founding publisher which had fallen on hard financial times)[61] but by Purnell himself and now titled *Him International*. Regardless, the political edge of *Him* was intact and the magazine remained steadfast in its desire to instruct readers 'how to fuck, suck, and love'.[62]

The magazine and the Him Bookstore (which went through various incarnations in Hammersmith, Earls Court and Notting Hill) continued to be subjected to periodic scrutiny and visits from the Obscene Publications Squad through the latter years of the decade. During the summer of 1976 the police 'harassed the magazine by visiting it three times without a search warrant' and continued its anti-gay campaign by raiding London bookshops and seizing magazines with homosexual content, actions that the Liberal MP David Steel characterised as 'ignoring the spirit of the 1967 Sexual Offences Act'.[63] In late 1978, Customs and Excise officers were ordered to seize and open packages from abroad addressed to some twenty-six different publishers and publications. Among those targeted were *Gay News*, Paul Raymond Publications (which printed a variety of magazines directed at a heterosexual male market) and Incognito (the initial publisher of *Him*).[64] The action produced something of an uproar among publishers of pornography (who threatened various forms of legal action) and some newspaper readers generally, who objected to a 'Victorian type backlash'.[65] Continued raids and seizures occurred during the final year of the decade. In May 1979, the Him store in Notting Hill had between 15,000 and 20,000 magazines as well as 'mail orders for a whole week and a file of all classified ads for the next issue of *Him*' confiscated.[66]

While many of these ventures continued as the winter of discontent morphed into Mrs Thatcher's Britain, the radical cultural moment that seemed to mark *Him*'s formative years gave way to a pornography more strictly devoted to pleasure. It was also a pornography that continued to be regulated and compromised by government attempts to censor it and control access through the passage of legislation like the Indecent Displays (Control) Act of 1981.[67] Indeed, by October 1982 *Him Monthly* (the successor to *Him Exclusive* and *Him International*) began to clothe its models in swimsuits and gym wear (returning, in part, to the physique aesthetic of the 1950s and 1960s) as a matter of self-preservation in a climate, as Alan Purnell noted, where government 'thought police' were launching a highly orchestrated 'attack on pornography and the civil liberties of British people'. Rather than reading this as a defeat, however, Purnell chose to interpret this shift in editorial policy as a victory: 'By adapting and changing the victim fights back.'[68] While the political edge of earlier issues was gone, editors and publishers like Purnell continued to see their enterprises as central to the fight for gay liberty and freedom.

British government officials were not the only ones who expressed concern about magazines like *Him*. Unsurprisingly, not all gay men characterised pornography positively or viewed the appearance of publications like *Him* as unfettered or unproblematic symbols of progress. Following the lead of some feminists (who saw all pornography as fundamentally sexist, exploitative and degrading to women and men who are 'blacker, weaker, younger, poorer')[69] and radical socialists (who questioned all forms of identity-driven consumption), certain gay men on the left wrote critiques of pornography that hinted at the contested nature of this particular mode of expression. For men like John Shiers, who described his own experience of coming out and involvement with the Gay Liberation Front in a 1978 article, the commercial gay scene (in the form of bars, shops and media), while appealing and satisfying on a visceral level, was also an indication of the 'capacity of capitalist enterprises to colonise gay men'.[70] Gregg Blachford, a Canadian living in London and involved in the gay socialist movement, engaged more specifically with issues of pornography in an article he published in a 1978 issue of *Gay Left*.

Within this piece, titled 'Looking at Pornography', Blachford's ideas were informed by the feminist principle that the personal is political. In keeping with this perspective, he began the article by asserting that 'masturbation, cruising, cottaging, S/M sex, and pornography' were 'not unimportant parts of many gay men's, including gay socialist men's lives'[71] and that the last of these, pornography, needed to be viewed through a critical lens. While Blachford maintained, throughout the essay, that heterosexual pornography was ultimately exploitative and sexist, when it came to questions of censorship or outright bans he remained decidedly ambivalent. Constantly thoughtful and reflective in his views, he also ruminated in his piece on the nature of objectification and inequality, recognising that different forms of 'non-exploitative and mutually enjoyable' sexual relationships were indeed possible. In formulating these ideas, Blachford drew on Carl Wittman's *A Gay Manifesto*, noting that the sexual objectification of male bodies by other men, the very thing that men are not supposed to do to each other, had the potential to liberate rather than oppress. Still, Blachford asserted that inequalities between men, particularly those between men of different social classes or of 'differential physical attractiveness', required at least some further reflection by people interested in righting social wrongs. To this end, he concluded his article with several questions: 'can we retain the erotic elements of sexual images and eliminate the sexist and exploitative elements? Can we wrench porn from its ideological moorings? Can we turn porn into art: that is, something that is utopian, ideal, and therefore anti-status quo?'[72]

While Blachford's ideas remain an interesting example of gay political thought and action in 1970s Britain, an assertion that came on the third page of his article revealed that even those who viewed the pornographic explosion of the 1960s and 1970s critically could simultaneously embrace the perspectives of people like Alan Purnell, who argued vociferously about the centrality of sexual images to the promotion of gay visibility. Blachford, in fact, highlighted the value of pornography to young gay men when he noted, 'I believe that these magazines cannot be dismissed so easily out of hand as their heterosexual equivalents because, although the context is clearly exploitative, the images presented are important to many gay men because they furnish evidence that gay male sexuality actually exists!' He then continued by providing readers with a few personal insights about his own responses to pornography: 'I remember the very exciting feeling I got when I first saw one of these magazines before I came out. There I saw men kissing and holding and loving each other; something that I never thought possible as the mainstream culture manifests itself in overwhelmingly heterosexual and macho terms.' Most important, for Blachford, was the way in which pornographic magazines like *Him* functioned as 'proof of a homosexual community'.[73]

## The cultural and personal meaning of pornography: evidence from the Williams Committee

Public and private conversations about pornography were not, of course, confined to gay publishing entrepreneurs and magazine correspondents or those officials concerned with policing public morals. Indeed, by the late 1970s, it appeared that broader social attitudes toward magazines like *Him* were starting to shift, despite the government's attempts at censorship in the middle part of the decade and the existence of conservative purity campaigns spearheaded by organisations like the Christian-inspired Nationwide Festival of Light. In 1977, a Committee on Obscenity and Film Censorship (known as the Williams Committee for its chair, the Cambridge Moral Philosophy Professor Bernard Williams) was created by the Home Office with the intention of reviewing laws on obscenity in publications (including indecency and violence) and film censorship.[74] Of particular concern to this committee, as Mary Warnock noted in a 1980 article in *Political Quarterly*, was 'not obscenity but pornography'. While actual changes to the laws were never implemented (owing, in part, to the Thatcher government's disagreement with its more liberal findings), the committee's report, when issued in 1979, highlighted some of the processes of redefinition that seemed to be occurring in society at large. Departing from Longford, Williams (who was driven by a 'presumption in favour of freedom') concluded that pornography could not be shown to be harmful to British citizens and paled in comparison to other social problems.[75] Despite such seemingly forward-looking assertions, the Committee's recommendations continued to place restrictions on the sale and distribution of pornography. Paedophilic images and those involving the infliction of harm were to be banned, while sanctioned material was to be sold in shops that children and 'unsuspecting members of the public' were unlikely to enter.[76] The Committee also recommended that these specialised shops and cinemas should be subjected to a system of licensing.

In collecting evidence, the Committee solicited reactions from concerned organisations and members of the ordinary public in daily newspapers including *The Times*, the *Guardian* and the *Daily Telegraph*. Many of these respondents railed against censorship and the 'infringement of liberty'[77] that they saw in the current laws and actions of the Director of Public Prosecutions. The Campaign for Homosexual Equality, as one of the concerned parties that submitted

an opinion to the committee, came down firmly on the side of freedom by asserting the following: 'as citizens we are entitled to expose
ourselves and others who wish it to the fullest and freest information
and entertainment, without interference from our fellow citizens dis-
guised as the law'. They indicated that the risk of becoming 'more
base and less civilised' was worth it if it meant eliminating the 'standards of the cotton-wool society, the kindergarten state' and not surrendering 'to the control of others the most sublime of human freedoms,
the cornerstone of human happiness, the ability to simply be ourselves'.[78] Despite such compelling calls for increased freedoms, not
all who wrote to the Committee wanted to see censorship eliminated.
A minority of respondents, for example, pleaded with government
representatives in their letters to 'move against those whose self-
interest is leading to such relaxation of past restraints that our nation
is increasingly manifesting deep sickness in mental, physical, social,
and spiritual health'.[79]

Contained within this collection of documents, housed in both the
London Metropolitan and the National Archives, are also a number of
letters from self-identified homosexual or gay men who commented
in their submissions to the Committee not only on the value of more
respectable publications like *Gay News* but also on magazines that
most in British society would have definitely deemed pornographic.
These letters ran the gamut in terms of content and arguments. All
expressed their support for a broad range of gay publications but
were careful, in most instances, to note that magazines like *Him
International, Man-to-Man Forum* or *Mister International* should not
be available to children under the age of sixteen (or sometimes eighteen), nor should they ever contain images of children or bestiality.
Many of the gay men who wrote to the Williams Committee (through
a Home Office official named Jon Davey) divulged quite intimate
details about their reading habits and their personal struggles with
the processes of sexual self-discovery. In these fascinating documents
they frequently employed rhetorical strategies that privileged notions
of community; ideas about freedom and persecution; and notions of
self-realisation, pleasure and normative socialisation and psychological development.

In a letter written on 25 September 1977, M. G. Colgate rejected
the belief that there was a connection between the enjoyment of pornography and perversion: 'I enjoy pornography and I do not regard
myself as a menace to the public.' More important for the purposes of

this study were Colgate's assertions about his right to view images of naked men (and thus achieve sexual satisfaction and pleasure) in an unimpeded fashion: 'I object to other people determining what I may, or may not, see. I believe that obtaining sexual pleasure is a matter for the individual and should only be restricted if it can be shown to be harmful.' Throughout this letter, Colgate linked his ability to enjoy photographs (a point reiterated time and again in *Him* editorials) with the positive assertion of his identity as a '32 year old homosexual'.[80] Other correspondents linked the right to see, to read and to learn about other gay men and gay issues as central to alleviating the isolation that some felt as they embarked upon journeys of sexual awakening; something, as Julian Carter indicated in his letter to the Committee, 'no person should have to feel today in any liberal society'.[81] Clearly influenced by the rise of the psychological self in the twentieth century,[82] W. J. Whitehead commented on developmental issues in his letter to the committee: 'Sexual feelings, especially if not conventional as portrayed in films, popular magazines, etc. can be disquieting, and counsel and expression are valuable. The other choice, ignorance or repression, can lead to frustration, isolation, mental pain, perhaps violence (probably not sexual violence, but sublimated outlets, e.g. over-masculinity, fighting, etc).'[83]

For some, the sense of isolation that Whitehead discussed in his letter was literally geographical. For others it was rooted in erroneous depictions of homosexuality in popular culture or the lack of sexual knowledge. D. P. Freeman from Swansea in 'still chapel-dominated Wales' argued forcibly in favour of his right to read and view what he liked: 'I don't see why I should not be allowed to buy and read magazines showing naked men in various poses provided I am over a certain age.' Freeman reasserted in several places in this letter that material of this nature did not cause any harm and might have, in fact, helped to 'relieve' a sense of 'frustration' that was most likely born out of sexual and social isolation.[84] Sean Barker, the Cambridge man introduced at the beginning of this chapter, highlighted the psychological isolation created by negative stereotypes by pointing to the dangerous absurdity of 'films which treat the subject by innuendo and as a source of laughter (e.g. "Are You Being Served", almost any "Carry On" film and so on)' that 'corrupt the ignorant (including naïve homosexuals), bolster prejudice and prevent true rational discussion'.[85] Finally, one correspondent who was living in a homosexual relationship but self-identified as bisexual noted how certain publications could lead to greater sexual awareness: 'I think a certain amount of magazines which are described as "pornographic" could be of very great benefit to sensible minded people.'[86] Many same-sex-desiring men thus served to underscore, in their letters, the positive benefits of publications like *Him* while still recognising the fraught nature of public and private debates about the nature of pornographic images and magazine content that dealt explicitly with sensitive sexual topics.

This chapter has illustrated how the close study of gay pornographic magazines, and the reactions of readers to them, can serve to illuminate several important themes in the history of gay men in Britain after 1967. As Marcus Collins has asserted, with respect to heterosexual pornography from the period, 'the history of the sixties and seventies cannot be written with the pornography left out'.[87] While some might question the boldness of this claim, it points researchers of postwar gay Britain in important directions. Aesthetic celebrations of the desirable and attractive male body signalled a new kind of political boldness that presented both opportunities and dangers for gay men. As contributors to *Him* articulated a new gay aesthetic, they provided a positive assertion of gay sexuality through the employment of new kinds of confrontational pornographic tropes (including sexualised images of male genitalia and highly eroticised as opposed to clinical descriptions of sexual practices and techniques). By exploiting the emergence of a new kind of gay consciousness among queer Britons, as well as a long national history of celebrating the beautiful man, gay pornographers and entrepreneurs like Alan Purnell helped to articulate components of gay male subjectivities and desires while carving out a market niche for themselves.

Curiously, it was the multifaceted nature of these publications and their transgressive aesthetic experimentation (and a general realisation, perhaps, that their publication signified a new moment in the sexual history of Britain) that led the Director of Public Prosecutions and the Metropolitan Police to monitor the images, articles and commercial activities of homosexual men. While gay men's private acts may have been partially decriminalised after 1967, their public culture and assertions of a new kind of sexual subjectivity continued to be scrutinised closely by the state, a situation that led publications like *Him*, as well as countless individuals, to become 'ardent campaigner[s] for all freedoms'.[88] This chapter thus reveals not only the centrality of pornography to post-1967 gay male culture but also how aesthetics, questions of censorship and the politics of liberation were intermingled during a decade that, for gay Britons, was marked by tumult, uncertainty and contingency as much as it was by increasing visibility and progress.

## Notes

1 Rupert Smith, *Physique: The Life of John Barrington* (London: Serpent's Tail, 1997), pp. 117, 121.
2 John S. Barrington, 'Editorial', *Male Model Monthly*, 1 (November 1954), 2.
3 Smith, *Physique*, 184.
4 See Frank Mort, *Capital Affairs: London and the Making of the Permissive Society* (New Haven: Yale University Press, 2010), pp. 1–24. On views of permissiveness, see Marcus Collins, 'Introduction: The permissive society and its enemies', in Marcus Collins (ed.), *The Permissive Society and Its Enemies: Sixties British Culture* (London: Rivers Oram Press, 2007), pp. 1–40.
5 On these developments, see Matt Cook, 'From gay reform to Gaydar, 1967–2006', in Matt Cook (ed.), *A Gay History of Britain: Love and Sex between Men since the Middle Ages* (Oxford: Greenwood, 2007), pp. 179–214.
6 For the perspective of an active participant in the gay press, see Peter Burton, *Parallel Lives* (London: GMP, 1985), pp. 106–7. On the political functions of gay publications and the rise of the gay press as an expression of community, see Stephen Jeffery-Poulter, *Peers, Queers and Commons: The Struggle for Gay Law Reform from 1950 to the Present* (London: Routledge, 1991), pp. 97, 107; Jeffrey Weeks, *Coming Out: Homosexual Politics in Britain from the Nineteenth Century to the Present* (London: Quartet Books, rev. edn, 1990), pp. 219–22.
7 Alan Purnell, 'Editorial Introduction', *Him Exclusive*, 1 (1974), 3.
8 On the history of pornography in the nineteenth and early twentieth centuries see Lisa Z. Sigel, *Governing Pleasures: Pornography and Social Change in England, 1815–1914* (New Brunswick, NJ: Rutgers University Press, 2002). On the pre-Stonewall history of the gay erotic image see Thomas Waugh, *Hard to Imagine: Gay Male Eroticism in Photography and Film from Their Beginnings to Stonewall* (New York: Columbia University Press, 1996).
9 C. H. Rolph, 'Introduction', in C. H. Rolph (ed.), *Does Pornography Matter?* (London: Routledge and Kegan Paul, 1961), p. 103, quoted in H. G. Cocks, 'Saucy stories: Pornography, sexology, and the marketing of sexual knowledge in Britain, c. 1918–1970', *Social History*, 29:4 (November 2004), 473.

10  See Cocks, 'Saucy stories', pp. 465–84. The point about genre mixing is also made in Marcus Collins, 'The pornography of permissiveness: Men's sexuality and women's emancipation in mid twentieth-century Britain', *History Workshop Journal*, 47 (Spring 1999), 99–120, and *Modern Love: Personal Relationships in Twentieth Century Britain* (Newark: University of Delaware Press, 2003).

11  Michael Denneny, 'Gay politics: Sixteen propositions (1981)', in Mark Blasius and Shane Phelan (eds), *We Are Everywhere: A Historical Sourcebook of Gay and Lesbian Politics* (New York: Routledge, 1997), p. 490. This idea also appears in Jeffrey Escoffier, *Bigger than Life: The History of Gay Porn Cinema from Beefcake to Hardcore* (Philadelphia: Running Press, 2009), p. 5.

12  National Archives (hereafter TNA), HO 265/86/103, Sean Barker to Jon Davey, Submission to Departmental Committee on Obscenity and Film Censorship (hereafter DCOFC), n.d.

13  Colin Clarke, 'The Colin Clarke portfolio', *Him Exclusive*, 2 (1975), 25.

14  'Man talk: Chat', *Him Exclusive*, 4 (1975), 18.

15  Advertisement for the Mr Playguy Contest, *Him Exclusive*, 5 (1975), 47. For an account of the cultural politics of drag in American gay culture, see Betty Luther Hillman, '"The most profoundly revolutionary act a homosexual can engage in": Drag and the politics of gender presentation in the San Francisco gay liberation movement, 1964–1972', *Journal of the History of Sexuality*, 20:1 (January 2011), 153–81.

16  On this, see Matt Houlbrook, *Queer London: Perils and Pleasures in the Sexual Metropolis, 1918–1957* (Chicago: University of Chicago Press, 2005), pp. 1–13, 139–66.

17  Alan Purnell, 'Hard dollar hustler', *Him International*, 9 (1977), 26.

18  *Him Exclusive*, 1 (1974), 19.

19  See H. L. Malchow, *Special Relations: The Americanization of Britain?* (Stanford: Stanford University Press, 2011).

20  For examples, see 'Preview: Footballin'', *Him Monthly*, 13 (1978), 32–6; 'Beach boy '75', *Him Exclusive*, 6 (1975), 16–19; and 'Hercules undressed', *Him Exclusive*, 4 (1975), 22.

21  'Private and personal', *Him Exclusive*, 5 (1975), 44.

22  Geoff Stout, 'Editor's perks', *Him Exclusive*, 14 (1976), 4.

23  Cook, *A Gay History of Britain*, pp. 187–8.

24  'Carnival', *Him Exclusive*, 10 (November 1975), 46–7.

25  'Mombasa & Amsterdam: Gay holidays – blow hot and cold', *Him Exclusive*, 12 (1976), 25–6.

26  'Black and white: Multi-racial sex', *Him International*, 12, (1978), 23, 26.

27  Alan Cartwright, 'Letter to the editor', *Him Exclusive*, 3 (1975), 20.

28  On the social and cultural history of the personal advertisement, see H. G. Cocks, *Classified: The Secret History of the Personal Column* (London: Random House, 2009).

29  'Man talk: Letters', *Him Exclusive*, 4 (1975), 18.

30  'Man talk: Letters', *Him Exclusive* (Special Edition), 8 (September 1975), 35. On the appeal of military uniforms, see Matt Houlbrook, 'Soldier heroes and rent boys: Homosex, masculinities, and Britishness in the Brigade of Guards, circa 1900–1960', *Journal of British Studies*, 42:3 (July 2003), 351–88.

31  'Him cruising classified', *Him International*, 1 (1976), 39.

32  *Him Exclusive*, 1 (1974), 19.

33  Paul Marshall, 'A bit of a mouthful: How you can do more than pay lip service to gay oral sex', *Him Exclusive*, 3 (1975), 4–5; Alan Purnell, 'Pleasure and pain', *Him Exclusive*, 4 (1975), 4–6; 'If you care for "cottaging"', *Him Exclusive*, 3 (1975), 7–8; and 'Gay movies for London', *Him International*, 8 (1977), 16.

34  'Man talk: Letters', *Him Exclusive*, 5 (1975), 19.

35  Hall-Carpenter Archives, London School of Economics (hereafter HCA), HCA/GLF/1, 'The Gay Liberation Front Demands', 1970.

36  Alan Purnell, 'Seduction: The gentle gay art', *Him Exclusive*, 1 (1974), 4–5, and Paul Marshall, 'Could you have a sexier body?', *Him Exclusive*, 1 (1974), 27.

37  For one example, see Len Richmond, 'Len Richmond's news of the gay', *Him Exclusive*, 13 (1976), 5–6. On gay male consumption, see Justin Bengry, 'Courting the pink pound: *Men Only* and the queer consumer, 1935–39', *History Workshop Journal*, 68 (Autumn 2009), 122–48; Houlbrook, *Queer London*, pp. 68–92; Frank Mort, *Cultures of Consumption: Masculinities and Social Space in Late Twentieth-Century Britain* (London: Routledge, 1996), pp. 164–70. On the importance of consumer culture to the formation of gay identities in the US, see David K. Johnson, 'Physique pioneers: The politics of 1960s gay consumer culture', *Journal of Social History*, 43:4 (Summer 2010), 867–92.

38  'The lure of denim', *Him Exclusive*, 10 (November 1975), 14.

39  '"T" appeal', *Him International*, 1 (1976), 9.

40  Cook, *A Gay History of Britain*, p. 180.

41  *Obscene Publications Act (1959)*, UK Statute Law Database, www.statutelaw.gov.uk/content.aspx?activeTextDocId=1128038, accessed 13 October 2010. On the larger history of censorship, see Alan Travis, *Bound and Gagged: A Secret History of Obscenity in Britain* (London: Profile Books, 2000).

42  HCA, Albany Trust 7/59, B. E. Nightingale ('Kebar') to Albany Trust, 4 September 1969.

43  Cook, *A Gay History of Britain*, p. 189.

44  HCA, Albany Trust 7/73/7, John D. Stamford to Lord Timothy
    Beaumont of Whitley, 26 October 1970.

45  Lesbian and Gay News Archive, Middlesex University (hereafter LGNA),
    Clipping File (Bb/Gay Porn), Chris Stretch, 'Men's Images of Men', *The
    Leveller* (30 October – 12 November, 1981), p. 12.

46  HCA, Albany Trust 7/73/18, Peter Moore to Michael De-la-Noy, 6
    January 1971.

47  LGNA, Clipping File (Bb/Spartacus), 'Homosexual magazine's editor
    sent for trial', *Scotsman* (26 January 1971).

48  One of the more famous cases related to the publication *Oz* (1967–73).
    See Gerry Carlin, 'Rupert Bare: Art, obscenity and the *Oz* trial' in
    Collins (ed.), *The Permissive Society and Its Enemies*, pp. 132–44.

49  'The law: Lord Porn's report', *Time* (2 October 1972), www.time.com/time/
    magazine/article/0,9171,906459,00.html, accessed 13 October 2010.

50  LGNA, Clipping File (Ba/Homosexuality as Perversion), John
    Chesterman, 'Porn: Gay witch-hunt?' *Guardian* (26 September 1972).

51  *Ibid.*

52  Jeffrey Weeks, *Sex, Politics and Society: The Regulation of Sexuality Since
    1800* (London: Longman, 1981), p. 280.

53  LGNA, Clipping File (Ba/Gay Circle), Michael De-la-Noy, '*Guardian*
    miscellany', *Guardian* (22 August 1975), p. 9.

54  John Sutherland, *Offensive Literature: Decensorship in Britain, 1960–1982*
    (Totowa, NJ: Barnes and Noble Books, 1982), pp. 164–71; Travis, *Bound
    and Gagged*, p. 214.

55  '*Him Exclusive* police raid', *Him Exclusive* (Special Edition), 8
    (September 1975), 10.

56  Alan Purnell, 'Editor's perks', *Him Exclusive*, 10 (November 1975), 5.

57  'Man talk: Letters', *Him Exclusive*, 10 (November 1975), 35.

58  Alan Purnell, 'Editor's perks', *Him Exclusive*, 12 (1976), 5.

59  Jeffrey Weeks has noted, 'Transgression, the breaching of boundaries,
    the pushing of experiences to the limits, the challenge of the law, what-
    ever it is, is a crucial moment in any radical sexual project.' See Jeffrey
    Weeks, *Invented Moralities: Sexual Values in an Age of Uncertainty* (New
    York: Columbia University Press, 1995), p. 108.

60  'Stop the press! *Him* found obscene, court case ends with destruction',
    *Him Exclusive*, 14 (1976), 17.

61  Some interesting details on the publication of pornographic magazines
    can be found on the Gay Erotic Archives website, maintained by the
    ONE Institute in Los Angeles, CA. While primarily American in focus,
    it does contain some information related to Britain. See www.gayerotic
    archives.com/02_pubs/Z/i/Zipper/index.html, accessed 11 January
    2012.

62  Alan Purnell, 'From Alan Purnell', *Him International*, 1 (1976), 5.

63   LGNA, Clipping File (Ba/Confiscation of Material), Nicholas de Jongh
     and Simon Hoggart, 'Steel attacks *Him* seizure', *Guardian* (27 August
     1976), 22.

64   LGNA, Clipping File (Ba/Confiscation of Material), Nicholas de Jongh,
     'Journals put on secret Customs list', *Guardian* (4 December 1978).

65   LGNA, Clipping File (Ba/Obscene Publications), Geoffrey Kenyon,
     'Notions of obscenity', *Observer* (31 December 1978).

66   LGNA, Clipping File (Ba/Confiscation of Material), '£8000 seizure
     of gay magazines' (no newspaper title included in the file) (3 May
     1979).

67   Alan Hunt, *Governing Morals: A Social History of Moral Regulation*
     (Cambridge: Cambridge University Press, 1999), p. 208.

68   'The new *Him*', *Him Monthly*, 51 (October 1982), 3, 7.

69   Stretch, 'Men's images of men', 14. Stretch is referring here to some of
     the classic feminist critiques of pornography, including those of Andrea
     Dworkin and Susan Griffin. On the pervasiveness of this critique, see
     Weeks, *Coming Out*, p. 234.

70   John Shiers, 'Two steps forward: Coming out six years on', *Gay Left: A
     Gay Socialist Journal*, 6 (Summer 1978), 12

71   Gregg Blachford, 'Looking at pornography: Erotica and the socialist
     morality', *Gay Left: A Gay Socialist Journal*, 6 (Summer 1978), 16.

72   *Ibid.*, 20.

73   *Ibid.*, 19.

74   On the history of the Williams Committee, see Travis, *Bound and
     Gagged*, pp. 262–7.

75   Mary Warnock, 'Reports and surveys: The Williams Report on Obscenity
     and Film Censorship', *Political Quarterly*, 51:3 (July 1980), 341.

76   Jane O'Grady, 'Obituary: Professor Sir Bernard Williams',
     *Guardian* (13 June 2003), www.guardian.co.uk/news/2003/jun/13/
     guardianobituaries.obituaries, accessed 13 October 2010.

77   TNA, HO 265/77/63, M. F. Boxall to Jon Davey, Submission to DCOFC,
     15 October 1977.

78   London Metropolitan Archives, LMA/4539/02/002, 'Submission by
     the Campaign for Homosexual Equality to the Williams Committee on
     Obscenity and Film Censorship', March 1978.

79   TNA, HO 265/80/90, Vicky Jiggins to Davey, Submission to DCOFC,
     28 October 1977.

80   TNA, HO 265/77/41, M. G. Colgate to Davey, Submission to DCOFC,
     25 September 1977.

81   TNA, HO 265/77/62, Julian Carter to Davey, Submission to DCOFC, 15
     October 1977.

82   Mathew Thomson, *Psychological Subjects: Identity, Culture, and Health in
     Twentieth-Century Britain* (Oxford: Oxford University Press, 2006).

83  TNA, HO 265/80/75, W. J. Whitehead to Davey, Submission to DCOFC,
    25 October 1977.
84  TNA, HO 265/80/45, D. P. Freeman to Davey, Submission to DCOFC,
    20 January 1978.
85  TNA, HO 265/86/103, Sean Barker to Davey, Submission to DCOFC,
    n.d.
86  TNA, HO 265/79/15, John Edward Prince to Davey, Submission to
    DCOFC, 16 December 1977.
87  Collins, 'The Pornography of Permissiveness', 100.
88  TNA, HO 265/86/103, Sean Barker to Davey, Submission to DCOFC,
    n.d.

# Index